A Heritage in Transition

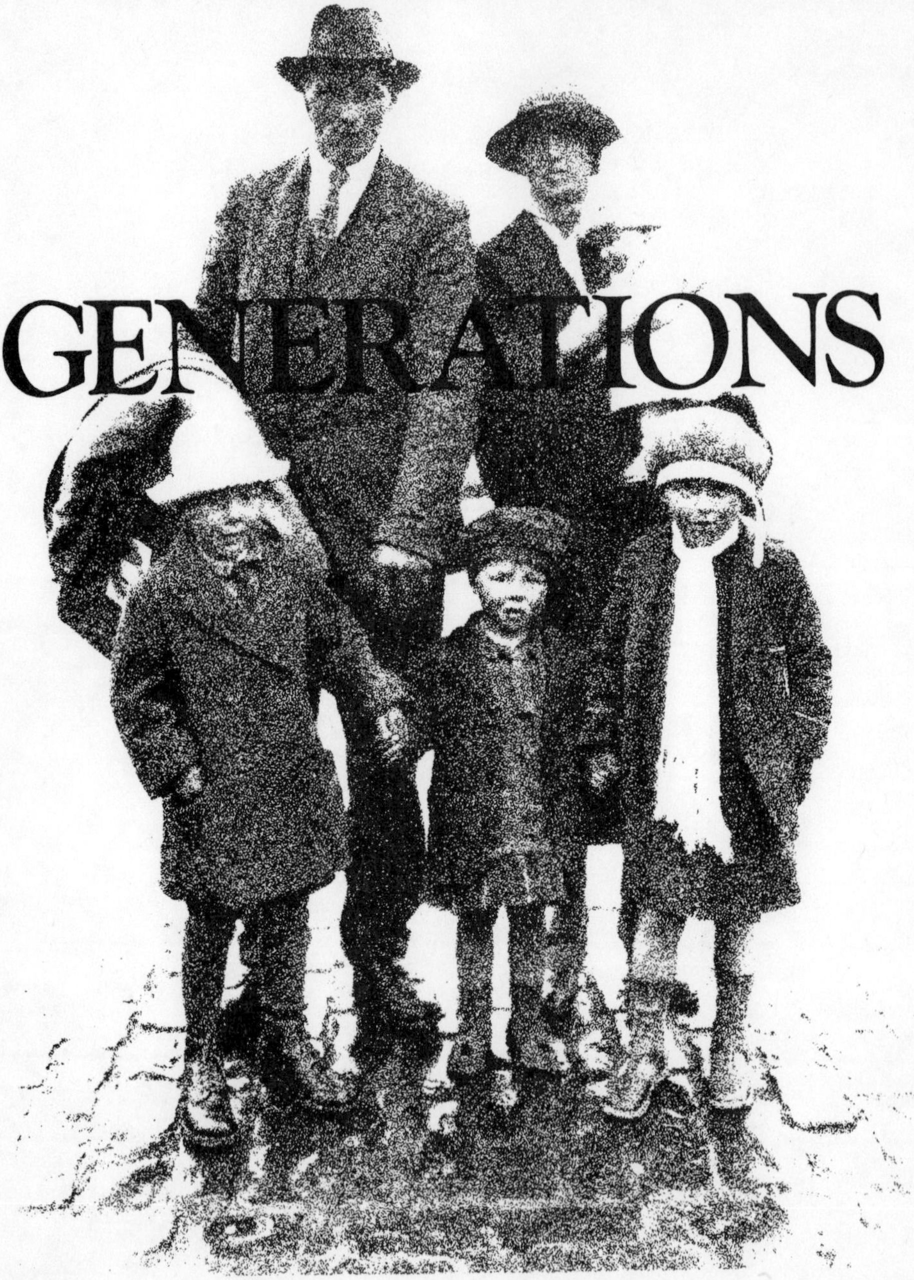
GENERATIONS

A History of Canada's Peoples

A Heritage in Transition

Essays in the History of Ukrainians in Canada

Edited by Manoly R. Lupul

[redacted]

Published by McClelland and Stewart Ltd. in association
with the Multiculturalism Directorate,
Department of the Secretary of State
and the Canadian Government Publishing Centre,
Supply and Services Canada.

Government Catalogue No. Ci 44-9-1982E

McClelland and Stewart Limited
The Canadian Publishers
25 Hollinger Road
Toronto, Ontario
M4B 3G2

Canadian Cataloguing in Publication Data

Main entry under title:
A Heritage in transition: essays in the history of
Ukrainians in Canada

(Generations: a history of Canada's peoples)
Includes bibliographies and index.
ISBN 0-7710-5388-6

1. Ukrainian Canadians – History – Addresses, essays, lectures.* I. Lupul, Manoly R., 1927- II. Series.

FC106.U5H47 971'.00491791 C82-094862-4
F1035.U5H47

Printed and bound in Canada

Contents

Editors' Introduction

Canadians, like many other people, have recently been changing their attitude towards the ethnic dimension in society. Instead of thinking of the many distinctive heritages and identities to be found among them as constituting a problem, though one that time would solve, they have begun to recognize the ethnic diversity of their country as a rich resource. They have begun to take pride in the fact that people have come and are coming here from all parts of the world, bringing with them varied outlooks, knowledge, skills and traditions, to the great benefit of all.

It is for this reason that Book IV of the *Report of the Royal Commission on Bilingualism and Biculturalism* dealt with the cultural contributions of the ethnic groups other than the British, the French and the Native Peoples to Canada, and that the federal government in its response to Book IV announced that the Citizenship Branch of the Department of the Secretary of State would commission "histories specifically directed to the background, contributions and problems of various cultural groups in Canada." This series presents the histories that have resulted from that mandate. Although commissioned by the Government, they are not intended as definitive or official, but rather as the efforts of scholars to bring together much of what is known about the ethnic groups studied, to indicate what remains to be learned, and thus to stimulate further research concerning the ethnic dimension in Canadian society. The histories are to be objective, analytical, and readable, and directed towards the general reading public, as well as students at the senior high school and the college and university levels, and teachers in the elementary schools.

Most Canadians belong to an ethnic group, since to do so is simply to have "a sense of identity rooted in a common origin . . . whether this common origin is real or imaginary."[1] The Native Peoples, the British and French (referred to as charter groups because they were the first Europeans to take possession of the land), the groups such as the Germans and Dutch who have been established in Canada for over a hundred years and those who began to arrive only yesterday all have traditions and values that they cherish and that now are part of the cultural riches that Canadians share. The groups vary widely in numbers, geographical location and distribution and degree of social and economic power. The stories of their struggles, failures and triumphs will be told in this series.

As the Royal Commission on Bilingualism and Biculturalism pointed out, this sense of ethnic origin or identity "is much keener in certain individuals than in others."[2] In contemporary Canadian society, with the increasing number of intermarriages across ethnic lines, and hence the growing diversity of peoples ancestors, many are coming to identify themselves as simple Canadian, without reference to their ancestral origins. In focusing on the ethnic dimension of Canadian society, past and present, the series does not assume that everyone should be categorized into one particular group, or that ethnicity is always the most important dimension of people's lives. It is, however, one dimension that needs examination if we are to understand fully the contours and nature of Canadian society and identity.

Professional Canadian historians have in the past emphasized political and economic history, and since the country's economic and political institutions have been controlled largely by people of British and French origin, the role of those of other origins in the development of Canada has been neglected. Also, Canadian historians in the past have been almost exclusively of British and French origin, and have lacked the interest and the linguistic skills necessary to explore the history of other ethnic groups. Indeed, there has rarely ever been an examination of the part played by specifically British - or, better, specifically English, Irish, Scottish and Welsh - traditions and values in Canadian development, because of the lack of recognition of pluralism in the society. The part played by French traditions and values, and particular varieties of French traditions and values, has for a number of reasons been more carefully scrutinized.

This series is an indication of growing interest in Canadian social history, which includes immigration and ethnic history. This may particularly be a reflection of an increasing number of scholars whose origins and ethnic identities are other than British or French. Because such trends are recent, many of the authors of the histories in this series have not had a large body of published writing to work from. It is true that some histories have already been written of particular groups other than the British and French; but these have often been characterized by filio pietism, a narrow perspective and a dearth of scholarly analysis.

Despite the scarcity of secondary sources, the authors have been asked to be as comprehensive as possible, and to give balanced coverage to a number of themes: historical background, settlement patterns, ethnic identity and assimilation, ethnic associations, population trends, religion, values, occupations and social class, the family, the ethnic press, language patterns, political behaviour, education, inter-ethnic relations, the arts and recreation. They have also been asked to give a sense of the way the group differs in various parts of the country. Finally, they have been asked to give, as much as possible, an insider's view of what the immigrant and ethnic experiences were like at different periods of time, but yet at the same time to be as objective as possible, and not simply to present the group as it sees itself, or as it would like to be seen.

The authors have thus been faced with a herculean task. To the extent that they have succeeded, they provide us with new glimpses into many aspects of Canadian society of the past and the present. To the extent that they have fallen short of their goal, they challenge other historians, sociologists and social anthropologists to continue the work begun here.

Jean Burnet
Howard Palmer

[1] *Report of the Royal Commission on Bilingualism and Biculturalism.*
[2] Ibid. Paragraph 8.

Introduction

Since Ukrainians began to settle in western Canada in the early 1890's, their growth in numbers and their achievements have been a dramatic part of the Canadian story. This book presents their accomplishments in numerous fields from the arts to agriculture, from politics to religion and education, and discusses the problems of adjustment which faced successive waves of Ukrainian immigrants. As a people from poverty-stricken eastern Europe whose numbers, especially before World War I, greatly alarmed the host society, they persevered through innumerable hardships to build for themselves and their children a better life in the New World. Today their number in Canada is over 600,000, with most in Ontario, where they constitute slightly over 2 per cent of the total population. They are most significant, however, in the Prairie Provinces, with the largest percentage (11.5) in Manitoba, followed by Saskatchewan (9.2) and Alberta (8.3). Their number in British Columbia has practically tripled since 1951, but today they are still less than 3 per cent of the whole. In Quebec the percentage (0.3) is minor by comparison and that in other parts of Canada is even smaller. Even with the substantial influx of new immigrants after World War II, today over 80 per cent of Canada's Ukrainians are Canadian-born.

The ancestral home of Ukrainians is a large land north of the Black Sea with a population of nearly fifty million, which today is part of the Soviet Union. Most Ukrainians in Canada emigrated from Ukraine's westernmost part – from Galicia and Bukovyna, two provinces once on the eastern periphery of the large Austro-Hungarian Empire. After World War I, most of Galicia and Bukovyna became part of Poland and Romania respectively. Not surprisingly, the small size of the two provinces, hemmed in by hostile neighbours, made for difficulty in identification, and the first Ukrainians were mistaken for Austrians, Poles, Romanians, and Russians and were known by various names – Galicians, Bukovynians, and later Ruthenians, after *Rutheni*, the traditional name used in documents of the Roman Catholic curia when referring to

Ukrainians or Belo-russians. Within the Austro-Hungarian Empire Ukrainians referred to themselves as *rusyny*, a term which led easily to further confusion of Ukrainians with Russians, for few among the first arrivals to Canada had sufficient knowledge of their own history to enlighten a host society equally uninformed about eastern Europe.

The historic roots of Ukrainians lie deep in the medieval princely era of Kievan Rus', which reached its zenith under Volodymyr (Vladimir) the Great (980-1015) and Iaroslav the Wise (d. 1054). Thereafter the Realm of Rus' gradually disintegrated amidst internecine princely quarrels and Tatar attacks (after 1223), and by the 1340's Ukraine was an easy prey to its marauding neighbours. In 1569, with the Union of Lublin, the Kingdom of Poland within the Commonwealth of Poland and Lithuania was given control over the greater part of the Ukrainian lands. The stage was thus set for the religious Act of Union in 1596, which gave birth to the Greek Catholic or Uniate Church, whose influence was greatest in Galicia, the territory nearest Roman Catholic Poland. With Orthodox Moldavia's control of most of Bukovyna firm, the westernmost part of Ukraine was thus divided along religious as well as political lines.

Opposition to Polish rule grew steadily and was led by the burghers, who disliked the acceptance of Polish values by most of the Ukrainian nobility. Orthodox church brotherhoods, encouraged by a small group of nobles who continued to value Ukrainian culture, became the vanguard of resistance to Polish rule. In addition, thousands of peasants resented the increased obligations of labour service (the dreaded *panshchyna*) imposed by the Poles. Many fled southeast to the Zaporozhian centre (*sich*), south of the Dnieper rapids, where the Cossacks had been living since the fifteenth century.

In 1648 Bohdan Khmelnytsky became the head (hetman) of the Cossack Zaporozhian Sich and with the support of the Crimean Tatars led a successful expedition westward, which liberated Lviv and penetrated deeply into Polish territory. In search of allies more reliable than the Turks and Tatars, he formed a military alliance with Moscovy in 1654. The treaty has been a subject of much controversy ever since (even in Canada), with some seeing it as an incorporation of Ukraine into the Muscovite state and others as merely a personal union between two monarchs. What is not in dispute, however, is that under Khmelnytsky, Ukraine once more became a force in European politics and for a brief period prior to his death in 1657 even an independent state.

With the end of Khmelnytsky's uprising, Ukraine was neatly divided along the Dnieper River into its right and left banks, with Poland in charge of the former and Russia the latter. In 1772, with the first partition of Poland, Russia acquired all Ukrainian lands under Polish rule except for Galicia, which was absorbed by the Austro-Hungarian Empire. Two years later, as a result of the Russo-Turkish war, Austria added

Bukovyna. (The Ukrainian lands south of the Carpathians were within the Kingdom of Hungary and thus already part of the Hapsburg Empire.) The destruction of the Zaporozhian Sich by Moscow in 1775 marked Ukraine's total denouement as a separate body politic; it became "Little Russia."

When World War I brought on the Russian Revolution of March, 1917, Ukraine reasserted its national character, demanding everything from the use of the Ukrainian language and access to Ukrainian schools to self-government within the Russian state and even complete independence. Ukrainians in Canada were much affected by these events, as several essays in this volume point out, but perhaps the most impressive fact is the great letdown that most Ukrainians experienced by 1923 when all political and military action had failed and the domination of Ukraine, Galicia, and Bukovyna by Russia, Poland, and Romania respectively was re-established.

The essays in this volume deal with a people who for most of their history had enjoyed only very brief periods of political independence. Even more rarely had all ethnic Ukrainian lands constituted a single, unified state, free of foreign occupants. This sense of statelessness is central to understanding most aspects of Ukrainian life in Canada. The importance attached to it divides the organized community, alienates others who might otherwise join, and differentiates the majority of ethnically conscious Ukrainians from most other ethnocultural groups and from the wider Canadian society. For the Canadian of Ukrainian origin, the fact of foreign domination underlies almost everything – from the very need to emigrate in the first instance to subsequent decades of preoccupation with linguistic and cultural survival. Others in Canada have shared similar concerns but seldom with the same sense of urgency as the Ukrainians. For Ukrainians, the fear of losing their ethnic identity through physical separation from the ancestral homeland has been greatly intensified by the perennial uncertainty of Ukraine's own political and cultural survival.

In this context, it should surprise no one that the leaders have always sought to foster national consciousness (especially among the first group of largely denationalized peasant-settlers); to insist upon correct collective identification as Ukrainians; to champion Ukrainian independence; to establish English-Ukrainian bilingual schools; to elect Ukrainians to political office; to contribute to Ukrainian causes; and to heal religious differences, especially in recent years. As a result, the first Ukrainians in Canada, in particular, acquired a reputation for being intensely nationalistic – a people who posed their own narrow "parochial" interests against the broad "patriotic" nation-building interests espoused by Anglo and Celtic Canadians determined to place the stamp of English-speaking Protestant Ontario upon the young and heterogeneous West.

The situation was fraught with ethnic and religious tensions born of insecurities in the Old and New Worlds, some of which remain to the present day.

The fifteen essays in this volume have no central theme. The approach is topical, with one large topic per essay. With several contributors, some duplication was inevitable. A work by a single writer may have been preferable, but the state of existing knowledge is still insufficient for a single author to attempt a comprehensive study. Most contributors, however, undertook considerable new research and synthesis of data, and the essays contain much new information and some fresh insights.

The book begins with the social situation in western Ukraine (Galicia and Bukovyna) on the eve of migration. John-Paul Himka discusses the peasant's growing political consciousness in the latter half of the nineteenth century. This consciousness was spurred on by liberal and radical influences. In the second essay the three waves of settlement and colonization are discussed by the late Vladimir J. Kaye (Kysilewsky), assisted by Frances Swyripa, and the evidence for changing the traditional date of the first Ukrainian contact with Canada is assessed. In the essay on economic development Wsevolod Isajiw examines how the low entrance status of Ukrainians as peasant-settlers and unskilled labourers has affected their subsequent social mobility. Three essays are devoted to political development because no scholar has yet produced a study of that difficult subject comparable to Paul Yuzyk's exhaustive work in the area of religion. While Bohdan Harasymiw's essay on the most recent political period is optimistic as to the impact of ethnicity on Canada's political system, Paul Yuzyk views the future viability of Ukrainian-Canadian religious organizations pessimistically. In the discussion of community organizations Ol'ha Woycenko chronicles their recent decline, although a distinctive feature of Oleh Gerus's sympathetic account of the Ukrainian Canadian Committee is the attention given to the role Ukrainian Canadians have played in bringing Ukrainians in all parts of the Western world together. My own account of the struggle to obtain Ukrainian-language instruction in provincial schools is the first attempt to take the story past the controversies of the pre-1916 period to the present day. In Frances Swyripa's essay on private education, the little-known efforts of the Protestant and Roman Catholic missions are brought together for the first time. Yuri Daschko then analyses the Ukrainian-Canadian press, and Robert B. Klymasz treats the varied manifestations of the Ukrainian-Canadian aesthetic experience in the performing and graphic arts.

The last two essays deal with both English- and Ukrainian-language works in the fields of poetry and prose, scholarship, and historiography. First, Yar Slavutych discusses the literary output on Canadian soil of Ukrainians who wrote primarily in Ukrainian or who may be termed Ukrainian-Canadian writers. Although narrower in scope than a study of the literary output of Canadian authors of Ukrainian origin who write in

English, the size of the undertaking and the difficulty of determining ethnic content in the English-language literature of Canadians of Ukrainian origin who explore universal themes necessitated the limitation. In the other essay Frances Swyripa reviews what non-Ukrainians and Ukrainian Canadians have written about Ukrainians in Canada in English and Ukrainian.

The inadequate state of research, already noted, is responsible for some limitations in the book at hand. The emphasis is too exclusively on the organized Ukrainian-Canadian community, where records are most readily available. As a result, certain important issues, problems, and themes are barely mentioned or are ignored altogether: the world view of the Ukrainian peasant-settler; the life of the Ukrainian navvy, urban labourer, and industrial employee; the nature and influence of the most successful individual Ukrainian entrepreneurs; the life of Ukrainians during the Great Depression and their involvement in the Communist Party; the nature and activities of the Ukrainian-Canadian extreme right; the orientation of Ukrainian Canadians to the issues and concerns which animate those who see themselves as part of the worldwide Ukrainian diaspora; and the role of youth and student groups. What is needed are social historians or sociologically oriented scholars who will probe the changes in family life, patterns of authority, and fundamental values and identity in the typical Ukrainian rural communities of western Canada and in the urban enclaves of the larger cities.

The development of Ukrainian communities in Ontario, Quebec, and British Columbia is given scant attention in this volume, partly because the interwar and post-war periods, when these areas became important to Ukrainian Canadians, have still to receive the scholarly attention they deserve. The Anglo-Celtic response to and perception of the first wave of Ukrainians, in particular, is touched upon in several essays, but the changing attitude toward Ukrainian Canadians since World War II, including the growing interest in Ukrainian food, folklore, and festivals on the part of Ukrainians and non-Ukrainians alike, is also given only passing attention.

This volume, then, is far from a definitive history of the Ukrainians in Canada. From the essays, however, the reader can obtain a fairly good idea of the history and the economic, political, and cultural development of the Ukrainians in Canada – a group large enough and old enough to place itself among the West's founding peoples. But the fate of Ukrainians in Canada is at best uncertain. Without fresh immigrants, and with a Canadian-style birth rate, the threat of complete assimilation is ever present. To identify oneself in ethnocultural terms has become easier since the last world war, but whether subsequent Canadian-born generations – tomorrow's focal point of *A Heritage in Transition* – will feel the impact of multiculturalism sufficiently to carry a dual identity remains to be seen. Their response will determine everything – including, of course, the nature of future histories about the life of Ukrainians in Canada.

In the meantime, it is well to note their rapid advance in educational level, their concomitant rise in occupational and socio-economic status, their leadership in pressing for a rethinking of ethnic policy in Canada, their scholarly and literary achievements, their range of community organizations, the incredible lengths to which some will go to retain their language and to manifest their culture, and their devotion to Canada in the face of discrimination experienced by few others in Canada. There is certainly cause to celebrate these achievements.

Numerous individuals play large roles in the preparation of such a volume. Foremost are the various authors who agreed "to essay" contributions and who accepted with such good grace modifications, criticisms, and deadlines. Their co-operation is gratefully acknowledged, with apologies for numerous unavoidable delays. Gratefully acknowledged also is the assistance provided during the early stages by Dr. Ivan L. Rudnytsky, professor of Ukrainian history, University of Alberta. I am pleased to record a special debt of gratitude to Mr. Orest Martynowych, without whose diligence as a research assistant the inadequacies of this volume would have been much more numerous. My thanks also go to Miss Jennifer McQueen, Mr. Steve Jaworsky, Mr. Myron Momryk, Mrs. Roberta Russell, and Ms. Yok Leng Chang in the Multiculturalism Directorate of the Secretary of State for many courtesies; to Ms. Diane Mew for editorial assistance; to Mr. Martynowych, Dr. John-Paul Himka, Dr. Andrij Hornjatkevyč, Mr. Jars Balan, and Mr. Nestor Makuch for assistance with translation and transliteration; and to Mrs. Doris Dobbin, Mrs. Luba Dzubak-Petryshyn, Miss Anhelyna Szuch, Miss Olenka Lupul, and Mrs. Khrystia Kohut for typing the manuscript. I am especially indebted to the series editors, Dr. Howard Palmer, University of Calgary, and Dr. Jean Burnet, Glendon College, York University, for their moral support and scholarly assistance. Finally, I wish to thank my wife, Natalie, for her usual understanding in coping with the impositions which accompany scholarly work.

M.R. Lupul
Edmonton, 1982

Note on Transliteration and Names

TRANSLITERATION

In the text and footnotes a modified Library of Congress system of transliteration is followed (but without diacritical marks and ligatures). Only in the essay on "Ukrainian Literature in Canada" has the Library of Congress system (again without diacritical marks and ligatures) been applied consistently.

Table of Transliteration

а	a	у	u
б	b	ф	f
в	v	х	kh
г	h	ц	ts
ґ	g	ч	ch
д	d	ш	sh
е	e	щ	shch
є	ie*	ю	iu*
ж	zh	я	ia*
з	z	ь	' (omitted, except in the word Rus' and in the essay on "Literature")
и	y		
й	i*		
і	i	-ий	y (in endings of personal names only*)
ї	i		
к	k		
л	l		
м	m		
н	n		
о	o		
п	p		
р	r		
с	s		
т	t		

* except in the essay on "Ukrainian Literature in Canada"

NAMES

Names of Persons

The personal names of Ukrainians who did not live in Canada, Britain, or the United States are cited according to their Ukrainian spelling and transliterated according to the Table of Transliteration. A notable exception is Joseph Oleskiw, who is cited in the Canadian context rather than the Ukrainian (Osyp Oleskiv) or Polish (Jósef, Josef Oleskόw).

The personal names of Ukrainian Canadians (as well as Ukrainians who lived in Britain or the United States) are cited either according to the spelling the person used (where known) when signing his or her name in English *or* according to well-established usage in Canada, Britain, or the United States. Where the discrepancy between the English spelling in common usage and the Ukrainian name might cause confusion, the Ukrainian name, spelled according to the Table of Transliteration, is included in parentheses: Paul Crath (Pavlo Krat), John Navis (Ivan Navizivsky).

Names of Newspapers and Periodicals

The names of Ukrainian newspapers and periodicals (Canadian, American, European) are transliterated according to the Table of Transliteration. Generally, English translations are included in parentheses only for those newspapers and periodicals published outside Canada. However, in the essay on the press and in the Index, English translations of all names are included in parentheses.

Where the name of a specific Ukrainian-Canadian newspaper or periodical is mentioned frequently in a single chapter, it has sometimes been abbreviated: *Ukrainskyi holos = Holos; Kanadiiskyi farmer = Farmer; Robochyi narod = Narod.*

Names of Ukrainian Organizations

The names of Ukrainian organizations which do not exist in Canada are transliterated according to the Table of Transliteration and the English translation is included in parentheses. The names of Ukrainian-Canadian organizations are given only in their English form in the text and in the Index. The names of a few (turn-of-the-century) Ukrainian-Canadian organizations which do not have English equivalents are transliterated according to the Table of Transliteration or spelled according to well-established usage: e.g., Zaporozhian Sich, Boyan Drama Society.

Abbreviations have been derived either from the Ukrainian or English name of an organization in order to comply with well-established usage and to avoid confusion: Ukrainian Catholic Brotherhood (BUK) not (UCB); Ukrainian Labour-Farmer Temple Association (ULFTA) not (TURF-Dim). In the Index, abbreviations for organizations are used sparingly.

Geographical Names

In general, geographical names within the current boundaries of the Ukrainian Soviet Socialist Republic appear in the Ukrainian form transliterated according to the Table of Transliteration. Thus, Bukovyna (not Bukovina), Polissia (not Polesie), Lviv (not Lvov or Lemberg). The following exceptions are established by standard English usage: Azov, Sea of; Crimea; Dnieper; Dniester; Galicia; Kiev; Odessa; Volhynia. Canadian geographical names of Ukrainian origin are spelled according to established English spelling: Stry (not Stryi); Trembowla (not Terebowla).

Contributors

YURI DASCHKO (M.A., University of Toronto). Policy analyst, National Revenue, Customs and Excise, Ottawa.

OLEH W. GERUS (Ph.D., University of Toronto). Associate professor, Department of History, University of Manitoba.

ROSE T. HARASYM (B.A., University of Western Ontario).

BOHDAN HARASYMIW (Ph.D., University of Toronto). Associate professor, Department of Political Science, University of Calgary.

JOHN-PAUL HIMKA (Ph.D., University of Michigan). Canadian Institute of Ukrainian Studies, University of Alberta.

WSEVOLOD W. ISAJIW (Ph.D., Catholic University of America). Professor, Department of Sociology, University of Toronto.

VLADIMIR J. KAYE (KYSILEWSKY), 1896-1976 (Ph.D., University of Vienna). Co-founder and first president of the Canadian Association of Slavists; associate professor, University of Ottawa.

NADIA KAZYMYRA (M.A., Carleton University). Public Archives of Canada.

ROBERT B. KLYMASZ (Ph.D., Indiana University).

MANOLY R. LUPUL (Ph.D., Harvard University). Professor, Department of Educational Foundations; director, Canadian Institute of Ukrainian Studies, University of Alberta.

OREST T. MARTYNOWYCH (M.A., University of Manitoba). Graduate student, University of Michigan.

YAR SLAVUTYCH (Ph.D., University of Pennsylvania). Professor, Department of Slavic Languages, University of Alberta.

FRANCES A. SWYRIPA (M.A., University of Alberta). Canadian Institute of Ukrainian Studies, University of Alberta.

OL'HA WOYCENKO. Author and historian, Ottawa.

PAUL YUZYK (Ph.D., University of Minnesota). Professor emeritus, Department of History, University of Ottawa; member of the Senate of Canada.

ONE

The Background to Emigration: Ukrainians of Galicia and Bukovyna, 1848-1914

John-Paul Himka

I

> "We don't need Peruvian gold mines. The skin of the peasant – that's the best Peru."
>
> – Prince Adam Czartoryski

Throughout the nineteenth century and until 1917, the Ukrainian people were divided between the large, multinational empires of the Romanovs and Hapsburgs. In 1900 some seventeen million Ukrainians lived in the Russian Empire; in the Austro-Hungarian Empire there were about three million Ukrainians in Galicia, 300,000 in Bukovyna, and 400,000 in Carpatho-Ukraine (Subcarpathia). The latter, in the Hungarian part of Austria-Hungary, sent few immigrants to Canada,[1] and the Ukrainians of the Russian Empire do not appear to have emigrated to North America in large numbers, preferring, if they left at all, to homestead on the virgin soil of southern Siberia. Thus, almost every Ukrainian who arrived in Canada before World War I was an emigrant from the Austrian crownlands of Galicia and Bukovyna.

Though they provided so many Ukrainian immigrants for Canada, Galicia and Bukovyna were not exclusively inhabited by Ukrainians. In fact, they were among the most heterogeneous regions in that collection of peoples known as Austria. Galicia's population was about 40 per cent Ukrainian, 40 per cent Polish, and 10 per cent Jewish, with a small German minority. In Bukovyna the population was about 40 per cent Ukrainian and 30 per cent Romanian, with the remainder German and Jewish. The Ukrainians inhabited the eastern part of Galicia and northern Bukovyna, which are today in the Ukrainian Soviet Socialist Republic (Lviv, Ternopil, and Ivano-Frankivsk oblasts or districts are eastern Galicia; Chernivtsi oblast is northern Bukovyna). The Poles and Romanians lived mainly in western Galicia and southern Bukovyna, which are today in Poland (the region south and east of Cracow) and Romania (the Suceava region). But Poles and Romanians also lived in eastern Galicia and northern Bukovyna, where they formed the upper class, owned the great estates, dominated the government, and together with the Jews and Germans made up about 75 per cent of the urban population. The Ukrainians lived in the countryside and worked the land. As late as 1900, 95 per cent of the Ukrainian population of Galicia and Bukovyna were peasants.

In the Hapsburg Empire, peasant emancipation came in 1848 with the abolition of *panshchyna*, the equivalent of the corvée, the peasants' compulsory, unremunerative labour on the lords' estates. The abolition of serfdom, however, did not end the long period of exploitation by Polish noblemen in Galicia and by their Romanian counterparts, the boyars, in Bukovyna. By the terms of emancipation, the lord retained his large estate and the peasant received small plots, the so-called rustical lands he had tended and which had sustained him for centuries. Despite the decidedly unequal division, it did appear at first that the nobility would be ruined. The large estates required labour, now subject to the vagaries of the market. For the first few decades after 1848, the peasant was reluctant to return to the estate, even for wages.[2] The respite ended, however, when the peasant's plot began to decrease in size while the demands of a money economy increased. The peasants who then glutted the labour market were obliged to work long hours for subsistence wages. *Panshchyna* returned in a new form, because the unequal division of land left the emancipated peasant in economic bondage to the lord.

However inequitable, the division of the land did at least delineate clearly what the nobleman and peasant owned. The same could not be said for the forests and pastures. Where previously the peasants had enjoyed the use of forest and pasture lands, with emancipation the nobles in Galicia and Bukovyna appropriated both. The peasants took to the courts, but by 1881, out of 32,000 cases in Galicia involving claims to forests and pastures, the peasants had won only 2,000 in a judicial system controlled by the nobility. As a result, if the peasant wished to graze his cow, build a cottage, heat his home, or even gather mushrooms, he had to pay the lord in cash or labour.[3]

The nobility, then, did not lose much from the abolition of corvée labour. Nonetheless, when a short-lived Austrian Parliament debated the subject in 1848, the nobles insisted on compensation. A Ukrainian peasant deputy, Ivan Kapushchak, strongly objected and suggested that the lords keep "the whips they used on our exhausted bodies."[4] The Austrian government, however, favoured the nobility, who were compensated by special supplementary taxes paid by the peasants. As late as the 1880's, these amounted to about 50 per cent of the regular state taxes in Galicia, a much higher rate than elsewhere in Austria: in Bohemia, Moravia, and Silesia the supplementary taxes were only 3 to 7 per cent.

Compensation in Galicia was paid for half a century after the abolition of serdom.[5]

Another form of peasant exploitation was propination or monopoly over the production and sale of alcoholic beverages. In the mid-1870's the nobles received five million gulden[6] annually from this source. The right was abandoned in 1889 on condition that the nobles receive 66 million gulden, a huge amount considering that one gulden could support an agricultural worker for two days.

The nobles frequently leased their right of propination to tavern keepers, who often doubled as money-lenders. While tavern loans provided the Ukrainian peasants with immediate relief from difficulty, drinking on credit or defaulting on a loan could lead to the ultimate tragedy: the loss of land. As a result, antagonism – tempered only by the peasant's dependency – developed between the innkeeper-lenders and the villagers, an antagonism with ethnic and religious dimensions, since most of the tavern keepers and money-lenders were Jewish.[7] This was the root cause of much of the anti-Semitism of the East European peasantry.

It would be wrong, however, to see the situation solely in terms of Poles, Romanians, and Jews living off the labour of the Ukrainian peasants. Polish and Romanian peasants in western Galicia and southern Bukovyna fared little better economically under nobles of their own nationality. Nor did the many poor Jews, the so-called *kaptsonim* and *Luftmenschen*, escape mistreatment from the wealthy of their community. Moreover, within Ukrainian society itself there were classes that exploited the peasantry. The few Ukrainian peasants who were better off acted much like the lords, money-lenders, and innkeepers of other nationalities. They hired landless or dwarf-holding peasants to work for them at subsistence wages, lent money at high interest,[8] and, especially in the years before World War I, occasionally came to control local taverns. The richer peasants also dominated the village government because of the procedure by which officials were elected. The village chief (*viit*), scribe, and councilmen often abused their considerable powers when assessing taxes, making loans, aiding the poor from the communal treasury, assigning peasants to repair roads, functioning as the village police, issuing various certificates, and granting exemptions from military service and licences to open shops.[9]

Rich peasants were not the only Ukrainians in the village to live off the labour of others. The priest, Greek Catholic in Galicia and Orthodox in most of Bukovyna, had three sources of income: a salary from the government, a sizable farm (twelve to fifty hectares), and fees for sacramental rites. Even the pastor of a poor parish of eighty households could make more than his salary (380 gulden) from burial fees,[10] not to mention the additional income from weddings, christenings, and prayer services. Moreover, since the priest farmed as one of the large landholders in the village, he could behave like the noble when the peasants claimed gleaning and pasturing privileges.[11]

Outside the village, too, there were Ukrainians who could thank the peasant for their daily bread. The secular intelligentsia, predominantly lawyers,[12] derived their livelihood directly or indirectly from the peasantry; among the more direct methods were court cases and investments in parcellation. By 1881, Galician peasants had paid an estimated fifteen million gulden for court cases involving only pastures and forests. Parcellation, the sale of large manorial estates in plots small enough for peasants to purchase, had become a special branch of commerce dominated by lawyers and merchants by the turn of the century. In about 65 per cent of the cases, speculating middlemen – and not the estate-owners themselves – initiated plans to parcel, with the middlemen generally reaping a 25 to 50 per cent profit on each sale. During the 1902-1904 period alone, Galician peasants paid eight to fifteen million crowns annually to the parcellation intermediaries.[13]

The Ukrainian peasant, then, was enmeshed in a system of exploitation. It is true that lawyers worked to defend the peasant in court cases, that lenders and investors risked their money, and that innkeepers and priests required a livelihood. (Some may even feel that the nobles had a legitimate claim to their economic privileges.) But the fact remains that the peasant worked to support a good many others besides himself. When the Ukrainian peasant looked up, he could see above him, riding on his back, the Polish noble, the Romanian boyar, the Jewish innkeeper-lender, and a few of his own people as well; but when he looked down, all he could see was earth, and precious little of that.

II

Hey! Who in the world has a better lot
Than he who plows the sacred earth?
Than he who falls in debt
  as deep as the bottomless sea,
Than he who struggles on
  till driven to auction his land,
Than he who reaps for someone else,
Hey! Who in the world has a better lot?

– Ivan Franko, "Khliborob" (The Farmer)

The typical Galician peasant farmed in a primitive manner, even in the late nineteenth century. He used a light plough, either completely or mostly of wood. Only wealthy peasants employed factory-made steel ploughs. They might also own a chaff-cutter powered by a treadmill, but only the manor could afford a threshing machine. Most peasants threshed with flails and winnowed with sieves. They used little artificial fertilizer, and crop rotation replaced the three-field system only at the turn of the century.[14] It is therefore not surprising that, as Table 1 shows, the Ukrainian peasant in eastern Galicia produced much less on a single hectare of land than did farmers elsewhere.

From Table 2, one can see that about half the landholdings came to less than two hectares, the great majority to less than five. The legal holding represented in the table was not identical with the size of the farm unit. Perhaps half the peasant families had two holdings, the husband's and the wife's. Even so, most peasant families owned less than five hectares, the minimum required to support a family. Not included in the table, of course, are landless peasants. The manorial estates, including the property of such institutions as the Greek Catholic Church, made up almost all holdings of over twenty hectares. Although estates accounted for only 2 per cent of all holdings, they occupied half the land used for agriculture, husbandry, and forestry.

TABLE 1

Grain Production (in Quintals) Per Hectare of Arable Land, 1907

	Eastern Galicia	*Bukovyna*	*Lower Austria*	*Denmark*
Wheat	10.8	13.6	15.5	31.0
Rye	8.6	11.4	13.8	19.0
Barley	8.0	12.8	14.7	—
Oats	6.5	10.9	11.6	—

Note: The figures for Denmark refer to the average harvest in 1903-12.

Source: W. Najdus, *Szkice z historii Galicji* (Essays on the History of Galicia), 2 vols. (Warsaw: 1958-60), I, p. 32. F. Buzek, *Wybór pism* (Selected Writings), 2 vols. (Warsaw, 1976), II, p. 390.

TABLE 2

The Size of Agricultural Landholdings in Galicia and Bukovyna, 1900-1902

Size of holding in hectares	*Galicia*		*Bukovyna*	
	Per cent of holdings	*Per cent of area*	*Per cent of holdings*	*Per cent of area*
Up to 2	49.0	9.2	56.6	
2-5	30.7	19.8	28.6	39
5-10	14.9	15.7	9.4	
10-20	3.8	8.1	3.1	
Over 20	1.6	47.2	2.2	61

Note: The data for Galicia refer to 1902, for Bukovyna to 1900.

Source: Najdus, *Szkice z historii Galicji*, I, p. 105. D. Kvitkovsky *et al.*, *Bukovyna. li mynule i suchasne* (Bukovyna: Its Past and Present) (Paris, 1956), pp. 449-50.

The small size of the Ukrainian farm unit was partly the result of a long historical process. The Ukrainian peasant divided his land among his children. Quite naturally, given the high birth rates,[15] each successive generation received less land than the previous one. Using statistics from 1819, 1859, and 1876, Ivan Franko calculated that the number of peasant holdings increased proportionally, 100:154:275, while the size of these holdings shrank proportionally, 100:67:37.[16]

The transition to a capitalist economy in agriculture accelerated the shrinking of peasant landholdings. Under serfdom, the lord of the manor had been, in theory and frequently in practice, responsible for feeding his serfs in the event of a bad harvest, cattle epidemic, fire, or other catastrophe. With emancipation, however, all mutual obligations ceased; in times of need, instead of applying to the lord for a subsidy, the peasant would have to borrow money or grain. The stage was thus set for a tragedy frequently enacted in Austrian Ukraine: the peasant would take out a loan, invariably at high interest; he would find that he could not pay his mounting debt; and a court would order him to auction his land, in part or entirely. In 1868 a series of laws abolished all limits on interest and all restrictions on the division of land.

The peasant would borrow at various crucial times: in the spring before sowing, when he had already consumed the produce of the last harvest; at tax collection time; on the eve of the great feast days; when involved in a court case; when the host at weddings or christenings; or, more rarely, when buying land, tools, or cattle. In some regions of Galicia in the 1870's nearly 90 per cent of the population was in debt.[17]

Generally, the annual interest rate was 52 to 104 per cent (one or two kreuzers weekly for every gulden borrowed), though rates were occasionally as low as 25 or as high as 500 per cent. Those who defaulted (no rare occurrence considering the high rates) were forced by the courts to auction their land. In the last quarter of the nineteenth century in Galicia the courts ordered over 2,400 auctions annually. In the mid-1890's almost a third of the land auctions paid for loans of less than 100 crowns. In many cases, peasants sold land to pay debts even without a court order.[18]

III

Oi pidu ia v Buryslavku hroshyi
zarobliaty,
Iak sia vernu z Buryslavky,
budu gazduvaty.

(Oy, I'll go to Buryslavka to
make some money,
When I return from Buryslavka,
I'll be farming my own land.)

– a Galician folksong

From the foregoing it should be clear why the Ukrainian peasant found it difficult to support himself and those who lived from his labour, and why many peasants simply lost out in the struggle for existence. A publicist in the late 1880's calculated that 50,000 Galicians died every year from hunger or diseases related to malnutrition.[19] To survive, many Ukrainian peasants were forced to seek supplementary incomes. Some went to work in "Buryslavka," the one sizable industry in Austrian Ukraine. Others hired themselves out as farm labourers. Still others, especially as the nineteenth century drew to a close, earned money through seasonal emigration.

"Buryslavka" was what the peasants called the extraction of oil and mineral wax (ozocerite) from the land around Drohobych and Boryslav. This was the most important, most lucrative, and unquestionably the most brutal industry in late nineteenth-century Galicia. It was also in some respects the most advanced economic enterprise in Austrian Ukraine, attracting investors from western Europe and the United States. Even Rockefeller's Standard Oil had holdings in Galicia.[20]

Galician law encouraged the most predatory exploitation of the oil and ozocerite deposits. Since companies could buy relatively small patches of land, rival companies set their rigs close together to work the same deposit. Because, by law, the oil belonged to whoever could extract it the fastest, everything, including the ecological balance and the workers' safety, was subordinated to the quickest possible extraction. The oil was collected in buckets by workers lowered on ropes into the wells. With the shafts poorly supported and the air thin and mixed with noxious gases, explosions, cave-ins, broken ropes, and asphyxiation were common occurrences in the oilfields.[21] For this dangerous work, the oilmen received from thirty to fifty kreuzers daily (1870). If they were fortunate enough to receive their full wage, they might save a few kreuzers. But numerous exploitative practices were prevalent: workers were fined for tardiness and insubordinate talk; paymasters extorted two kreuzers from each day's pay; and sometimes oilmen were paid in tokens which shopkeepers discounted at 80 to 95 per cent of their face value.[22]

Still, many young Ukrainian peasants risked life and limb in the shafts of Boryslav. Some bragged about working three twelve-hour shifts in succession and sang about oilmen buying cigars and braided loaves (*kolachyky*).[23] It is difficult to say how many workers Boryslav employed, but a safe estimate for the 1870's would be 15,000, more than half of whom were Ukrainian peasants from the surrounding countryside.[24]

The most common way, by far, for Ukrainian peasants to supplement their income was to hire themselves out as farm labourers, those with small holdings on a daily basis and the landless ones annually. For working fourteen to eighteen hours a day, the day labourer might receive every twelfth sheaf he cut, or he might, depending on the season, earn half a crown or a full crown in cash. Women and children received considerably less than adult males. Men in summer received 110 hallers, women only seventy-five.[25] At times, the manor hired children to tend cattle, with food and shelter as recompense. By 1900, perhaps a million Ukrainian peasants in Galicia and Bukovyna were working at least occasionally as agricultural labourers.[26]

Toward the end of the nineteenth century, more ambitious peasants left Galicia and Bukovyna for a few months or years to earn money elsewhere. In 1910 over 82,000 Ukrainians from Galicia worked in Prussia, either in agriculture (about 60 per cent) or industry (40 per cent).[27] The emigrant working in Prussia could set aside 100 to 200 gulden after eight to ten months. If the peasant ventured to work in the coal mines of Pennsylvania, he might earn 600 gulden a year. After three or four years in America, he could return a wealthy man, able to lend money, hire farm hands, and, most importantly, buy land.

Emigration, then, could produce the most radical improvement in the peasant's prosperity. In the early twentieth century hundreds of thousands of Ukrainian peasants left their homeland either temporarily or permanently. By 1910, the income of one in four Galician inhabitants was largely derived from seasonal emigration.

IV

I am a son of the people,
  the son of a nation on the rise . . .
I am a peasant: not epilogue,
  but prologue.

– Ivan Franko, "Dekadent"

Powerful socio-economic forces were pushing the Ukrainian peasants into the mines of Boryslav and back to the lord's estate. Eventually, they even pushed them across the ocean. But the Ukrainian peasants did not leave without a struggle. Major revolts in Bukovyna and Galicia occurred in the 1840's, when peasants refused to work for the manor and seized the nobles' woods and pastures. Like most peasant revolts, they were defeated, though they did strengthen the government's determination to abolish corvée labour. In the decades following emancipation, many observers predicted Galicia would be the scene of bloody peasant rebellions.[28] Although no full-scale jacquerie occurred, there were sporadic incidents of violent peasant resistance to the lord or the tax collector. In the village of Khorostiv, for example, a group of peasants attacked a hunting party of nobles for trampling on the winter sowing. In Cherliany in 1880, 150 peasants assaulted an armed detachment of tax collectors who had confiscated their property.[29] Although such acts were important for the peasants' sense of dignity, they held no prospect of changing the grim realities of life. The peasants were too uneducated and isolated in their villages to initiate any political movements in Ukraine. Instead, the initiative for political organization passed to the educated strata of Ukrainian society – the intelligentsia and the clergy.

Ukrainian politics in Austria[30] were born amid the upheavals in Europe stemming from the revolutionary year of 1848. From the viewpoint of the all-European revolution, the restive Polish gentry in Galicia seemed to be in the forefront of the democratic, anti-monarchist struggle. From the Ukrainian viewpoint, however, the Polish revolutionary movement signified the greater ascendancy of Poles over Ukrainians and of the gentry over the peasants. In opposition, the Ukrainians of Galicia and Bukovyna (then united in a single administrative unit) established the Supreme Ruthenian Council (*Holovna ruska rada*). This was a turning point in the Ukrainian national awakening. Previously, because Polish nobles had set the tone in cultured society, educated Ukrainians in Austria had also considered themselves Polish. Although in 1848 many of the members of the Supreme Ruthenian Council were still more comfortable in the Polish language than in Ukrainian, they now asserted their separate national identity. This was the heritage of the romantic nationalism that had made some progress in the preceding generation. Significantly, the first Ukrainian-language periodicals began to appear precisely during the revolution of 1848. The Supreme Ruthenian Council sought to defend the rights of Ukrainians by demanding the partition of Galicia into separate Polish and Ukrainian crownlands. The Council in Lviv and its branches in the countryside collected over 200,000 signatures on petitions for the division of Galicia, thus indicating that the Ukrainian national idea was beginning to penetrate among the peasantry.[31]

During the decade of absolutism that followed the stifling of the revolution in 1850, Ukrainian national life entered a state of hibernation, with national leadership in the cautious hands of the Greek Catholic hierarchy in Lviv. Under the surface, however, an important debate began on the question of national identity. The 1848 revolution had established the Ukrainians, in their own and in others' minds, as a people distinct from the Poles. This settled who the Ukrainians were not, but not who they were. Some Ukrainians argued that they were really part of the Russian nation. The Russophiles, who first appeared in the 1850's, advocated a close political and cultural relationship with tsarist Russia, and several factors supported them. Ukrainians and Russians did share many linguistic, religious, and cultural traits that distinguished both from the Poles. The Russian government and Slavophiles supported the Russophile movement financially and morally. Moreover, many Ukrainians in Austria looked for aid to Russia because they felt betrayed by the Austrian government and threatened by Polish domination. Finally, some educated Ukrainians suffered from an inferiority complex because of their peasant culture and lack of a tradition of independent statehood. Through union with the Russian nation, they could claim as their own not only a powerful state but a highly developed culture. Russophilism was a strong current in Ukrainian cultural and political life until the mid-1880's, when it began to lose influence in both Galicia and Bukovyna.

Opposed to the Russophiles were the Ukrainophiles or national populists (*narodovtsi*). They emerged in the 1860's and ultimately came to dominate the national movement. The national populists argued that the Ukrainians of Austria belonged to the same nation as the Ukrainian people who lived in the Russian Empire. They favoured using the Ukrainian vernacular in literature and lionized the heroes of the Ukrainian movement in Russian-ruled Ukraine. Among these, pride of place belonged to Taras Shevchenko, a ransomed serf whose poetry expressed the anger and melancholy of a peasant nation.

Two social movements, radicalism and social democracy, adopted the basic tenets of national populism (use of the Ukrainian vernacular, identification with the Ukrainian nation), but both moved beyond purely cultural matters to the question of socio-economic liberation. Radicalism was a non-Marxist, agrarian socialist, and anti-clerical movement. Its first spokesman was a political theorist from Russian-ruled Ukraine, Mykhailo Drahomanov, who argued that the Ukrainian intelligentsia, "which could educate itself only because the people work and sweat," had to dedicate itself "to serving the people morally, politically, and socio-economically with the goal of ridding the people of ignorance, tyranny, and exploitation."[32] Drahomanov's credo made a great impression on Ukrainian university students of the 1870's, especially on two peasants' sons, Ivan Franko and Mykhailo Pavlyk. Franko, a gifted writer, and Pavlyk, less gifted but more tenacious, remained the leaders of the radical movement into the late 1890's. Social democracy was, at first, a current within radicalism. Marxist in orientation, it wished to organize a Ukrainian industrial proletariat that did not then exist. Its chief contribution to Ukrainian political development was that, in the 1890's, it was the first political group to call for the establishment of an independent Ukrainian state.[33]

The ideas of Russophilism, national populism, radicalism, and social democracy reached the peasantry through village institutions that dramatically increased the peasants' cultural level and political awareness. The institutional transformation of the Ukrainian village began in the 1860's, when Austria entered its constitutional era. At first, Ukrainian politics were limited to the educated classes, which constituted only a small minority of the Ukrainian nation. As late as 1900 only 1 per cent of the Ukrainians in Austria were employed in government, the free professions, or the church. If the political movements they initiated were to have any significance, they required the participation of the peasantry, who constituted the overwhelming majority of the nation. The very existence of the constitution and parliamentary system required that the intelligentsia and clergy draw the peasant into political life. The constitution fortunately provided the means to this end through freedom of association, assembly, and press. In the 1860's, then, Ukrainian politics entered a new stage of development characterized by mass participation in national institutions. Institutional development reached maturity by the turn of the century, when modern political parties emerged. Ukrainian political currents had existed before, but only in 1890 did the Galician radicals establish the Radical Party, the first Ukrainian political party in Austria-Hungary. The national populists, with the right wing of the radicals, founded the National Democratic Party in 1899. In the same year left-wing radicals formed the Ukrainian Social Democratic Party in Galicia. In 1906 the Ukrainians in Bukovyna founded both Radical and Social Democratic Parties. From being the concern of an educated elite, Ukrainian politics was being transformed into the concern of the nation as a whole, including the peasantry.

The transformation owed much to the reading club (*chytalnia*), a village organization that met on Sundays and holidays for public readings. One of the few literate peasants in the village, perhaps a church cantor or sacristan, would read aloud to the members from popular newspapers specifically designed for the purpose: *Russkaia rada* (Russian Counsel), founded by the Russophiles in 1871; *Batkivshchyna* (Fatherland), founded by the national populists in 1879; and *Khliborob* (The Farmer), founded by the radicals in 1892. The clubs also read popular booklets published by the same political groups.

All popular periodicals contained practical information on agricultural techniques and the law. Russophile publications stressed saints' lives and liturgical matters more than did the national-populist publications. The radicals and social democrats ridiculed religion and the church and railed against the clergy. The periodicals contained political news, which reflected the program of the publishers and advised the peasant how to vote. Letters from the villages, written by activists in the reading clubs and containing such complaints as one about a village chief bribed with sausage to vote for the Polish candidate and boasts about a village's own co-operative granary, were a regular feature of all popular periodicals. These letters allowed villages to compare themselves on such matters as the number of co-operatives established or Ukrainian candidates elected. In short, the letters – and the reading clubs as a whole – linked the peasants in one village with other peasants in other villages and with writers and editors in the cities. By joining the reading club, the peasant joined the nation.

In spite of opposition from the government, Ukrainian reading clubs flourished. From a handful in the 1870's, thousands existed by 1910.[34] Several umbrella organizations fostered them and published their booklets. The first was Prosvita (Enlightenment), founded by national populists in Lviv in 1868. Six years later the Russophiles set up a rival organization, the Mykhailo Kachkovsky Society in Kolomyia. The Bukovynian equivalent was Ruska Besida (Ruthenian Club), established in 1869. Until the mid-1880's it had a Russophile orientation; thereafter, it was purely Ukrainian and closely allied with Prosvita. The radicals established Narodna Volia (People's Freedom) in Kolomyia in 1893.

Although important for the maintenance of reading clubs, the umbrella organizations were not responsible for their existence in thousands of individual villages. In the nineteenth century the clubs were promoted by the rural clergy, who alone had the educational and financial resources to provide leadership. A vital link between the non-radical intelligentsia and peasantry, the clergy enjoyed exceptional influence in the national movement in Austrian Ukraine. However, when the peasants themselves took over and the reading clubs became forums for their interests, they took even the clergy to task if they charged too much for a christening or if their moral admonitions were considered a nuisance.[35] The radicals, of course, encouraged such conflict and some radical clubs even introduced secular funerals with banners and processions that rivalled the pageantry of the church service. The growth of anticlericalism in the Ukrainian village was one symptom of the larger process of change within the peasantry, concerned to take charge of their own affairs.

Although the great majority of Ukrainian peasants remained illiterate into the twentieth century,[36] the public readings in the reading clubs provided a partial substitute for literacy. The readings allowed the attentive peasant to acquire knowledge about farming, politics, and even about the existence of free lands across the sea. Moreover, the cultural activities of the clubs quickly expanded into areas beyond the printed word. Many had their own choir and some even had amateur theatrical troupes. On such festive occasions as the anniversary of the abolition of serfdom, they would hold evenings of song and verse. Imitating the more elaborate affairs in Lviv and Chernivtsi, they would also arrange commemorative programs in honour of Taras Shevchenko, where peasants would sing and declaim his poetry and someone would read aloud about the life of the former serf, or perhaps the priest or a visiting intellectual might give a talk about the poet's significance. Outside lecturers also visited reading clubs at other times. In the 1880's, in fact, Lviv students spent their summers touring the countryside and speaking to the reading clubs on such topics as the 1848 revolution and the Austrian constitution.

Reading clubs also frequently agitated for the establishment of co-operative stores and loan societies and thus came into conflict with the local tavern keepers and village elite, whose economic monopolies they threatened. Despite numerous difficulties associated with the first peasant business ventures, the co-operative movement flourished in Austrian Ukraine. Co-operative stores in the villages joined the larger organization, Narodna Torhivlia (National Commerce), founded in Lviv in 1883. In 1898 a credit co-operative, Kraiovyi Soiuz Kredytnyi (Crownland Credit Union), was established in Galicia. Agricultural co-operatives were organized as branches of Silskyi Hospodar (Village

Farmer), the first appearing in the village of Oleske in 1899 with an all-Galician organization of the same name founded in Lviv three years later. In 1907 the first dairy co-operative was formed near Stryi.[37]

In politics, too, the Ukrainian peasant gradually became a more important factor, as the newspapers introduced him to the whole range of political issues, national and social. He began to take his vote seriously and to choose his candidates with care. At first, he voted for electors (generally the village chief and a few councilmen) who then participated directly in elections. The system was easily abused by the lords of the manors who bribed or threatened the handful of electors to sway their votes. In response to popular agitation throughout Austria, the electoral procedure was reformed at the turn of the century. In 1897 the direct franchise was extended to all adult males, though the indirect franchise was also retained; in 1907 universal male suffrage completely replaced the indirect franchise.[38] The electoral reforms enhanced the vote of each peasant, but without the political awareness developed in the reading clubs this vote would have meant little. Although electoral abuses did not disappear in Austrian Ukraine, the peasant could send enough national populists and radicals to Parliament to make his presence felt throughout the Empire.

At the same time the peasant began to organize in defence of his class interests. In the late 1890's the radicals began to publish articles and booklets about strikes, and the first strikes of agricultural labourers in Galicia and Bukovyna followed. The momentum of the strike movement surprised even the radicals and social democrats. Agricultural labourers in most of eastern Galicia went on strike in 1902. In 1906-1907, under the influence of the first Russian revolution, another wave of farmworker strikes swept Galicia and Bukovyna. As a result, the wages of the Ukrainian agricultural labourers rose.[39] In the same period, in 1904, the oil workers of Boryslav organized their first successful mass strike, another indication that the Ukrainians of Galicia and Bukovyna were taking command of their own destiny.

In summary, the Ukrainian peasants of Austria knew the hopelessness of working a grudging, shrinking patch of land. They also were tired of the fetid holes of Buryslavka and had had enough of the landlords and their large estates. They found intolerable a system in which most of what they earned seemed to accrue to the nobles, the innkeepers, the mine owners, the priests – to everyone but themselves. In the end, many decided to turn their backs on this and strike out for lands across the ocean.

But during the same period, an organized political and economic struggle was already under way in the homeland. Thus, those who left Galicia and Bukovyna were under the influence, directly or indirectly, of the social and national awakening back home; and this they brought with them to Canada. Many may not have been able to read and write, but they nonetheless understood much. They knew what injustice was and they were learning how to organize to fight it. These were the men and women who stepped off the boat onto Canadian soil.

NOTES

1. Although most Carpatho-Ukrainians emigrated to the United States, some did settle in Canada, e.g., near Lethbridge, Alberta.
2. The labour shortage and the nobility's reaction to it is discussed by K. Wyka, *Teka Stańczyka na tle historii Galicji w latach 1849-1869* ("Stańczyk's File" and the History of Galicia in 1849-1869) (Wrocław: Zakład Narodowy im. Ossolińskich, 1951), pp. 25-30. See also B.P. Murdzek, *Emigration in Polish Social-Political Thought, 1870-1914* (Boulder, Colorado: East European Quarterly, 1977), pp. 84, 88-9.
3. Unless otherwise indicated, the information on agrarian relations is drawn from W. Najdus, *Szkice z historii Galicji* (Essays on the History of Galicia), 2 vols. (Warsaw: Książka i Wiedza, 1958-60), I, pp. 99-170; I. Franko, "Zemelna vlasnist u Halychyni" (Land Ownership in Galicia), *Tvory* (Works), 20 vols. (Kiev: Derzhavne vydavnytstvo khudozhnioi literatury, 1950-56), XIX, pp. 278-304; F. Bujak, *Wybór pism* (Selected Writings), 2 vols. (Warsaw: Państwowe Wydawnictwo Naukowe, 1976), II, pp. 279-397; D. Kvitkovsky *et al.*, *Bukovyna. Ii mynule i suchasne* (Bukovyna: Its Past and Present) (Paris: Zelena Bukovyna, 1956); V. Kurylo *et al.*, *Pivnichna Bukovyna. Ii mynule i suchasne* (Northern Bukovyna: Its Past and Present) (Uzhhorod: Karpaty, 1969).
4. Quoted in R. Rosdolsky, *Die Bauernabgeordneten im konstituierenden österreichischen Reichstag 1848-1849* (The Peasant Delegates in the Constituent Austrian Reichstag 1848-1849) (Vienna: Europaverlag, 1976), p. 138.
5. The financial details of Galician compensation are both complex and tragic. See L. Caro, "Sprawa indemnizacyjna w Galicyi" (The Indemnization Affair in Galicia), *Studya społeczne* (Social Studies), 2nd ed. (Cracow: Czas, 1908), pp. 1-31; I. Franko, "Halytska indemnizatisiia" (Galician Indemnization), *Tvory*, XIX, pp. 456-87.
6. In the second half of the nineteenth century the standard currency in Austria was the gulden (*zolotyi rynskyi*) made up of 100 kreuzers. In the early 1870's one gulden was worth forty-six cents (U.S.) or 2.5 centimes (French). Beginning in 1892 gulden were gradually replaced by crowns, each worth half a gulden or 100 hallers. The currency reform of 1900 established crowns and hallers as the sole units of currency.
7. According to the census of 1900, Jews made up 85 per cent of those who produced or distributed alcoholic beverages in Galicia. In the later 1870's, in the numerous cases when land was auctioned to pay a debt, 94 per cent of the debtors were Christian and 6 per cent Jewish, while 73 per cent of the creditors (excluding institutions) were Jewish and 27 per cent

Christian. J. Buzek, *Stosunki zawodowe i socyalne ludności w Galicyi według wyznania i narodowści, na podstawie spisu ludności z 31. grudnia 1900 r.* (Occupational and Social Relations of the Galician Population by Religion and Nationality, Based on the Census of December 31, 1900), Wiadomości statystyczne o stosunkach krajowych (Statistical Information about the Crownland), tom XX, zeszyt 2 (Lviv, 1905), "Tablice," p. 6. Zwillig, "Gerichtliche Feilbietungen bäuerlicher und kleinstädtischer Realitäten in Galizien in den Jahren 1875 bis inclusive 1879" (Court Auctions of Peasant and Small-town Real Estate in Galicia in the Years 1875 through 1879), *Statistische Monatschrift* (Statistical Monthly) (Vienna), 1880, pp. 476-8.

8. In 1886 in the village of Kotsiubyntsi one peasant borrowed forty gulden from another. The creditor charged only 5 per cent annual interest, but he also took from the debtor and farmed for six years a plot of land measuring a hectare and a half. How high this payment was should be clear from a glance at Table 2, which shows the size of landholdings in Galicia and Bukovyna. Caro, "Lichwa na wsi w Galicyi" (Usury in the Galician Village), *Studya społeczne*, p. 220.
9. The electoral procedure is described in "Iak vybyraietsia radu hromadsku?" (How is the Communal Council Elected?), *Batkivshchyna* (Fatherland), 1885, nos. 37-38. Some powers of local government and their abuse are described in V. z Sokalshchyny, "Iaki oboviazky" (What Obligations), *ibid.*, 1887, nos. 39-40; see also Najdus, *Szkice z historii Galicji*, I, pp. 114-16.
10. For the budget of one priest published by Ivan Franko in *Molot* (Hammer) in 1878, see "Dokhody i vydatky vbohoho sviashchenyka" (Revenue and Expenditures of a Poor Priest), reprinted in M.F. Nechytaliuk, *Publitsystyka Ivana Franka (1875-1886 rr.). Seminarii* (Ivan Franko's Publicistic Writings (1875-1886); Seminar Handbooks) (Lviv: Vyd. Lvivskoho universytetu, 1972), pp. 60-5.
11. Incidents such as the following, which took place in Volia Iakubova in the mid-1880's, contributed to the emergence of anti-clerical sentiment in the villages. For years Rev. Harbinsky had rented his pasture to the speculator Chaim for 90-110 gulden, who, in turn, subleased it to the peasants for an additional 100 gulden. When villagers asked the priest to rent the pasture directly to them, he agreed and asked 200 gulden, the same rate as Chaim. [P. Melnyk], "Pysmo z pid Drohobycha" (A Letter from the Drohobych Region), *Batkivshchyna*, 1884, no. 31, p. 194.
12. Law was the profession most favoured by the secular Ukrainian intelligentsia. This is confirmed by the statistics of Ukrainian university students, 1861-1901. Excluding those preparing for the priesthood (55 per cent of the total), nearly 70 per cent of Ukrainian university students studied law. Buzek, *Stosunki zawodowe*, pp. 42-3.
13. F. Bujak, "Parcelacja" (Parcellation), in S. Kieniewicz (ed.), *Galicja w dobie autonomicznej (1850-1914). Wybór tekstów* (Galicia in the

Autonomous Era (1850-1915): Selected Texts) (Wrocław: Zakład Narodowy im. Ossolińskich, 1952), pp. 329-32.

14. Najdus, *Szkice z historii Galicji*, I, p. 32; Polska Akademia Nauk (PAN), *Historia Polski* (History of Poland), 4 vols. (Warsaw: Pánstwowe Wydawnictwo Naukowe, 1967), III, part 1, pp. 200, 528-9. F. Bujak, in an essay on the Polish-inhabited West Galician village, maintains that fertilizer was in universal use by the turn of the century and that, for the most part, the steel plough had replaced the wooden one. *Wybór pism*, II, pp. 289-92.
15. The average Galician family had five members. The population of Galicia was 4.6 million in 1857, 5.4 million in 1869, nearly 6 million in 1880, 6.6 million in 1890, and 7.3 million in 1900. In 1880 there were 76 persons per square kilometre, in 1890, 84, in 1900, 93, and in 1910 (in spite of massive emigration), 102.
16. Franko, "Zemelna vlasnist" (Land Ownership), *Tvory*, XIX, pp. 285-6. For the most thorough study of the proliferation and simultaneous shrinking of peasant holdings, see W. Styś, *Rozdrabnianie gruntów chłopskich v byłym zaborze austrjackim od roku 1787 do 1931* (The Division of Peasant Land in the Former Austrian Sector from 1787 to 1931) (Lviv: Nakładem Towarzystwa Naukowego, 1934).
17. Because of abuses, a special law of 1877 reimposed interest limits in Galicia and Bukovyna. It failed, however, owing to numerous loopholes. The account of lending in the Galician village is based on Caro, *Studya społeczne*, pp. 125-238. Caro's account, however, may exaggerate how high interest rates were. A peasant angry about usury complained in the mid-1880's that one lender "does not take less than 25 per cent, and at the moments of lending and repayment he 'only' takes a couple of chickens and five or ten dozen eggs." *Batkivshchyna*, 1884, no. 41, p. 254. A non-peasant stated that usurers lent at 18 per cent and credit unions at 12 per cent. *Ibid.*, p. 253.
18. Nearly 90,000 peasants in Bukovyna sold part or all of their land in the years between 1868 and 1892. Kurylo *et al.*, *Pivnichna Bukovyna*, p. 56.
19. S. Szczepanowski, *Nędza Galicyi w cyfrach i program energicznego rozwoju gospodarstwa krajowego* (The Poverty of Galicia in Numbers and a Program for the Energetic Development of the Crownland's Economy) (Lviv: Gubrinowicz i Schmidt, 1888), pp. 55-7. Epidemics also took their toll. In 1873, for example, over 90,000 Galicians died of cholera. *Statistische Monatschrift*, I (1875), p. 136.
20. PAN, *Historia Polski*, III, part 2, p. 173.
21. The conditions in the Boryslav mines provided the subject matter for one of the greatest achievements of Ukrainian prose, a series of stories and novels by Ivan Franko, some of which are available in English: *Boa Constrictor and Other Stories* (Moscow: Foreign Languages Publishing House, n.d.).
22. I. Franko, "Promyslovi robitnyky v Skhidnii Halychyni i ikh plata r. 1870. Statystychna studiia" (Industrial Workers in Eastern Galicia and

Their Pay in 1870: A Statistical Study), *Tvory*, XIX, p. 226. Ie. A. Iatskevych, *Stanovyshche robitnychoho klasu Halychyny v period kapitalizmu (1848-1900). Narys* (The Condition of the Working Class of Galicia in the Epoch of Capitalism (1848-1900): An Outline) (Kiev: Vyd. AN URSR, 1958), p. 71, includes a photograph of some metal tokens issued to Boryslav workers in lieu of cash payment. See also *Bericht der k.k. Gewerbe-Inspectoren über ihre Amtsthätigkeit im Jahre 1884* (Report of the Imperial and Royal Industrial Inspectors Concerning Their Official Activities in the Year 1884) (Vienna, 1885), p. 255.

23. I. Franko, "Deshcho pro Boryslav" (A Note on Boryslav), *Vybrani statti pro narodnu tvorchist* (Selected Essays on Folklore) (Kiev: Vyd. AN URSR, 1955), p. 147.

24. The 1869 census recorded 2,876 workers in extractive industries and metallurgy in the Drohobych district and 498 in chemical works (which included petroleum refining). These numbers, supplied by employers who wished to avoid the head tax on workers, are undoubtedly low. A contemporary industry expert reported that, in 1874, 10,500 workers were employed in Boryslav and the suburban village of Volianka. Soviet economic historians have calculated that by the primitive techniques then employed, 17,000 workers would have been required just to mine the 19,650 tons of mineral wax acquired in 1873 from Boryslav alone. In the censuses of this period, occupation was not correlated with nationality. It is therefore impossible to determine the national composition of the Boryslav workers. When Ivan Franko visited a petroleum refinery in 1880, he noted that 45 per cent of the workers were Ukrainian. In the oilfields themselves Ukrainian peasants probably counted for a larger percentage of the work force, for here no skill was required. *Bevölkerung und Viehstand von Galizien nach der Zählung vom 31. December 1869* (Population and Cattle in Galicia According to the Census of December 31, 1869) (Vienna, 1871), pp. 42-9; E. Windakiewicz, *Olej i wósk ziemny w Galicyi* (Oil and Earth Wax in Galicia) (Lviv, 1875), p. 6; Iatskevych, *Stanovyshche*, pp. 31-2; J. F[ranko], "Korespondencje. Drohobycz" (Reports: Drohobych), *Praca* (Labour), 1880, no. 17, p. 67, and 1881, nos. 2-3, p. 10.

25. The cash wages cited are from official statistics for Galicia in 1897. They are based on information from the employers and, as contemporaries declared, they overstated the actual wages paid by 100 per cent. The problem of payment for agricultural labour is a complex one, involving contradictory evidence and the mingling of payment in kind and cash. Najdus, *Szkice z historii Galicji*, I, pp. 140-8. F. Bujak, who knew best the agrarian structure of Galicia, wrote that in western Galicia a work day in summer paid thirty kreuzers until the turn of the century and fifty kreuzers thereafter. Bujak, *Wybór pism*, II, p. 305. The agricultural worker in Bukovyna earned ten to forty kreuzers daily: Kurylo *et al.*, *Pivnichna Bukovyna*, p. 56.

26. The Austrian census of 1900 listed 67,557 Ukrainian Galicians as

agricultural workers (*robotnicy*), another 126,170 as agricultural wage-earners (*zarobnicy*), and 995,324 as agricultural helpers (*pomagający*). The latter included some agricultural workers and children of peasants helping around the farm at home. Moreover, a percentage of the 495,000 independent farmers (*samoistni*) undoubtedly hired themselves out from time to time. Statistics on Ukrainians engaged in agriculture are in Buzek, *Stosunki zawodowe*, "Tablice," p. 3.

27. I.I. Kompaniiets, *Stanovyshche i borotba trudiashchykh mas Halychyny, Bukovyny ta Zakarpattia na pochatku XX st. (1900-1919 roky)* (The Condition and Struggle of the Toiling Masses of Galicia, Bukovyna, and Transcarpathia at the Beginning of the 20th Century [1900-1919]) (Kiev: Vyd. AN URSR, 1960), p. 67.
28. O.A. Kupchynsky *et al.* (eds.), *Klasova borotba selianstva Skhidnoi Halychyny (1772-1849). Dokumenty i materialy* (The Class Struggle of East Galician Peasantry [1772-1849]: Documents and Materials) (Kiev: Naukova dumka, 1974), pp. 264-512; Kvitkovsky *et al.*, *Bukovyna*, p. 230. Mykhailo Drahomanov, for example, wrote in 1881: "When we take into account everything that is going on in Galicia, we . . . think that an insurrection of the peasants there is inevitable, an insurrection against all the upper classes, who have not so much as a spark of compassion for the peasant, let alone for the peasant-Ruthenian." M. Drahomanov, "Nauka z poperednykh opovidann" (Lessons from the Foregoing Stories), *Hromada* (Commune), V, 2 (1881), p. 221. Polish nobles feared a peasant rebellion at the end of the 1860's.
29. In Khorostiv, the peasants were imprisoned. Ostap, "Pysmo z Husiatynskoho" (A Letter from the Husiatyn Region), *Batkivshchyna*, 18 March 1881, no. 6, pp. 48-9. In Cherliany, the leaders were arrested. "W Czerlanach" (In Cherliany), *Gazeta Lwowska* (Lviv Gazette), 25 September 1886, no. 220, p. 3. On rebellions in Bukovyna, see Kurylo *et al.*, *Pivnichna Bukovyna*, p. 57.
30. Most of this part of the essay is based on original research in primary sources (archives and the contemporary press). Some points are elaborated in J.-P. Himka, "Polish and Ukrainian Socialism: Austria, 1867-1890" (Doctoral dissertation, University of Michigan, 1977), chapters 2, 3, 5, 6. There are several good articles in English on the political development of the Galician Ukrainians: I.L. Rudnytsky, "The Ukrainians in Galicia under Austrian Rule," *Austrian History Yearbook*, III, part 2 (1967), pp. 394-429; P. Brock, "Ivan Vahylevych (1811-1866) and the Ukrainian National Identity," *Canadian Slavonic Papers*, XIV, 2 (Summer, 1972), pp. 153-89; P.R. Magocsi, *The Language Question in Galicia*, Ukrainian Heritage Notes, no. 2 (Cambridge, Mass.: Harvard Ukrainian Research Institute, 1978); J.P. Himka, "Voluntary Artisan Associations and the Ukrainian National Movement in Galicia (the 1870s)," *Harvard Ukrainian Studies*, II, 2 (June, 1978), pp. 235-50. For the wider context of Ukrainian history, see R. Szporluk, *Ukraine: A Brief History* (Detroit: Ukrainian Festival

Committee, 1979); D. Doroshenko, *A Survey of Ukrainian History* (Winnipeg: Humeniuk Publication Foundation, 1975) and *Ukraine: A Concise Encyclopaedia*, 2 vols. (Toronto: University of Toronto Press, 1963-71).

31. On the 1848 revolution, see M. Bohachevsky-Chomiak, *The Spring of a Nation: The Ukrainians in Eastern Galicia in 1848* (Philadelphia: Shevchenko Scientific Society, 1967); J. Kozik, *Między reakcją a rewolucją. Studia z dziejów ukraińskiego ruchu narodowego w Galicji w latach 1848-1849* (Between Reaction and Revolution: Studies in the History of the Ukrainian National Movement in Galicia in the Years 1848-1849) (Cracow: Państwowe Wydawnictwo Naukowe, 1975); R. Rosdolsky, *Zur nationalen Frage: Friedrich Engels und das Problem der "geschichtslosen" Völker* (A Contribution on the National Question: Frederick Engels and the Problem of the "Nonhistoric" Peoples) (Berlin: Olle & Wolter, 1979).

32. M. Drahomanov, "Druhyi lyst do redaktsii 'Druha.' Ukrainshchina ili rutenshchina?" (Second Letter to the Editorial Board of *Druh* (Friend): Ukrainianism or Ruthenism?) *Literaturno-publitsystychni pratsi* (Literary-Publicistic Works), 2 vols. (Kiev: Naukova dumka, 1970), I, p. 411.

33. The first formulations of the demand for an independent Ukrainian nation-state were those of Viacheslav Budzynovsky (1890) and Iuliian Bachynsky (1893), both then members of the Radical Party's social democratic current. Because they argued from Marxist positions, they have been neglected in nationalist historiography, which prefers to view Mykola Mikhnovsky as the first advocate of independent statehood (1900). As "national communists" Budzynovsky and Bachynsky were far ahead of their time. I have discussed their programs in depth in "Young Radicals and Independent Statehood: The Idea of a Ukrainian Nation-State, 1890-95," paper presented to the American Association for the Advancement of Slavic Studies, 12 October 1979. For a shorter version, see my "Ukrainskyi sotsiializm u Halychyni (do rozkoly v Radykal'nii Partii 1899r.)" (Ukrainian Socialism in Galicia, up to the Split in the Radical Party in 1899), *Journal of Ukrainian Graduate Studies*, IV, 2 (Fall, 1979), pp. 43-6. The fullest programmatic statements by Budzynovsky and Bachynsky are in S.V. Budzynovsky, *Kulturnaia nuzhda Avstriiskoi Rusy* (The Cultural Poverty of Austrian Ruthenia), 2 parts (Lviv, 1891); V. Budzynovsky and I. Hrynevetsky, "Materiialy do revizii prohramy Rusko-ukrainskoi radykalnoi partii" (Materials for the Revision of the Program of the Ruthenian-Ukrainian Radical Party), *Narod*, 1891, pp. 155-9; Iu. Bachynsky, *Ukraina irredenta* (Lviv, 1895).

34. Only two reading clubs had figured in the membership list of Prosvita in 1868-74. By 1908, however, Prosvita was the patron of 2,048 Galician reading clubs. "Chleny tovarystva 'Prosvita' " (Members of the Society Prosvita), *Spravozdanie z dilanii "Prosvity" vid chasu zavia-zania*

tovarystva – 26. lystopada 1868 roku, do naivnoviishoho chasu (Report on the Activities of Prosvita Since the Time of the Society's Founding, 26 November 1868 to the Most Recent Times) (Lviv, 1874), pp. 26-32; M. Lozynsky, *Sorok lit diialnosty "Prosvity"* (Forty Years of Prosvita's Activity) (Lviv, 1908), pp. 46-7. On the development of reading clubs in Bukovyna, see St. Smal-Stotsky, *Bukovynska Rus'* (Bukovynian Rus') (Chernivtsi, 1897), p. 288. The best study of reading clubs is M. Pavlyk, "Pro rusko-ukrainski narodni chytalni" (On Ruthenian-Ukrainian Reading Clubs), *Tvory* (Works) (Kiev: Derzhavne vydavnytstvo khudozhnioi literatury, 1959), pp. 416-549.

35. See J.P. Himka, "Priests and Peasants: The Greek Catholic Pastor and the Ukrainian National Movement in Austria, 1867-1900," *Canadian Slavonic Papers*, XXI, 1 (March, 1979), pp. 1-14.

36. Excluding children under six years of age, illiterates made up 77 per cent of Galicia's population in 1880, 67 per cent in 1890, and 57 per cent in 1900. Bujak, *Wybór pism*, II, p. 320. The illiteracy rate for Ukrainian peasants, however, was higher, for a great number of Galicia's literate inhabitants lived in cities, not in the countryside; western Galicia was more literate than Ukrainian-inhabited eastern Galicia; and in the countryside, non-peasants (nobles, stewards, tavern keepers, priests, teachers) made up a significant percentage of the literate group.

The illiteracy of the Ukrainian peasantry was inherited from the era of serfdom. In 1845, 97 per cent of the school-age children in Lower Austria attended school; but in Galicia, only 17 per cent. In 1840 the Greek Catholic bishop of Przemyśl, Snihursky, had proposed to the Galician Diet that more elementary schools be established in the villages. The Polish nobility almost unanimously rejected his proposal, concerned that schools in the countryside would lead the peasants to complain more about the nobility to the local representatives of the central government. Rosdolsky, *Die Bauernabgeordneten*, p. 7.

37. The most detailed (and enthusiastic) history of the Ukrainian co-operative movement is I. Vytanovych, *Istoriia ukrainskoho kooperatyvnoho rukhu* (History of the Ukrainian Co-operative Movement) (New York: Naukove tovarystvo im. Shevchenka/Tovarystvo ukrainskoi kooperatsii, 1964). For the Soviet view, see L.O. Olesnevych, *Kooperatyvni mify i kapitalistychna diisnist. Zakhidnoukrainska burzhuazna kooperatsiia (1883-1939)* (Co-operative Myths and Capitalist Reality: The West Ukrainian Bourgeois Co-operative Movement [1883-1939]) (Kiev: Naukova dumka, 1974).

38. The electoral system had been based on curias. Until 1897, there were four curias, one each for the noble estate owners, chambers of commerce, large cities, and everybody else (i.e., mainly the peasants). The franchise was indirect only in the fourth curia (the peasants'). The political weight of each voter depended on the curia to which he belonged. Fifty or sixty landlords sent one delegate to Parliament; it took 10,000 peasants to do the same. The 1897 reform added a fifth curia in

which each adult male voted directly. The 1907 reform abolished the curial system altogether and replaced it with the principle of one man, one vote. The reforms of 1897 and 1907 only affected the central Parliament in Vienna. The Galician Diet (the crownland's legislative assembly in Lviv) retained the curial system until World War I.

39. To date, the best study of the agrarian strikes in Galicia is Najdus, *Szkice z historii Galicji*, I, pp. 259-86, II, pp. 274-362. For Bukovyna, see V.M. Botushansky, "Pidnesennia straikovoi borotby selian Pivnichnoi Bukovyny na pochatku XX st. (1900-1907 rr.)" (The Taking up of Strike Warfare by the Peasants of Northern Bukovyna at the Beginning of the Twentieth Century [1900-1907]), *Mynule i suchasne Pivnichnoi Bukovyny* (Past and Present of Northern Bukovyna) (Kiev: Naukova dumka, 1972), I, pp. 18-29.

TWO

Settlement and Colonization

Vladimir J. Kaye (Kysilewsky) and Frances Swyripa *

Ukrainian immigration to Canada has occurred in three waves. Each was sufficiently prominent and distinct to characterize a period of Ukrainian-Canadian development and to provide a framework for writing history. The first settlers laid the foundations of community life, shaped the initial group outlook, and determined its public image. Succeeding waves introduced their own institutions and attitudes, modifying existing structures and creating new tensions in the established community.

A handful of families enticed to Alberta from Galicia in the early 1890's by former German neighbours launched the first immigration. The large-scale movement of Ukrainian peasants to western Canada, however, began in 1896 through the initiative of Joseph Oleskiw, professor of agriculture at the Teachers' Seminary in Lviv. It was facilitated by the receptive atmosphere in the Department of the Interior under Clifford Sifton, the minister responsible for immigration in Sir Wilfrid Laurier's Liberal cabinet. This first and largest immigration ceased with the outbreak of war in 1914. It had peaked the previous year when 22,363 Ukrainians landed in Canada. The settlers located almost exclusively on western agricultural lands, in blocs that preserved unique customs and an alien language in the midst of a predominantly Anglo-Celtic or northern European society. The first immigrants came overwhelmingly from the Austrian provinces of Galicia and Bukovyna – hence the identification of Ukrainian immigrants as "Galicians," "Bukovynians," and "Austrians" by many Canadians during the first two decades of the century. Limited emigration from Russian Ukraine after 1905 primarily affected the industrial east – Ontario, Quebec, and Nova Scotia – although small numbers gravitated to Alberta mines, western urban centres, and rural settlements. Official census statistics and sailing records indicate that during this period approximately 170,000 Ukrainians entered the Dominion.[1]

* Prepared before Dr. Kaye's death in 1976; revised with additions by Frances Swyripa.

The second or interwar immigration opened with a trickle between 1920 and 1924 when a total of 1,503 immigrants arrived. These were principally war refugees and sponsored relatives of Canadian citizens. During the next decade (1925-34), 59,891 Ukrainians came to Canada, although annual figures dropped with the onset of the Great Depression. When World War II terminated the migration, it had reached 67,578 individuals. Western Ukraine, divided among Poland, Romania, and Czechoslovakia, continued to furnish the bulk of the newcomers. The decennial census in 1941 reported 305,929 Canadians claiming Ukrainian ethnic origin and 313,273 who spoke Ukrainian as their mother tongue. Ukrainians formed 2.6 per cent of the population.

The third and, to date, last wave coincided with the international resettlement of displaced persons who had been separated from their homelands by World War II and were unwilling or unable to return. Between 1947 and 1953, Canada accepted 33,304 Ukrainians, encompassing all Ukrainian territory, from Kuban to Carpatho-Ukraine. By the end of 1959, with the borders of the Ukrainian Soviet Socialist Republic sealed, only 3,143 additional Ukrainian refugees had come to Canada. Subsequent numbers have been insignificant. As a result, today over 80 per cent of Ukrainians in Canada are Canadian-born (see Table 3).

All three immigrations contributed materially and spiritually to the Ukrainian-Canadian community and influenced its composition, structure, and growth. Not unnaturally, the first arrivals were most crucial. They encountered an inhospitable physical environment; a host society whose attitudes were frequently hostile; and unfamiliar social, religious, and cultural institutions. They had to grapple with the new homeland without the aid of fellow countrymen already used to its customs and peculiarities. They planted the roots of Ukrainian-Canadian organizational life, and subsequent immigrants came not to a socio-cultural void but to an established community, although adaptation of the three immigrant groups to each other was not without its problems. The early immigrants tackled homesteading with little capital and no acquaintance with North American farming methods, and they entered the urban labour force without industrial skills. Immigrants of the second and third waves profited from their experiences. Because of the fundamental role of the first wave of immigration in Ukrainian-Canadian development, this account will focus primarily on this first Ukrainian immigration.

ARRIVALS BEFORE 1891

Ukrainian-Canadian history officially dates from 1891 with the coming of Wasyl Eleniak and Ivan Pillipiw, but fact and tradition suggest earlier, isolated arrivals, though the attempt to name and date them has not been too successful. The possibilities of Ukrainian immigration before 1891 have been linked to Russian colonization on the West Coast,

TABLE 3

Number and Percentage of Ukrainians in Canada and Percentage Canadian-born, 1901-71

Year	*Canada*	*British Columbia*	*Alberta*	*Saskatchewan*	*Manitoba*	*Ontario*	*Quebec*	*New Brunswick*	*Nova Scotia*	*Prince Edward Island*	*Percentage Canadian-born*
1901	5,682(.10)	23(.01)	634(.87)	1,094(1.2)	3,894(1.5)	31*	6*				
1911	75,432(1.0)	682(.17)	17,584(4.7)	22,276(4.5)	31,053(6.7)	3,078(.12)	458(.02)	4*	292(.06)	4*	
1921	106,721(1.2)	793(.15)	23,827(4.0)	28,097(3.7)	44,129(7.2)	8,307(.28)	1,176(.05)	3*	389(.07)		
1931	225,113(2.1)	2,583(.37)	55,872(7.6)	63,400(6.8)	73,606(10.5)	24,426(.71)	4,340(.15)	12*	871(.17)		57.0
1941	305,929(2.6)	7,563(.92)	71,868(9.0)	79,777(8.9)	89,762(12.3)	48,158(1.2)	8,006(.24)	22(.01)	711(.12)	2*	65.7
1951	395,043(2.8)	22,613(1.9)	86,957(9.2)	78,399(9.4)	98,753(12.7)	93,595(2.0)	12,921(.32)	129(.03)	1,235(.19)	47(.05)	69.6
1961	473,337(2.5)	35,640(2.1)	105,923(7.9)	78,851(8.5)	105,372(11.4)	127,911(2.0)	16,588(.31)	379(.06)	1,763(.24)	66(.06)	76.7
1971	580,660(2.7)	60,145(2.8)	135,510(8.3)	85,920(9.2)	114,410(11.5)	159,880(2.1)	20,325(.30)	600(.09)	2,315(.29)	125(.11)	81.7

* Percentage lower than .01

Source: Report of the Royal Commission on Bilingualism and Biculturalism, *The Cultural Contribution of the Other Ethnic Groups,* Book IV (Ottawa: Queen's Printer, 1970), pp. 247-66; 1971 Census of Canada, *Population Ethnic Groups,* I, part 3 (Bulletin 1.3-2), October, 1973; I.J. Tesla, "The Ukrainian Canadian in 1971," in O.W. Gerus *et al.* (eds.), *The Jubilee Collection of the Ukrainian Free Academy of Sciences* (Winnipeg: UVAN, 1976), p. 508.

the composition of the mercenary De Meuron and De Watteville regiments, Mennonite and other German immigration in the 1870's, and the proximity of the United States.

Russian interest in North America, aroused first during Peter the Great's reign by the explorer Vitus Bering, led to a flourishing trade with the Aleuts and to pockets of Russian settlement as far south as California. The most persistent claim of Ukrainian involvement comes from the writings of Ahapii Honcharenko, a Russian Orthodox priest of Ukrainian origin serving the Pacific Coast from San Francisco in the late 1880's. He supported the participation of Kamchatka Cossacks in both exploration and settlement and maintained that 20,000 Ukrainians lived in California and Alaska in 1865. Honcharenko's statements and figures are probably impossible to verify, but he himself was sufficiently confident of Ukrainian readership to publish articles with Ukrainian themes in his Russian-English bilingual newspaper, *Alaska Herald*.[2]

Evidence of possible Ukrainians among the De Meuron and De Watteville regiments, sent by Great Britain to protect Canada in the War of 1812, is more substantial. With demobilization, some of the soldiers settled in Ontario. Among them were Ivan Diakovsky, born in Brody, Petro Barko (Barkov), born in Ternopil, and Andrii Mykhailiuk, whose birth place is unknown.[3] In 1816 others were hired by Lord Selkirk to help pacify the Métis in the Red River colony. While Anglo-Canadian writers have alluded to foreigners with the De Meuron and De Watteville settlers in Selkirk's colony, it was not until 1954 that Poles were identified among them.[4] From the list, Ukrainian-Canadian historian Paul Yuzyk then extracted three possible Ukrainian names: Jankofsky, Kaminsky, and Wasilowsky.[5] Others have since added to them by utilizing Selkirk's own documents.[6]

The Mennonite movement to Canada, which began in 1874, included colonists living in ethnically Ukrainian territory. It is conceivable that Ukrainians were among the immigrants, but to date there is little evidence to corroborate such a position.[7] With Ukrainian immigration to the United States predating that to Canada by fifteen years, there is some evidence that Ukrainians came to Canada from the south. Among the settlers from Pennsylvania brought out in 1885 by the Hungarian Count Esterhazy to Hun's Valley (later Polonia and Mountain Road), Manitoba, were some who called themselves Ruthenians, the term commonly used before the twentieth century to identify Ukrainians in Austria-Hungary. There were also Ukrainians in Esterhazy, founded by the Count in 1886 in eastern Saskatchewan.[8] Ukrainians were also part of the American Slovak movement to the coal mines around Lethbridge after 1885; in that year, for example, twelve Carpatho-Ukrainians travelled from "Grand Forks, Montana [?]," to the area.[9] The pre-1891 arrivals, however, are only an interesting footnote to Ukrainian-Canadian history, for they came out as individuals and failed to leave any Ukrainian imprint on the communities in which they lived.

THE FIRST IMMIGRATION

In the 1890's conditions in Canada and Austrian Ukraine were ideal for large-scale Ukrainian immigration. Not only were Canadian authorities and railway companies anxious to populate the Prairies, but Galician and Bukovynian Ukrainians were just as anxious to escape political oppression and economic destitution. Contrary perhaps to popular Canadian opinion, the initiative was not solely Canadian. While Canada was still soliciting immigrants from "preferred" and traditional sources - Great Britain, the United States, and northern Europe - the Ukrainian peasants were anxious to investigate rumours of free land in western Canada. As a result, on September 7, 1891, Wasyl Eleniak and Ivan Pillipiw, two peasants from the village of Nebyliv in Galicia, landed in Montreal.

Pillipiw and Eleniak

The initiative to emigrate lay with Pillipiw, one of six sons of a prosperous farmer who owned forty morgen (approximately twenty-seven acres) of land. Pillipiw's marriage brought additional land, which he gradually sold to finance various unsuccessful business ventures. By the 1890's, his fortunes had so declined that he elected to emigrate. Although unimpressed with a visit east to the Kuban in the Russian Empire, he returned enthused by reports of Canada given to him by Germans from Galicia, whose compatriots had chosen Canada over the Kuban. Obtaining the Canadian address of John (Johan) Krebs, a German acquaintance from his school days in Stanyslaviv, Pillipiw wrote and learned that there was plenty of good, cheap land in Canada, although Medicine Hat, where Krebs had settled, lacked rain and so Krebs was contemplating a move to the Edmonton area. Pillipiw convinced about twelve villagers to accompany him to Canada, but first three men would investigate settlement possibilities. Only two actually went; accompanying Pillipiw was Wasyl Eleniak, an illiterate peasant who had once worked for Pillipiw on a logging contract.[10]

From Hamburg, Pillipiw and Eleniak sailed to Liverpool and then to Canada on the *Oregon*. Arriving in Winnipeg with $240 between them, they proceeded to Langenburg and filed on homesteads among some German loggers whom Pillipiw had once employed. Never occupied or developed, the homesteads in time reverted to the Crown. Hearing of more desirable land and a better climate near Edmonton, Pillipiw and Eleniak reached Calgary but had to return for lack of funds. After harvest, when they worked for the Mennonites at Gretna for $1.50 per day, Eleniak remained at Gretna while Pillipiw returned to Galicia to bring both families to Canada.

Pillipiw's arrival in Nebyliv early in 1892 and his tales of 160 acres of free Canadian land created a sensation. Eager peasants visited him in great numbers, and he actively encouraged them to emigrate. He had contracted with Messrs. Spiro and Co. in Hamburg to book passages to Canada, collecting advance payments from the emigrants and receiving five dollars for each family head and two dollars per family member. Although several families were willing to leave, others questioned the whereabouts of Eleniak and wondered if Pillipiw had actually seen Canada. Some thought he was merely promoting emigration to swindle fares. The Austrian authorities, too, were uneasy, as emigration depleted the labour supply and provoked unrest. On May 12, 1892, he was arrested for sedition, for inciting the people to emigrate, and for defrauding them of their advance money for fares. After three months in prison, he was tried, found guilty, and imprisoned an additional month.

Pillipiw's arrest and imprisonment cooled the ardour of many prospective emigrants. On the other hand, the publicity generated by his trial advertised Canada more effectively than he himself could have done, and even before his release six families and a single male, thirty-five individuals in all, had left Nebyliv for Canada. Some of the group initially selected homesteads near Stuartburn, Manitoba, but the majority eventually settled near John Krebs in Alberta, establishing the settlement of Edna-Star. Antin Paish and Nykola Tychkovsky, who filed in August on S.E. of 28-55-21-4 and S.W. of 22-55-21-4 respectively, went immediately to Alberta. The remainder came later after working for the Gretna Mennonites for sorely needed cash.

On his release from prison, Pillipiw found his resources depleted and turned to timber contracting to obtain the money needed for emigration. In the spring of 1893 he and his family left Nebyliv. After filing in the infant colony east of Edmonton, he returned to work in Gretna for the Mennonites and also in North Dakota, where wages were higher. In December, Pillipiw purchased some livestock, implements, and staple foods in Winnipeg, rented a boxcar, and brought his family to their new homestead. Fire took his house, contents, cow, and calf in May, 1894, and he and his wife were reduced to begging in Edmonton. Abandoning his original homestead, Pillipiw moved several miles east and filed close to Edna-Star. When he died in 1936 the peasant from Nebyliv owned 800 acres. Meanwhile, Eleniak had spent almost two years at Gretna. In the spring of 1893 he returned to Nebyliv to bring his family. As the ferment about Canada still angered the Austrian authorities, he sold his land with difficulty and received only $160. On his return to Canada, Eleniak worked for a time at Gretna, but late in 1898 or early in 1899 he settled in the Chipman district, where he died in 1956 in his ninety-eighth year.

Pillipiw and Eleniak did not continue to promote Ukrainian immigration; nor did they participate much in organized community life. On coming to Canada, Pillipiw had embraced Russian Orthodoxy while Eleniak remained Greek Catholic. Although only a few miles apart, their religious differences might partially explain their limited contact. For many years their place in history was not recognized. In 1932 Professor Ivan Bobersky (sent abroad in the 1920's by the Ukrainian Citizens'

Committee of Lviv to collect funds) became interested in the "first" Ukrainian Canadian. Hearing of Pillipiw and Eleniak, still alive in Alberta, he went to Lamont to interview them and his reports bestowed upon them the role of "founding fathers."[11] Pillipiw's initiative and courage were mainly responsible for the venture into the unknown. However, his death was untimely and fate was kinder to Eleniak.[12] He received recognition within his own community and in 1947 was the fourth Canadian to receive a citizenship certificate at a special ceremony in Ottawa.

Pillipiw and Eleniak undoubtedly stimulated the first sustained interest in Canada among the Ukrainian peasantry. What is less certain is whether the movement would have assumed mass proportions without such additional catalysts in Galicia as Joseph Oleskiw, whose writings and speeches gave wide publicity to the free lands in Canada.

The Role of Joseph Oleskiw

Joseph Oleskiw was born on September 28, 1860, into a clerical family. He obtained his Ph.D. at Lviv University and did post-graduate studies at the University of Erfurt in Germany, where he specialized in botany, agriculture, and political economy. Until his appointment as professor of agriculture at the Lviv Teachers' Seminary, he lectured at the Agricultural College in Dubliany. Oleskiw was one of the generation influenced by populism and the desire to better the economic and political conditions of the Ukrainian peasantry in Galicia. To escape alien landlords, constantly shrinking landholdings, debts, and taxes, it was proposed to channel the surplus rural population to a country with agricultural opportunity and political freedom. After familiarizing himself with Brazil, Argentina, the United States, Siberia, and Canada, he selected the last for the permanent resettlement of rural Ukrainians.

The material Oleskiw collected on Canada included data on the latest Canadian census, free homesteads, employment opportunities, the location of homestead and railway lands, climate, precipitation, vegetation, and livestock prices.[13] Drawing on the literature forwarded to him by the Department of the Interior, he produced his first booklet on Canada, *Pro vilni zemli* (About Free Lands), a remarkably accurate account of Canada's geography, economy, people, and government. It was published as the July, 1895, issue in a series sponsored by the Prosvita Society of Lviv. *Pro vilni zemli* informed its readers of Oleskiw's intent to visit Canada to obtain his own impressions, assess the land, and discuss with Canadian government representatives the possibility of settling large numbers of Ukrainian peasants on prairie homesteads. It also warned prospective emigrants against hasty departures to other parts of the world and suggested that they wait for his first-hand report on Canada. The Prosvita Society endorsed Oleskiw's journey and its emigration committee recommended that two well-known peasant farmers accompany him to provide their own accounts of the country.

However, only Ivan Dorundiak from the district of Kolomyia obtained the necessary travel documents. In Canada the Department of the Interior promised "to facilitate [Oleskiw's] seeing the country as thoroughly as possible."[14]

Oleskiw squeezed a full itinerary into less than three months, leaving Lviv on July 25, 1895, and returning to Liverpool on October 14.[15] He arrived in Montreal on August 12, after a lengthy interview with Sir Charles Tupper, Canada's high commissioner in London, and proceeded to Ottawa, where he visited the Dominion Experimental Farm. In Winnipeg the Commissioner of Dominion Lands assigned Hugo Carstens as interpreter and guide for the duration of the western tour.

Oleskiw visited the few Ukrainian families in the Winnipeg area and examined selected farms around Calgary, but the lands immediately surrounding Edmonton interested him most. Already impressed by the soil and crop yields in the German settlements north and west of Edmonton, he turned to the northeast – to Beaverhill, Victoria Trail, Beaver Creek, Whitford, Limestone Lake, and the homesteads of the Ukrainian families who had emigrated between 1892 and 1894. The soil was rich, water was plentiful, and there were sufficient trees for fuel and housing. Satisfied, Oleskiw returned to Edmonton, where he met T. Mayne Daly, the Minister of the Interior in the Conservative government, and explained his scheme for settling Ukrainian peasants on Canadian homesteads, assuring Daly of their desirability. The minister promised to place his proposals before cabinet. On his return journey, Oleskiw visited the Indian Head Experimental Farm for information on farming conditions in Assiniboia and Saskatchewan, toured local Mennonite colonies, and inspected land open for homesteading on the Red River south of Winnipeg.

While in the East, Oleskiw visited Shamokin, Pennsylvania, where he advised the Ruthenian National Association to encourage American Ukrainians to obtain homesteads in western Canada. Some eight months later, the Association's official organ, *Svoboda*, published a lengthy appeal to American Ukrainians, urging them to accept "free" homesteads in Canada and outlining details of the agreement reached with the Canadian government agent who visited Shamokin in June, 1896.[16] A special three-man committee formed to supply prospective emigrants with essential information advertised regularly throughout 1896 and 1897 that in Canada one could "become the owner of his land . . . be his own lord and not a servant of others. . . ." In February, 1897, Nestor Dmytriw,[17] editor of *Svoboda*, urged that those with the necessary savings ($300 to $400) and desire to homestead in Canada contact him for further information so that a party could be ready to leave in early April. However, in spite of the efforts of Oleskiw, the committee, and Reverend Dmytriw, the response was limited, and in comparison with the mass movement from Europe, relatively few Ukrainian Americans emigrated to Canada.

On his return to Galicia, Oleskiw reported to a conference of prominent Ukrainians, who established an Emigrants' Aid Committee to assist in preparation and protection against exploitation. Oleskiw's second booklet on Canada, *O emigratsii* (About Emigration), was published by the Mykhailo Kachkovsky Society in Lviv in December, 1895. *Pro vilni zemli* and *O emigratsii*, issued by two popular societies, made information available to the widest possible rural audience. Oleskiw, who also lectured publicly, was swamped by individuals and peasant delegations with requests for additional material and advice.[18]

In Canada, Oleskiw had prepared numerous memoranda for the Canadian authorities on how to assist the Ukrainian immigrants. For example, he advocated farm co-operatives:

> The . . . people will be organized on a cooperative basis as companies of farmers, because the singel [*sic*] farmers would not succeed. These companies receive on the arrival on their grounds bonusses [*sic*] of at least 50-60$ per each homestead, taken up by a member of company. The company warrant, that the homestead, for which is paid bonuss [*sic*], will not be abandoned, respective will be settled again. The bonusses [*sic*] will build a fundation [*sic*] store of an institution, which shall make easier the life of farmers. At first the institution which will be whole under control of companies, will serve to common buying of such objects as seed, victuals, stoves, agricultural machines and tools etc. then to common purchase of products, to building of elevators, mills, establishing creameries, cheese factorys and other agricult. factorys, for improving of cattle breeding by buying of generous reproducteurs etc. It will be my care to convey [communicate] through this organisation.[19]

In spite of the awkward English, the idea was sound and, if implemented, could have helped the Ukrainian settlers. Oleskiw also proposed homesteader loans of up to $400 "at an interest not exceeding six per cent as a mortgage on his homestead." He asked that the "Cooperating Farming Company" be permitted to make homestead entries prior to the arrival of settlers and to plough ten acres "on settler's account," enabling a family arriving in the spring to settle on a registered homestead, sow grain and vegetables without delay, and harvest a crop the first year.[20] In a letter to the Commissioner of Immigration in Winnipeg, Oleskiw suggested that simple but comfortable dwellings be constructed at a cost not exceeding $100 on the allotted homesteads upon notice of the settlers' impending arrival. Building costs could be repaid immediately or entered as a mortgage on the homestead. Another request that the Canadian government provide a Greek Catholic priest with a modest stipend until the settlers could support him received a quick and negative reply.[21]

The implementation of even a few of Oleskiw's numerous suggestions would have prevented many hardships experienced by the early Ukrainian immigrants and certain problems subsequently faced by Canadian immigration officials. Before the federal cabinet could act, however, a general election in June, 1896, defeated the Conservative government, and the officials with whom Oleskiw had been communicating were replaced by Liberal appointees. Although Clifford Sifton, the new Minister of the Interior, soon became Oleskiw's supporter, the latter's proposals were not adopted to any significant extent.

The year 1895 was the turning point in the immigration of Ukrainian peasants to Canada. Beginning in 1896 numbers increased rapidly.[22] In 1900 Oleskiw was transferred to the directorship of the Teachers' Seminary in Sokal, where his health worsened and his activities in Ukrainian immigration dwindled and ceased. He died in 1903, but the movement he initiated continued to grow. It was not, however, the orderly and controlled immigration of selected farmers with means, assisted by the Canadian government, that he had envisaged. Attempts to regulate Ukrainian immigration on both sides of the Atlantic failed, as the movement assumed mass proportions and steamship agents in both Hamburg and Austria frustrated Oleskiw's efforts. Eventually, glowing letters from settlers replaced Oleskiw and steamship agents as the major catalyst of further emigration.

Obstacles to Emigration

The Ukrainian immigrants were overwhelmingly from the peasantry, whose world was restricted to the circumference of a few miles. The decision to depart created many problems. The scarcity of money forced them to dispose of their plots, houses, and livestock for a fraction of the actual value. Once emigration boomed, it was even more difficult to sell their land, and land values dropped while credit charges rose. The peasants usually borrowed from credit unions, innkeepers, or loan sharks, who demanded that the high interest be paid immediately. Steamship agents had to be contacted, transportation arranged, railway and steamship tickets bought, and passports obtained. Fares averaged $85 for adults and half that amount for children under ten. Frequently, the unworldly peasants placed their trust (and money) in the hands of unscrupulous agents who fleeced them. Some agents sold worthless steamship advertising cards in lieu of tickets or charged exorbitant prices. Food purchases en route and lengthy delays at ports of departure, where they were prey to all types of exploitation, further eroded the peasants' cash reserves.

Although unable to prohibit emigration, the landlords strongly opposed it to prevent the increased wages a diminished agricultural labour supply would impose. The Austrian government co-operated with the landlords in various ways.[23] Young men of military age were not permitted to emigrate before they had completed their three years of service, a state of affairs conducive to illegal border crossings and steamship agents who doubled regular ticket prices. Former soldiers were "liable under oath to return to Austria to fulfill military duties when called upon."[24] Emigrants were urged to retain Austrian citizenship, "to look upon Austria as their home," and to send back their sons at military age for Austrian military service. But in spite of strict border surveillance, Austrian authorities were unable to detain the hundreds of young men of military age determined to cross the Austrian border without a passport. Border guards were bribed by steamship agents, and work permits to Germany enabled a young man to join his waiting family in Hamburg or Bremen. As Canada did not require passports, the personal documents and cards prepared by steamship companies sufficed.[25]

Leaving friends and relatives and the ancestral village was a traumatic experience, affecting both travellers and those staying behind. This departure remained vividly engraved in one emigrant's memory:

> When the third of March 1900 came, the time to leave the village came; we were due to meet the train at the railway station in Vydyniv at two in the afternoon. We hardly slept that night and when the morning dawned, we packed our belongings, changed our peasant garments for city clothing, stored food for the long journey in bags, sewed money in our garments for safety, and started to board the waiting wagons. The people of the whole village assembled in our yard to say farewell to us, and when the church bells started to ring, all the people started to cry as if it were a funeral.[26]

Sometimes entire families emigrated together, but often the man went first, sending or returning for his wife and children once he had a foothold in Canada. In addition to homesickness, the voyage itself was lengthy and exhausting, especially for steerage passengers. The ships waiting in Hamburg, usually German vessels, were ancient, small, and dirty, and they transported cattle or grain on their return journeys to Europe. Memoirs can seldom recapture the human tragedy, fears, and uncertainties the immigrants experienced.[27]

Treatment in Canada

Sir John A. Macdonald's National Policy to promote industrialization, transcontinental railway traffic, and western settlement in Canada was ultimately fulfilled by the Liberal government elected in 1896. Depression in the early 1890's was followed by slow recovery and then rapid progress; by 1898, prices, government revenues, and exports had recuperated, and immigration surged forward at a pace hitherto unknown. The Canadian West was attracting investment and settlers, but not in sufficient quantity to satisfy Clifford Sifton, who now launched an ambitious immigration policy to obtain the farmers necessary to bring the land in western Canada into production.

Americans, with their capital and knowledge of dry farming methods, were eagerly sought, and exhibits of Canadian farm products at local American fairs supplemented substantial advertising literature. Similar programs were begun in Great Britain and northern and western Europe.

Sifton established an inspector of Canadian agents in Europe, removing immigration from the high commissioner's office and placing it under a person specifically concerned with attracting people to Canada. As the free homesteads in the United States had been occupied by 1890, many Europeans were diverted north. The traditional sources, however, in spite of lectures, slide shows, fair booth displays, a network of immigration offices, and brochures designed to entice them, failed to supply the number and type of immigrants Sifton desired. He turned to previously unsolicited sources in central, eastern, and southern Europe, where he found scores of peasants happy to accept 160 acres of free land. This was the type of agricultural immigrant Sifton wanted, and soon circulars publicizing Canada were issued in various languages. His agreement in 1899 with the North Atlantic Trading Company covered Ukrainians and other East Europeans; it stipulated that the company would receive five dollars for each family head and two dollars for other family members it recruited.

Throughout this period Canada opposed unrestricted immigration to prevent undue increase in urban population and problems similar to those in American cities. Farmers, farmworkers, and domestics were solicited. By 1914, several inadmissable categories appeared in immigration regulations: criminals and "other vicious classes," paupers and destitute immigrants, diseased persons (including the physically and mentally infirm), prostitutes and procurers, and "subversives." After 1906, those becoming criminals, public charges, or infirm after arrival in Canada could be deported. A 1908 requirement that immigrants land with the sum of $25 or $50 (depending on summer or winter arrival) was waived for agriculturalists, domestics, and those joining relatives.

Sifton admitted that the state had a certain responsibility for newcomers to Canada. They were not to be "turned loose on the country without any instruction being given them as to methods to follow."[28] Another Member of Parliament, drawing on the advice of an experienced immigration agent, expanded:

> . . . the moment he [the immigrant] arrives in this country, we must apply ourselves to helping him. He must be taken in hand; he must be settled in the part of the country where his settlement will be the most advantageous to himself and to the country, and he must be followed up for one or two years, made acquainted with the system of government, with our municipal institutions; in short, with the manners of our people, and kept in view until he is in a position to assume the quality of a citizen.[29]

However, while Canadian government bodies provided a modicum of guidance, there was no centrally directed program to ease the transition of the East European from his traditional peasant world to the North American environment. The work of Canadianizing was left largely to local schools, churches, and social institutions and concerned itself mainly with the language, religion, manners, and dress of the immigrants.

The Ukrainian immigrant was highly visible with his strange speech, unusual peasant garb, unfamiliar customs, and concentration in ethnically exclusive bloc settlements. He encountered much hostility and suspicion from Anglo-Celtic Canada, which feared his "questionable" moral standards, "authoritarian and ritualistic" religion, and simple way of life. One Presbyterian minister warned in 1913:

> The close relations into which we are brought with these people who are now degraded and vicious ought to force us to do them good in self-defence. Either we must raise them or they will lower us.[30]

Negative attitudes led to labelling all East Europeans as "Galicians," a term that rapidly acquired derogatory connotations, second only to "bohunk." Hostile public attitudes in the early years became a weapon in the hands of political agitators. Opponents of Laurier's Liberal government launched venomous tirades against "Sifton's sheepskins" and an immigration policy that permitted thousands of such undesirables to settle in Canada. The bitterness engendered by this initial contact between two widely divergent cultures and outlooks often persisted for decades in the memories of the Ukrainian pioneers.

Official supervision of immigrant parties occasionally extended from disembarkation to location on the homestead. Sometimes the larger parties were accompanied by interpreters, who were responsible for a safe and comfortable journey inland - well-heated, well-lit, and uncrowded railway cars; a plentiful fresh water supply; and medical aid in case of illness. They also recorded the names, ages, nationalities, number, and destinations of their charges to facilitate movement from the Immigration Hall in Winnipeg, the major immigration centre, where care of the new arrivals was transferred to colonization agents from the local commissioner's office. Several days in the Immigration Hall might follow to complete arrangements for satisfactory settlement on the land. Officers who accompanied immigrant parties to their final destinations either remained until they were settled or until local agents or land guides assumed responsibility for settlement and purchase of livestock and implements. A register of vacant positions advised immigrants of employment opportunities in Winnipeg.[31] Interpreters were also stationed at the immigration halls. Their departmental reports carry references to escorting parties of Ukrainians across Canada and to the problems and frustrations which plagued them. This terse but revealing comment captures the immensity of their task very well: "The whole party of 1100 came in within six hours of each other, and you may depend upon it it was no easy task to manage them."[32]

Oleskiw had suggested that Ottawa engage an interpreter to help the immigrants and had recommended Cyril Genik, a school teacher emigrating with one of his first groups, who knew Ukrainian, Polish, and

German and who had begun studying English before his departure for Canada. The Department of the Interior endorsed Oleskiw's choice and early in 1897 Genik became the first civil servant of Ukrainian origin in Canada. As the flow of settlers increased, an additional Ukrainian interpreter or immigration officer was needed, and Reverend Dmytriw received a temporary appointment.[33]

The number of Ukrainian immigrants grew so rapidly that the Commissioner of Immigration in Winnipeg, W.F. McCreary, had difficulty coping with them and those who preyed upon them. Exploiters sold substandard food and clothing as well as non-existent land around Winnipeg to the gullible immigrants. In 1898 McCreary wrote to the Superintendent of Immigration in Ottawa:

> I think you are already aware of the difficulties we have at this point with such large number as this. They get off here without having any destination in view, and are immediately met by a lot of Poles, Jews, and even Canadians, who try to take all the money they have from them for useless goods, and persuade them to give every resistance to our efforts to locate them. This became so serious last spring that we had to call in the Police, and if possible I want to avoid this condition of affairs this year, I believe by taking these people off at Montreal and keeping them in the sheds for one or two days, ascertaining what money they have and also where they have friends, if any, that they can be put into the cars with their destination clearly before them, and given tickets to the point to which they decide to go.[34]

The early colonies were largely forgotten once the immigrant had been located, though officials did investigate complaints of destitution. In proven cases, the government supplied flour, cornmeal, and potatoes, and sometimes, if a family had small children, cows on loan.[35]

The Settlements

Selecting a homestead, obtained for the registration fee of $10, was not an unregulated decision, for several factors influenced the choice. Most accessible homesteads, located near towns and railways or roads, had been occupied in the 1880's by settlers from eastern Canada, the United States, and Great Britain. However, plenty of virgin land, submarginal or far from established transportation routes, had been bypassed and the Ukrainians took it, often paying dearly where the soil was poor. For the Ukrainian immigrant, proximity to other Ukrainians was crucial, and to 1896 most settlers clustered around the growing colony at Edna-Star. Sometimes submarginal lands were deliberately chosen on this account, and in 1898 the Stuartburn region of Manitoba was settled because of nearby Ukrainian-speaking Mennonites. The government, for its part, was not averse to locating the Ukrainians near Mennonite colonies as the prosperous German farms provided work and badly needed cash.

With the explosion of Ukrainian immigration after 1896, one huge Ukrainian colony, closed to assimilating influences, began to stretch from its nucleus at Edna-Star east to Saskatchewan. Strong Conservative and public opposition forced the Liberal government to come to terms with the issue of Ukrainian bloc settlement. As the law did not permit coercing the Ukrainians to settle where the government wished, it could only rely on unofficial pressure or persuasion tactics, as well as "a variety of underhanded, if not illegal, devices"[36] to dictate the location of new colonies, especially where immigrants had no specific destination in mind. In 1897 an immigration agent located a party of Bukovynians in the Yorkton area over the objections of the immigrants, who wanted to go to Alberta,[37] but officials generally did not meddle with the plans of immigrants who already had relatives in Canada and a known destination.

Liberal policymakers in Ottawa and agents in the field were not always in agreement. With no law forcing the Ukrainians to settle in areas they selected, the agents found that it greatly simplified their work to heed the wishes of the immigrants and place them in existing colonies:

> Government Colonization Agents in the West were generally well disposed toward the concept of block settlement because planning and organization were greatly facilitated when immigrants were settled in discrete groups. Such settlements, moreover, were generally more successful. Social and spiritual needs were more easily provided for and co-operation between settlers was usually better than in ethnically mixed areas. There were fewer crises in settlement, fewer cases of destitution requiring Government assistance, and a concomitant decrease in the workload of the Government officials concerned.[38]

The government also recognized that bloc settlements, although retarding assimilation, facilitated administration and cut costs as land agents could work out of one area.

As it was neither prudent nor possible to disperse the Ukrainians entirely, especially in the light of their own preference to settle together, the government reached a compromise that acknowledged the realities of the situation. While Edna-Star did not become the centre of only one large, continuous homogeneous bloc, the government established several smaller blocs across western Canada. This fragmentation of the ethnic bloc concept never did become articulated government policy, but the drive to create new nuclei of Ukrainian settlement was sufficiently pronounced to lead to the conclusion that it was "more than simple expediency or pragmatism."[39]

In selecting new settlement centres, the government looked for areas with potential for expansion and, particularly until the railways and mines absorbed larger numbers of Ukrainian labourers, potential for capital acquisition. The benefits from location close to Mennonite communities have been mentioned; submarginal land was frequently good for picking seneca roots (bringing in a dollar a day) and wooded land made cutting cordwood possible (one cord yielded between $1.25 and $1.75).[40] The Ukrainians themselves were responsible for the concentration in the parkland belt, as they shunned the prairie in favour of wooded land. Their preference was strong enough to come to the attention of immigration officials:

> These Galicians are a peculiar people; they will not accept as a gift 160 acres of what we should consider the best land in Manitoba, that is first class wheat growing prairie land; what they particularly want is wood, and they care but little whether the land is heavy soil or light gravel; but each must have some wood on his place.[41]

The initial years in Canada were the most trying as the new settlers eked out an existence on land hitherto untouched by the plough, while coping with unfamiliar cultural, political, and socio-economic factors. Often without capital, livestock, or implements, the Ukrainian immigrant and his family had to work hard for whatever the soil yielded. Frequently, the wife and children erected the first crude dwelling, broke the first acres of land, and sowed the first seeds, while the husband and father pursued seasonal work in the lumber camps or mines and on railway or construction gangs. His wages purchased machinery, staple foods, cattle, and horses.

In most cases, the wife of the homesteader remained isolated on the farm with social contacts limited to those of her own nationality and language. The psychological and physical hardships were great. One child of immigrant parents in Alberta recounted how her mother, pregnant and alone in charge of her children and the farm, tied her four-year-old son to a post, provided him with food, and walked twenty miles to mail a letter to her husband who was working elsewhere for much-needed cash.[42]

The wisdom of allowing Ukrainian settlement in homogeneous ethnic blocs, closed to outside influences, was hotly debated in later decades. Both rural colonies and urban ghettos, however, were perhaps inevitable. They resulted primarily from an almost instinctive urge of self-preservation in alien surroundings. In addition, it was only natural that friends and relatives or village neighbours would wish to locate adjacent to one another. That the extensive Ukrainian rural blocs retarded "assimilation" or adaptation to Canadian societal norms cannot be denied, for they ensured that the Ukrainian immigrant's primary, and to a large extent secondary, relationships would be restricted to his ethnic group. Frequently, the school was the only Canadian agent to penetrate the colony and to affect its orientation meaningfully. Simultaneously, however, the rural Ukrainian bloc eased the transition process for its inhabitants, and many of the adjustment problems – juvenile delinquency, mental illness, crime, and alcoholism – that plagued urban immigrants, cast abruptly into a foreign environment, were avoided or minimized.

Similarly, ethnic urban ghettos cushioned adjustment. A certain number of Ukrainian immigrants had gone directly to urban centres, some with the intention of remaining only long enough to earn the money needed to start farming. Others became permanent members of the urban labour force. The latter, the more stable element, included families, while the former (a fluid and transient group) consisted largely of single males or men who had temporarily left their homesteads and families. Both groups, initially locating close to each other and establishing their neighbourhood institutions, formed the nucleus of urban Ukrainian communities across Canada. Their ghettos acquired physical limits and a visible Ukrainian character. In North End Winnipeg, for example, there were in time several Ukrainian churches, organizational headquarters, and shops along Main Street. The reaction of the host society to the rural bloc and urban ghetto was negative and full of concern that their perpetuation would create numerous "Little Ukraines," detrimental to the Canadian way of life because their main loyalty was outside Canada.

By 1905, the pattern of Ukrainian settlement on the Canadian Prairies was firmly established; thereafter, settlement expanded outward from the original nodes. Ukrainian colonies extended in a belt "north from southeastern Manitoba to east of Winnipeg, and from there to Edmonton along the line of the Canadian National Railway."[43] They included the Stuartburn, Interlake, and Dauphin regions in Manitoba; Yorkton, Canora, Insinger, Prince Albert, Wakaw, Rosthern, Radisson, Krydor, and Hafford in Saskatchewan; and, in Alberta, a bloc extending east of Fort Saskatchewan practically to the Saskatchewan border with Vegreville and Vermilion as major centres. Within this extensive bloc, a Ukrainian way of life, modelled on that practised in old country villages, emerged. A profusion of Ukrainian names of schools, churches, and post offices proclaimed the Ukrainian influence in the districts. To a great extent, the marks placed on the landscape by the Ukrainian immigrants – especially their distinctive church and cottage architecture – remain.

THE SECOND IMMIGRATION

Following World War I, the Treaty of Riga divided the greater part of Ukraine between Poland and Russia. Romania, Poland's ally, received Bukovyna, while newly created Czechoslovakia acquired Carpatho-Ukraine. As conditions in Europe stabilized, substantial numbers of Ukrainian immigrants entered Canada in the years after 1924, with Poland readily issuing passports to persons wishing to emigrate. The old provinces of Galicia and Bukovyna continued to supply the bulk of the immigrants, though Volhynia, now Polish but formerly in tsarist Russia, became an additional source. Half of the total interwar Ukrainian migration to Canada arrived in the three years between 1927 and 1929.

Much of Ukraine had been ruined by years of war – villages burned,

Figure 1. Ukrainian Bloc Settlements in 1905

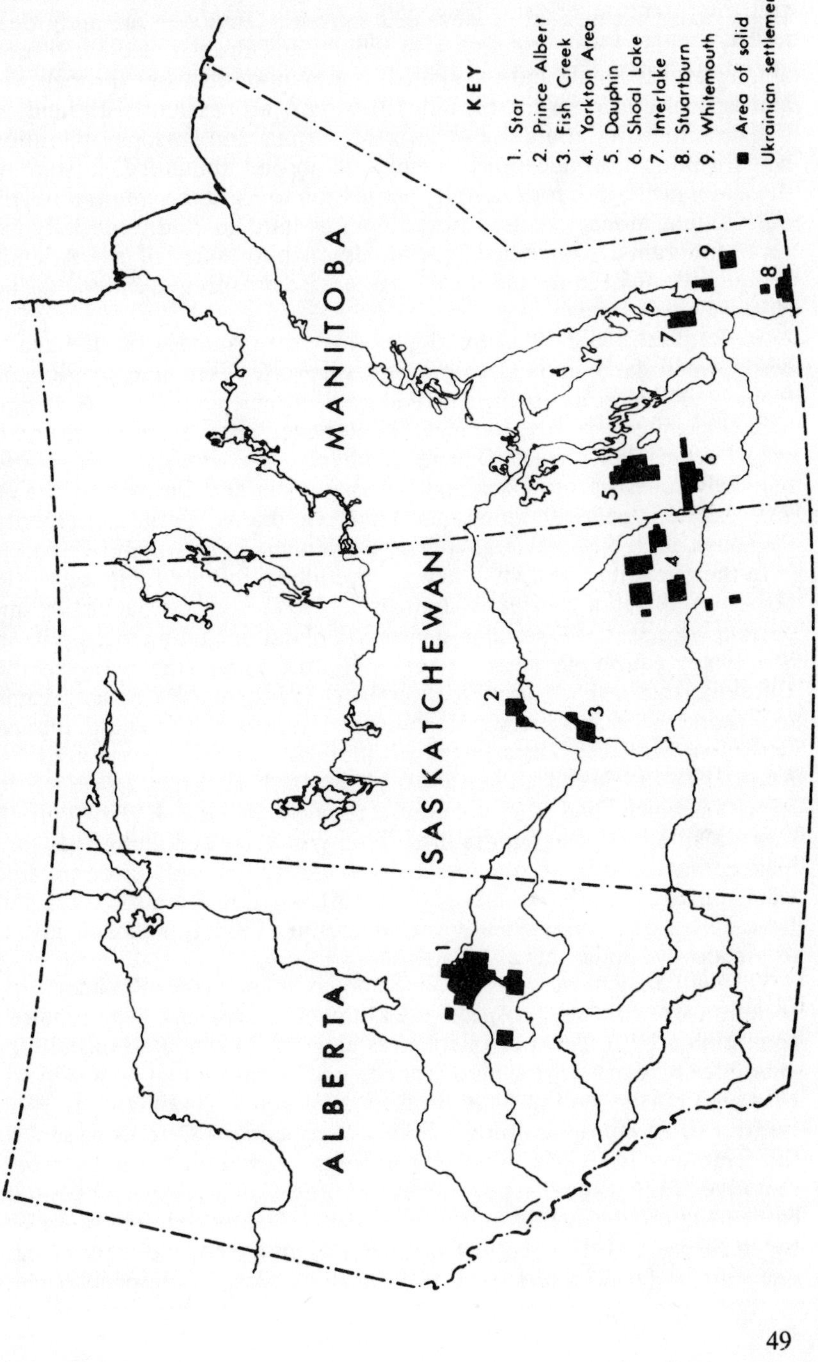

Source: *Canadian Ethnic Studies*, IX, 2 (1977), p. 50. Reprinted with permission.

farm buildings and equipment destroyed, and livestock slaughtered. The losses set back the economy of the countryside and farmers suffered. High taxes because of a devalued currency imposed an additional burden. Poland was attempting to rebuild and discouraged emigration among professionals and the skilled, but manpower losses through war and agricultural reforms still failed to supply all peasants with land. A fledgling industry could not absorb the surplus and seasonal migration was forbidden. Applications to emigrate abroad abounded, in spite of the many problems: for example, permission to leave the country was required, and money for transportation was hard to find, especially for rural emigrants. Concerned individuals on both sides of the Atlantic recognized the need for aid societies to advise prospective emigrants and to assist them financially.

St. Raphael's Ukrainian Immigrants' Welfare Association of Canada was formed early in 1924 to aid and supervise Ukrainian immigrants from their departure to their arrival and settlement in Canada. It also helped reunite separated families. St. Raphael's concentrated on immigrants from Polish-ruled Galicia, Volhynia, and Polissia, but it also handled requests from Ukrainians in Bukovyna and Carpatho-Ukraine and assisted political emigrants from Germany, France, Bulgaria, Romania, and Yugoslavia as well as Ukrainians in Brazil and Cuba.

In the meantime, in Lviv a new group, the Ukrainian Emigrants' Aid Society, received a charter on January 25, 1925.[44] It was backed by important segments of Ukrainian society in Poland, including Metropolitan Sheptytsky, although some sectors felt that emigration betrayed the Ukrainian cause. The committee secretary, Volodymyr Bachynsky, came to Canada in 1925 to investigate immigration possibilities and to discuss settlement with the Department of Immigration. He reorganized St. Raphael's Association and established several branches, particularly in Alberta, which had the greatest settlement potential. Recognizing Canada's desire for agriculturalists, Bachynsky assured authorities that his committee would screen applicants to ensure that only those suitable were approved. Both societies gathered information from the Canadian Department of Immigration on the admission of immigrants and gave it to prospective emigrants and potential sponsors.

Through agreement with the Canadian government, St. Raphael's Association was to clear prospective Ukrainian immigrants, who required sponsorship by a friend or relative residing on a farm. Responsible for guaranteeing work for the immigrant and for assuring that he would not become a burden on the state, St. Raphael's urged Ukrainian-Canadian farmers to accept agricultural workers. Applications were to be sent to the committee in Galicia, which expanded its operation, and to the representative of the Canadian government in Europe, who issued a permit of entry to approved immigrants.[45] Applicants, legally required to be between fifteen and fifty years of age, had to sign a pledge to work at least one year as farm labourers or as farm domestics. Tradespeople, merchants, city labourers, and individuals unconnected with agriculture were not encouraged, although there is little doubt that some falsified their occupations. Immigrants had to possess proper passports issued by the state of which they were citizens. Refugees residing in foreign countries submitted special applications to secure permits of entry to Canada.

With Canada stressing the admission of agriculturalists, peasant farmers continued to dominate the second wave of Ukrainian immigration. Nonetheless, a considerable number of immigrants gravitated to urban centres after completing or feigning their obligatory year on the farms. They became industrial workers or enrolled in schools and courses in order to resume former professions. Many were veterans of the Ukrainian army, which had fought against Poland and the Bolsheviks. After the collapse of the Ukrainian republic, they had sought asylum in Czechoslovakia and had come to Canada as sponsored immigrants, where they began to settle in British Columbia and in eastern Canadian cities. Toronto began to supplement Winnipeg and Edmonton as a focal point of Ukrainian social and cultural life, as Ontario's Ukrainian population grew: 3,078 in 1911, 8,307 in 1921, 24,426 in 1931, and 48,158 in 1941.[46]

Whole families were encouraged to emigrate in the 1920's, but again many men came first. As before, uninterrupted family life alleviated dislocation and had a stabilizing influence. Financially more secure than their predecessors, the interwar immigrants began life in Canada with higher socio-economic status. War veterans also had a worldliness lacking in the peasants who came to Canada before 1914. Some interwar immigrants, particularly those arriving around 1930, lost their jobs during the Great Depression and faced deportation. As a result, farmworkers, domestics, labourers, and relatives of Canadian residents were deleted from the classes of immigrants admitted to Canada. In 1930 promotional activity by the Canadian government stopped. As only immigrants able to establish themselves were accepted, few Ukrainians qualified, and St. Raphael's Association also moved away from immigration work to cultural and then political activities.

The interwar immigrants, as already noted, encountered a well-organized community life with churches, reading halls, religious and socio-cultural organizations, and a number of Ukrainian-language newspapers to serve their needs. While peasants who emigrated intended to remain in Canada (those of the first immigration largely viewed their relocation as an upgrading), urban immigrants, usually better educated, often exhibited politico-refugee characteristics and expected to return to Ukraine when conditions permitted. To them, Canada was at best a second choice, and the state of transiency discouraged efforts of adjustment and accommodation.

However, as hopes for Ukrainian independence faded, the nationalistic political refugees somewhat grudgingly accepted Canada as the new homeland, although without relinquishing their identification with

Ukraine and its welfare. The younger generation, particularly those with secondary or university education, entered professional schools or universities. On completion of their studies they joined the ranks of Canadian professionals or were absorbed by the industrial sector. The older immigrants, less adaptable and with poor knowledge of English, became teachers of Ukrainian parish schools, choir masters, editors of Ukrainian newspapers (either those already in existence or others founded by the newcomers), or small businessmen.

The second immigration had few illiterates; most new arrivals possessed at least an elementary education and some had attended higher educational institutions. Because of the continued association with Ukrainian affairs abroad, lively contacts were established between Canada and Ukrainian centres in Western Ukraine, Germany, and Czechoslovakia. Soviet Ukraine, its borders a barrier to the movement of people and ideas, lay outside this exchange. Visits to Canada by Ukrainian journalists, political figures, women's representatives, and academics to solicit financial and moral support for the "Ukrainian cause" were accompanied by a more modest return of concerned individuals to Europe. This intercommunication elevated the national consciousness of Ukrainian Canadians and injected a more pronounced Ukrainian orientation into the Ukrainian-Canadian community.

THE THIRD IMMIGRATION

The third phase of Ukrainian immigration to Canada began in 1947 with the arrival of 2,044 displaced persons from camps in Europe. The largest group, 10,041 individuals, came in 1948.[47] Fewer arrived in each subsequent year, although the number rose temporarily in 1951 with the cessation of International Refugee Organization (IRO) activities and the need to resettle the refugees before the camps were liquidated. By 1953, Ukrainian immigrants to Canada had dwindled to a few hundred each year. In all, the period from 1947 to 1953 brought 30,834 Ukrainians to Canada.

The great displacement of civilian population during World War II created millions of refugees. Rescued by the Allies in 1945, they could choose repatriation or displaced-person status and emigration to another country. Western Europe, ravaged by war, was unable to accommodate them. Close to one million refugees, almost half of them Ukrainian, refused to return to their homeland, which was totally in Soviet hands as the result of war. During the war approximately five million Ukrainians were deported by the Germans to labour farms and war industries. The numbers of conscripted civilians were swollen by political prisoners, underground supporters, prisoners of war, and those who had simply fled. Many died in concentration camps in Germany and Poland. In 1947 official statistics reported 54,580 Ukrainians in the British, 104,024 in the American, and 19,026 in the French occupation zones of Germany; the three Austrian zones had 21,893 Ukrainians and the large camp at Rimini, Italy, 11,000. An estimated 100,000 Ukrainians were living in the forests or with civilians.[48]

In 1945 Member of Parliament Anthony Hlynka toured the refugee camps to determine why such large numbers of Ukrainians refused repatriation. The reasons were several: opposition to dictatorship; a desire for religious, national, economic, and political freedom impossible under Communism; danger from the NKVD, the Soviet secret police; and rumours that those forcibly repatriated had been sent to Siberia. Accordingly, the Ukrainian Canadian Committee urged the Canadian government to accept Ukrainian displaced persons. Canadian immigration law was gradually amended to satisfy not only ethnic groups and the foreign countries facing over-population, but the needs of national development as well. By 1947, besides numerous classes of relatives, any Canadian resident could sponsor an immigrant if he could ensure his employment in agriculture, mining, or lumbering.[49] The policy was designed to attract such immigrants as the national economy could absorb. In the same year Canada joined the IRO and agreed to accept thousands of displaced persons.

The Ukrainian Canadian Relief Fund formed in 1944 under the War Charities Act provided immediate moral and financial aid to Ukrainian camp inmates. By 1950, 90 per cent of the Ukrainian displaced persons had been resettled. The refugees remaining in camps were primarily those unable to pass medical examinations. With the dissolution of the IRO in 1951, the Ukrainian Canadian Relief Fund changed its form. The European mission was liquidated and "patron" work was organized to care for the sick, establish kindergartens and schools, and look after the needy in the British zone of Germany.

The third-phase immigration included fewer peasants and a much higher percentage of persons with university, college, or technical education. Realizing that residence in Canada might be permanent, many immigrants in the camps had taken advantage of IRO language and occupational training classes oriented toward Canada. Many who failed to locate employment to match their training embarked upon supplementary education late in life, frequently with considerable dissatisfaction, resentment, and frustration. However, addition of numerous new members to the Ukrainian intellectual community, who founded Canadian branches of the Shevchenko Scientific Society and the Ukrainian Free Academy of Sciences, created an atmosphere highly favourable for scholarly pursuits. Again, unlike the two preceding Ukrainian immigrations, the third group was almost entirely urban.

The majority of new arrivals were channelled to Ontario, where nearly 50 per cent found employment in such industries as lumbering, the Ontario Hydro Electric Power Commission projects, and mining. With a labour shortage in low-skilled occupations, such immigrants were especially welcome. Farmers were also needed, and a high percentage of

Ukrainian immigrants (50 per cent) claimed farming as their occupation.[50] Toronto and area absorbed 80 per cent of the newcomers, mainly skilled labourers and professionals.

Some of the post-1945 immigrants joined existing Ukrainian institutions. Others, like the interwar immigrants, established their own organizations based on Ukrainian political factions with exiled headquarters in western Europe (particularly Germany) and followed trends and events in Ukrainian life in the homeland and in neighbouring European states. The newcomers disapproved of the Canadian orientation of the Ukrainian bodies they encountered in Canada and the friction that attended the accommodation of the second-phase immigrants was repeated. In many cases, the hostile or suspicious attitudes of the Ukrainian Canadians of the first two immigrations alienated the third and provoked conflict. The new immigrants were highly politicized and, in general, strongly anti-Soviet and self-proclaimed missionaries on behalf of Ukrainian liberation. Nevertheless, the most recent immigrants greatly revitalized the Ukrainian-Canadian community, then on the verge of losing its influence over an ever larger proportion of Ukrainian Canadians.

CONCLUSION

The three waves of Ukrainian immigration to Canada determined the orientation and composition of today's Ukrainian-Canadian community. The group's future rests with the descendants of each wave, as additional immigration seems highly unlikely. A fourth large movement of Ukrainians to Canada, either directly from Ukraine in response to relaxed Soviet emigration policies or from other parts of the world, would, of course, revitalize the Ukrainian-Canadian community and give it yet another dimension. But the future of what is generally recognized as a well-organized and articulate Canadian ethnocultural group is most uncertain; with the percentage of Canadian-born increasing steadily, it remains to be seen whether institutional adjustments can be made in time to give the Ukrainians in Canada indefinite viability.

NOTES

1. All immigration statistics are based on W. Darcovich and P. Yuzyk (eds.), *Statistical Compendium on the Ukrainians in Canada 1891-1976* (Ottawa: University of Ottawa Press, 1980), pp. 513-14.
2. See J. Stechishin, *Istoriia poselennia ukraintsiv u Kanadi* (History of Ukrainian Settlements in Canada) (Edmonton: Ukrainian Self-Reliance League, 1976), pp. 84-5.
3. *Ibid.*, pp. 105-6.
4. V. Turek, "Poles Among the De Meuron Soldiers," *Transactions of the Historical and Scientific Society of Manitoba*, series III, no. 9 (1954).

5. Stechishin, *Istoriia*, p. 104. Yuzyk supported his claims by noting that Jankofsky came from Ternopil and Wasilowsky from Tuchyn.
6. See M.H. Marunchak, *The Ukrainian Canadians: A History* (Winnipeg: Ukrainian Free Academy of Sciences, 1970), p. 25.
7. For a discussion of specific individuals, see A. Czumer, *Recollections about the Life of the First Ukrainian Settlers in Canada* (Edmonton: Canadian Institute of Ukrainian Studies, 1981), p. 23; I. Goresky, "Stefan Koroluk," in *Ukrainians in Alberta* (Edmonton: Ukrainian Pioneers' Association of Alberta, 1975), pp. 249-53.
8. Esterhazy imported a group of Pennsylvania miners to strengthen the settlement. Severe conditions drove many to Alberta's mines, while others either returned to the United States, went to Winnipeg, or began farming on their own. Not all Ukrainians deserted the colony, for among the founders of Esterhazy are such Ukrainian names as Babiak, Chorniak, and Krupka. See Stechishin, *Istoriia*, p. 93.
9. *Ibid.*, p. 92.
10. The third member was turned back at the border by the authorities for lack of money. Some controversy exists as to whether Tyt Ziniak or Iurii Panishchak was to accompany Pillipiw and Eleniak on their historic voyage. Disregarding the popularity of the latter version among Ukrainian-Canadian historians, arguments for the former are convincing. The Stanyslaviv court records for 1892 state that at his trial Pillipiw named Ziniak as the third party. His statement under oath shortly after the event was apt to be more accurate than his claim forty years later that it had been Panishchak. See *ibid.*, p. 122.
11. Bobersky's interview with Eleniak was published in *Kalendar kanadiiskykh ukraintsiv - "Providnyk"* (Calendar of Ukrainian Canadians - *The Leader*) (Winnipeg: St. Raphael's Ukrainian Immigrants' Welfare Association, 1933), while that with Pillipiw appeared in *Iliustrovanyi kalendar-almanakh "Kanadiiskoho farmera"* (Illustrated Calendar-Almanac of the *Canadian Farmer*) (Winnipeg: Kanadiiskyi farmer, 1937).
12. According to Bobersky: ". . . Pillipiw died at a wedding in the home of a relative in North Bank, Alberta. Leaning too far out of a window to cool himself on a hot day, Pillipiw lost his balance and fell out of the window killing himself instantly." A second account stated that the occasion was a wedding at the home of Pillipiw's cousin, Vasyl Kulka of North Bank. Pillipiw had been drinking and was helped to one of the bedrooms upstairs to rest. During the night, mistaking the large window for a door, he walked through it and fell to the ground, killing himself instantly. The doctor who was called affirmed the cause of death as a broken neck. Stechishin, *Istoriia*, p. 129.
13. V.J. Kaye, *Early Ukrainian Settlements in Canada, 1895-1900: Dr. Josef Oleskow's Role in the Settlement of the Canadian Northwest* (Toronto: University of Toronto Press, 1964), pp. 3-4.

14. *Ibid.*, p. 4. Although the Austro-Hungarian government and the landlords opposed large-scale emigration, Oleskiw was not prevented from making his trip to Canada because Austrian law formally guaranteed personal liberty to its subjects and allowed anyone to emigrate who had a legal passport and had fulfilled his military service requirements. Moreover, the prime minister of the Austro-Hungarian Empire, Count Casimir Badeni (1895-97), had formerly been governor of Galicia, knew Oleskiw personally, and was favourably disposed to an undertaking which promised to divert Galician immigrants from Brazil. Badeni, however, was not prepared to tolerate the promotion of large-scale emigration schemes. See *ibid.*, pp. 25, 48-9, 92-4.
15. Oleskiw's journey is described fully in J. Oleskiw (O. Oleskiv), *O emigratsii* (About Emigration) (Lviv: Vyd. Obshchestva im. M. Kachkovskoho, 1895); and Kaye, *Early Ukrainian Settlements*, pp. 3-131.
16. See *Svoboda*, 25 June 1896.
17. On the recommendation of Oleskiw, Dmytriw was appointed a Canadian immigration agent and departed for Canada in April, 1897, released from his parish duties at Mount Carmel, Pennsylvania, for two months. Following permanent transfer to Canada, he resided in Winnipeg, working as both an immigration agent and pastor to the rapidly growing Ukrainian community. The tasks proved onerous and Dmytriw fell ill, resigned, and returned to the United States in August, 1898.
18. A peasant delegation, which journeyed from the village of Synkiv to Lviv to consult Oleskiw about Canada after reading Oleskiw's booklets, stimulated a mass migration from that village and led to the establishment of a settlement bearing its name in the Stuartburn district. See J. Kohut, *Narys istorii ukrainskoi katolytskoi tserkvy sv. Troitsi v Stuartburn, Man. Moi spomyny* (A Sketch of the History of the Holy Trinity Ukrainian Catholic Church at Stuartburn, Man.: My Memoirs) (Yorkton: Redeemer's Voice, 1958), p. 6.
19. Oleskiw to the Minister of the Interior, 22 September 1895, quoted in Kaye, *Early Ukrainian Settlements*, pp. 41-2.
20. Public Archives of Canada (hereafter PAC), Oleskiw to the Department of the Interior, 6 September 1895, file 21103, Immigration, vol. 1, no. 31442.
21. Oleskiw had persuaded Rev. Ostap Nyzhankivsky, a Greek Catholic priest and noted composer, to emigrate to Canada to serve the spiritual needs of the Ukrainian settlers. Oleskiw's request for financial support needs to be understood in the context of Old World practice, where the state supported the church. The Canadian government passed his letter to the Roman Catholic hierarchy in Winnipeg, which opposed Nyzhankivsky's coming, probably because he was married.
22. Ukrainian immigration to Canada from 1891 to 1903 is indicated by the following figures: 1891:2; 1892:52; 1893:44; 1895:452; 1896:616;

1900:6,734; 1901:4,014; 1902:8,377; 1903:10,451. See Darcovich and Yuzyk (eds.), *Statistical Compendium*, pp. 507, 514.

23. Wasyl Zahara, one of the earliest settlers from the village of Bridok, district of Zastavna, Bukovyna, made nine trips to the district town of Zastavna to obtain his passport:

> The sheriff of Zastavna, the county in which Wasyl Zahara lived, refused to issue an exit permit and reprimanded him for gossiping about land grants to Canada. He warned him not to mention the subject to any one lest the rumours agitate the peasants. After making nine trips to the sheriff's office for an exit permit, Wasyl Zahara finally threatened to leave without one. (I. Panchuk, *A Sketch of Wasyl Zahara* (Battle Creek, Michigan: n.p., 1956)), p. 2.

24. PAC, Report of W.T. Preston, Commissioner of Immigration, London, England, to W.D. Scott, Superintendent of Immigration, Ottawa, 8 July 1905, Department of the Interior, file 1980.
25. The inspection cards issued to the immigrants by officials at the port of arrival in Canada included a declaration of the amount of money brought, vaccination protection, name, boat, European port of departure, and date of entry into Canada. They were to be kept three years and produced when requested.
26. P. Svarich, "Z ridnoi zemli v svit dalekyi" (From the Native Land into the Far-off World), *Kalendar "Ukrainskoho holosu"* (Calendar of the *Ukrainian Voice*) (Winnipeg: Ukrainian Publishing Company, 1942), p. 72.
27. For a description of one ocean crossing, see D. Romanchych, "Ukrainski kolonii v okruzi Davfyn, Man." (Ukrainian Colonies in the Vicinity of Dauphin, Man.), in D. Doroshenko and S. Kowbel (eds.), *Propamiatna knyha ukrainskoho narodnoho domu u Vynypegu* (Commemorative Book of the Ukrainian National Home in Winnipeg) (Winnipeg: Trident Press, 1949), p. 511.
28. *Debates of the House of Commons*, 1899, col. 8507.
29. *Ibid.*, col. 8531.
30. W.D. Reid, "The Non-Anglo-Saxons in Canada - Their Christianization and Nationalization," *Address Delivered at the Presbyterian Pre-Assembly Congress . . . with Reports of Committees* (Toronto: Board of Foreign Missions of the Presbyterian Church in Canada, 1913), p. 126.
31. PAC, Memorandum on "Handling of Immigrants," 25 February 1902, Records Centre, Department of the Interior, file 13098 (1).
32. W.F. McCreary, Commissioner of Immigration, Winnipeg, to James A. Smart, Deputy Minister of the Interior, 6 May 1897, quoted in Kaye, *Early Ukrainian Settlements*, p. 280.
33. *Ibid.*, pp. 114-17, 163.
34. *Ibid.*, pp. 105-6.

35. For one example of such aid, where the loan was repaid, see Marunchak, *Ukrainian Canadians*, p. 72.
36. J.C. Lehr, "The Government and the Immigrant: Perspectives on Ukrainian Block Settlement in the Canadian West," *Canadian Ethnic Studies*, IX, 2 (1977), p. 48.
37. For a detailed account of the difficulties presented by this party of Bukovynians, who proved to be particularly obstinate and uncooperative in their demands, see Kaye, *Early Ukrainian Settlements*, pp. 281-2.
38. Lehr, "Government and Immigrant," p. 46.
39. *Ibid.*, p. 47.
40. *Ibid.*, p. 48.
41. PAC, W.R. McCreary to J.A. Stuart, 18 May 1897, file 34214(1), no. 37514. As we have seen in Chapter One, the terms of emancipation in Galicia had allowed the landlord to retain control of the forests; the peasants now sought to escape similar inconveniences in Canada.
42. See O.R. Fry, *My Heritage from the Builders of Canada* (New York: Carleton Press, 1967), p. 24.
43. C.H. Young, *The Ukrainian Canadians: A Study in Assimilation* (Toronto: Thomas Nelson & Sons, 1931), p. 58. For a detailed account of the establishment and development to 1900 of the Ukrainian colonies at Stuartburn, Dauphin, Pleasant Home, Strathclair, Shoal Lake, Yorkton, Rosthern, and Edna-Star, based on official government records and communiqués as well as pioneer memoirs, see Kaye, *Early Ukrainian Settlements*, pp. 135-360.
44. *Nove pole* (New Field) (Winnipeg: St. Raphael's Ukrainian Immigrants' Welfare Association, 1927), p. 121.
45. Marunchak, *Ukrainian Canadians*, p. 363.
46. Darcovich and Yuzyk (eds.), *Statistical Compendium*, p. 33.
47. *Ibid.*, p. 17.
48. M.H. Hykawy, "Ukrainian Displaced Persons," *Opinion*, III, 6 (1947), p. 13.
49. Individual lumber and mining companies agreed to guarantee employment for ten months or to release an individual only with the permission of the Department of Labour. See *ibid.*, pp. 6-8, for a discussion of procedures followed by some mining and lumbering companies.
50. Marunchak, *Ukrainian Canadians*, p. 569.

THREE

Occupational and Economic Development

Wsevolod W. Isajiw

The relationship established when ethnic groups first come into contact with one another may have a greater impact than can be foreseen at the time. For an immigrant group, a pattern is formed when its members are funnelled primarily into one type of occupation, and once established, this "entrance status" can be changed only gradually, usually over the lifespan of two or three generations. Additional waves of immigrants of the same ethnic background usually have little influence in bringing about a change in status.

Ukrainians as a group entered Canadian society as settler-farmers and manual labourers and their economic history in Canada has been largely a process of shedding these roles for more diverse occupations. These initial roles have largely determined their social mobility, and consequently, a brief examination of economic conditions in the Prairie Provinces at the time of the Ukrainians' first contact with Canadian society is most important.

Before the Canadian Pacific Railway was built in 1885 and for some ten years after, Canadian agriculture had few outside markets, because wheat was too difficult and too expensive to transport in large quantities. The government land settlement policies at the time were therefore population policies rather than ones aimed primarily at economic development. A number of land and colonization companies were given land grants on condition that they brought out settlers; most, however, failed to live up to their contracts.[1] In 1871 the total population of the Canadian West was 73,228, composed primarily of native peoples; twenty-five years later it was only about 200,000.

Government land settlement policies failed for at least three reasons. First and perhaps most important, immigration was drawn off to the United States, where the western plains were more attractive than the Canadian Northwest. Second, the economic policies of the railway companies discouraged large settlements. In order to cover their construction and operating costs and yield a profit, the companies not only tried to sell their lands at high prices but also charged high freight rates that discouraged mass migration.[2] Third, because of economic depression, the price of wheat, the mainstay of the prairie economy, remained consistently low. Thus, the first Ukrainian immigrants who settled the Prairies did not come because wheat offered an opportunity to become rich quickly, but because land was abundant; the federal government's 160 acres was about thirty times the average peasant holding in Galicia.

By 1896, the policy of population development related to railroad construction was well-established, and when Clifford Sifton took over as Minister of the Interior, he only added vigour and determination to the old policy. Circumstances, moreover, favoured him. Changes in the world economic situation had created a need for raw materials, and the price of food rose more rapidly than that of manufactured goods. Through its policy of prairie settlement, Canada was ready for the economic boom. By 1914, the average price of Canadian grain exports had increased by 66 per cent, and in the first three decades of the twentieth century the Prairie Provinces constituted the prime investment area in Canada. Indeed, by World War I, wheat had replaced timber as Canada's largest export.[3] By the turn of the century, then, immigration to the Prairies became economically profitable. The rapid economic development of the West would not have been possible without immigration, but it was not as important as were markets, capital, technology, and resources.[4]

Most Ukrainians who came did not settle the best or the most fertile lands. From the standpoint of the group's economic history, this is very important because it determined their entrance status or their actual economic level upon arrival and their potential for future social and economic development. It also affected the perception of them by the general population, with which they had to cope in the years to come.

The settlement by Ukrainians of specific areas was a result of several interrelated factors. Much of the best land had already been settled by the British and Germans, and places like southern Alberta were being settled by the Americans. Government agents who guided Ukrainian immigrant groups often took them to homesteads which had been worked by others and then abandoned because of the poor quality of the soil. Within these general areas the immigrants had a choice of land. The attitudes toward land and its cultivation that the immigrants brought with them led them to choose land that was often most difficult to work:

> Due to his own or his father's economic subjection to Austro-Hungarian or Russian feudalism he [the Ukrainian immigrant farmer] felt literally that he could earn his bread only by the bitter sweat of his brow, and hence no amount of hard labour, even with no immediate evident return, discouraged him; and thinking in terms of the self-sufficient rural family economy of his native land, he prized soil with brush or forest and with lakes and small sloughs

> rather than bald prairies. These attitudes, and in part his ignorance of the actual toil that this involved with little return, made him an attentive listener to the suggestions of government dominion lands and immigration agents that he take out his homestead in such areas.[5]

As a result, the land the immigrants usually settled possessed any or all of the following features: thick brush, low-lying swamp, stone, sand, heavy clay soil, or hills. The poorest land was in Manitoba, west and south of Lake Winnipeg; the best was in Alberta where, particularly in the Vegreville area, Ukrainian homesteads were as good as those of other settlers. The Ukrainian lands in Saskatchewan, though better than those in Manitoba, were frequently covered with thick brush and difficult to clear. Moreover, except for a few small colonies around Winnipeg, all settlements were far removed from rail facilities, with most at least fifty miles from a railroad station. The only roads at the time (and for a long time after) were prairie trails on which oxen were the surest means of transportation.

STAGES OF AGRICULTURAL DEVELOPMENT

There were four stages of agricultural development among Ukrainians: early homesteading, intensive grain farming, mixed farming, and mass-production farming. The most dramatic was undoubtedly the early homesteading stage during which the immigrant farmers literally started from scratch. Clearing of the land with axe, ox, and fire usually took at least five years. In the beginning, with animal power scarce, it was not unusual for individuals to hitch themselves to the plough and break the ground for seeding. Soil was raked with a hand-rake and sown by hand; the grain was cut with a scythe or sickle brought from the old country, stooked and threshed with a flail, and ground with a quern by hand. Few immigrants possessed enough capital to buy oxen or cattle. A survey of Ukrainian rural settlements in 1917 showed that out of 832 families, 50 per cent had no money on arrival in Canada and 42 per cent had less than $500. Yet it took at least $250 to begin a homestead. In the first four or five years, therefore, the typical pattern was for the men to hire themselves out in the summer either as farm or railroad labourers to earn enough money to buy cattle.[6] In fact, by means of the Alien Labour Act of 1897, Sifton tried to prevent railway construction workers from the United States from working on government-subsidized projects, so as to keep the jobs for Canadian settlers who needed money to establish themselves on the land.[7]

Even so, few could earn more than $50 in an average season, and the early period for the Ukrainian settler was essentially one of subsistence agriculture. The grain produced was only sufficient for the settler's use. Not until about 1914 did most farmers possess the horses and machinery to farm for profit through more intensive grain cultivation. The change from oxen to horses was almost as much an advance as the transition from horses to power machinery. In 1909 the first steam-powered threshing machine was bought by six farmers to thresh their own fields and then, for a fee of $15 per farm, those of their neighbours.[8]

The war increased wheat prices greatly and by 1919 they were 134 per cent above the pre-war average. This, and the greater availability of farm machinery, pushed the farmers into intensive wheat production, to the exclusion at times of other farm products. The years 1918-19 were the most prosperous Ukrainian Canadians experienced prior to World War II. Farmers bought more machinery and more land, the latter of better quality and adjacent to Anglo-Celtic districts and hence acquired at exorbitant prices.[9]

Economic depression followed the war. By 1923, the price of Canadian grain had fallen 7 per cent below the pre-war average. Many Ukrainian farmers had to give up their newly acquired farms;[10] others, especially in Manitoba, took up mixed farming. By 1925, districts such as Stuartburn, Elma, Mid-Lake, and Glenella were engaged primarily in dairying and stock-raising with forage crops replacing cereals. Others, such as Brokenhead and Ethelbert, split their farming between grain-growing and dairying and stock-raising. At Birch River cordwood was important and at Sifton a trend to poultry-raising was established. While grain-growing continued to predominate in Saskatchewan and Alberta, in some districts bee-keeping, rabbit-hunting, and the gathering of seneca root for medicinal purposes brought profitable returns.[11]

An important economic element to the Ukrainian farmer was his garden. Every farm had one - an object of display to friends and guests, and even more significantly, a source of food when other farm products failed. "The ability of Ukrainians to succeed where other nationalities have failed, was due to the farmer making such remarkably good use of garden products."[12]

In the last stage of Ukrainian agricultural development, the transition to the use of machinery, which made mass production of farm products possible, was complete. This development, which saw the younger generation enter farming, took place during the 1930's and 1940's and coincided with the Great Depression.

The Depression heralded an unprecedented slump in prices; average annual wheat production for the nine years 1920-28 was 220.5 million bushels, and for 1929-37 only 138.6 million. At the same time, the value of the 1929 wheat crop had shrunk to about two-thirds of that in 1928; the 1930 crop to two-fifths; 1931 to one-fifth; 1932 to one-quarter; and the crops of 1935 and 1936 to about one-third each. The wheat crop of 1932 was the largest since 1928 and was graded higher than any in the previous twenty years. It was sold at an average price of 35 cents a bushel, compared to 77 cents for the low-grade crop of 1928.[13] The sudden disappearance of markets for export staples, especially agricultural goods, was at the root of Canada's economic decline, as agricultural exports fell from $783 million in 1928 to $253 million in 1932.[14] In spite of this, some prairie farm areas provided work for a temporary influx of unemployed males from the cities, while a significant number of females from rural areas found employment in domestic service in the cities, thus partially supplementing the reduced income of the farms.[15]

The slump caused Ukrainian farmers to retrench. Most turned to mixed farming and to their gardens to carry them through the difficult period. By the late 1930's, and especially in the 1940's, Ukrainian agriculture felt the impact of a new Canadian-born generation, better educated and eager to apply electric and motor power to farm machinery.[16] The period also witnessed the beginning of an exodus from the farms. In 1941 at least 55 per cent of the total Ukrainian labour force was still involved in agriculture; by 1951, the percentage had fallen to 35. By the mid-fifties, the character of the typical Ukrainian farmer in Canada had changed. Few of the post-war immigrants became independent farmers, although some gravitated toward fruit farming in southern Ontario and British Columbia. The grain farmer, however, was no longer a peasant. Although he inherited many cultural traditions from his parents, he was not rooted, like them, in a feudal social system, subordinate to the aristocracy and their administrators. The second-generation farmer lived in a world that considered farming a business enterprise rather than a way of life. He was, in fact, a professional farmer.

SOCIAL ASPECTS OF AGRICULTURAL GROWTH

From the outset, the homesteading farmer depended on the co-operation of others: first, the informal co-operation of family, relatives, neighbours, and friends, and with time the formal co-operation of agricultural organizations.

Before mass-production farming, the entire family was involved. The role of the woman was especially important; she was often in charge of the entire household and farm, especially during the early period when men had to hire themselves out. According to a survey conducted by J.S. Woodsworth in 1917, two-thirds of all the Ukrainian women worked in the fields. The sociologist, C.H. Young, in 1931, described a typical summer day:

> The average Ukrainian woman often contributes more to the work of the farm than does the average hired man, whether in the interest, strength and ability she brings to the task, or in the variety of work she performs. A Ukrainian woman in the Canora district, Saskatchewan, gave us an outline of her day's work in the summer. She gets up between four and five in the morning and goes to bed at eleven at night. When she gets up she does the chores outside, feeds the cattle and milks the cows. She then prepares breakfast and washes the dishes, after which she follows the family to the field where she may

> hoe or drive a gang-plow, stook, etc. She comes in shortly before dinner, prepares it and cleans up, a matter of one and a half or two hours, then returns to the field until eight o'clock when she milks, after which she gets supper. This is a man's share in any other community. Along with the contribution of all the other members of the family – and they are usually several – the woman's labour goes far to explain the undeniable progress of the Ukrainian farmer.[17]

Friends and neighbours were often relied upon, especially during the homesteading stage. With oxen scarce, deals would be made to plough the land. Querns, too, were shared, sometimes for a fee, but just as often in exchange for reciprocal service in the future.[18] Economic need, in the early days and in times of depression, was largely a private matter, since government assistance, even when available, was slight. In the 1890's newly arrived immigrants would walk fifty or sixty miles for provisions and return empty-handed because there was not enough to go around.[19] Survival depended on self-reliance or on the support of friends and relatives, and many successful early farmers planted their crops with the understanding that they would be shared with the next batch of new arrivals.[20]

The prejudice of the host society against Ukrainian farmers was revealed, among other ways, through news items and editorials in the press. On December 23, 1896, Winnipeg's influential *Daily Nor' Wester*, under a heading "Unwanted Immigrants," claimed that Slavs, dirty and uneducated, were the least hopeful material for nation-building. On another occasion, the same paper, protesting against the settlement of "Galician paupers," warned that the immigrants' methods of farming would lower the quality of the community's products and their farms would be centres for the spread of weeds and animal diseases.[21] Similar editorials can be found in the *Edmonton Bulletin* of this period.[22]

A study of three papers, the Toronto *Globe*, the *Manitoba Free Press*, and the *Dauphin Press*, however, shows that in the 1890's there were actually fewer prejudicial attitudes than in 1914. In the early period, descriptions of Ukrainian immigrants as "progressive and industrious," "good agriculturalists" with a "good future" and "healthy appearance" predominated. By 1913-14, however, such epithets as "ignorant and uneducated," "open to manipulation," "poor," "dirty," and "unhealthy" were common.[23]

Prejudice and accompanying discrimination caused the Ukrainians to withdraw even further into their own community. Mistrust and suspicion of Canadian officials, government programs, agricultural organizations, and political parties resulted.[24] The informal system of mutual support was reinforced and contributed to the formation of ethnic organizations. On a more formal level, Ukrainian farmers created their own wheat pool organizations and co-operative movements.

The prairie farmers' co-operative movement grew out of fears of monopoly in transportation, marketing, and finance, and out of the dissatisfaction with the tariff. In 1901 the Territorial Grain Growers' Association was formed, the precursor of the United Farmers of Alberta and the Saskatchewan Grain Growers' Association. In 1903 the Manitoba Grain Growers' Association was established, the future Grain Growers' Grain Company. Besides storing and marketing grain, the associations soon purchased farm supplies and leased flour mills. In 1909 government ownership of elevators failed in Manitoba and in 1912 they were leased to the Grain Growers' Grain Company. This precipitated further formation of independent farmers' co-operatives in Saskatchewan and Alberta, so that at the outbreak of World War I co-operatives handled one-third of the prairie grain and competed successfully with private companies.[25]

By that time, Ukrainian farmers were out of the homesteading stage. Because of the language problem, the prejudice and discrimination from local farmers, and the risky nature of the general co-operatives, Ukrainian farmers tended to distrust them and attempted to establish co-operatives and flour mills of their own. Most were failures. Among the bigger and more successful ones was the Ruthenian Farmers' Elevator Company founded in 1917. At its peak, it operated eleven elevators in Manitoba and four in Saskatchewan, but in spite of its early success it went bankrupt in 1930.[26]

Much more successful were the Ukrainian consumer co-operatives. At least nine co-operative stores were established in Alberta: Vegreville (1929), Smoky Lake (1934), Willingdon and Myrnam (1938), Derwent (1940), Chernhill (1941), Mundare (1942), Thorhild (1944), and Boyle (1945). In Saskatchewan, co-operatives were established in Regina (1932), Ituna (1937), Smuts and Alvena (1938), Arrau and Wishert (1940). The most active co-operative movement was in Manitoba. Kalyna Co-op in Winnipeg, established in 1930, had about 300 members; another large co-operative in Winnipeg was the National Consumers' Co-operative established in 1937. Others included Fisher Branch (1929), Sandy Lake (1935), Broad Valley (1936), Britestone (1938), Dauphin (1945), Gilbert Plains (1947), and Ethelbert (1949). Manitoba also had several Ukrainian fuel co-operatives, in particular the North Winnipeg Co-operative (1932) and the Co-operative Union of St. Boniface (1936).[27]

The rise of the co-operative was sparked by the Depression and by the existence in the Ukrainian community of many knowledgeable younger people. Consumer co-operatives had also begun to flourish in Western Ukraine in the 1920's and 1930's, and recent immigrants who had had some experience with them encouraged their development in Canada.[28]

By the 1930's, the general wheat pool co-operatives became more acceptable to Ukrainians, partly because of articles in the Ukrainian press on the advantages of wheat pools but more significantly because of the attitude of the younger generation of farmers who knew English and against whom there were fewer prejudices. As a result, once wheat pools became stable, successful enterprises, earlier inhibitions against participating in co-operative ventures with non-Ukrainians disappeared.

In Manitoba, by the end of the 1930's, only the Germans outnumbered the Ukrainians as the largest non-Anglo-Celtic group in the Wheat Pool. By 1950, Ukrainians formed the majority of members in the Manitoba Vegetable and Potato Growers' Co-operative Association and the People's Co-operative Creamery Limited with its branch, the People's Cooperative Fuel Limited. In 1948, 10 per cent of prairie Wheat Pool membership was Ukrainian. Large numbers of Ukrainians joined the Dairy, Egg and Poultry Pool, the Livestock Pool, and the Canadian Cooperative Implements Limited.[29]

URBAN ECONOMIC DEVELOPMENT

About 1900 circumstances began to favour immigration to urban areas. In the next decade, even though prices remained high and excellent crops were harvested in all but four years, the homestead dream gradually vanished, as good homesteads disappeared. In eastern Canada manufacturing took on a new lease on life; new companies were organized, construction booms succeeded one another, and railway construction was particularly active. Labour was in short supply and wages increased rapidly. Although a recession in 1907 broke the advance, manufacturing revived two years later and prospered until 1914.[30]

Many unskilled immigrants joined the ranks of industrial labour immediately upon their arrival in Canada. The official policy was still immigration for agricultural settlement, but the government did not oppose the growing tendency of immigrants to settle in urban industrial areas. On the contrary, it stopped directing East European immigrants to rural settlement and allowed immigrants to remain in the cities, especially those of Ontario and Quebec where labour was badly needed.[31]

The number of Ukrainian immigrants entering the industrial labour market increased rapidly after 1900. In 1901-02, 25.5 per cent went to work at jobs other than farming; by 1903-04 the percentage had jumped to 40. In sharp contrast to the early immigrants, almost all of whom gave their destination as the Prairie Provinces, between 1904 and 1919 only 55.3 per cent of Ukrainian immigrants came west. After World War I, the pattern continued. Between 1921 and 1931, 89.2 per cent of the Ukrainian immigrants settled in urban areas. Many who initially occupied rural areas moved to urban centres, mainly the industrial areas of Ontario and Quebec.[32] The post-World War II immigrants settled almost entirely in the urban areas, principally in Toronto, Winnipeg, and Edmonton.

THE CHARACTER OF URBAN SETTLEMENT AREAS

All cities have attracted immigrants because of the work opportunities they provide. Jobs and housing in the city are found through friends and friends of friends. Ethnic immigrant communities thus become a source of important information for new arrivals. Ethnic residential communities offer not only opportunities for social and cultural participation with one's own people, but in the absence of other effective communication networks, they offer significant economic advantages.

Historically, Winnipeg, Edmonton, Toronto, and Montreal have had large concentrations of Ukrainians, and in each the patterns of residential segregation have been similar. Three types of residential areas are found: areas of tenement houses; areas of working-class, one-family houses; and one-family houses in suburban areas. The first two overlap in time, both predominating before World War II; the third is mainly a post-war phenomenon. Each wave of Ukrainian immigrants has begun in the poorer areas, with the second generation gradually migrating to economically better districts. Since the 1960's, however, because new waves of Ukrainian immigrants have not been forthcoming, the first two areas have been taken over by more recent immigrants of other ethnic groups.

C.H. Young described the tenement area of the second and the third decades of this century as a deteriorating section on the outskirts of the business section, with low rents and high land values because of its potential for future business expansion. The original owners having moved out, the low rents made the area an "immigrant reception area." The aging tenements housed from two to fifteen families each - many more than originally intended - with about 47 per cent of all families living in three rooms or less. Often the families took in roomers to help pay the rent. In the Winnipeg housing survey of 1918 there were 428 roomers among 641 families. In Winnipeg this area was located roughly at Point Douglas on the south and north sides of the Canadian Pacific Railway depot, between Higgins, Henry, Dufferin, and Sutherland Avenues. In Montreal the same type of area was near St. Lawrence and Main, between St. Urbain and Sauguinet; in Toronto it encompassed Bathurst Street, from McCaul to Claremont Streets, between Queen and Dundas, and the King Street East section, west of the Don River, near Parliament Street.[33]

The working-class area of one-family dwellings contained no tenements and had a relatively high percentage of homeowners. It was inhabited by more established workingmen and tradesmen. A few families might still have boarders, but overcrowding was unknown. Some such areas were adjacent to the immigrant reception centres, but most represented residential colonies away from the original areas.[34] More established or younger people with better jobs moved into them, and with time the relocation of ethnic institutions followed. The areas represented social mobility of the Ukrainian immigrants into the upper-lower and to some extent the lower-middle classes.

The third type of residential area - the suburban - arose once Ukrainians moved into the middle class. Two sub-types can be distinguished, the new suburbs and the old. The new suburbs were the products of the post-war mass development of family homes. The old suburbs were sections of the city, once suburbs, now engulfed by urban sprawl. Old or new, both were far from the old immigrant reception area, geographically and economically, reflecting the rapid occupational mobility of Ukrainians in Canada since 1945. Although less solidly Ukrainian than the other types of residential areas, many still remain areas of Ukrainian residential concentration.

URBAN OCCUPATIONS

The history of urban occupations among Ukrainians in Canada can be divided into three periods: from the beginning of immigration to the 1920's; the transitional period from the end of the 1920's to the 1940's; and the period from the end of World War II to the present. In the beginning, the bulk of urban workers were unskilled and the number in skilled and professional occupations increased slowly. But after the 1920's specialization and diversification were rapid, so that by 1941, the percentage of unskilled labourers among Ukrainians had dropped substantially. The shift out of unskilled work was, in fact, faster than that of most other ethnic groups and of Canada as a whole.

Before examining the statistical data on the shifts in the occupational structure of Ukrainians in Canada, let us take a brief look at the types of Ukrainian urban workers and some of the forces which influenced them.

The Workers

In the early period, Ukrainian immigrants came from the peasant ranks; very few could be classified as other than farmers or unskilled labourers. Between 1904 and 1919, only about 8 per cent of all Ukrainian immigrants in Canada could be classified as clerks, traders, mechanics, miners, or female domestics.[35] Unlike the homesteader, however, the urban immigrant was much more often a single male. Within the same period close to 70 per cent of Ukrainian immigrants were males, which explains the large number of roomers in the early city settlements.

The Ukrainian urban unskilled workers of that period fall into three types: resident labourers, seasonal labourers, and female labourers.[36] The resident labourers were those with regular jobs: the yardmen on the railways, workers in the sugar refineries, men in manual labour in the packing plants. Their wages were better than those of the seasonal labourers and they provided the element of stability in the residential neighbourhoods.

The seasonal labourers used the city as their base but moved around with their work, which was usually in railway or road construction. Their season started in the spring and lasted until about September, depending on the work available. Their wages varied from one sub-contractor to another; in the 1920's they averaged about 25 to 30 cents an hour for a ten-hour day, with 90 cents a day deducted for board and lodging.[37] The seasonal construction worker lived, worked, and moved with his camp.

In the work camps groups of men from different ethnic groups were thrown together during the day, yet segregated at night in different bunkhouses, each characterized by a discipline of rigid obedience to the Anglo-Celtic bosses. About 3,000 camps operated in certain years, employing around 200,000 men, more than 5 per cent of the total Canadian male labour force. They existed from the early days of settlement down to the 1920's, with some surviving into the 1970's.[38]

The number of Ukrainians in the camps is unknown, but the percentage must have been high. Many employment bureaus reported that their long line-ups of unemployed were mostly Ukrainian, and an employment agency in Montreal reported in 1928 that out of the 350 workers it supplied for the bush, 250 were Ukrainian.[39] Often employment agencies would sign up more men than the camps could hire. It was not unusual to see fifty workers sent to the bush, with only ten hired. The remainder would often wait around the camps for a few days in the hope of being hired, only to return to the cities, usually on foot.[40]

Ukrainian workers were also employed in the mines, although fewer than in construction work. They worked in Sudbury, Ontario, in mines as far east as Sydney, Nova Scotia, and as far west as the coalfields of Alberta and British Columbia. Wages in the mining industry were higher than those in construction work. In the 1920's an average wage was about 53 cents an hour on the surface, with the pay higher underground, undoubtedly the highest wage earned by any Ukrainian workers, including the farmers.[41]

In the years up to World War II many Ukrainian women in urban areas were employed as domestic servants and restaurant workers, with a few in the food-processing industry. Young girls from rural areas often worked in the cities for a definite period and then returned home. There was hardly a Ukrainian settlement in the West from which girls and young women did not go to work in the cities. New immigrant girls who spoke no English found it hard to get work, except in the eastern European Jewish homes of Montreal, Toronto, and Winnipeg, where Ukrainian was understood. The wages were usually low, though somewhat better than in restaurants. C.H. Young reports that in the 1920's Ukrainian girls could be found in most Winnipeg restaurants, though seldom in the most expensive ones. Although a minority, many women with families worked in the cities, mostly as housekeepers. In Toronto Ukrainian women were also employed by the two largest meat-packing houses, Swift's and Harris's.[42]

Unemployment

By 1931, although the occupational structure of Ukrainians in Canada was beginning to change, at least 40 per cent of the urban labour force was still unskilled and subject to chronic unemployment. For the unskilled worker there were several periods of particularly high unemployment and the outbreak of war in 1914 intensified the problem. Large numbers of immigrants were dismissed from their jobs for "patriotic reasons." Many government officials and Canadian employers thought that immigrants, especially those from eastern Europe, were not loyal to Canada and were a security risk. Some Canadians, to forestall the spread of socialism, insisted that the unemployed be forced to work even at the point of a bayonet. Others agitated for the mass internment of the "idle and impoverished aliens." Arthur Meighen, Solicitor General in the Borden government in 1914, disagreed and suggested that each unemployed alien be granted forty acres of land to be cultivated under government supervision, since "these Austrians . . . can live on very little." Even the Trades and Labour Congress in 1915 suggested that the unemployed workers be placed on homesteads in northern Ontario.[43]

Unemployment for Ukrainians and other immigrant workers did not cease with the end of the war. In 1919 the government received many petitions, particularly from veterans' organizations, demanding mass deportation of enemy aliens. At the same time demands were made for discriminatory economic regulations on the ground that returned soldiers deserved the jobs held by enemy aliens. In 1919 the International Nickel Company of Northern Ontario, with 3,200 employees, bowed to public pressure and dismissed 220 of its foreign-born employees.[44] Other companies followed.

In 1928-30 the problem of unemployment was again unusually severe, especially among the unskilled and seasonal workers. After the bush season was over in spring, many men returned to the cities, especially Winnipeg, looking for work. In the fall the farm labourers, after harvesting the grain, returned to Winnipeg for the same reason. Because of a severe drought in 1928, Winnipeg was overrun by unemployed farm labourers. In the parades and daily meetings of the unemployed in the market square in 1928, anywhere from 1,500 to 2,000 men participated. The bulk were undoubtedly Ukrainians. When the government decided to register the unemployed, out of the 837 men, 548 were classified as being "non-preferred," most being Ukrainians, as Ukrainians headed the list of labourers from "non-preferred" countries.[45]

Another severe period of unemployment was, of course, the Great Depression. Besides farmers, the groups hit hardest were the unskilled and young people entering the labour market for the first time,[46] both categories in which the Ukrainians were highly represented. In his book *The Winter Years*, historian James H. Gray, who was himself on relief, gives a graphic description of the unemployed in Winnipeg:

> With boundless leisure, there was an almost infinite variety of things to be done. Along north Main Street, all the neighbourhood stores were equipped with chess tables, and the unemployed Jews and Ukrainians in the stores outnumbered the customers four and five to one.

The unskilled workers suffered most, but even for Ukrainians with skills, training, or ability, only unskilled jobs were usually available, according to Gray.

> In my search for employment I was free to range over the whole of commercial Winnipeg and nobody denied me a job from any ulterior motive. This did not hold true for the Ukrainians, Poles, and Jews. For them Winnipeg was far from being a city of 250,000 in which they too were free to search for work. As much as two-thirds of it was barred and bolted against them.
>
> None of the city's chartered banks, trust companies, or insurance companies would knowingly hire a Jew, and anyone with a Ukrainian or Polish name had almost no chance of employment except rough manual labour. The oil companies, banks, mortgage companies, financial and stock brokers, and most retail and mercantile companies except the Hudson's Bay Company discriminated against all non-Anglo-Saxons. For the young Ukrainians and Poles there was a possible solution if they could beat the accent handicap. They could change their names. So they changed their names, sometimes formally and legally, but mostly informally and casually.

The change of name, however, did little to help the unskilled. Ethnic discrimination, Gray observed, was so prevalent that it drove the minorities into economic ghettos.

> Jews tried to live off the trade of other Jews; and Ukrainians, Poles, and Germans tried to live off other Ukrainians, Poles, and Germans. This drive to survive in a prejudice-ridden community produced the rash of small industry and of bootstrap manufacturing that developed in Winnipeg. . . .
>
> The North End filled up with home-based contractors. When a Ukrainian went into the construction business, he trailed a small army of other Ukrainians behind him – a Ukrainian excavator, a Ukrainian concrete-mixer, a Ukrainian plumber, a Ukrainian carpenter, a Ukrainian painter, a Ukrainian plasterer.[47]

The government's relief efforts helped many to survive, but they were largely insufficient. Besides assistance to farmers, government programs included meals and bed services for the transients, relief land settlement, public works, and direct employment aid,[48] but the sheer number of transients defied assistance. The land settlement program was no great success either. The costs of transporting families from the cities to rural areas were high and many would give up farming after a year or two. The public works projects, however expensive to government, especially at the municipal level, were unable to employ all who needed work, and most of them kept men busy only temporarily.

Involvement in the Labour Movement

The involvement of Ukrainians in the labour movement in Canada still requires research, but it seems likely that Ukrainians were active in establishing unions in lumber camps, mines, and factories by 1910. Historian C. Lipton claims that immigrants took the lead in developing such unions, and Ukrainians were probably involved in the organization of the carpenters' union in Toronto in 1913. They were also involved at that time in organizing the rock miners at South Porcupine and Cobalt, the coalminers in western Canada, and the Amalgamated Clothing Workers of America in Toronto.[49]

Ukrainians also participated in the radical labour movement in Winnipeg. Both the Ukrainian Social Democratic Party and its organ, *Robochyi narod*, played an important role in the July, 1917, construction workers' strike which hastened recognition of the construction workers' union in Winnipeg.[50] The role played by Ukrainians in the Winnipeg General Strike is more difficult to assess. All the strike leaders were of British origin and no Ukrainians were among those leaders arrested in the raids of June 17, 1919, although the Ukrainian Labour Temple was searched by the authorities.[51] There seems to have been little direct contact between the strike leaders and prominent Ukrainian socialists, probably because the latter had not achieved prominence in the unions or trades councils. However, most Ukrainian workers in the city seem to have sympathized with the strike and participated in the rallies and demonstrations. Two immigrant labourers killed on June 21, Bloody Saturday, may have been Ukrainians. As many as thirty Ukrainians were also injured and one hundred arrested on that day.[52]

In 1918 a broad-based organization, the Ukrainian Labour Temple Association, was established by the Ukrainian social democrats. When the Ukrainian Social Democratic Party and its paper were banned in September, 1918, the new organization assumed responsibility for the dissemination of socialist and Marxist ideas among Ukrainians and began to espouse a pro-Soviet orientation. In 1924 the organization was renamed the Ukrainian Labour-Farmer Temple Association (ULFTA), and by 1939 it boasted over 10,000 members in 201 branches across Canada. Prominent members of the ULFTA were involved with the Communist Party of Canada from its inception and constituted the core membership of several Communist trade union organizations.[53]

After the outbreak of World War II, Canada's massive unemployment problem was over. At the same time the number of unskilled workers in the Ukrainian population in Canada began to drop drastically. By 1961, the proportion of unemployed Canadian-born Ukrainians dropped slightly below the Canadian average. In the 1960's and 1970's the unemployed foreign-born Ukrainians have been mostly older people. Compared with 1921 or 1931, by 1971 the occupational structure of Ukrainians in Canada had also changed substantially.

Men with Front-window Stores and White-collar Shirts

By 1931, over 75 per cent of Ukrainians were still either farmers or unskilled labourers. However, the percentage of skilled workers, craftsmen and tradesmen, and persons in a variety of specialized occupations was increasing rapidly. Even in 1921 the government census housing survey in Winnipeg counted 564 persons engaged in specialized occupations in one Ukrainian district of the city. The most numerous were clerks and store-keepers (92), merchants (69), building tradesmen (68), railway employees (52), tailors (42), plumbers and steam fitters (33), mechanics (27), and painters and decorators (24).[54] The merchants and businessmen merit closer examination.

Lacking experience, skills, and capital, the peasant who would be a businessman had to operate by trial and error. It was difficult to attract non-Ukrainian customers, though some tried by Anglicizing their names. The first customers were therefore largely Ukrainians. Even here competition was keen. Ukrainians were not accustomed to dealing with Ukrainian businessmen and preferred Jewish merchants because the Jews had frequently migrated from Ukraine and were familiar with the language and the psychology of the Ukrainian peasant. As a result, the slogan "svii do svoho" (patronize your own) became an important part of Ukrainian business promotion in Canada.[55]

The first Ukrainian grocery store was opened in 1902 by Paul Rudyk in Edmonton. He later turned to real estate and in 1913 organized a loan company. The pattern was typical. The general store, selling groceries and dry goods, was the most popular early business venture. Barber, beauty, book, tailor, gift, smoke, shoe, flower, and jewellery shops followed. The second stage of business development included gas stations, hotels, dairies, bakeries, vegetable, fruit, and meat-packing plants, furniture manufacturing, the supply of transportation equipment, and the formation of construction companies.[56]

Table 4 indicates the selected businesses owned by Ukrainians and the number in selected professions between 1946 and 1952. The prominence of grocery stores, general stores, and hotels suggests that many Ukrainian businessmen were still in the first stage of business development. The table does not indicate the variety of businesses or professions in which Ukrainians have been engaged; the directory from which the data are taken contained some 215 business and professional categories.

The Credit Unions

One of the more important developments in the economic life of the Ukrainian business community in Canada has been the credit union movement. The first savings and loan association had been established in Ukraine in 1896. Between the two wars, they became more common in western Ukraine and to some of the immigrants of that time they were familiar institutions. The credit unions established in Canada, however, followed the model set up in 1900 by A. Desjardins in Quebec.

The first Ukrainian credit union, New Community, was organized in Saskatoon in 1939. The Carpathia Credit Union followed in Winnipeg

TABLE 4

Selected Businesses Owned by and Professions of Ukrainians in Canada, 1946-52*

Type of Business	*1946-47*	*1950-51*	*1951-52***
Farm Implements	17	98	27
Grocery Stores	271	295	148
General Stores	158	302	187
Hotels	37	164	115
Insurance	43	67	49
Real Estate	41	86	72
Restaurants, Cafes	74	99	55
Service Stations	42	147	63
Shoemaker/Repairs	109	—	3
Professions			
Accountants	5	12	8
Barristers/Solicitors	38	58	58
Clergy	153	256	224
Dentists	14	40	37
Pharmacists	24	41	30
Physicians	40	86	84

* Includes Manitoba, Saskatchewan, Alberta, Ontario, and Quebec.

** The 1951-52 directory was not as extensive as that in 1946-47 and 1950-51.

Source: F.A. Macrouch, *Ukrainian Business Directory* (Winnipeg: n.p., 1946-47, 1950-51, 1951-52).

(1940), Hamilton (1943), Toronto (1944), and then Sudbury, Sifton, Poplarfield, and Fisher Branch (1945). After the war, credit unions grew rapidly and by the 1970's over forty were avowedly Ukrainian and in twenty more Ukrainians were prominent. The first group had about 40,000 members and a cash turnover of about $100 million. In the same period there were 4,122 credit co-operatives in Canada as a whole, with close to seven million members and almost $9 billion in assets.[57] The largest Ukrainian credit union in 1974 was the Ukrainian Credit Union of Toronto with 5,553 members and over $15 million in assets. By the end of 1976, membership had increased to 6,320 and the assets had risen to over $22 million. The second largest was Carpathia of Winnipeg with 5,225 members in 1974 and over $13 million in assets. Ranking third was Buduchnist of Toronto with 4,487 members in 1974 and over $11 million in assets.[58]

Several factors have been responsible for the success of the credit union movement among Ukrainians: more favourable interest rates, free cheque-writing privileges, and Ukrainian-speaking tellers in the ethnic neighbourhood or near institutions regularly patronized by Ukrainians. Historically, also, the economic crisis of the 1930's and the association of East Europeans with Communism made banks consider foreign-born Ukrainians as bad credit risks.[59] The formation of co-operative loan associations was one way to meet financial difficulties. The fact that such institutions ingeniously combined the motive of personal gain with the feeling of community obligation has always been significant where children are taught to participate in ethnic organizations and to believe that every Ukrainian has an obligation to his community.

What economic impact have credit unions had on their members and what kind of benefits have the latter derived from them? In the Ukrainian Credit Union of Toronto the average savings per member in 1976 were $3,286.[60] Far more important were the loans for the purchase of a multitude of goods and services:

83 purchasing homes and land	$2,449,400
35 refinancing mortgages	812,700
32 purchasing cars	163,600
9 investments	127,000
14 purchasing businesses	118,100
7 building houses	95,500
18 home repairs	83,800
16 refinancing other debts	73,400
6 purchasing furniture	10,700
5 travel	7,300
3 school needs	3,200
1 a wedding	2,000
1 medical purposes	1,900
5 other purposes	10,300
	$3,958,900

The report for 1976 in which these figures were published concluded, with apparent self-satisfaction, that the above were given in large measure to young married couples and to young businessmen.[61]

UP FROM THE SOIL: CHANGES IN THE OCCUPATIONAL STRUCTURE

To assess adequately the changes in socio-economic status which have taken place among Ukrainians in Canada since the homesteading days, it is necessary to resort to statistical data. Tables 5, 6, 7, and 8 present the occupational composition of the Ukrainian male labour force in Canada for four decades, 1941 to 1971. Only the data on the male labour force are used, since they are a better, more stable indicator of the socio-economic status of households and families. What have been the significant shifts in the occupational composition? How do they compare with the changes which have taken place in the general Canadian labour force?

First, most striking among the Ukrainian male labour force is the decrease in the proportion of people engaged in agriculture. Thus in 1941, 54.6 per cent or more than half of the Ukrainian male labour force was still agricultural. By 1951, the percentage had decreased to 35.3, by 1961 it was 23.0, and by 1971, 13.2, a decrease more rapid than that for the Canadian male labour force as a whole. Second-generation Ukrainians moved quickly out of farming. They did not, however, move out as rapidly as did other East Europeans, and by 1971 they were still over-represented in agriculture by more than 6 per cent.[62]

The second discernible pattern involves labouring and manufacturing occupations. In 1931, 23.9 per cent of the Ukrainian male labour force were still labourers and unskilled workers.[63] By 1941, the percentage had dropped to 9.2 and, except for 1951 when it rose to 10.5, continued to

TABLE 5

Occupational Composition of Male Ukrainian and Total Male Canadian Labour Force, 1941*

Occupational Category	*Male Ukrainian* No.	*Male Ukrainian* %	*Total Male Canadian* %
Clerical	1,051	1.1	5.4
Trade and finance	3,612	3.7	9.0
Service	3,722	3.8	5.9
Transportation and communication	6,675	6.8	7.6
Agriculture	53,849	54.6	31.7
Logging	1,520	1.5	2.4
Fishing, hunting, trapping	197	.2	1.5
Mining and quarrying	2,904	2.9	2.1
Manufacturing and construction	14,346	14.5	23.1
Labourers	9,048	9.2	7.5
Professional	1,478	1.5	3.5
Not specified elsewhere	166	.2	.3
Total	98,562	100.0	100.0

* Total male labour force: 3,363,111.

Source: *Census of Canada*, 1941, vol. 6, Table 6; vol. 7, Tables 5 and 12.

decline to 3.5 in 1971. The 1951 increase probably reflects the influx of post-war immigrants. Although better educated than the two earlier waves, and with many possessing professional and clerical qualifications acquired in Ukraine, most of them lacked knowledge of the language and appropriate contacts and took on unskilled work.

TABLE 6

Occupational Composition of Male Ukrainian and Total Male Canadian Labour Force, 1951*

Occupational Category	*Male Ukrainian No.*	*%*	*Total Male Canadian %*
Managerial and proprietary	6,560	5.0	9.0
Clerical	4,139	3.1	5.9
Commercial and financial	3,249	2.5	5.3
Service	7,102	5.4	6.6
Transportation and communication	11,442	8.7	9.2
Farming	46,438	35.3	19.4
Logging	1,461	1.1	2.5
Fishing, hunting, trapping	160	.1	1.2
Mining and quarrying	3,044	2.3	1.6
Manufacturing, mechanical, power production engineering, construction	29,537	22.5	25.0
Labourers	13,757	10.5	8.0
Professional	3,390	2.6	5.1
Not specified elsewhere	1,135	.9	1.2
Total	131,459	100.0	100.0

* Total male labour force: 4,121,832.

Source: *Census of Canada*, 1951, vol. IV, Table 12; vol. V, Tables 11 and 21.

By 1971, however, for the first time the proportion of labourers in the Ukrainian male labour force was no higher than that in the total Canadian male labour force. This decrease was accompanied by a rapid increase in manufacturing, construction, and related occupations. In 1931 only 7.8 per cent of the Ukrainian male labour force was engaged in manufacturing and construction. By 1941, the percentage had almost doubled to 14.5 and by 1971 it had risen to 27.7. This reflected the general post-war industrial development in Canada, but Ukrainians showed a steady influx into the manufacturing occupations. Under-represented in manufacturing by 8.6 per cent in 1941, by 1951 Ukrainians were under-represented by only 2.5 per cent, and by 1971 they were slightly over-represented (by 0.7 per cent).

TABLE 7

Occupational Composition of Male Ukrainian and Total Male Canadian Labour Force, 1961*

Occupational Category	*Male Ukrainian No.*	*Male Ukrainian %*	*Total Male Canadian %*
Managerial	9,710	7.1	10.2
Clerical	7,687	5.7	6.9
Sales	4,788	3.5	5.6
Service and recreation	9,948	7.3	8.5
Transportation and communication	8,739	6.4	7.5
Farmers and farmworkers	31,225	23.0	12.2
Loggers	897	.6	1.7
Fishing, hunting, trapping	129	.1	.8
Mining and quarrying	2,398	1.8	1.4
Production workers and craftsmen	40,218	29.6	28.8
Labourers	9,343	6.9	6.2
Professional and technical	7,928	5.8	7.6
Not specified elsewhere and not stated	2,977	2.2	2.6
Total	135,987	100.0	100.0

* Total male labour force: 4,705,518.

Source: *Census of Canada*, 1961, vol. III, Table 17; vol. III: I, Table 21; vol. III: 3, Table 21.

The third significant pattern is the change in the managerial and proprietary, clerical, commercial and sales, and professional categories. In 1931 only 2.1 per cent of the entire Ukrainian male labour force was engaged in trade and only 0.4 per cent occupied clerical, financial, and public administration categories. Only 0.8 per cent of the same force did professional work. The trade and sales category, which had increased only slightly by 1951, almost doubled between 1961 and 1971. The clerical category showed a steady increase from 1.1 per cent in 1941 to 6.7 per cent in 1971. The managerial and proprietary category has experienced a sharp decline in both the Ukrainian and the general labour force. Some of this decline is probably the result of the change of classification of occupations on this level by the census bureau.

TABLE 8

Occupational Composition of Male Ukrainian and Total Male Canadian Labour Force, 1971*

Occupational Category	*Male Ukrainian No.*	*Male Ukrainian %*	*Total Male Canadian %*
Managerial, administrative, and related	6,555	3.9	5.5
Clerical	11,380	6.7	7.6
Sales	11,580	6.8	9.9
Service and recreation excluding labourers	14,660	8.6	8.6
(including labourers)	(15,375)	(9.0)	(9.1)
Transportation and communication excluding labourers	17,365	10.2	9.8
(including labourers)	(18,190)	(10.7)	(10.8)
Farming, horticultural, and animal husbandry	22,400	13.2	7.1
Forestry and logging	1,095	.6	1.2
Fishing, hunting, trapping	120	.1	.5
Mining and quarrying	2,305	1.4	1.0
Manufacturing, processing, construction, and related (excluding labourers)	47,050	27.7	27.0
Labourers (except those in agriculture, fishing, logging, and mining)	6,005	3.5	3.5
Professional and technical	14,945	8.8	9.9
Not specified elsewhere (excluding labourers)	2,200	1.3	1.1
Occupations not stated	12,440	7.2	7.3
Total	170,100	100.0	100.0

* Total male labour force: 5,736,560.

Source: *Census of Canada*, 1971, Catalogue 94-734, vol. III, Part 3 (Bulletin 3.3-7), February, 1975.

Participation in professional occupations of Ukrainian males has shown a definite, steady increase with the gap between them and the general male labour force gradually narrowing. Thus in 1941, 1.5 per cent of the Ukrainian male labour force was professional, in 1951, 2.6 per cent and by 1971, 8.8 per cent. Whereas in 1941 the under-representation in this category was 3 per cent and in 1951, 2.5 per cent, by 1971 it had decreased to 1.1 per cent. However, it should be noted that in spite of decreasing under-representation in the trade and sales, managerial, clerical, and professional categories, Ukrainians were still under-represented in each of these categories, trailing other ethnic groups, including other Slavic groups such as the Poles and Russians.[64]

The 1971 census statistics on educational attainment and average income corroborate this conclusion. Of all Ukrainians twenty-five years and over, 49.3 per cent gave elementary school as their highest educational attainment, 43.1 per cent had one to five or more years of secondary education, and 7.6 per cent had either some university education or had obtained a university degree. In regard to the university educational attainment, out of twelve selected ethnic groups only the French, Italians, and native peoples had smaller percentages. On the other hand, the percentage for the Poles was 8.5, the British 11.3, the Jews 23.6, and the Asians 27.7.[65]

As to average annual incomes, for persons fifteen years and over in the same twelve groups, only the native peoples, with $2,976, earned less than the Ukrainians. Ukrainians earned on the average $4,637; the French, $4,711; the Poles, $4,843; the British, $5,162; the Italians, $5,219; the Asians, $5,292; and the Jews, $7,631.[66]

CONCLUSION

There have been three stages of socio-economic development experienced by ethnic groups whose occupational history in Canada has been similar to that of the Ukrainians. The first stage emphasizes work in primary occupations such as agriculture and other unskilled jobs. The second stage is movement into manufacturing and skilled occupations until equal representation with other groups is attained, with a concomitant assumption of such tertiary occupations as trade, sales, clerical, management, and professional. The third stage is a decrease in participation in manufacturing occupations and an increase in trade, sales, finance, management, and professional occupations.

Ukrainians in Canada have lived through the first and second stages and only recently have entered the third stage. Although the majority of Ukrainians have moved out of agriculture and unskilled jobs, they, along with the Germans, Dutch, and Scandinavians, are still more engaged in Canadian agriculture than other ethnic groups. In the tertiary occupations they have not yet reached the point of equal representation with other ethnic groups. They have now to compete with groups whose entrance status in Canada was higher, groups who did not have to move up from the soil.

NOTES

1. C.A. Dawson and E.R. Younge, *Pioneering in the Prairie Provinces:*

The Social Side of the Settlement Process (Toronto: Macmillan of Canada, 1940), pp. 11-16.

2. A.W. Currie, *Canadian Economic Development*, 4th ed. (Toronto: Thomas Nelson & Sons, 1968), p. 177.
3. V.C. Fowke, *The National Policy and the Wheat Economy* (Toronto: University of Toronto Press, 1957), pp. 70-84; also R.C. Brown and R. Cook, *Canada 1896-1921: A Nation Transformed* (Toronto: McClelland and Stewart, 1974), p. 20.
4. D.C. Corbett, "Immigration and Economic Policy," *Canadian Journal of Economics and Political Science*, XVII (1951), p. 364.
5. S.W. Mamchur, "The Economic and Social Adjustment of Slavic Immigrants in Canada with Special Reference to the Ukrainians in Montreal" (Master's thesis, McGill University, 1935), p. 34. For the role of immigration agents and immigrant land-settlement psychology, see Report of the Commissioner of Immigration, Winnipeg, 1897, *Sessional Papers of Canada*, 1898, no. 13, part IV, p. 171; M. Ewanchuk, *Spruce, Swamp and Stone, A History of the Pioneer Ukrainian Settlements in the Gimli Area* (Winnipeg: n.p., 1977), pp. 3-25, 30; J.C. Lehr and D.W. Moodie, "The Polemics of Pioneer Settlement: Ukrainian Immigration and the Winnipeg Press," *Canadian Ethnic Studies*, XII, 2 (1980), pp. 88-101.
6. See Woodsworth report in C.H. Young, *The Ukrainian Canadians: A Study in Assimilation* (Toronto: Thomas Nelson & Sons, 1931), pp. 43-4, 78-80, 94.
7. M.F. Timlin, "Canada's Immigration Policy, 1896-1910," *Canadian Journal of Economics and Political Science*, XXVI (1960), pp. 517-32.
8. O. Woycenko, *The Ukrainians in Canada* (Ottawa: Canada Ethnica, 1967), pp. 66-7.
9. Young, *Ukrainian Canadians,* pp. 80-1.
10. *Ibid.*, p. 81.
11. *Ibid.*, pp. 82-4.
12. R.W. Murchie and H.C. Grant, *Unused Lands of Manitoba* (1926), quoted in *ibid.*, p. 84.
13. W.L. Jacobson, "Prairie Relief and Rehabilitation," in L. Richter (ed.), *Canada's Unemployment Problem* (Toronto: Macmillan of Canada, 1939), pp. 226-7.
14. M.C. Urquhart (ed.), *Historical Statistics of Canada* (Toronto: Macmillan of Canada, 1965), p. 178, cited in L.M. Grayson and M. Bliss (eds.), *The Wretched of Canada* (Toronto: University of Toronto Press, 1971), p. viii.
15. L.C. Marsh, *Canadians In and Out of Work* (Toronto: Oxford University Press, 1940), pp. 285-9.
16. For brief selected biographical sketches of the younger farmers, see V. Lysenko, *Men in Sheepskin Coats: A Study in Assimilation* (Toronto: The Ryerson Press, 1947), pp. 255-64.
17. Young, *Ukrainian Canadians*, p. 88.

18. M.H. Marunchak, *The Ukrainian Canadians: A History* (Winnipeg: Ukrainian Free Academy of Sciences, 1970), pp. 84, 94.
19. J.G. MacGregor, *Vilni Zemli (Free Lands): The Ukrainian Settlement of Alberta* (Toronto: McClelland and Stewart, 1969), p. 155.
20. *Ibid.*, p. 66.
21. M.H. Marunchak, *Studii do istorii ukraintsiv Kanady* (Studies in the History of Ukrainians in Canada), 4 vols. (Winnipeg: Ukrainian Free Academy of Sciences, 1964-65), I, pp. 52-3.
22. MacGregor, *Vilni Zemli*, pp. 155-6.
23. D. Daschko, "Attitudes Toward Ukrainians in Canada Between 1896 and 1914: A Content Analysis of Three Canadian Newspapers," unpublished paper, University of Toronto, Department of Sociology, 1974.
24. For an illustration of this, see W.A. Czumer, *Recollections about the Life of the First Ukrainian Settlers in Canada* (Edmonton: Canadian Institute of Ukrainian Studies, 1981), pp. 98-102, 106-12.
25. W.T. Easterbrook and H.G.J. Aitken, *Canadian Economic History* (Toronto: Macmillan of Canada, 1968), pp. 500ff.
26. P. Yuzyk, *The Ukrainians in Manitoba: A Social History* (Toronto: University of Toronto Press, 1953), p. 50.
27. Marunchak, *Studii*, I, pp. 106-7; Yuzyk, *Ukrainians in Manitoba,* p. 60.
28. Marunchak, *ibid.*
29. Yuzyk, *Ukrainians in Manitoba*, p. 60; Young, *Ukrainian Canadians*, p. 89; Woycenko, *Ukrainians in Canada*, p. 69.
30. Mamchur, "Slavic Immigrants," pp. 38ff; also J.W. Dafoe, "The Economic History of the Prairie Provinces 1870-1913," in A. Shortt and A.G. Doughty (eds.), *Canada and Its Provinces: A History of the Canadian People and their Institutions*, 23 vols. (Toronto: Publishers Association of Canada, 1913-17), XX, pp. 283-330.
31. Mamchur, "Slavic Immigrants"; also D.H. Avery, "The Immigrant Industrial Worker in Canada 1896-1919: The Vertical Mosaic as an Historical Reality," in W.W. Isajiw (ed.), *Identities: The Impact of Ethnicity on Canadian Society* (Toronto: Peter Martin Associates, 1977), p. 17.
32. Mamchur, "Slavic Immigrants," pp. 41, 50.
33. Young, *Ukrainian Canadians,* pp. 107-9.
34. *Ibid.*, pp. 110-11.
35. Mamchur, "Slavic Immigrants," p. 38.
36. Young, *Ukrainian Canadians*, pp. 114ff.
37. E.W. Bradwin, *The Bunkhouse Man: A Study of Work and Play in the Camps of Canada, 1903-1914*, 2nd ed. (Toronto: University of Toronto Press, 1972).
38. J. Burnet, "Introduction," in *ibid.*, p. vii.
39. Young, *Ukrainian Canadians*, p. 116.
40. Czumer, *Recollections,* p. 72.
41. Young, *Ukrainian Canadians*, p. 117.
42. *Ibid.*, pp. 122-3.

43. Avery, "Immigrant Industrial Worker," pp. 20-1.
44. *Ibid.*, pp. 23-4.
45. Young, *Ukrainian Canadians*, pp. 118-19.
46. Grayson and Bliss, (eds.), *Wretched of Canada*, pp. i-viii.
47. J.H. Gray, *The Winter Years: The Depression on the Prairies* (Toronto: Macmillan of Canada, 1966), pp. 49, 126-7, 132, 133.
48. Richter (ed.), *Canada's Unemployment Problem*, chapters 4 to 7.
49. C. Lipton, *The Trade Union Movement of Canada 1827-1959* (Montreal: Canadian Social Publication, 1967), p. 125.
50. D. Avery, "The Radical Alien and the Winnipeg General Strike of 1919," in C. Berger and R. Cook (eds.), *The West and the Nation: Essays in Honour of W.L. Morton* (Toronto: McClelland and Stewart, 1976), pp. 214-15.
51. *Ibid.*, p. 223. Avery states that one of the four non-Anglo-Celtic labour activists arrested on June 17 was Michael Charitinoff, whom he refers to as the "former editor of *Robochy Narod*" and as a "young Ukrainian socialist." In fact, Charitinoff was of Russian Jewish origin, and had in all probability been editor of the Russian-language *Rabochii narod*, a weekly published for some time in 1918 by the Russian Social Democratic Party in association with the Ukrainian social democrats and *Robochyi narod*.
52. For a general account of the strike, see D.J. Bercuson, *Confrontation at Winnipeg: Labour, Industrial Relations and the General Strike* (Montreal: McGill-Queen's University Press, 1974), pp. 126-7, 186. The information regarding Ukrainian casualties is taken from A. Gregorovich, *Chronology of Ukrainian Canadian History* (Toronto: Ukrainian Canadian Committee, 1973), p. 22. According to Gregorovich, the two men killed were Mike Sokolowski and Steve Shcherbanovich. It is difficult to determine the nationality of the two victims because the spelling of their names is inconsistent in the press. Shcherbanovich, for example, appears as J. Szczerbaniewicz (Shcherbanovych?). Sokolowski (Sokolovsky?) may have been Ukrainian. The Ukrainian press, including *Ukrainski robitnychi visti*, the pro-Communist successor to *Robochyi narod*, did not attempt to make martyrs out of either, nor did it identify them as being Ukrainian. *Ukrainski robitnychi visti*, 12, 16 July 1918.
53. J. Kolasky, *The Shattered Illusion: The History of Ukrainian Pro-Communist Organizations in Canada* (Toronto: Peter Martin Associates, 1979), pp. 1-26.
54. Young, *Ukrainian Canadians*, p. 124.
55. Woycenko, *Ukrainians in Canada*, pp. 53-6.
56. For specific names of businessmen and their companies, see *ibid.*, pp. 51-3, 58, 61; Yuzyk, *Ukrainians in Manitoba*, pp. 57-9.
57. M. Plawiuk, "Ukrainian Credit Unions in Canada," in *Slavs in Canada* (Ottawa: Inter-University Committee on Canadian Slavs, 1968), pp. 146-8; see also A. Kachor, *75-littia kredytovoho rukhu v Kanadi (1900-1975)* (75th Anniversary of the Credit Union Movement in

Canada, 1900-1975) (Winnipeg: Kooperatyvna hromada, 1976), pp. 13-14.

58. Kachor, *75-littia*, pp. 14-15; also *Ukrainian (Toronto) Credit Union, 1976*, Board of Directors' Report, p. 4.
59. Plawiuk, "Credit Unions," pp. 147-8.
60. Board of Directors' Report, p. 19.
61. So-Use (Toronto) Credit Union, *27th Annual Report for 1976*, p. 12.
62. The measure of over, under, and equal representation is a measure of comparison of proportions of quantitative characteristics within an ethnic group with those of society as a whole. Thus, if in 1971 the proportion of the Ukrainian male labour force in agriculture was 13.2 per cent and the proportion of the Canadian male labour force in agriculture was 7.1 per cent, then Ukrainian males were over-represented in agriculture by 6.1 per cent. Under-representation occurs when the total societal percentage is higher than that for the ethnic group. Equal representation can be said to exist when the percentages for the ethnic group and society as a whole are the same.
63. For all 1931 census data on Ukrainian occupational composition, see Dominion Bureau of Statistics, *Seventh Census of Canada, 1931*, VII, Occupations and Industries (Ottawa, 1936), p. 22.
64. W.W. Isajiw and N.J. Hartmann, "Changes in the Occupational Structure of Ukrainians in Canada: A Methodology For the Study of Changes in Ethnic Status," in W.E. Mann (ed.), *Social and Cultural Change in* Canada, 2 vols. (Toronto: Copp Clark, 1970), I, pp. 96-112.
65. W. Kalbach and W.W. McVey, Jr. (eds.), *Demographic Basis of Canadian Population*, rev. ed. (Toronto: McGraw-Hill Ryerson, 1978), Table 8:8.
66. *Census of Canada*, 1971, *Profile Studies: Ethnic Origins of Canadians*, V, part 1 (Bulletin 5.1-9), May, 1977. Figures rounded off to nearest dollar.

FOUR

Political Activity in Western Canada, 1896-1923

Orest T. Martynowych and Nadia Kazymyra

Prior to 1914, Ukrainian political activity was limited to the municipal and provincial levels. As struggling rural settlers and frontier labourers, Ukrainians were naturally concerned with issues related to everyday life and were thus drawn into local politics. By the early 1920's they controlled a number of rural municipalities, had freed themselves from local party machines, and in Manitoba and Alberta had achieved a legislative presence that reflected a growing independence and maturity. Not until World War I brought the need to protest the suspension of their rights in Canada, and to appeal on behalf of Ukraine's struggle for independence, did they come to appreciate the importance of active participation at the federal level.

THE SOCIO-ECONOMIC MILIEU

The majority of Ukrainians who emigrated between 1891 and 1914 to western Canada were politically unsophisticated peasants. However, as we have seen in Chapter One, public education in their native land was beginning to reach broader segments of the Ukrainian population through Prosvita societies and a growing network of recreational associations, co-operative stores, credit unions, and agricultural marketing associations. Politically, too, the Radical, Social Democratic, and National Democratic Parties had begun to concern themselves with the plight of the Ukrainian peasant and labourer and had published a number of newspapers which encouraged mass participation in the struggle for social and political reform. Successive waves of strikes during the first decade of the twentieth century demonstrated the growing politicization of Ukrainian peasants and labourers, and it is likely that an influential and articulate (if not very large) minority of the pre-1914 immigrants to Canada did have some practical political experience and fairly definite ideas about the national and class interests of their countrymen.

Those who provided political leadership among Ukrainians in Canada at this time were usually young men born in Galicia during the last quarter of the nineteenth century. Although generally of peasant background, a few had origins in the impoverished lower gentry, which, while economically indistinguishable from the peasant masses, had never been enserfed and continued to cherish "traditions of status, learning and leadership."[1] A handful of the most prominent came from districts where the radicals, social democrats, and national democrats were influential. Most were literate, a minority having attended secondary schools, a teachers' or theological seminary, or even university. After learning English in Canada, they acquired considerable political influence as interpreters for government officials, politicians, teachers, and missionaries. They were elected to municipal office, provided with opportunities to improve their education, and gradually acquired a better understanding of Canadian society and politics. Above all, they began to realize that men like themselves could be agents of social change and progress, that they could shape their own destiny.

The desire to ameliorate living and working conditions prompted the politically experienced immigrants to mobilize their countrymen for political activity. During this period the vast majority of Ukrainian immigrants continued to occupy the bottom rung of the social ladder, just as they had in Galicia and Bukovyna. Recruited to satisfy the demand for agricultural settlers and cheap labour, they were isolated from centres of political power and cultural activity, left without basic social services, and were expected to perform the type of menial and unremunerative labour which Canadians of Anglo-Celtic and northern European backgrounds shunned. Surveys during the next decade revealed that many Ukrainian rural settlers led lives that were materially and culturally impoverished.[2]

In view of the inadequate state of social utilities and services in rural areas, this was hardly surprising. Municipalities controlled by established settlers were usually unwilling or unable to provide the newcomers with roads, bridges, and other facilities. In remote pioneer regions the settlers remained destitute and without local administration for years. Medical care was almost impossible to obtain. Had it not been for the Presbyterian and Methodist medical missionaries, many Ukrainian settlements would have been totally without such services. Educational facilities were equally inadequate, largely owing to the unwillingness of municipal councils to approve the construction of new schools, the low level of financial support from provincial governments, and the reluctance of English-speaking teachers to go into "Galician" settlements. The special schools for "foreigners" to train teachers for rural Ukrainian settlements were subject to political expediency. Constantly attacked for impeding "Canadianization," they were ultimately abolished during the war years.

Well over 20 per cent of the Ukrainian immigrants on the Prairies remained in urban centres, and over 50 per cent of all Ukrainian agricultural settlers spent many years as labourers, drifting in and out of cities and frontier camps before establishing themselves on the land. The number of Ukrainian non-agricultural immigrants rose rapidly between 1907 and 1913, when railroad construction was booming and federal restrictions on Oriental immigration caused Canadian railroad companies to turn to southern and eastern Europe for cheap labour.[3]

The plight of the urban immigrants was even more alarming than that of the farmer-settlers. Working conditions on the railroads and in the mines, the urban ghettos, and the factories were deplorable, and wages, especially on the railroads, were irregular and exploitative. Living conditions in frontier bunkhouses and urban tenements were crowded, with the most basic social amenities practically non-existent. The incidence of tuberculosis in Winnipeg's immigrant quarter, the North End, was especially high, and the infant mortality rate in 1912 reached the astounding figure of 28.2 per cent.[4]

When the economy went into recession the immigrant was the first to feel its effects. In the summer of 1913, when thousands of unemployed Ukrainians, formerly railroad navvies, began to congregate in western urban centres, some were arrested for loitering and a number were deported. By the war's outbreak, thousands of unemployed Ukrainian labourers were wandering vainly in search of work, and the war only aggravated their unhappy condition. Large numbers of "enemy aliens," immigrants from non-Allied countries, were dismissed from their jobs. Only critical manpower shortages caused by the war enabled many to find employment after 1917.

More subtle were the efforts of the dominant Anglo-Celtic group to Canadianize the immigrants. The Protestant church and the public school were viewed as the vehicles with which to forge a homogeneous English-speaking people free of all class and ethnic tensions by moulding all immigrants into loyal English-speaking citizens who would in the process forfeit their culture and language. At first, Presbyterian and Methodist missionaries were the Canadianizing agents, bent on isolating and socializing a loyal immigrant elite with the culture, values, and ideology of the Anglo-Celtic Protestant majority. Anti-clerical sentiments, engendered by radicals from Ukraine hostile toward the Catholic clergy, encouraged the Protestant missionaries and led them to believe that ministers of the Presbyterian-sponsored Independent Greek Church could constitute an intermediary elite. By 1912, however, it was clear that the conversion of Ukrainians to Protestantism and the prospect of Canadianization would not come easily.

Accordingly, the public school became the prime agency of Canadianization and attacks on the bilingual school system in Manitoba and on the provisions for instruction in languages other than English in the public schools of Saskatchewan and Alberta escalated. Teachers who had graduated from the special training schools were accused of incompetence and their schools were criticized as "hotbeds for the propagation of foreign racial prejudice" that transformed western Canada into another Austria-Hungary – "the home of a dozen races each adhering with desperation to its mother tongue."[5] After the outbreak of war, the training schools were abolished, and the use of languages other than English in the public schools was not only outlawed but reproved by corporal punishment. Objects representative of the Ukrainian heritage were removed and the schools became instruments of cultural domination.[6]

The outbreak of war also made it easier for the government to implement anti-foreign political measures. In May, 1914, the British Nationality, Naturalization and Aliens Act had already made it more difficult to obtain naturalization certificates.[7] In August, 1914, Parliament passed the War Measures Act, which permitted the government to make decisions by Orders-in-Council. Enemy aliens were ordered to report or register monthly with the police. Those who failed to report or who were deemed to be a threat to national security were detained in internment camps. A total of 8,579 individuals were thus affected, among them 5,954 of Austro-Hungarian citizenship, many of whom were unemployed Ukrainian labourers.[8] In July, 1915, a Press Censorship Board was established to monitor the ethnic press in Canada. Finally, in September, 1917, the Wartime Elections Act disfranchised all citizens born in enemy countries and naturalized after 1902.

By 1917, the Canadian economy had suffered heavy manpower losses as a result of the war. Even though they had been deprived of their civil rights, those formerly considered enemy aliens were now needed to stem the growing labour shortage, and all above the age of sixteen were registered with the Canadian Registration Board. An "anti-loafing law," enacted in April, 1918, required that all male residents of Canada be "regularly engaged in some useful occupation." In September, 1918, as a result of growing fears that labour unrest among workers was connected with Bolshevism, all foreign-language publications were suppressed and fourteen left-wing organizations were outlawed. A month later the Public Safety Branch was set up to enforce the legislation.

Many Ukrainian immigrants experienced the full weight of these enactments, while the whole community, especially in urban centres, was exposed to outbursts of nativist hostility and intimidation by private individuals and citizens' groups. In Winnipeg, for example, Ukrainians were prevented from participating in the Dominion Day parade in 1915, and three years later Ukrainian and other foreign institutions were vandalized by war veterans who demanded that aliens be dismissed from their jobs and deported.[9] In February, 1919, an Alien Investigation Board was established in Manitoba by the provincial government to determine who among the aliens had been "loyal" and who had to be deported.[10] Later in 1919 growing labour unrest and the presence of unemployed war veterans resulted in more immigrants being laid off and in amendments to the Immigration Act, which brought Canada's "open door" policy to an end.

MUNICIPAL POLITICS

Ukrainians became directly involved in municipal politics shortly after the turn of the century. This was accomplished with difficulty, however, since established settlers monopolized municipal councils and urban property qualifications excluded most Ukrainians. Nevertheless, by 1914 Ukrainians had made such rapid progress, especially in rural areas, that a prominent westerner observed: "one fact stands out with tremendous clearness - the Ruthenians have become a force . . . throughout the prairies."[11]

Interest in municipal politics developed when Ukrainian immigrants realized that it was incumbent upon them to take the initiative if roads and bridges were to be built and post offices erected. Thus Stefan Shandro (who had been active on his village council in Bukovyna) and his sons established Shandro as a centre in Alberta and provided it with a post office, a road, and a telephone. Likewise, Pavlo Melnyk and Wasyl Romaniuk, with experience acquired in Galicia, petitioned for the formation of the Ukraina Local Improvement District and established the post office at Myrnam, Alberta.[12]

Where municipal councils already existed, the awareness that their needs were being neglected pushed Ukrainians into municipal politics. Ukrainian settlers in the municipality of Franklin in Manitoba entered municipal politics in 1902 because their requests for roads, bridges, and schools were being ignored. When the provincial government also failed to support their request for a school, Theodosy Wachna convinced the settlers to break away from Franklin and create the municipality of Stuartburn. Except for the reeve, all members of the new municipality's council were Ukrainians, with Wachna the first Ukrainian municipal secretary-treasurer in Canada. Within a year three schools and a post office were built. In 1908, with the election of Ivan Storosczuk as reeve, the Stuartburn council became the first all-Ukrainian municipal council in Canada.

The situation in the Interlake region of Manitoba was similar. In Gimli the council was dominated by Icelandic settlers who had been concentrated near Lake Winnipeg since the 1870's. They were not anxious to spend municipal funds for improvements in the interior settled by Ukrainians. In 1913 the Ukrainians, aided by a few German and Icelandic settlers, finally broke away and gained considerable influence in the new municipality of Kreuzberg.[13]

By the early 1920's, rural Ukrainians controlled several municipal councils: Stuartburn, Ethelbert, Dauphin, Gimli, Kreuzberg, Brokenhead, Chatfield, Rossburn, and Mossy River (in Manitoba); Rosthern, Hafford, and Yorkton (in Saskatchewan); and Vegreville, Myrnam, Mundare, Two Hills, and Smoky Lake (in Alberta). The councils in Ethelbert, Stuartburn, Rossburn, Vegreville, and Hafford were bilingual, corresponding with other levels of government in English while carrying on local business in Ukrainian.[14]

It was much more difficult for Ukrainians to win election to city councils. Property qualifications enabled commercial elites to control such councils, particularly in Winnipeg, which had the largest urban concentration of Ukrainians in Canada. In 1906 fewer than 8,000 of the city's 100,000 residents were registered voters, and election to any municipal office required backing from powerful business interests. In practice this meant endorsement by one of the two major parties.

Toma Yastremsky, a veteran Conservative Party worker, was the first to enter Winnipeg city politics. In 1907 he ran unsuccessfully as an independent aldermanic candidate to represent the Ukrainian and German voters of Ward Six. The following year he failed to win one of the four city controller seats on a Conservative ticket.[15]

In 1910 another prominent Conservative Party member, Theodore Stefanyk, contested the same aldermanic seat. Although supported by the Ukrainian press, he lost by sixty-seven votes. But in 1911 he was elected with support from the Conservative Party and a committee of Ukrainian, Polish, and German voters. In the summer of 1912 he helped Ukrainians employed on water main construction in the North End obtain wage parity with workers employed in other parts of the city. Stefanyk, however, survived in office for only one year. His open association with the unpopular provincial Conservative administration of Rodmond P. Roblin repelled most immigrant voters. It was not until 1926 that a second Ukrainian - William Kolisnyk, a Communist - was elected to the city council in Winnipeg.[16]

PROVINCIAL POLITICS

Success and the experience acquired in municipal politics encouraged Ukrainian participation on the provincial political level on the eve of World War I. Disgusted with the corrupt electoral practices of the Conservative and Liberal Parties, incensed by unfair criticism of bilingual instruction, and frustrated by their inferior socio-economic status and ethnic prejudice, Ukrainians moved to elect their own independent candidates in Manitoba and Alberta.

The first politically active Ukrainians in Manitoba were Cyril Genik, Ivan Bodrug, and Ivan Negrich. All came from the same village in Galicia, where the radicals had been very active. Each had a sound secondary education, had taught in village schools, and had assisted the first groups of peasant immigrants organized by Joseph Oleskiw to settle in

1896 and 1897. Because of their knowledge of German, all at one time or another were employed by the Immigration Branch.[17]

Their radical sympathies inclined them toward the Liberal Party in politics and to the Protestant church in religious matters. Although vaguely socialist in personal convictions, they favoured the Liberals, who had supported large-scale Ukrainian immigration to Canada, distributed the homesteads, and consistently defended the Ukrainian presence during the early years. Conservative spokesmen, on the other hand, had described Ukrainian immigrants as "foreign scum," and in Manitoba the Conservative government had extended the period of enfranchisement for all East Europeans from three to seven years.[18] Moreover, the Conservatives were seen as the party of the eastern capitalists and their local agents, while the Liberals were reputed to be the champions of the farmer and the little man. Socialist parties, which might have appealed to Genik, Bodrug, and Negrich, had still to become established on the Prairies during the early period (1896-1904).

Protestantism, especially Presbyterianism with its "rational, ethical and intellectual" quality,[19] impressed the three men because of their deep hostility to Catholic clericalism and their desire to base the life of Ukrainian immigrants on what they thought were enlightened and rational foundations. In 1903, with financial assistance from the Liberals, they established the first Ukrainian newspaper in Canada, the weekly *Kanadiiskyi farmer*, which disseminated their political and religious views. The following year they campaigned for Liberal candidates during the federal election.

The close identification of the Liberals with Galician radicalism and Anglo-Protestantism alienated tradition-oriented peasant immigrants and the more conservative political and social immigrant activists. The Liberals, who controlled *Kanadiiskyi farmer*, found a new editor in 1905 and instructed him to steer clear of religious polemics, which would suggest that the party was concerned with its image among Ukrainian voters. Nevertheless, by 1904-05, the more traditional Ukrainian elements in Manitoba were beginning to gravitate toward the Conservatives.

The fact that the Conservatives, as the government party, were in a position to provide for the immigrants' educational needs, including their desire to retain their language, helped to tilt the balance in their favour. As early as August, 1901, Toma Yastremsky was disturbed to see Genik and his associates distributing radical pamphlets and had urged Conservative representatives to organize a special school to train Ukrainian teachers. To this end, he had even built a non-denominational hall in Winnipeg. Early in 1903, anticipating a provincial election, Yastremsky devised a scheme to naturalize 1,500 Ukrainian immigrants in Winnipeg. He approached Conservative organizers and promised to deliver 1,500 votes if the party pledged to establish a teacher-training school for Ukrainians. He then invited the recently naturalized Ukrainians to a meeting in support of Samson Walker, the Conservative candidate in

North Winnipeg. After Walker's election, Premier Roblin assured Yastremsky that the school would be established.[20] It opened its doors in 1905.

With the Ukrainian population on the increase, in 1904 the Conservatives reversed their discriminatory franchise legislation and began subsidizing a Ukrainian newspaper, *Slovo*. As a result, the party emerged as the benefactor of the Ukrainian community, with the bilingual school system affording an excellent opportunity to consolidate the Conservative hold on Ukrainian voters. The men appointed bilingual school organizers in Ukrainian districts - John Baderski, Michael Rudnicki, Theodore Stefanyk, and Paul Gigeychuk - were loyal party members who spent more time organizing voters than school districts.[21] Prior to elections, they agitated in favour of Conservative candidates, received generous travel subsidies, and distributed bribes. Although there is no evidence that bilingual teachers participated in such activities, a number did campaign for Conservative candidates, especially as political patronage often determined who was admitted to the Ruthenian Training School and who retained his teaching post.[22]

During the ensuing decade, prior to every provincial and federal election, the Conservative machine in Manitoba was set in motion in ridings populated by Ukrainians. Appointees of the Conservative government - school organizers Stefanyk and Gigeychuk, immigration officer Yastremsky, weed inspector Fred Bodnar, and a host of minor personalities - campaigned, agitated, cajoled, and paid Ukrainian immigrants to vote Conservative. Districts that failed to vote Conservative ran the risk of remaining without educational facilities. In rural and urban areas voting lists were falsified, impersonation at the booths was encouraged, money and liquor were distributed, and unsophisticated immigrants were instructed in the fine art of casting the ballot. Road construction crews, sent into Ukrainian districts shortly before an election, were plied with liquor, given the day off, paid overtime, and transported to Liberal rallies which they promptly disrupted.[23]

The Liberals, too, were not above this type of activity. In 1908 the Ruthenian Liberal Club was organized in Winnipeg by Zygmunt Bychynsky, editor of *Kanadiiskyi farmer* and a minister of the Independent Greek Church. Ukrainians of Protestant sympathies supported the Liberals because Catholic immigrants tended to be in the Conservative camp. Although Liberal campaigns were not as corrupt as Conservative ones, they too demoralized many immigrants and reduced elections to internecine squabbles. A low point was reached in the Gimli by-election in July, 1913, when Stefanyk, Yastremsky, Gigeychuk, Bodnar, and other Conservatives confronted Ostrowsky, Dyma, Shandro, and an assortment of Liberals. A bilingual teacher in the district informed the *Manitoba Free Press* (July 16) that most meetings had been reduced to drunken orgies, while his pupils had been exposed to an endless procession of cars filled with drunken men passing their school.

It is difficult to determine how successful the Conservative machine was among Ukrainians in Manitoba.[24] During the 1907 election it appears that rural Ukrainians supported the Liberal Party quite consistently, although in North Winnipeg Yastremsky's activity on behalf of the Conservatives helped to elect John Mitchel.[25] The 1910 election, however, saw a definite shift toward the Conservatives. Although Mitchel unexpectedly lost in North Winnipeg, three heavily Ukrainian constituencies – Gimli, Dauphin, and Gilbert Plains – previously Liberal or Independent, all returned Conservatives.

It was not, however, until the by-elections of 1913 that Ukrainian voters lined up squarely behind the Conservatives. Indeed, it was generally conceded that the Roblin regime held on to office because of the Ukrainian vote. The reasons for the new alliance were complex. By 1913, Conservative corruption and support of the bilingual school system had sent most Protestant Anglo-Celtic advocates of Canadianization into the Liberal ranks. Convinced that the bilingual school system impeded the emergence of a homogeneous English-speaking Canadian society, the Liberals launched a determined campaign against bilingualism in the schools. Although abolition was never formally a campaign plank, Liberal criticism, on the heels of a similar campaign in Alberta, increased indignation among Manitoba's Ukrainians and consolidated their support for the Conservatives. Only *Kanadiiskyi farmer* and the Presbyterian *Ranok* stood by the Liberals; *Kanada*, the new pro-Conservative weekly, *Kanadyiskyi rusyn*, the Ukrainian Catholic organ, and *Ukrainskyi holos*, the Ukrainian bilingual teachers' publication, all supported the Conservatives in 1914.

Ukrainskyi holos, established in Winnipeg in 1910 by fairly well-educated and politically sophisticated immigrants, was distressed by the manner in which Ukrainians were manipulated by both missionaries and politicians. As the first Ukrainian paper not affiliated with any political party or religious denomination, it criticized the electoral practices of both parties and challenged the notion that Ukrainians could advance their interests by working for established parties and extracting favours in return. Accordingly, Ukrainians would have to nominate and elect dedicated, selfless Ukrainians, with or without the support of established parties, if their interests were to be taken seriously. The expansion of Ukrainian national awareness and the cultivation of personal self-respect were the foundations for the type of collective political action needed. To the editors, bilingual education was imperative, for it developed a sense of solidarity and helped overcome feelings of inferiority among the immigrants and their children.

The opportunity to put these principles to the test came in 1915 after the fall of the Roblin government following charges of corruption concerning the new Parliament buildings. Taras Ferley, the manager of *Holos* and a Ukrainian teacher at the Ruthenian Training School, decided to run as an Independent Liberal in the election after losing the official Liberal nomination to a popular local municipal official. To prevent the Conservative incumbent from winning because of a divided Liberal vote, Ferley's supporters prevailed upon the Liberal nominee to withdraw. With the support of local bilingual teachers and the Ukrainian press, Ferley won by a margin of more than 600 votes. He had advocated compulsory education and the teaching of English, but he defended the right of all children to learn their mother tongue in the public schools.[26]

The election of the Liberal Party in 1915 virtually assured the abolition of bilingual education early in 1916, and Ferley and the Franco-Manitoban representatives were powerless against an overwhelming Liberal majority. Even so, an important hurdle had been crossed. Political leadership in Manitoba had passed "from the hands of personally motivated agents who manipulated the Ukrainian vote on behalf of a given party to community-oriented leaders."[27]

Unlike Manitoba, Saskatchewan and Alberta were practically without a two-party system until the interwar years. The Liberals, benefiting from the patronage flowing from their federal counterparts, entrenched themselves in both provinces and retained the sympathy of Ukrainians for many years. Nor were Saskatchewan Ukrainians inclined to assert their independence in provincial politics. Most had received fairly good land, much better than that of the Ukrainians in Manitoba. It was therefore easy to identify with the pro-farmer Liberal Party. The absence of large urban centres and industry meant that there were fewer politically experienced immigrants, so that the leadership vacuum was initially filled by Independent Greek Church ministers with their Liberal sympathies. The Saskatchewan Liberals, too, had learned a lesson from Manitoba's Conservatives and made concessions to the Ukrainians in matters of education.

From the outset, the Liberals used the Independent Greek Church ministers as intermediaries. Ivan Bodrug and Zygmunt Bychynsky, both ministers of that church and former editors of *Kanadiiskyi farmer*, became the first school organizers in Ukrainian districts and acted as staunch Liberal boosters. James A. Calder, the Deputy Minister of Education, was informed that Bychynsky was "highly thought of by our [Liberal] Party friends in Canora during the late Provincial Campaign . . . [he was] quite effective and . . . would have the Party interest in view in all dealings with Galicians."[28]

For the first few years after 1905, the government allowed both graduates of Manitoba's Ruthenian Training School and permit teachers to teach in the schools established among the Ukrainian settlers. The co-operation of Manitoba Liberals was also enlisted to find "bright young men . . . to counteract the Tory work" as teachers in Saskatchewan.[29] When it became difficult to find such men, the Saskatchewan government created a school of its own – the Training School for Teachers for Foreign Speaking Communities – on the recommendation of Joseph

Megas, the school organizer at Rosthern and a former editor of *Kanadiiskyi farmer*.

Megas was helpful to the Liberals on a number of occasions. He established a pro-Liberal newspaper, *Novyi krai*, through which he sought to influence the Ukrainian vote. *Novyi krai*, founded as the organ of the Association of Canadian Ruthenian Farmers, promoted bilingual education and rural co-operatives, but its primary function was to endorse the activities of Premier Walter Scott and his close friend, J.A. Calder, the Minister of Education. It urged Ukrainians to support Liberal rather than independent Ukrainian candidates. It was not enthusiastic, therefore, when Mykhailo Gabora was nominated by a group of homesteaders in Canora to run as an Independent in the 1912 provincial election. Even though Gabora's campaign was poorly organized and he himself lacked leadership qualities, *Novyi krai*'s excessive praise of the Liberals and its references to the impropriety of independent Ukrainian candidates betrayed its intense Liberal partisanship.

Aside from Gabora's ill-conceived attempt, however, Ukrainians did not enter provincial elections in Saskatchewan. When bilingual instruction was abolished late in 1918, they were too involved in religious disputes and in promoting the Petro Mohyla Institute to challenge the Liberals.

In Alberta the situation was very different. Alberta's Ukrainians were initially part of the mighty Liberal machine. Men like Peter Svarich, Paul Rudyk, Dmytro Solianych, and Hryhorii Kraykiwsky provided leadership comparable to that of Genik, Bodrug, Ferley, and the *Ukrainskyi holos* group in Manitoba. In fact, Svarich and Rudyk were major shareholders in the Ukrainian Publishing Company which published *Holos* and communicated with the editors on a regular basis. Their cooperation with the provincial Liberals was motivated by a desire to secure educational concessions similar to those in Saskatchewan.

In December, 1909, shortly after Alberta's second provincial general election, a convention organized by prominent Ukrainian Liberal activists was held in Edmonton. The 200 participants passed several resolutions: that the provincial government fulfil its pre-election promises to appoint school organizers and to establish a training school for Ukrainians; that it appoint only Ukrainian teachers to schools in Ukrainian districts and allow them to teach Ukrainian; that a national council be established consisting of organizers from all Ukrainian settlements; that a student residence be established in Edmonton if the government refused to open a training school for Ukrainian teachers; and that the national council be entrusted with the organization of a democratic political party among Ukrainians in Alberta.[30]

The provincial government finally established a training school, the English School for Foreigners, in 1913. Its inadequacies made it clear that Ukrainians had to be represented in the legislature if their demands were to be taken seriously. In the election in April, however, the only Ukrainian candidate nominated by the Liberal Party was Andrew Shandro in the Whitford constituency. No Ukrainian candidate managed to win a nomination for the Conservatives, so four prominent Ukrainians entered the elections as Independents: Peter Svarich (Vegreville), Hryhorii Kraykiwsky (Vermilion), Michael Gowda (Victoria), and Paul Rudyk (Whitford). All were defeated.[31]

Although Shandro captured Whitford and technically became the first Ukrainian MLA in Canada, relations between the Ukrainians and the Liberals steadily deteriorated. Within a month the Alberta government dismissed all Ukrainian permit teachers in Alberta and uncovered a "conspiracy" led by a "definite outside organization . . . determined to break up the educational system of the province."[32] The fact that John R. Boyle, Minister of Education, referred to Ukrainian as a "dialect of Russian" and to Ukrainians as "Little Russians" revealed the Russophile influences within the Alberta Liberal organization and alienated nationally conscious Ukrainians, who would be among those who abandoned the Liberals in subsequent elections.

FEDERAL POLITICS

The First World War brought Ukrainians face to face with the federal government. Disillusioned by the abrogation of civil rights and anxious to support the struggle for Ukrainian national independence in Europe, they became more concerned with being heard at the federal level. Their growing alienation from the two traditional parties, evident before the war at the provincial level, was exacerbated. By 1923, the six Ukrainian MLAs on the Prairies were either Independents or third-party representatives, while none of the Ukrainians who had contested federal seats had run on a Liberal or Conservative ticket.

The war brought socialism, a new political philosophy within the Ukrainian immigrant community, into general prominence.[33] Although some of the immigrants with radical sympathies – Genik, Bodrug, Ferley, Svarich – had flirted with socialism, prior to 1905 the social base for such an orientation among Ukrainians was slight. The influx of Ukrainian recruits for frontier labour between 1907 and 1913 provided a base, but socialism remained a marginal movement within the community. The first organized Ukrainian socialist groups, all affiliated with the Socialist Party of Canada (SPC), emerged in 1907. The first socialist paper, *Chervonyi prapor*, appeared only eighteen times in Winnipeg before folding in 1908. Another attempt to mobilize Ukrainian workers was launched in Winnipeg in May, 1909, through *Robochyi narod*. The response was strong enough to organize a conference of the ten existing Ukrainian socialist groups in Canada, which culminated in the formation of the Federation of Ukrainian Social Democrats in Canada (FUSD).

The men who led the Ukrainian socialist movement through the pre-war years – Paul Crath (Pavlo Krat), Myroslaw Stechishin, Toma Tomashevsky, Wasyl Holowacky – had all been associated with radical and socialist groups in the old country.[34] Although they referred to themselves as social democrats, they were ethical socialists rather than doctrinaire Marxists. In 1910 the FUSD broke its ties with the SPC and participated in the formation of the Social Democratic Party of Canada. Stechishin and other FUSD leaders criticized the SPC for its ultra-radical posturing and its refusal to recognize the FUSD's autonomy.

Between 1910 and 1914, leadership within the movement passed from its founders to younger, more radical men. The change in leadership reflected changes in the composition of the Ukrainian labour movement. As single males recruited by the railroad companies became more numerous, the movement became more narrowly class-oriented. By 1915, Tomashevsky, Stechishin, Holowacky, and Crath had left the socialist camp for more moderate Ukrainian circles.[35] The new socialist leaders – Matthew Popowich, John Navis (Ivan Navizivsky), and Danylo Lobay – stood closer to the Galician social democrats than to the Galician radicals and were moving leftward on the eve of war.[36] They maintained ties with Ukrainian social democrats in Galicia, Bukovyna, Russia, and Europe. The change in leadership was followed by a change of name. In 1914 the FUSD became the Ukrainian Social Democratic Party in Canada (USDP).

Prior to the war, the founders of the movement had concentrated on developing a sense of class consciousness and international working-class solidarity among Ukrainian immigrant labourers. They urged that workers join unions organized by the International Workers of the World (IWW) and that farmers establish co-operatives. The new leaders tended to be more doctrinaire. They believed that capitalism was an inherently exploitative system of production which could not be reformed. Consequently, they looked forward to the day when all workers, "united under one red banner," would seize control of the state, socialize the means of production, and establish a just and equitable social order. However, this commitment did not prevent them from organizing dramatic and choral groups or from expressing their support for the principle of bilingual education.[37]

Deteriorating economic conditions and the outbreak of war made the new leaders impatient with the moderate non-socialist Ukrainian leaders, whom *Robochyi narod* mocked as "spineless plebians." In August, 1917, at the second congress of the USDP, an amendment to the party's constitution declared that "no branch of the USDP may co-operate with any group of people who do not recognize the class struggle and the necessity of abolishing the capitalist order."[38]

After the war's outbreak, Ukrainian social democrats were increasingly drawn into the Bolshevik sphere of influence. Even before the war, their more experienced organizers had tried to organize Ukrainian and Russian workers in Canada and the United States. Matthew Popowich, for example, had established contacts with the Russian social democratic editors of the increasingly pro-Bolshevik *Novyi mir* while in New York. After 1914, Alexandra Kollontai, Vladimir Volodarsky, Nikolai Bukharin, and Leon Trotsky were associated with that paper. Thus, by 1917, *Robochyi narod* had begun to feature articles by leading Bolsheviks, including Lenin. In April, 1917, Ivan Kulyk, a high-ranking Ukrainian Communist in the 1920's, attempted to join the staff of *Robochyi narod* but was kept out of Canada by immigration officials.[39]

The social democrats' exposure to Bolshevik views coincided with the curtailment of civil liberties in Canada and an unprecedented eruption of nativist hostility toward enemy aliens. As the distinction between conditions in the British Empire and the despotic empires abandoned by the immigrants became increasingly blurred, Bolshevik declarations became more relevant to the immediate experience of some Ukrainians in Canada.

During the war the social democrats were fairly prominent on the radical labour scene in Winnipeg. In April, 1915, they organized a demonstration of unemployed workers in Winnipeg, and in July they campaigned actively in support of R.A. Rigg, an Independent Labour candidate in North Winnipeg. Thereafter, activity subsided as organizers and members left the country or were interned. It resumed in 1917 when economic conditions began to improve. In June the USDP played a prominent role when Winnipeg's unskilled construction workers struck on the issue of collective bargaining. Although arrests and internments ensued, working conditions in the industry improved and the construction workers' union was recognized. *Robochyi narod* saw the strike as a major victory.[40]

Throughout 1917 *Narod* consistently criticized the federal government and predicted its demise. By late December, its editorials declared that

> There can no longer be the slightest doubt that the present bloody carnage . . . will . . . administer the death blow and dig the grave of the present social order. . . . the Russian Revolution is the prologue to the inevitable proletarian revolution which must sweep across the entire world destroying the present intolerable order.

Needless to say, the federal government became alarmed by the socialist activity among European immigrants and by the fact that the IWW was simultaneously trying to reconcile the interests of immigrant and English-speaking workers. As a result, in September, 1918, two Orders-in-Council authorized the suppression of the ethnic press and outlawed a number of socialist and anarchist organizations. *Robochyi narod* and the USDP, which had over 2,000 members organized in twenty-six branches concentrated primarily in western Canada, were affected by the coercive measures.

The non-socialist community also became more militant as the war progressed. The suspension of civil liberties, the intimidation by private groups, and the calculated misrepresentation of Ukrainians as "reds," plus a desire to win Canadian support for the Ukrainian independence struggle overseas, mobilized the more moderate elements within the community, and a number of representative committees to co-ordinate campaigns for just and equitable treatment were organized. The Ukrainian Canadian Citizens' League (UCCL),[41] a body representing several lay and parish organizations, carried the brunt of the burden between 1917 and 1919. Its executive was dominated by members of the *Ukrainskyi holos* group, but it also included representatives from the Catholic camp. On February 20, 1918, a UCCL delegation met with Prime Minister Borden. They protested the designation of Ukrainians as enemy aliens, the internment of non-registered Ukrainians, and disfranchisement, and expressed concern about rumours that unnaturalized Ukrainians would have their lands confiscated.[42] A few months later, another delegation focused on the issue of Ukrainian Canadians who had enlisted in the Canadian armed forces and their status in Canada.[43]

Within a year the religious controversy that enveloped the community (see Chapter Seven) caused Catholic members of the executive to leave the UCCL and create the Ukrainian National Council (UNC). Roman Kremar, editor of Edmonton's *Novyny*, was the most influential member of the UNC, and their spokesman in Ottawa was East Edmonton MP, H.A. Mackie, a Unionist. The existence of two committees prevented a truly effective Ukrainian lobby in Ottawa. Nevertheless, Ukrainian delegations did manage to obtain some concessions. Although banned in September, 1918, later in the year the Ukrainian press was permitted to resume publication upon receipt of special authorization from the Secretary of State and the Postmaster General, provided that a parallel English translation accompanied the Ukrainian text. These restrictions remained in force until the following spring. Ukrainians in internment camps because of their "Austrian" origin were also released.

With rumours rampant that Ukrainians in Springfield, Manitoba, were planning to establish Bolshevik rule,[44] the UCCL protested to the federal Minister of Justice and demanded a royal commission to investigate the origin of the rumours. The Criminal Code, too, they asserted, had to be amended "to protect classes and groups of people, just as individuals were protected against the dissemination of slanderous statements."[45]

The Winnipeg General Strike, which paralysed the largest city in western Canada for almost two months, followed on the heels of these developments. Despite the attention focused by forces of law and order on the aliens in the city, Ukrainians and other minority groups played a secondary role in a strike precipitated by a dispute about the right of collective bargaining.[46] Although a few thousand Ukrainian workers did participate, it is difficult to assess the role of prominent leaders such as Popowich and Navis.[47] The authorities did raid the Ukrainian Labour Temple, established by the Ukrainian social democrats in 1918, and a number of immigrants, including a few Ukrainians, were arrested, interned, and ultimately deported without due process of law. The issue of "alien" participation was magnified out of all proportion by Winnipeg's powerful business elite, which hoped to mask the real causes of the strike – low wages and high living costs – and was eager to take advantage of the widespread fear of Bolshevism to break the Winnipeg labour movement. As a result of the strike, the widening gap between British and other labourers increased, as the former tried to dissociate themselves from the latter. This only reinforced the Ukrainian social democrats' drift into the Communist camp.

THE POST-WAR PERIOD

With the collapse of the Romanov and Hapsburg Empires and the proclamation of the Ukrainian National Republic (January, 1918) in eastern Ukraine, followed by the Western Ukrainian National Republic (November, 1918) in Galicia and their subsequent unification in January, 1919, non-Communist Ukrainian Canadians became actively involved in aiding and publicizing the cause of independence. Hundreds of telegrams to Allied diplomats were sent, requesting that Ukrainian independence be recognized in accordance with the principle of national self-determination. For the next four years the UCCL and the UNC assumed responsibility for promoting the cause of Ukrainian independence in Canadian government circles.

In the summer of 1918 the UCCL decided to send a Ukrainian-Canadian delegation to the peace conference at Versailles to assist representatives of the Ukrainian National Republic and to act as advisers to the Canadian delegation. Although Ukrainian Canadians were hopeful that their delegates would receive full accreditation from the Canadian government and thus form an integral part of the Canadian mission, they were only provided with letters of introduction and passports to England. The delegates' expenses were to be financed by a fund-raising campaign, which ran into a snag when the Catholic members of the UCCL disapproved of both delegates – Joseph Megas, an Orthodox sympathizer, and Ivan Petrushevich, the former editor of the Catholic *Kanadyiskyi rusyn*, who appeared to be moving toward the *Ukrainskyi holos* group since early 1918.[48]

The achievements of Petrushevich and Megas, like those of the Ukrainian mission generally, were minimal. The Allies refused to recognize the united Ukrainian National Republic, since its representatives in Kiev had concluded a separate peace treaty with the Central Powers at Brest-Litovsk on February 8, 1918 (almost a month before the government of Soviet Russia). De facto occupation by Polish forces considerably minimized the Western Ukrainian National Republic's bargaining power. Disputes within the Ukrainian delegation added to the confusion. By the fall of 1919, the Bolsheviks were in control of eastern

Ukraine, while the fear that the Bolshevik presence could easily spill over into Europe led the Allies to place Galicia under Polish protection in order to create a buffer zone. The news spurred massive protests by Ukrainians throughout Canada. On November 21, 1919, almost 5,000 packed the Industrial Bureau in Winnipeg in a futile attempt to urge "the Dominion government . . . [to] do everything in its power to secure recognition of the Ukrainian republic by the Allied Powers."[49]

Subsequent developments provided little cause for rejoicing. For the next three and a half years, until the Council of Ambassadors allowed Poland in March of 1923 to annex Galicia outright, a government-in-exile of the Western Ukrainian National Republic continued to function. Osyp Nazaruk and Ivan Bobersky, its representatives in Canada, managed to collect over $33,000 during that period, while the immigrants sent successive appeals to the government to raise the question of eastern Galicia at the League of Nations. With Canada's isolationist foreign policy growing, when the issue of eastern Galicia was raised in the Commons on February 26, 1923, Prime Minister King declared he did not wish to involve Canada.[50] Once news of the dissolution of the government-in-exile, based in Vienna, reached Ukrainian Canadians, a profound apathy set in. The fund-raising campaign had accomplished little, and some, thinking they had been betrayed, became indifferent and cynical about overseas Ukrainian causes.

Meanwhile, in domestic politics the mounting rural dissatisfaction with the provincial governments in Manitoba and Alberta also influenced the Ukrainians, who entered the post-war provincial election campaigns with a new display of energy. In Manitoba the Ukrainian press, anticipating the 1920 provincial elections, encouraged its readers to exercise rights, only recently restored. As a result, four Ukrainian candidates were nominated. Taras Ferley and J.W. Arsenych ran as Liberals in Gimli and Fisher, while Dmytro Yakimischak, like Ferley and Arsenych a founder of the UCCL, and Nicholas Hryhorczuk, reeve of Ethelbert since 1916, ran as Independent Farmer candidates in Emerson and Ethelbert. The two Liberal candidates lost tight races to Farmer candidates. Yakimischak and Hryhorczuk, on the other hand, won as a result of determined efforts by the Ukrainian communities in Ethelbert and Stuartburn. Both pressured the minority Liberal government to return control of school districts to Ukrainian trustees.[51] In the Manitoba provincial elections in July, 1922, there were eleven Ukrainian candidates: six Independent Farmer and/or Liberal, two United Farmers of Manitoba (UFM), two Labour, and one Conservative.[52] In addition to Yakimischak (Independent Farmer) and Hryhorczuk (UFM), Michael Rojeski (Independent Liberal, Gimli), a former municipal reeve, and Nicholas V. Bachynsky (UFM, Fisher), a teacher and founder of the UCCL, were elected. For the first time two of the Ukrainian members belonged to the governing party – the UFM.

In Alberta, William Fedun (United Farmers of Alberta, Victoria), a general store owner, and Andrew Shandro (Liberal, Whitford) ran successfully in 1921. However, Shandro, elected by acclamation because his opponent was disqualified on a technicality, was defeated in a by-election on July 10, 1922. In Alberta, as in Manitoba, Ukrainian farmers had joined other farmers to break with the two traditional parties, which had ignored and mishandled their interests.

Only Saskatchewan's Ukrainians remained in the grasp of the Liberal Party. Two Ukrainians, Hryhorii Slipchenko (Pelly) and Wasyl Sawiak (Canora), ran as Independents in the 1921 provincial election and lost. Prior to Sawiak's nomination in Canora, an unsuccessful attempt had been made to obtain the Liberal nomination for Wasyl Baleshta. Sawiak finished last in a field of three, Slipchenko third in a field of four. Ukrainians in Saskatchewan, however, did establish a precedent of sorts. During the 1921 federal election Wasyl Swystun, a member of the *Ukrainskyi holos* group, became the first serious Ukrainian federal candidate.[53] Running as an Independent in Mackenzie, Swystun emphasized economic security and proposed a wheat marketing board, stabilized prices, and easy credit terms at the banks.[54] He finished third in a field of four.

Even so, the election of six Ukrainian MLAs in Manitoba and Alberta marked a major breakthrough. Many peasant immigrants realized for the first time that they could determine their representatives in provincial and federal assemblies. The sense of collective self-respect and confidence, necessary for sustained interest and involvement in politics, had been all but absent before the war. In the interwar period that sense would gradually transform immigrant politics into minority group politics with an ethnic flavour.

NOTES

1. V.J. Kaye, *Early Ukrainian Settlements in Canada, 1895-1900* (Toronto: University of Toronto Press, 1964), pp. xiii-xiv.
2. See C.H. Young, *The Ukrainian Canadians: A Study in Assimilation* (Toronto: Thomas Nelson & Sons, 1931); R. England, *The Central European Immigrant in Canada* (Toronto: Macmillan, 1929); J.S. Woodsworth, "Ukrainian Rural Communities: Report of Investigation" (Winnipeg: Bureau of Social Research, Governments of Manitoba, Saskatchewan and Alberta, 1917).
3. The best study of Canadian immigration policy during this period is D.H. Avery, "Canadian Immigration Policy and the Alien Question, 1896-1919: The Anglo-Canadian Perspective" (Doctoral dissertation, University of Western Ontario, 1973).
4. The incidence of tuberculosis in the Point Douglas area was 3.8/1000 and in the North End it was 3/1000. *Report on Housing Survey of Certain Selected Areas: May-December 1918* (Winnipeg: City of Winnipeg Health Department, 1919); *Manitoba Free Press*, 27 May 1913.

5. *Ibid.*, 20 October 1911; 25 September 1912.
6. P. Melnycky, "A Political History of the Ukrainian Community in Manitoba, 1899-1922" (Master's thesis, University of Manitoba, 1979), pp. 186-91.
7. Formerly the submission of an affidavit to a commissioner, establishing that the immigrant had been domiciled in Canada for three years, was sufficient to obtain a naturalization certificate. The new Act required five years residence in Canada, adequate knowledge of English or French, and acceptance of the application by a superior court judge. In addition, the Secretary of State was empowered to withhold certificates from applicants whom he deemed to be a threat to the "public good." *Statutes of Canada*, 4-5 Geo.V, c. 44, s. 2 (1914).
8. Sir William Otter, *Internment Operations 1914-1920* (Ottawa: King's Printer, 1921), p. 6. Ukrainians were concentrated in camps at Brandon (800), Kapuskasing (500), and Spirit Lake (800). *Robochyi narod*, 28 October 1915; *Kanadyiskyi rusyn*, 3 November 1915; J.A. Boudreau, "Western Canada's 'Enemy Aliens' in World War One," *Alberta Historical Review*, XII (1964), pp. 1-10; D. Morton, "Sir William Otter and Internment Operations in Canada during the First World War," *Canadian Historical Review*, LV (1974), pp. 32-58.
9. M. Mandryka (ed.), *Pivstolittia pratsi ukrainskoho tovarystva Chytalni Prosvity v Vinnipegu* (A Half Century of the Prosvita Ukrainian Reading Association's Work in Winnipeg) (Winnipeg: Ukrainske t-vo Chytalnia Prosvity, 1958), p. 180.
10. See T. Peterson, "Ethnic and Class Politics in Manitoba," in M. Robin (ed.), *Canadian Provincial Politics: The Party System of the Ten Provinces* (Scarborough: Prentice-Hall of Canada, 1972), p. 80; and M.K. Mott, "The 'Foreign Peril': Nativism in Winnipeg, 1916-1923" (Master's thesis, University of Manitoba, 1970), pp. 25-6.
11. E.H. Oliver, *The Country School in Non-English Speaking Communities in Saskatchewan* (Saskatoon: Saskatchewan Public Education League, 1915), p. 17.
12. M.H. Marunchak, *V zustrichi z ukrainskymy pioneramy Alberty* (Among Ukrainian Pioneers in Alberta) (Winnipeg: Zahalna biblioteka UKT, 1964), p. 27.
13. M. Ewanchuk, *Spruce, Swamp and Stone: A History of the Pioneer Ukrainian Settlements in the Gimli Area* (Winnipeg: n.p., 1977), pp. 136-44.
14. M.H. Marunchak, *The Ukrainian Canadians: A History* (Winnipeg: Ukrainian Free Academy of Sciences, 1970), pp. 219-24.
15. T.A. Yastremsky, *Kanadyianizatsiia. Politychnyi rozvytok kanadyiskykh ukraintsiv za poslidnykh 46 rokiv ikhnoho pobutu v Kanadi* (Canadianization: The Political Development of Canadian Ukrainians During the Preceding 46 Years of Their Sojourn in Canada) (Winnipeg: n.p., 1946), pp. 88-9; *Winnipeg Tribune*, 1, 9 December 1908.
16. In December, 1914, Taras Ferley failed as an Independent candidate,

though supported by a committee of Ukrainian, German, and Polish electors. Matthew Popowich, a Communist, failed in 1924 and in 1925.

17. Genik (1857-1925) was the oldest of the three. In Galicia he had been a close friend of Ivan Franko, one of the most prominent Ukrainian radicals and a major Ukrainian novelist, poet, and literary critic. Bodrug and Negrich were about twenty years younger.
18. Individuals who were not British by birth and who had not resided in Canada for seven years were granted the franchise in Manitoba after they had passed a literacy test administered in English, French, German, Icelandic, Swedish, Norwegian, or Danish. This applied whether the individual was naturalized or not. An immigrant who passed the test was enfranchised after three years' residence and naturalization; illiterates and those literate in other languages were enfranchised four years after being naturalized. Melnycky, "Political History," p. 98; M.S. Donnelly, *The Government of Manitoba* (Toronto: University of Toronto Press, 1963), p. 72.
19. For the origins of the Protestant movement among Ukrainians in Canada, see the serialized reminiscences of Ivan Bodrug, "Spomyny pastora Ivana Bodruga" (Reminiscences of Pastor Ivan Bodrug), *Ievanhelska pravda*, XVIII-XIX (1957-58).
20. Yastremsky, *Kanadyianizatsiia*, pp. 31, 46-53.
21. Stefanyk resigned his position as school organizer in 1910 after being accused of damaging school property when trustees refused to let him use their school for a Conservative campaign meeting. The accusations were made by a Liberal MLA. See Melnycky, "Political History," pp. 130-1.
22. When Michael Drabiniasty, a graduate of the Ruthenian Training School, was reported to have "a library full of Liberal material," Deputy Minister of Education Robert Fletcher dispatched Inspector Fallis to verify the situation and stated, "these teachers have been trained at considerable expense to the Government . . . and it is up to them to return in kind." When it was discovered that the man who had recommended a student to the Training School was working for the Liberals, Fletcher informed Principal J.T. Cressey that as far as the student was concerned, "We may have to declare that he is too weak in English. Kindly say nothing whatsoever of this." On the other hand, a man who spoke no English was given a permit to teach on a school organizer's recommendation because he had worked on behalf of Glen Campbell, the Conservative MP, during the 1908 federal election. When it was discovered that Myroslaw Stechishin was a frequent contributor to the socialist press, Fletcher informed Cressey: "If he has been doing much of this we may find it necessary to ask him to settle his account and retire." Public Archives of Manitoba, Robert Fletcher Letter Book, 1905-11, pp. 273, 276, 373-4, 525, 286, 625, 809, 921.
23. *Manitoba Free Press*, 6 July 1914; Melnycky, "Political History," p. 155.

24. For an assessment, see Melnycky, "Political History," pp. 118-25, 129-30, 133-5.
25. Yastremsky, *Kanadyianizatsiia*, p. 95.
26. Melnycky, "Political History," pp. 165-7.
27. *Ibid.*, p. 262.
28. Saskatchewan Archives, J.A. Calder Papers, H.E. Perry to J.A. Calder, 2 April 1909.
29. *Ibid.*, H.E. Perry to J.A. Calder, 18 January 1911.
30. Marunchak, *Ukrainian Canadians*, p. 170.
31. An editorial in the *Ukrainskyi holos* (7 May 1913) ascribed their defeat to several factors: they had to contend with the corrupt practices of the Liberal and Conservative political machines; Ukrainian Catholic and Russian Orthodox clergy thought they were strongly anti-clerical and opposed their election; the candidates entered the campaign less than two weeks before the election; many English-speaking settlers thought they saw a conspiracy in their initiative; some of the less enlightened Ukrainian settlers were consumed by envy. The *Holos* itself was encouraged by the fact that over 50 per cent of the Ukrainian vote supported the Independent candidates.
32. *Manitoba Free Press*, 11, 18, 19, 27 September 1913. During the campaign both Shandro and Rudyk employed irregular tactics. Rudyk flaunted a letter from a Liberal official which stated that he should be the Liberal candidate. Shandro retaliated by having Rudyk arrested on charges of false pretences and he was held in jail for a few days before the election. After Shandro's victory, Rudyk brought court action on two counts against Shandro: the first concerned damages caused by Shandro's allegations about the letter, the second declared the election null and void because of corruption on Shandro's part. Although Rudyk prevailed, Shandro again won the seat in a special by-election on March 15, 1915, and held it until 1921. J.M. Lazarenko, "Ukrainians in Provincial Politics," in *The Ukrainian Pioneers in Alberta* (Edmonton: Ukrainian Pioneers' Association, 1970), pp. 43-6; J.G. MacGregor, *Vilni Zemli (Free Lands): The Ukrainian Settlement of Alberta* (Toronto: McClelland and Stewart, 1969), pp. 240-3; *Ukrainskyi holos*, 28 May 1913; 25 November 1914; 3, 24 February 1915.
33. This discussion of the socialist movement is based on O.T. Martynowych, "Village Radicals and Peasant Immigrants: The Social Roots of Factionalism among Ukrainian Immigrants in Canada, 1896-1918" (Master's thesis, University of Manitoba, 1978), pp. 241-52; O.T. Martynowych, "The Ukrainian Socialist Movement in Canada, 1900-1918," *Journal of Ukrainian Graduate Studies*, I (Fall, 1976), pp. 27-44, and (Spring, 1977), pp. 21-31. For the Ukrainian Communist point of view in Canada, see P. Krawchuk, *Ukrainskyi sotsiialistychnyi rukh u Kanadi, 1907-1918* (The Ukrainian Socialist Movement in Canada, 1907-1918) (Toronto: Vyd-vo. Kobzar, 1976).

34. Crath (1882-1952), unlike the other three, had been born in Russian-occupied eastern Ukraine. He came from a wealthy, educated family and arrived in Winnipeg in 1907 after having belonged to the Revolutionary Ukrainian Party and its leftist splinter group, which constituted itself as the Ukrainian Social Democratic Union (*Spilka*). He had participated in the revolution of 1905 and in student demonstrations at the University of Lviv in 1907 after fleeing from the Russian Empire. See N. Kazymyra, "The Defiant Pavlo Krat and the Early Socialist Movement in Canada," *Canadian Ethnic Studies*, X (1978), pp. 38-54. Stechishin and Tomashevsky were born in 1883 and 1884 respectively and emigrated to Canada in 1902 and 1900. Holowacky, born between 1880 and 1885, like the others, had come into contact with the Radical Party prior to emigrating from Galicia.
35. Martynowych, "Ukrainian Socialist Movement," II, pp. 23-7.
36. Popowich, Navis, and Lobay were born around 1890 and had come into contact with Ukrainian social democratic groups. Lobay, unlike the other two, left the Canadian Communist Party and the pro-Communist Ukrainian Labour-Farmer Temple Association in 1935.
37. Martynowych, "Village Radicals and Peasant Immigrants," pp. 255, 260; *Robochyi narod,* 28 February 1917.
38. *Robochyi narod*, 29 August 1917.
39. Kulyk was detained by Canadian immigration officials in Vancouver and prevented from entering Canada. During the 1920's he was a Soviet consul in Canada. *Robochyi narod*, 13 April 1917.
40. D. Avery, *"Dangerous Foreigners": European Immigrant Workers and Labour Radicalism in Canada, 1896-1932* (Toronto: McClelland and Stewart, 1979). p. 72.
41. The Ukrainian Canadian Citizens' League (UCCL) was also known as the Ukrainian Canadian Citizens' Committee (UCCC).
42. *Kanadiiskyi farmer*, 22 February, 8 March 1918.
43. Marunchak, *Ukrainian Canadians*, p. 331.
44. *Manitoba Free Press*, 1, 14, 15 May 1919; *Ukrainskyi holos*, 7 May 1919.
45. Melnycky, "Political History," p. 228.
46. See D.J. Bercuson, *Confrontation at Winnipeg: Labour, Industrial Relations and the General Strike* (Montreal: McGill-Queen's University Press, 1974); D.C. Masters, *The Winnipeg General Strike* (Toronto: University of Toronto Press, 1950); K. McNaught and D.J. Bercuson, *The Winnipeg Strike* (Don Mills: Longman's, 1974); D. Avery, "The Radical Alien and the Winnipeg General Strike of 1919," in C. Berger and R. Cook (eds.), *The West and the Nation: Essays in Honour of W.L. Morton* (Toronto: McClelland and Stewart, 1976), pp. 209-31.
47. Michael Ewanchuk suggests that Popowich and Navis had taken refuge in Gimli at the time of the strike: *Spruce, Swamp and Stone*, p. 115. Peter Krawchuk, on the other hand, states that both were members of the strike committee and were obliged to flee Winnipeg and hide with Ukrainian farmers in Gimli. H. Potrebenko, *No Streets of Gold: A*

Social History of Ukrainians in Alberta (Vancouver: New Star Books, 1977), p. 146.

48. Petrushevich (1875-1950) had attended the July, 1918, conference, which ultimately led to the formation of the Ukrainian Greek Orthodox Church in Canada.
49. *Ukrainskyi holos*, 26 November 1919.
50. *Ibid.*, 28 February 1923.
51. *Manitoba Free Press*, 4, 9 March 1921; *Ukrainskyi holos*, 12 January, 9, 16 March 1921; Melnycky, "Political History," pp. 244-5.
52. The Independent Farmer/Liberal candidates were Yakimischak (Emerson), M. Vonitovy (Russell), B. Zaporzan (Gilbert Plains), M. Rojeski (Gimli), and I. Bilash (St. Clements). Vonitovy, Zaporzan, and Bilash seem to have withdrawn before the election, as they were not listed in any of the election results. United Farmer candidates were Hryhorczuk (Ethelbert) and N.V. Bachynsky (Fisher). Labour candidates were Popowich (North Winnipeg) and W.N. Kolisnyk (St. Clements). The lone Conservative was E. Grabosky (Gimli). Melnycky, "Political History," p. 246.
53. In 1904 Mykhailo Gabora ran as an Independent in Mackenzie (Saskatchewan). He obtained 6 out of a total of 2,495 votes. *Canadian Parliamentary Guide* (1905), p. 187. In 1911 Wasyl Holowacky ran as an Independent (socialist) in the Manitoba riding of Selkirk. He obtained 234 of 6,343 votes cast and also finished last in a field of three. *Ibid.* (1912), p. 257.
54. Swystun obtained 1,896 of 11,640 votes cast. *Ibid.* (1923), p. 246. See *Ukrainskyi holos*, 2 November 1921.

FIVE

Ukrainians in Canadian Political Life, 1923-45

Rose T. Harasym

In the period 1923 to 1945 Ukrainians in Canada used the political system to achieve cultural recognition and full and equal social participation. Their efforts, in the face of assimilationist pressures and discriminatory tendencies, ensured their survival as a distinct and viable ethnic community.

The political socialization of Ukrainian Canadians was well under way by 1923. Ukrainians had been elected to local school boards and municipal councils and eight had served in provincial legislatures. Although the voting power of Ukrainian Canadians had still to be effectively harnessed by 1923, some members of the community were politically experienced and could act as spokesmen for Ukrainian-Canadian interests. To increase the political participation and voting cohesion of the group, they relied on Ukrainian-Canadian newspapers to mould political opinion.

Such nationalist newspapers as *Ukrainskyi holos, Ukrainski visti*, and *Ukrainskyi robitnyk*[1] often did little more than attempt to coax the voters into supporting a particular candidate, especially one of Ukrainian origin. Occasionally, they performed a broader function and explained the electoral platforms of the political parties. Their editorials dealt with the social, economic, and political situation in the various provinces. Discrimination, the problems of the economy, and the workings of the parliamentary system were discussed. The views of Ukrainian Canadians on a wide range of issues were also communicated. Signed articles expressing individual viewpoints created an editorial forum that encouraged Ukrainian Canadians to debate political issues.

This account does not take into consideration the views expressed in the Ukrainian Communist press and only reflects briefly on Communist activities among Ukrainian Canadians. The history of the Communist movement among Ukrainian Canadians is an involved one and deserves more detailed treatment than can be given here.[2]

THE DEVELOPMENT OF POLITICAL ATTITUDES

The attitudes of Ukrainian Canadians toward politics and government in the period from 1923 to 1945 were influenced by several factors: (1) memories of discriminatory treatment during and immediately after World War I; (2) Ukraine's struggle for independence between 1917 and 1920 and the subsequent arrival of a second wave of Ukrainian immigrants to Canada, including a large number of political refugees; (3) the emergence of the Ku Klux Klan in Saskatchewan in the late 1920's; (4) the Depression and the prairie drought during the 1930's; and (5) political events preceding World War II (and the war itself), especially developments that created an unstable situation in Europe and revived hopes for an independent Ukraine. The net effect heightened the political awareness of the Ukrainian group and reinforced feelings among Ukrainians that they were on the defensive in both Canada and Europe.

The 45,000 Ukrainians who arrived between 1925 and 1930 reinforced the trend toward urbanization and diversification in occupation evident among the hitherto predominantly rural Ukrainian-Canadian population. The new immigrants, however, were at times politically disruptive. Many refused to participate in the organized life of the established Ukrainian community, which to them was too "Canadian," too concerned with preserving Ukrainian culture and language in Canada, and not involved enough in the political issues of the Old World. They established their own parishes, press, and other secular institutions. Hopeful of returning to their former homeland, the newcomers established politically oriented organizations (primarily monarchist and nationalist), each with its own women's and youth affiliates. The divisions bred suspicion and weakened all efforts to organize on Ukrainian issues in Canada and overseas.

Despite the urbanization and disunity, the large influx of new immigrants ensured that Ukrainians would remain a highly visible ethnocultural group in Canada. Refusing to disappear into the mainstream of Canadian society while eager to benefit from the opportunities the latter offered, they became victims of extreme prejudice and discrimination, particularly with the introduction of the Ku Klux Klan into Canada in the late 1920's and the onset of the Great Depression shortly thereafter.

In the anti-foreign and predominantly anti-Catholic emotionalism, most pronounced in Saskatchewan, "prejudices . . . were skillfully sought out, fanned into overt animosity, and capitalized upon by an organization strange to the Saskatchewan scene, the Ku Klux Klan."[3] A primary thrust of the attack was concern about the "invasion" of immigrants from southern, eastern, and central Europe. Typical was the following warning of one Klan leader:

> I want to tell you tonight, men and women of Saskatchewan, that

> the time has come when you must, as you never did before, guard your Dominion. You must awaken to the situation you are facing, and as men, stand as a solid wall against invasion of your Dominion by those who cannot be assimilated.[4]

The Klan found many able assistants, including members of the Orange order and Bishop Lloyd of the Prince Albert Anglican diocese. When, in May, 1929, the latter, in a racist condemnation of the central and southeastern Europeans, referred to them as "dirty, ignorant, garlic-smelling, [and] unpreferred," Michael Luchkovich, the sole Ukrainian Member of Parliament, defended them:

> Hon. members will agree with me . . . that there is some sinister power in Canada whose main purpose is to engineer a so-called pogrom against Ukrainians in Canada, to compromise them in every possible manner, and whose despicable plans have no doubt gained the sympathy and unqualified support of . . . Bishop Lloyd, the would-be Bismark of Prince Rupert. . . .[5]

In the 1929 Saskatchewan election, the Conservative Party successfully capitalized on the emotionalism which made religion and race major electoral issues. Both before and after the election, the Ukrainian press strongly criticized J.T.M. Anderson, the Conservative leader to whom the party's shortcomings were attributed.[6] By the early 1930's, the Klan disappeared in Saskatchewan but prejudices against "foreigners" remained, as Anglo-Celtic opposition to Ukrainian candidates in the 1934 election would show.

During the Depression years, it was not uncommon for Ukrainians to feel that they suffered more than the average Canadian. Some Ukrainian immigrants, arriving relatively late in western Canada, had settled the less productive farm lands, and during the thirties they joined many others who could not meet their mortgage payments and had to abandon their homesteads. Some, however, felt they had a special grievance:

> One retired farmer told how his neighbours received monthly relief packages but he did not because, as he claimed, he was discriminated against. This was not an unusual complaint among Ukrainians of this period. The Ukrainian communities sent delegations to both provincial and federal capitals to have this practice rectified.[7]

In recalling the Depression years, one Ukrainian woman also spoke of discrimination:

> We lived in the marsh. The land was no good. It was boggy and wouldn't drain. We dug canals. . . . We did everything. We starved, and nobody in the village knew us. Everybody else got credit, because they were all old-time Scots and Irish settlers from Christ knows where. . . .

> We felt it deeply. We knew we were poor, very poor. You didn't need to be a genius to see that my Dad was wearing himself out on that lousy 160 acres that nobody wanted, land that had been picked out so some Bohunk could be sold a bill of goods in Minneapolis and passed on to some shyster in Winnipeg. . . . I watched my mother go down, and you tell me how a woman can go 16 hours a day working in the fields, in the barn, in the house, and still look like something Frank Sinatra would take out. . . .
>
> I haven't put this well, right? I know it, but if you were a Bohunk kid growing up in an all-Scots plus Irish and English community, a farm community, you had a fight on your hands. It made you tougher, and now we're on top.[8]

Ukrainians who had taken urban employment also encountered difficulties. They were usually located at the blue-collar level, which had the highest level of unemployment during the thirties. For the Ukrainian unemployed applying for relief, there was the ever-present threat of deportation. In relating his experiences during that period, James Gray commented on the predicament of the non-Anglo-Celtic worker:

> I came to appreciate for the first time the tremendous advantage it was to be a Canadian Anglo-Saxon in Winnipeg. And as time passed, the advantage widened when, as if racist intolerance was not enough, a new terror for the non-Canadian began to stalk the land in the form of Immigration Officers with deportation orders in their hands.[9]

In the cities of eastern and western Canada, large numbers of Ukrainian labourers took part in Communist-organized hunger strikes, thereby earning a reputation for being strong Communist supporters. After one such protest held in Toronto in 1935, the mayor claimed, incorrectly, that of the estimated 15,000 workers involved, at least 80 per cent were of Ukrainian origin.[10] *Holos* deplored the fact that the majority of Canadians believed that Ukrainian Canadians were mostly Communists, stating that, as a result of the stigma, Ukrainians had been excluded from many job opportunities in factories and mines.

Considering the general discriminatory tenor of the time, it was not surprising that great numbers of Ukrainians changed their names in an effort to pass as Anglo-Celts. As late as May, 1944, *Holos* noted that the local papers daily listed Ukrainians who had changed their names to "Smith, Johnson, Jackson, Russell, Williams, etc.," because they were of the impression that "the English were better than the Ukrainians."

The events of the twenties and thirties demonstrated to Ukrainians that they were not considered equal citizens by many members of the Canadian community and were generally misunderstood. Thus the onset of war in 1939 aroused apprehensions among Ukrainians that prejudices on the part of the wider Canadian public would result in discriminatory legislation similar to that enacted during World War I. In September,

1939, *Robitnyk* warned its readers to be careful about what they said or wrote in wartime or their loyalty might be questioned. *Holos* also reminded its readers of the discriminatory treatment during the First World War, followed by an editorial in January, 1940, entitled "We Are Not Immigrants," in which it declared, somewhat defensively, that the majority of Ukrainians either were born in Canada or had arrived as small children.

The growing spectre of war in Europe unsettled the Ukrainian-Canadian community for still another reason. Hopes were high that a confrontation between the Soviet Union and Nazi Germany would result in a readjustment of European borders in Ukraine's favour. The primary objective was an independent and united Ukraine, free of the oppressive tyranny of foreign rule. The aspirations were based on more than national sentiment. Throughout the interwar period Ukrainian Canadians had received reports of the persecution of their kin in Europe by Soviet, Polish, Romanian, and Czechoslovakian authorities. Ukrainian communities across Canada had held protest meetings and numerous petitions had been sent to the Canadian and British prime ministers and to the League of Nations, urging remedial action.[11] The ill-treatment of Ukrainians was made a subject of debate in the House of Commons by Ukrainian and non-Ukrainian members.

As war became imminent, Ukrainian Canadians became more insistent in their demand that the government take an active interest in "The Ukrainian Question." Through correspondence and private meetings with members of the government (in particular the Department of External Affairs), representatives of the Ukrainian community argued that a free and united Ukraine would act as a buffer to Soviet and Nazi expansionist ambitions in eastern Europe.[12] Similar representations were made to the British government by Ukrainian Canadians who felt that Ukraine's best interests would be served by an alliance with Great Britain. British and Canadian government officials were at best sympathetic, but no action followed as neither wished to risk alienating possible allies in the event of war.[13]

Not all Ukrainians could agree on the manner in which a united and independent Ukraine might emerge. Opinions also varied as to the best form of government for an autonomous Ukraine, as attested by the bitter and extensive polemics in the Ukrainian-Canadian press. With the outbreak of war, the Canadian government became concerned about the political disputes raging within the Ukrainian-Canadian community, especially such pro-Communist and pro-Nazi sympathies as could be detected.

When Carpatho-Ukraine made its brief bid for independence in 1939, some Ukrainians hoped that Nazi Germany would support Ukrainian self-determination. Once Hitler permitted his satellite, Hungary, to invade Carpatho-Ukraine in March, 1939, the pro-German sentiment quickly disappeared. With the outbreak of war, the majority of Ukrainian organizations declared their loyalty and dedication to the Canadian war effort. Government officials, however, remained suspicious of pro-German sympathies and Ukrainian newspapers were censored and meetings observed.[14] On January 24, 1940, *Holos* commented facetiously that the RCMP knew far more about Ukrainian Canadians than about Anglo-Canadians.

Communist sympathies were also a concern. The Ukrainian Labour-Farmer Temple Association (ULFTA), which advocated social revolution for Canada, strongly opposed the Canadian war effort during the time of the Stalin-Hitler alliance (1939-41). By June, 1940, the group's activities provoked the government to confiscate all ULFTA meeting halls and property. With Hitler's attack on the Soviet Union in the summer of 1941, the ULFTA made a complete about-face.

By 1939, debate within the Ukrainian-Canadian community had shifted to the feasibility of establishing a nation-wide organization to represent the community on a variety of issues, including ambitions for an independent Ukraine, the preservation of Ukrainian culture, and effective measures to decrease discrimination. The following year the Ukrainian Canadian Committee was founded to co-ordinate Ukrainian-Canadian activities and represent Ukrainian interests before various government bodies. (See Chapter Nine.)

THE ROLE OF THE UKRAINIAN-CANADIAN PRESS IN POLITICAL LIFE

By the 1920's, the Ukrainian press was firmly convinced that being industrious and law-abiding was insufficient to achieve equal status. What Ukrainians required was better education, more organization, and especially greater political participation. Through education, they would exercise their citizenship obligations in a more responsible fashion and also improve their overall economic and social status and image in Canada. Through greater organization, they would be in a stronger position to fight assimilationist forces by making their aspirations known across Canada. Through the political process – as voters, party members, and candidates – the issues of education and organization were linked: Ukrainians had to participate in politics in an informed and disciplined manner if they wished the political system to work for them.

To further the education of their Ukrainian readers, the newspapers, accordingly, provided articles on the value of democratic government, the workings of the Canadian parliamentary system and its British traditions, and the need to be constantly on guard against despotism in any form. Political commentary naturally increased around election time, when party platforms were discussed and candidates evaluated – usually in terms of which party or individual could be expected to serve Ukrainian interests best. Post-election results were also analysed with the emphasis on why Ukrainian candidates did or did not succeed. Frequently, the advice offered revealed the political attitudes and motivations of the Ukrainian-Canadian leadership in general.

A great deal of emphasis was placed on the character of those running for election. Even when the newspapers came out in favour of a particular party, they did so usually in terms of the personalities involved. For instance, in 1925 *Holos* observed that members of former Liberal and Conservative governments in Manitoba had been paternalistic toward Ukrainians, while Progressive Party members had treated them as equal citizens. In 1935 *Robitnyk* supported R.B. Bennett's social reforms and condemned Mitchell Hepburn's impulsive, dictatorial behaviour and excessive pro-farmer attitudes. Prior to the 1945 federal election, both *Visti* and *Holos* provided lists of Liberal and Conservative candidates who had demonstrated a sympathetic attitude toward Ukrainian Canadians.

The newspapers, however, seldom supported any one party strongly. In the early twenties they tended to suspect the motives of Canadian parties, which, it was thought, were only concerned with organizing the "foreign vote" to win elections and not with bringing the so-called foreigners into the political system. Despite such misgivings, the Ukrainian press urged its readers to get involved in party politics. A 1925 editorial in *Holos* was typical:

> It would be advisable for Ukrainians to have representatives in all parties . . . but they should become active and continuous members of the parties and not temporary paid agents and agitators. Participation in various parties, especially in the leading parties, is a prerequisite for Ukrainians if they wish to free themselves from political humiliation in Canada.[15]

Participation in party politics would give Ukrainians a voice in the formation of party policy and influence in the choice of electoral candidates. The nomination of Ukrainian candidates was particularly important, especially as few parties were receptive to the election of non-French or non-Anglo-Celtic candidates. Ukrainians generally enjoyed greatest success within protest parties, from whose ranks came most of the Ukrainian federal and provincial candidates in the interwar period. Few Ukrainians, however, joined political organizations and acted in an organized manner – the key to political success, according to the press. Whenever a Ukrainian failed to secure the nomination of his party, the press blamed the lack of organization among Ukrainian party members. It was also particularly critical when two or more Ukrainians ran for election from the same riding. Candidates should choose the most popular party in their riding, preferably that most likely to form the next government. If elected, Independent Ukrainians or those who ran as part of "political experiments" would command little respect from the governing parties and would therefore be weak spokesmen for Ukrainian interests.[16] The press, however, was less opposed to Ukrainians as candidates in protest parties when the latter had a strong chance to succeed – as in the case of the United Farmers of Alberta prior to 1935. Above all, only capable and sincere individuals should compete, individuals who would be a credit to their Ukrainian origin.

The press freely admonished Ukrainians on how they should vote at election time. The most important criterion was an able Ukrainian candidate who was not a Communist. Otherwise, the affiliation of Ukrainian candidates, according to *Holos*, was of secondary importance:

> One member more or less from a particular party in Parliament in Ottawa will not make a difference. However, for Ukrainians every member of Parliament of Ukrainian origin, no matter what his party, will be worth his weight in gold.

Where no Ukrainian candidate existed, *Holos* advised readers to support the party or individual who had demonstrated a sympathetic attitude toward Ukrainians. The key always, however, was to maximize possible benefits and to avoid the image of Ukrainians as "oppositionists" or radicals.

Despite the political education, it is doubtful whether the Ukrainian press succeeded in directing much political activity. It hoped that ethnic communality would override cleavages rooted in class or region of settlement, and occasionally ethnicity did influence the manner in which Ukrainian Canadians voted. But the Ukrainian electorate frequently ignored the advice of the press. Not only were two or more Ukrainian candidates sometimes nominated to run in the same riding, but not all Ukrainians attached the same importance to voting for Ukrainian candidates as did the editors.

INVOLVEMENT AT ALL LEVELS OF GOVERNMENT

During the period under consideration the Ukrainian group matured politically. Prior to World War I Ukrainian-Canadian participation in politics at the local level – in the Stuartburn municipal council in 1902 and Theodore Stefanyk's election to the Winnipeg city council in 1911 – was a momentous event. Not until 1926 was another Ukrainian Canadian elected as alderman in Winnipeg, but thereafter, except for the occasional break during the 1930's, Ukrainian Canadians were regularly represented on the Winnipeg city council and school board.

Not unnaturally, experience in local government gradually became a stepping stone to higher office. The practical training gained in municipal politics was of particular importance to the early Ukrainian candidates who lacked the formal education of many of their Anglo-Canadian opponents and colleagues. Two of the first Ukrainian MLAs in Alberta, William Fedun and Michael Chornohus, for example, did not have any post-secondary education. However, both had served as municipal councillors before running in the provincial elections. According to one account, "of the 44 Ukrainian Canadians who served as members of the various legislative assemblies and the House of Commons during 1913-53, 21 went through such practical training."[17]

With increased social integration, Ukrainian Canadians became more involved in politics at higher levels. Prior to 1923, only eight MLAs of Ukrainian origin had been elected; by 1945, the figure had quadrupled and during the same period three Ukrainian Canadians were elected to the House of Commons. Fluency in English, greater familiarity with Canadian politics, and a relative degree of financial security were factors which determined who could run for election. But the success of Ukrainian candidates depended on several additional factors.

The bloc vote was probably the most important. With the Ukrainian immigrants in Canada's prairie West settled in compact groups and with several ridings boasting a Ukrainian majority, candidates relied on solid Ukrainian votes for their nomination and election. Usually they were successful. In the 1920's and 1930's, also, the dominance of the Liberal and Conservative Parties was challenged by new political parties, usually more receptive to the problems of the non-Anglo-Celtic and non-French elements of the population. As a result, prospective Ukrainian candidates who failed to secure the nomination in a traditional party often ran as Independents or as third-party candidates. In 1934 in Saskatchewan, for example, W. Burak and M. Daneleyko ran as CCF and Independent candidates respectively after being spurned by the Liberals.

Although the new parties provided greater opportunities for Ukrainian Canadians who wanted to get involved in politics, it was always difficult for a Ukrainian to secure the nomination or get elected in a riding that did not have a Ukrainian majority. It is not surprising, then, that many of the first Ukrainian candidates felt they had a special obligation to represent Ukrainian interests before the Canadian government and public. The three Ukrainian MPs elected by 1945 – Michael Luchkovich (Vegreville, UFA, 1926-35), Anthony Hlynka (Vegreville, SC, 1940-49), and Fred Zaplitny (Dauphin, CCF, 1945-49, 1953-58) – all introduced issues of concern to Ukrainian Canadians as subjects of debate in the House, and the Ukrainian press praised them not only for representing their constituencies well but for speaking out on behalf of Ukrainian interests. Many MLAs of Ukrainian origin also furthered the interests of Ukrainian Canadians. For instance, William Fedun, Isidore Goresky, and William Tomyn, MLAs in Alberta, were recognized for their efforts to have more Ukrainian representation in the civil service.[18]

Very little is known about the political activities of Ukrainian Canadians outside the Prairie Provinces during this period. Some insight, however, is provided by Toronto's *Ukrainskyi robitnyk*. Much to *Robitnyk*'s chagrin, by 1945 Ontario's Ukrainians had still to elect one candidate to either the provincial or federal legislatures. In fact, when the paper began publication in 1934, it criticized Ukrainians severely for failing to make inroads even at the municipal level. This lack of success can be attributed not only to the comparatively recent date of immigration, but also to the fact that in Ontario Ukrainians did not settle in compact groups as did their predecessors in western Canada.

ELECTORAL BEHAVIOUR IN MANITOBA

As the largest Ukrainian community in Canada, Ukrainians in Manitoba were also the most aggressive and successful politically in the period prior to 1945, electing fourteen Ukrainian representatives to the provincial legislature and one member to Ottawa. The second largest ethnic group after Canadians of Anglo-Celtic origin, Manitoba's Ukrainians were also more urbanized than Ukrainians in the other Prairie Provinces. The numerous bloc settlements placed the Ukrainians in a strong position to elect their own candidates:

> While the Germans remained out of the main stream of provincial life, however, a newer group, the Ukrainian, was thrusting aggressively in. The Ukrainians, fired by the recent birth of national sentiment among their people in Europe and in the majority opposed to the incorporation of the Ukrainian Republic in the Soviet Union, turned the zeal of their nationalism to the preservation of their group in Manitoba and to making their way in business and politics. Their drive and courage won them reluctant admiration from the British-Ontario majority and entrance to business and public life. So virile was the Ukrainian group that while avoiding complete assimilation itself, it was tending still more at first to absorb the Poles, a leaderless group scattered among the Ukrainian settlements.[19]

The Ukrainian electorate, exposed to a broad spectrum of political philosophies and party platforms, elected candidates from several different parties. Almost invariably Ukrainians in Manitoba, as elsewhere, voted for Ukrainian candidates, regardless of party affiliation. Only the United Farmers of Manitoba (the Progressives) drew consistent support during this period, even in times of economic distress. Unlike the patronizing Conservatives and disdainful Liberals, the Progressives accepted Ukrainians as social equals. Their "fundamental principle of local representation by local men was to bring Ukrainians into the mainstream of Manitoban political life."[20]

During the 1920's the Progressives attempted to restore economic stability by curtailing government expenditures, particularly in health, education, and welfare. By the end of the twenties, the policy increased the hardships of those with low incomes, among whom the Ukrainians predominated. With the onset of the Depression, Premier Bracken's government became even more determined to cut costs and balance budgets. Unemployment in the province soared and Winnipeg in 1932 showed the second highest urban unemployment rate in Canada. For the unemployed Ukrainian worker, relief was not always easy to obtain, as one Manitoba politician informed the *Winnipeg Tribune* in the summer of 1930: "In our town [Winnipeg] when these foreigners from across the tracks apply for relief we just show them a blank application for voluntary deportation. Believe me, they don't come back. It's simple, but it has saved the city a lot of money." At a meeting held in Winnipeg in 1932, members of the Ukrainian community expressed their concern, voicing the opinion that "those law-abiding persons who were legally admitted to Canada should not be deported when they are compelled by impaired health or unemployment to ask for assistance."[21]

Notwithstanding the hardships inflicted by his policies, the Ukrainian press remained staunchly loyal to the Bracken government in 1932. *Ukrainskyi holos* endorsed Bracken's attempts to balance the budget and noted that the problems were worldwide; the social costs simply had to be endured. *Kanadiiskyi farmer* was also reluctant to offend the governing party:

> Canadian Ukrainians do not have any influence. We are poor and need political help. Ukrainian farmers and workers depend for their livelihood on the more powerful. This forces us to support a politically influential party. Affiliation with small and radical parties brings us [Ukrainians] only discredit and ruin. . . . All signs show that we have to elect candidates put forward by the governing party. . . . Candidates from parties making strange and impossible promises will bring us no advantage, only national dishonour.

The Progressives' inability to come to grips with the economic and social problems of the Depression prompted some interest in opposition parties, but political alternatives were limited substantially by the Progressives' ability to co-opt their opponents into coalition governments. The first coalition between the Progressives and the Liberals in 1932 confined the opposition to Independent Labour (Co-operative Commonwealth Federation) and Social Credit.

In early 1934 *Holos*, in a long series of articles, explained the philosophy and platform of the Social Credit Party. Without actually supporting it, the paper's extensive coverage indicated growing dissatisfaction with the ruling party, and by 1936 there was sufficient interest in Social Credit to elect five Socreds in the poorer ethnic communities, including one Ukrainian candidate, William Lisowsky, who defeated Nicholas Hryhorczuk, a Liberal-Progressive member since 1920 in the largely Ukrainian constituency of Ethelbert. Lisowsky later led the Social Credit Party, but the protest was short-lived. Immediately after the 1936 election, Social Credit was co-opted into a new coalition government, and the CCF became the only effective opposition voice in Manitoba politics. To many Ukrainian spokesmen, the labour-oriented CCF appeared to be Communist-inclined and it faced major difficulties in obtaining the support of the Ukrainian community. While one Ukrainian CCF candidate, Joseph Wawrykow, was elected in 1936, the reaction of the Ukrainian press was anything but favourable. In 1940 *Holos* expressed disdain for the CCF by refusing to comment on its political platform, and suspicion continued throughout the period under review.

ELECTORAL BEHAVIOUR IN SASKATCHEWAN

By 1945, the salient fact about Ukrainian political life in Saskatchewan was that not a single federal candidate and only four MLAs had been elected in the province. Ukrainians in Saskatchewan gradually gave their allegiance to the CCF and, in fact, played a prominent role in the ethnic revolt against traditional political parties in the 1930's.[22]

Initially, Ukrainians, like the majority of the Saskatchewan electorate, supported the Liberal Party. In 1929 the support continued, as the Conservative Party failed to dissociate itself from the Ku Klux Klan and was largely discredited among Ukrainians because of its xenophobic attitudes toward immigration and assimilation and its attacks on sectarianism in the public schools. In the next election the Liberals made a concerted, if not entirely sincere, attempt to retain the Ukrainian vote. They benefited from the fact that they were still the only established political alternative to the Conservatives. To the CCF, established in 1932 out of the farmer-labour group, the 1934 election was its first political test, and its platform, with its unorthodox and unpopular land tenure policy, was no match for the sophisticated campaign waged by the Liberals. An observer described the strategy which allowed the Liberals to capture the Ukrainian vote:

> Liberals in Saskatchewan were not surprised some weeks before the election to learn there was some talk going around among Ukrainian voters that, though they had always voted Liberal, they had not received due recognition. They did not have a candidate of their own in the campaign. As there are between 40,000 and 50,000 Ukrainian voters in Saskatchewan, this report created a problem requiring the closest attention of the inner circle of the party. . . .
>
> Here is what happened. The Ukrainians got one of their own prairie-born sons, a Saskatoon doctor, as a candidate in one of the northeastern constituencies. Despite reports in the daily papers that an 'outside' candidate would not be welcome, the Ukrainian candidate arrived, received the support of the nominating convention, and any ruffled feelings among local Liberals were smoothed over. It was a situation that required finesse. . . .
>
> Political dopesters said it was a sacrifice hit on the part of the Liberal party. A Ukrainian candidate in one constituency would keep the Ukrainian vote in eight or ten other constituencies in line. It did not matter whether or not he was elected. . . .

> Came the election. The Ukrainian-Canadian candidate not only won the seat, but he piled up a majority of about 2,000, out of only some 6,000 votes in the riding.[23]

Not surprisingly, though the Liberals won a landslide victory and elected their Ukrainian candidate, George E. Dragan, there were rumblings of discontent within the Ukrainian community. Factions within the Liberal Party had opposed the nomination of a Ukrainian in Kelvington South and held conventions at which two non-Ukrainians were nominated to run for the same seat as Dragan. Two other Ukrainians met with similar Liberal opposition and were forced to run as non-Liberals. Outraged, *Holos* declared that Anglo-Canadians had made ethnicity an election issue and it was both necessary and justifiable that Ukrainians did the same by voting only for Ukrainian candidates. After the election, the paper thought Ukrainian candidates in Saskatchewan had little chance to succeed because of constituency boundaries which ensured that Ukrainians could obtain no majority anywhere.

For Saskatchewan's Ukrainian population, the discrimination experienced with the Liberal Party was indicative of a wider prejudice against ethnic groups in the province. By the late 1920's, Canadian-born Ukrainians, because of the economic depression, were under greater pressure to leave their rural enclaves for urban centres, where they faced stiff competition from the established Anglo-Canadian community for scarce education, jobs, and business opportunities. The discrimination they encountered there gradually broke the inhibition to vote against the traditional political parties. Moreover, the radical land reform policy proposed by the CCF prior to the 1934 election was muted by the late 1930's. As a result, in the 1938 election the CCF's overall philosophy of economic justice with implications of social equality appealed to numerous Saskatchewan voters, including those of Ukrainian origin.[24] A general ethnic revolt against traditional political forces was brewing:

> The importance of the socialist element in the CCF appeal to minority ethnics might now be underlined. Within the framework of conventional socialist thought one can suggest that a "just" society is identified with a just economic society. This identification was a political advantage for the party, because it enabled the CCF to speak in terms of the type of new society which would be the answer to social aspirations of ethnic minorities in the province. Thus, because the party would be unable to separate an interpretation of social problems from its recommendations for economic reform it would have a distinct political advantage in appealing to restive ethnics searching for social equality.[25]

In 1944 the CCF captured sufficient votes to win the provincial election with 53 per cent of the popular vote. The growing popularity of the party in Saskatchewan made it easier for Ukrainians to vote against the traditional provincial parties, since they did not have to fear the stigma of being considered more radical than the majority. Despite the doubts expressed by *Holos* about the integrity of the CCF, Ukrainian voters in Saskatchewan elected two Ukrainian CCF candidates, Daniel Z. Daniels (Pelly) and Dmytro Lazarko (Redberry), both victorious against the Ukrainian candidates of other parties. Moreover, so strong was the CCF tide that in June *Holos* noted that Ukrainian majorities in Touchwood and Canora constituencies preferred non-Ukrainian CCF candidates to Ukrainians from other parties.

ELECTORAL BEHAVIOUR IN ALBERTA

The Ukrainian community in Alberta, though smaller than in Manitoba and Saskatchewan, achieved a relatively high degree of political involvement by 1945, electing nine provincial and two federal representatives. It was the first province to elect Ukrainian candidates to a provincial or federal legislature. A major factor in the success was the nature of the provincial political parties. Between 1923 and 1945, neither the Liberals nor Conservatives were strongly established in the province and the populist United Farmers of Alberta and Social Credit, which dominated, encouraged ethnic participation in politics.

Although the UFA, formed in 1909 as a pressure group for farm interests and in power since 1921, was primarily concerned with forming a government founded upon "functional representation by occupational groups,"[26] there is some evidence that it recognized the significance of expanding the idea to include the representation of ethnic communities. In 1929, for example, *Ukrainski visti* praised the UFA for its concerted effort to broaden support among Ukrainian voters in Alberta by organizing party locals in Ukrainian ridings and suggested that the action had been taken to interest the communities in a more active civic life. The UFA put forward candidates of Ukrainian origin in ridings with Ukrainian majorities – a sign to the Ukrainian press that the UFA recognized the right of Ukrainians to be represented by candidates of their own ethnic background. Between 1921 and 1930, four Ukrainian UFA candidates were elected in constituencies with substantial Ukrainian majorities, and in 1926 Michael Luchkovich, the first federal representative of Ukrainian origin, was also elected under the UFA banner in the Vegreville constituency.

By 1929, however, the original fervour for the UFA had begun to decline. *Visti* warned that Ukrainian members in the party would have to achieve a higher level of organization if the Ukrainian representatives were to be re-elected. In 1935 the UFA was overwhelmed by the Depression and although *Ukrainskyi robitnyk* found the Social Credit economic policies too idealistic, particularly the promise of a $25 monthly dividend, at least part of Alberta's Ukrainian electorate disagreed. In the federal election of 1935 not only did the predominantly Ukrainian constituencies of Sturgeon and Willingdon elect Ukrainian Social Credit candidates, but in Vegreville the Ukrainian incumbent was defeated by a non-Ukrainian Social Credit candidate. Amazed, *Ukrainskyi holos* berated the Vegreville Ukrainians:

> . . . we lost him [Luchkovich] through the shortsightedness and naivete of our own Ukrainian voters. . . . Obviously, they feared that if they did not elect a Social Credit candidate, then they would not get the $25 that Aberhart had promised them.

In the 1940 and 1944 provincial elections, out of a total of twenty-two candidates of Ukrainian origin, only six Social Credit candidates were elected (three each year).

No doubt Ukrainian candidates for the UFA and Social Credit Parties were largely successful because they could count upon a bloc of Ukrainian votes, but there is some evidence that in supporting protest parties the Ukrainian electors were frequently perplexed and voted "marginally less in favour of the UFA and Social Credit, than did the Anglo-German-Scandinavian majority":

> Agrarian populism was not a culturally neutral political movement; its norms of direct democracy and participation are singularly American, or in a wider sense, north European; while it has also had a definite Protestant tone. In many respects, western populism must have been at least partially alien to the ethnic minorities of northern Alberta, which were imbued neither with Protestantism nor with the participatory norms of American democracy.[27]

CONCLUSION

During the 1923-45 period the discriminatory tendencies of Canadian society, while motivating greater Ukrainian participation in Canadian political life, also affected the nature and scope of that participation. Ukrainian Canadians became increasingly determined to elect Ukrainian-Canadian candidates to municipal, provincial, and federal governments to ensure a sympathetic representation of their interests before these governments and the general public. Ukrainian community leaders were especially concerned that such spokesmen express not only the socio-economic goals of their group but also the national and cultural aspirations of Ukrainians in general, including those in the old country. Very seldom did a Ukrainian candidate fail to get elected in a riding with a Ukrainian majority. When two Ukrainians with similar qualifications ran, the Ukrainian voters, again concerned to improve their position in Canadian society, tended to support the candidate most likely to be on the side of the victorious party. Because of a lack of receptiveness on the part of the traditional parties, most of these candidates were forced to run as Independent or third-party candidates.

The voting behaviour of Ukrainian Canadians was less predictable when they did not have "one of their own" in the riding. With Ukrainian-Canadian society becoming increasingly diversified and Ukrainians more widely dispersed across Canada, particularly with the post-World War I influx of new immigrants, on some issues Ukrainian Canadians had more in common with their non-Ukrainian neighbours than with members of their own group in the next province or even in the next city or town. From the editorials in the Ukrainian press, it is clear that all Ukrainians did not have the same views on tariffs, freight rates, or unemployment. In general, Ukrainians, usually on the defensive, tended to vote conservatively, often supporting the party most likely to win the election and hesitating frequently to cast a protest vote for fear of adding to their reputation of being overly radical. Thus, it is not surprising that Ukrainian voters in Alberta did not re-elect Luchkovich of the UFA in 1935 and voted instead for a non-Ukrainian Social Credit candidate. The extreme hostility Ukrainians encountered in Saskatchewan might explain why they joined in the protest vote against the traditional parties, but even in this case they were in step with a more widespread shift of voters' allegiance toward the CCF in Saskatchewan.

NOTES

1. The "nationalist newspapers" advocated a united, independent, and democratic Ukraine, free of foreign domination, and espoused the preservation of Ukrainian language and culture in Ukraine and elsewhere. The views of the Ukrainian Communist press were unpopular with the great majority of Ukrainian Canadians and are not considered here. *Ukrainskyi holos* after 1927 had become the organ of the Ukrainian Self-Reliance League. It was particularly emphatic that Ukrainian organizations in Canada should have no political ties with European-based Ukrainian political factions. *Ukrainski visti* began publishing in Edmonton in 1928 as the *Zakhidni visti*. It espoused Christian (Catholic) principles and favoured monarchism as the government of any future independent Ukraine. *Ukrainskyi robitnyk* originated in Toronto in 1934 and claimed the largest circulation of any Ukrainian newspaper in eastern Canada by 1945. As the official organ of the Hetmanite movement, it was devoted to monarchist principles and favoured the Ukrainian Catholic Church. It was concerned primarily with the concerns of the Ukrainian-Canadian labouring or blue-collar class.
2. For a discussion of the Communist movement among Ukrainians in Canada, see J. Kolasky, *The Shattered Illusion: The History of Ukrainian Pro-Communist Organizations in Canada* (Toronto: Peter Martin Associates, 1979), pp. 1-47; also I. Avakumovic, *The Communist Party of Canada: A History* (Toronto: McClelland and Stewart, 1975), p. 35.
3. P. Kyba, "Ballots and Burning Crosses: The Election of 1929," in N. Ward and D. Spafford (eds.), *Politics in Saskatchewan* (Don Mills, Ont.: Longmans, 1968), p. 108.
4. Quoted in *ibid.*, p. 110.

5. *House of Commons Debates*, 1929, col. 2902.
6. *Ukrainskyi holos*, 23 January 1929; *Ukrainski visti*, 11 April 1930.
7. S.I. Pobihushchy, "The Development of Political Socialization of Ukrainians in Alberta," in *Slavs in Canada* (Ottawa: Inter-University Committee on Canadian Slavs, 1968), pp. 26-7.
8. Quoted in Barry Broadfoot, *Ten Lost Years, 1929-1939* (Toronto: Doubleday, 1973), pp. 165, 167.
9. James Gray, *The Winter Years* (Toronto: Macmillan, 1966), pp. 157-9.
10. *Ukrainskyi robitnyk*, 5 March 1935.
11. See Public Archives of Canada (hereafter PAC), Department of External Affairs Records, vols. 1673, 1873, 1896, for numerous petitions from Ukrainian communities across Canada.
12. *Ibid.*, vol. 1896, file 165-1, George E. Dragan to William Lyon Mackenzie King, 23 January 1939, and "Memorandum from O.D. Skelton [Undersecretary of State for External Affairs] to the High Commissioner for Canada." Skelton referred to a meeting between himself and W. Kossar of the Ukrainian National Federation regarding the need for Canada and Great Britain to direct their efforts toward achieving autonomy for Ukraine.
13. *Ibid.*, William Burianyk to O.D. Skelton, July, 1939, one of a series of letters between the two men in 1939 on "The Ukrainian Question"; *ibid.*, vol. 1673, file 742, O.D. Skelton to Sir William Clark, 17 February 1934.
14. *Ibid.*, vol. 1896, file 165-11, O.T. Wood, RCMP Commissioner, to O.D. Skelton, 27 May 1940.
15. Quoted in O. Woycenko, *The Ukrainians in Canada* (Ottawa: Canada Ethnica, 1967), p. 114.
16. *Ukrainskyi holos,* 15 April 1925; *Ukrainski visti*, 22 August 1930.
17. V.J. Kaye, "Political Integration of Ethnic Groups. The Ukrainians," *University of Ottawa Review*, XXVII (1957), p. 473.
18. For praise of M. Luchkovich, see *Ukrainskyi holos*, 5 June 1929; *Ukrainski visti*, 31 May 1929; and *Ukrainskyi robitnyk*, 8 October 1935. For A. Hlynka, see *Ukrainskyi holos,* 30 May 1945; and *Ukrainski visti*, 29 May 1945. For information on Fedun, Goresky, and Tomyn, see J.M. Lazarenko, "Ukrainians in Provincial Politics," in *The Ukrainian Pioneers in Alberta* (Edmonton: Ukrainian Pioneers' Association, 1970), pp. 47, 51, 53, 55.
19. W.L. Morton, *Manitoba: A History* (Toronto: University of Toronto Press, 1967), p. 409.
20. *Ibid.*, p. 384.
21. PAC, C.N.R. Records, vol. 5635, file 5500-4, "A bulletin published by the St. Raphael's Ukrainian Immigrants Welfare Association."
22. A. Milnor, "The New Politics and Ethnic Revolt, 1929-1938," in Ward and Spafford (eds.), *Politics in Saskatchewan*, pp. 151-77; see also D. Smith, *Prairie Liberalism: The Liberal Party in Saskatchewan, 1905-71* (Toronto: University of Toronto Press, 1975), p. 220.

23. B.R. Richardson, "High Politics in Saskatchewan," *Canadian Forum*, XIV (September, 1934), p. 462.
24. *Ukrainski visti*, 20 June 1944.
25. Milnor, "The New Politics," p. 171.
26. J.A. Long and F.Q. Quo, "Alberta: One Party Dominance," in M. Robin (ed.), *Canadian Provincial Politics: The Party Systems of the Ten Provinces* (Scarborough: Prentice-Hall, 1972), p. 4.
27. T. Flanagan, "Ethnic Voting in Alberta Provincial Elections, 1921-1971," *Canadian Ethnic Studies*, III (1971), p. 147.

SIX

Political Participation of Ukrainian Canadians Since 1945

Bohdan Harasymiw

The major question facing every ethnic group is that of persistence and change. Are the elements of its ethnicity – the distinctive identity, bonds, and interests – being preserved or assimilated (i.e., eradicated by the dominant culture) or integrated (i.e., added onto the dominant culture thus modifying it)? In the political realm it is commonly assumed that ethnicity becomes less relevant with time and economic development. That is certainly not true for the Québécois or the Dene in Canada. What of the much less visible minority, Canadians of Ukrainian origin? How relevant is ethnicity to their participation in Canadian politics?

The political participation of Ukrainian Canadians in the post-war period has increased noticeably, influenced by numerous variations resulting from social cleavages, themselves rooted in differences in immigration and generation, foreign and native birth, social class, rural and urban residence, religious persuasion, adherence to old-country radical (left-wing, collectivist, socialist) *versus* conservative (patriotic, nationalist, self-reliant) traditions, and perhaps even the rivalry of East and West in Canada.

Of particular importance to Ukrainian Canadians in the post-1945 period have been the rejuvenating impact on identity of the third wave of immigration and the largely contrary influence of urbanization and assimilation into mainstream Canadian society. With immigration at a standstill, the impact of mainstream society has come to challenge group survival. The remarkable fact about Ukrainian-Canadian political participation since the war has been that survival as an issue moved beyond politics within the group and became not only an interest pursued openly in the wider political arena but a major motivator of political activity. The new, urban, middle-class, third-wave immigrants, however, were more interested in European than Canadian politics. Their ideologies and organizations in Canada tended to reproduce the Ukrainian émigré experience in Europe. Of the four major political tendencies to emerge – centre-democratic, nationalist, socialist, and monarchist – the strongest was nationalist, exemplified in the right-wing Canadian League for Ukraine's Liberation, linked ideologically with its European-based counterpart.[1] Largely because of its European orientation, the third immigration has not figured prominently in Canadian politics. Indirectly, however, it has promoted increased participation by heightening the sense of Ukrainian identity and by strengthening the community's associations; by the mid-1960's Ukrainians had the largest number of organizations and the most politicized members of any of the major ethnic groups in Canada.[2] Membership in organizations is the most important factor associated with involvement in politics[3] and may explain the extraordinary vitality of Ukrainian-Canadian political participation. But in this the third immigration was more of a catalyst than an active element.

Several external factors contributed to the upsurge in political participation by Ukrainian Canadians. One was the Diefenbaker phenomenon. John Diefenbaker was not only of non-Anglo-Celtic and non-French origin, but under his leadership the Progressive Conservative Party took a strong anti-Soviet stand in foreign policy. The Quiet Revolution in Quebec, followed by the creation of the Royal Commission on Bilingualism and Biculturalism, also helped. Appointed to the latter was Jaroslav B. Rudnyckyj, a member of the third immigration and an effective spokesman for what some saw as the "third element" in Canadian society. The commission spurred Ukrainian-Canadian political participation, with attention focused on whether Canada was a bicultural or multicultural society; once the Canadian political system accepted the concept of multiculturalism and the legitimacy of ethnically based interests and claims, political attention shifted to the implementation of multiculturalism.

In the political culture of Ukrainian Canadians, it is possible to discern three general orientations. One has been the concern with cultural survival and a determination that public facilities be used to assist it. This has led to changes in educational policies in several provinces. A second orientation has been opposition to bilingualism and biculturalism, when confined exclusively to French and English. This opposition was sufficient to influence the Trudeau government to adopt a policy of multiculturalism in 1971. When Joe Clark's Progressive Conservatives threatened to abandon the policy in the 1979 federal election the move reportedly cost them votes among Ukrainian Canadians (and other ethnic voters) in such places as Toronto.[4] The idea of Canada as a multicultural society undoubtedly appeals because of its promise to assist in survival.[5] A third orientation has been concern for the homeland. Most Ukrainians manifest this in a degree of anti-Communism (or perhaps, more properly, anti-Sovietism) far greater than is usual among Canadians.[6] Depending on the receptiveness of the government in power, this sentiment could influence the articulation of Canada's foreign policy.

Beyond these very broad common elements, the Ukrainians divide considerably on more specific political attitudes, and although direct studies have been few, some generalizations are possible.[7] Immigrants differ from the Canadian-born in being more concerned with the independence of Ukraine and with representation in the federal and provincial legislatures by fellow Ukrainians. Rural residents are likely to be more willing to participate in organized political and social life than urban dwellers. The two demographic features – immigrant/native born and rural/urban – differentiate the group regionally, with those in central Canada more urban and more recent and those on the Prairies more rural and Canadian-born.[8] The relevance to political activity of being Ukrainian, therefore, is likely to vary in different parts of the country. Religious affiliation may also differentiate the members of the community, with Catholics likely more anti-Communist and more conservative. Ideologically, the Orthodox appear to be more influenced by their more varied socio-economic status, and they are usually distributed more randomly along the political spectrum. Education tends to eradicate ethnic consciousness, and the better educated members of the group are likely to be more assimilationist in attitude. Socio-economic status, however, which is commonly assumed to be an assimilating factor, does not appear to have had this effect on the community: persons of higher status do not tend to be more assimilated; they tend, in fact, to be more ethnically conscious. If this higher consciousness is translated into political leadership it can delay assimilation, despite the contrary effects of education and generational change. In sum, in terms of political culture or basic political attitudes, Ukrainian Canadians are not a homogeneous group that can be easily mobilized *en bloc* behind any political party, platform, or idea. And they are equally diverse as to political participation.

Another feature that sets the Ukrainian-Canadian community off from the rest of society politically is the higher degree of alienation when compared to most Canadians, according to the limited studies available.[9] Ethnic consciousness for the group is not just a matter of identity or concern with cultural survival. It is reinforced by feelings of social disadvantage, of not quite fitting in, of not deriving equal advantage from the political system. Consequently, Ukrainians are not randomly distributed on the continuum of political participation: while more conservative, they are also more marginal, hugging the ends rather than the middle of the political spectrum. As a result, most are not likely to espouse middle-of-the-road ideas or to follow such parties.

In the midst of this alienation and unpredictability, there has been a continued preoccupation with unity in support of Ukrainian candidates. Outsiders have reinforced this tendency with their view of Ukrainian Canadians as an undifferentiated, malleable mass, who tend to vote as directed. Thus the notion that Ukrainian Canadians should or actually do vote as a bloc is very common. Outsiders expect Ukrainians to support one political party or another; insiders expect them to support "their own" candidates. This era in Canadian politics, however, was given a major jolt in 1949 when two Ukrainians contested the federal riding of Vegreville for different parties. Criticized by many in the community for challenging the incumbent (Anthony Hlynka, Social Credit Member of Parliament since 1940), the newcomer (Liberal John Decore) nevertheless won.[10] The predominantly Ukrainian electorate could not place ethnicity ahead of party affiliation. Although the "bloc vote" may survive in the imaginations of some politicians, its force has diminished in the hands of Ukrainian voters and as a fact of life in Canadian elections.[11] Indeed, since 1968, there have been several instances in federal and provincial elections where all of a constituency's candidates have been Ukrainians.[12]

If the Ukrainians neither voted exclusively for ethnic candidates nor *en bloc* for a particular political party, then how did they vote in the post-war period? At the federal level they tended to support the Liberal Party during the first decade.[13] With John Diefenbaker's rise in the mid-1950's, Ukrainians began leaning toward the Progressive Conservatives.[14] In the lead were probably Ukrainians of Catholic persuasion, drawn by Diefenbaker's anti-Communism. By 1962, Diefenbaker's appointment of Michael Starr (Starchevsky) to the federal cabinet established the Conservatives with Ukrainians throughout Canada, and ethnic aspects were played up in the election of that year with notable success. Most Ukrainians, especially in rural constituencies, continued to support the Conservatives throughout the 1960's.[15] At the same time, there are signs that in urban areas, both on the Prairies and in eastern Canada, Ukrainians began splitting their vote among the Liberals, the New Democrats, and Social Credit.[16] These patterns survived into the 1980's, indicating that Ukrainians are reasonably well-integrated into the overall political system in terms of electoral behaviour: rural people tend to support the Tories, while urbanites tend to favour the Liberals or New Democrats.

On the provincial level the electoral behaviour of Ukrainians, at least as observed in the Prairie Provinces, shows no overall uniformity except that sooner or later they come around to support the governing party. Thus in Manitoba in 1945, Ukrainians in Winnipeg voted for left-wing and Ukrainian candidates.[17] But throughout the province in the next two decades, Liberals and Conservatives managed to appeal successfully to the group's older voters. This persisted even to 1969, when the NDP came to power with the support of young non-Anglo-Celtic voters, Ukrainians included.[18] This split between generations appears to have lasted to the present day. In Saskatchewan, several studies indicate that Ukrainians were slow to line up behind the NDP government.[19] As yet, no satisfactory explanation has been offered. In Alberta, Ukrainians again hesitated to back Social Credit after it came to power, and they were not among the early switchers to the Lougheed Conservatives.[20] Thus, they are not the political trend-setters in the provinces but those who join the bandwagon late. At the same time, no particular party appears to hold their loyalty across provincial boundaries.

In Winnipeg, where ethnically motivated electoral behaviour by Ukrainians predates World War I, the first Ukrainian mayor, Stephen Juba, was elected in 1956 and held office without a break for twenty-one years. His counterpart in Edmonton during the same period was William Hawrelak, who despite two judicial removals was also re-elected twice. Both men were strongly supported by Ukrainians. Besides them, there have been several Ukrainian aldermen in various Canadian cities, but it does appear that representation of Ukrainians in municipal politics is less than statistical chances would allow. That Ukrainians have elected two chief magistrates in two prairie cities is no doubt significant (such representatives are probably closer to the electors than are MPs or MLAs), but the phenomenon may be part of a passing era. Ukrainians are increasingly either too preoccupied with their private affairs to engage in municipal politics on a scale commensurate with their concentration in the population, or, having tasted success, are less drawn to local politics than others.

Increased political participation during the period under review, however, can be seen in the number of Ukrainian Canadians among candidates for election to Parliament and the provincial legislatures. In the 1945 federal election, for example, only twelve of 952 candidates could be identified as Ukrainian; in 1980, there were thirty-four out of 1,496.[21] The proportion, however, is lower than the percentage of Ukrainians in the population. Perhaps a fairer comparison would be to concentrate on the country west of the Ottawa River, since nearly all members of the ethnic group (95.3 per cent in 1971) reside there. On that basis, the percentage of Ukrainian candidacies on the federal level rose from 2.1 to 6.3 (in 1974) and then declined to 3.9 (1980); meanwhile, the Ukrainian share of the population slipped from 4.6 per cent in 1951 to 4.1 per cent in 1971. This represents rough parity and may be interpreted as an indication of successful integration. But some questions remain. Was the over-achievement of the 1970's a phase in the group's adjustment process? Or was it an aberration? Without knowledge of the details of candidate selection – did they recruit themselves or were they chosen by party notables? – it is impossible to say. Has their participation as candidates perhaps slackened since the 1970's because of a realization that the actual role of legislatures everywhere has declined significantly, and that ethnic interests are better promoted elsewhere? To answer such questions, the motives behind political involvement need to be studied.

If the Ukrainian-Canadian electorate is politically conservative, its candidates for Parliament have not been exclusively so. In fact, the one party in which they have been consistently over-represented has been the Communist Party of Canada and its predecessor, the Labour Progressive Party. As standard-bearers for other parties, they tended disproportionately to be Social Crediters in the forties and fifties, to have flocked to the CCF-NDP thereafter, and then moved in the direction of the Liberal and Progressive Conservative Parties. In the 1980 election, they were clearly not interested (or not welcome) in the middle ground of the political party spectrum: they were over-represented by comparison with their overall share of candidates in not only the PC and Social Credit Parties, but in the Communist and Marxist-Leninist groupings, and they were correspondingly under-represented among Liberal, NDP, and independent and other fringe groups. In regard to the parties for which they choose to run for Parliament, therefore, Ukrainians are not well-integrated; they appear rather to be addicted (within the limits of the Canadian political system) to the extremes or, less dramatically, they tend to prefer the margin.

There is one sense in which Ukrainian-Canadian parliamentary candidates can be considered well-integrated, however, and that is in their chances of being elected. Statistically speaking, there is now no special advantage or disadvantage in a candidate's being Ukrainian: the chances of election are about the same as anyone else's, although in certain provinces and at certain times being Ukrainian has appeared significant. For instance, it was a definite disadvantage to be Ukrainian in Ontario (1965, 1979, and 1980) and Manitoba (1979), but a positive advantage in Alberta (1979, but less so in 1980) and Saskatchewan (1980). What likely matters most is party affiliation.

The percentage of Ukrainian MPs in the House of Commons representing Ontario and the West climbed from 0.7 in 1945 to 3.5 in 1980. Closer inspection shows a very erratic history: representation rose to 3.9 by 1957, fell to 1.9 in the 1963 and 1965 elections, jumped to 5.1 in the seventies, and has declined since then. Just as relatively fewer Ukrainian Canadians are running for Parliament, fewer are being elected. Altogether, there have been twenty-six MPs of Ukrainian origin in the period between 1945 and 1980 inclusive. Most belonged to the Progressive Conservatives, represented Alberta, and were born in Canada's smaller prairie towns and villages. To date, only one has come from the third immigration. Less highly educated than other MPs, only sixteen (or 61.5 per cent) attended university. They represented thirty-two occupations, mostly the professions (11), business and management (4), and teaching (7), with a sprinkling of others (three newspapermen, three farmers, and one each as railroad section foreman, pastor, social worker, and politician's executive assistant). Overall, the group resembles less the Canadian political elite generally (university-educated lawyers and businessmen) and more the Ukrainian-Canadian community.[22]

Four of the twenty-six Ukrainian MPs have been cabinet ministers, all but one in Conservative governments.[23] Ukrainians have found the Liberal Party less congenial and, as a result, have missed out on sharing power and the benefits of patronage from the post-war era's main governing party. The tradition of a Ukrainian in cabinet is not yet firmly established, notwithstanding the long tradition of sectional and regional cabinet representation.

On the other hand, both Conservative and Liberal prime ministers seem to have accepted as customary the appointment of two Ukrainian Canadians to the Senate. William Wall (Wolochatiuk), a Liberal and former school principal, was the first appointed in 1955, serving until his death in 1962. John Hnatyshyn, a Progressive Conservative and a lawyer, held office from 1959 until he died in 1967. Paul Yuzyk, also a Progressive Conservative who had been a school teacher and then a history professor, was summoned in 1963. John Ewasew, a lawyer and president of the Liberal riding in Mount Royal (Prime Minister Trudeau's constituency), was named in December, 1976, but died in March, 1978. In September, 1979, Martha Bielish, a schoolteacher and farmer from Alberta and a Progressive Conservative, was appointed.

It is probably easier for senators than MPs to be effective spokesmen for the Ukrainian-Canadian group, for it is understood that senators have special interest or socio-economic constituencies, while those of the MPs are geographical, embracing an ethnic cross-section in each riding. Few serving MPs identify themselves as Ukrainians in their official biographies; Senator Yuzyk, by contrast, does so by reference to parentage, marriage, religion, and membership in numerous associations. Although generally regarded like their Jewish counterparts, but unlike those of German or Scandinavian extraction, as spokesmen for their ethnic group[24] Ukrainians in the Commons appear willing to be so only symbolically.

The percentage of Ukrainians among candidates for the legislatures of Ontario and the Prairie Provinces, as well as among MPPs and MLAs, has been closer than in federal politics to the population as a whole. Perhaps the smaller constituencies, where ethnic surnames may be more familiar and party organizations more receptive, facilitate the higher participatory rate. In any case, as Tables 9 through 12 show, there has been an apparent downturn in the rate in all four provinces between the sixties and seventies. It may be that the peak in each indicated a brief period of overachievement common among minorities before more integrated forms of behaviour and proportionate representation settle in.[25] Or it may be an indication of the group's perception of the inefficacy of legislatures and its relapse into an alienated, less participatory role. Or it may just be an aberration.

In the post-war period, being Ukrainian has generally neither enhanced nor hindered a candidate's chances of election to a provincial legislature. Statistically, it appeared as a hindrance in four of Ontario's eleven post-war elections and in two of the most recent three in Manitoba. In Saskatchewan it has either made no difference or been a slight handicap (with the single exception of 1971, when no fewer than seven of ten Ukrainians were elected). On the other hand, in Alberta in the seventies, during three successive elections, the association between being

Ukrainian and getting elected became progressively stronger as Ukrainian candidates gradually gravitated toward the Progressive Conservative Party. As candidates for provincial legislative seats, Ukrainians as a rule are not swept along by the tide of the dominant political party. If this were so, in Tables 9 through 12 higher percentages in the MPP/MLA columns than in the candidate columns would appear more consistently. Of the thirty-nine elections reported in the tables, only twelve show such results and five of these are in Alberta. While the electorate may tend to line up behind the governing party, Ukrainian Canadians generally do not. However, the lack of uniformity here and in the matter of electoral chances again indicates the variations – especially regional ones – beneath the label "Ukrainian."

The party affiliations of Ukrainian provincial candidates have differed somewhat from those at the federal level, but this does not just reflect the different complexions of government at each level. While the percentage of Social Credit and Communist candidates has been higher in federal elections, the percentage of Liberal, PC, and CCF-NDP candidates has been greater in provincial contests, indicating that Ukrainians are apparently more in the mainstream of Canadian politics provincially than federally. With the Conservatives fielding fewer Ukrainian candidates than the other two parties, and the Liberals putting forward as many as the CCF-NDP, Ukrainian political activists obviously differ from the Ukrainian community at large, and the character of partisan activity

TABLE 9

Percentage of Ukrainians Among Candidates in Provincial General Elections, Elected MPPs, and in Population, Ontario, 1945-81

	Candidates	*Elected MPPs*	*Population*
1945	0.6	0	
1948	0.3	0	
1951	0.7	0.1	2.0
1955	1.9	1.0	
1959	1.0	1.0	
1961			2.0
1963	1.2	0.9	
1967	1.9	1.7	
1971	2.1	1.7	2.1
1975	1.8	1.6	
1977	1.5	0.8	
1981	2.3	2.4	

TABLE 10

Percentage of Ukrainians Among Candidates in Provincial General Elections, Elected MLAs, and in Population, Manitoba, 1945-77

	Candidates	*Elected MLAs*	*Population*
1945	12.0	10.9	
1949	12.5	12.3	
1951			12.7
1953	9.8	14.0	
1958	12.3	14.0	
1959	11.5	12.3	
1961			11.4
1962	13.5	10.5	
1966	15.1	12.3	
1969	12.0	8.8	
1971			11.6
1973	11.3	10.5	
1977	11.9	7.0	

TABLE 11

Percentage of Ukrainians Among Candidates in Provincial General Elections, Elected MLAs, and in Population, Saskatchewan, 1948-78

	Candidates	*Elected MLAs*	*Population*
1948	6.7	3.8	
1951			9.4
1952	6.2	5.7	
1956	7.6	7.5	
1960	6.7	9.1	
1961			8.5
1964	8.0	3.4	
1967	7.9	8.5	
1971	7.2	11.7	9.3
1975	10.6	8.2	
1978	8.6	8.2	

TABLE 12

Percentage of Ukrainians Among Candidates in Provincial General Elections, Elected MLAs, and in Population, Alberta, 1948-79

	Candidates	*Elected MLAs*	*Population*
1948	7.5	7.0	
1951			9.3
1952	8.2	6.6	
1955	7.4	4.9	
1959	7.9	7.7	
1961			8.0
1963	8.0	9.5	
1967	8.5	10.8	
1971	7.8	14.7	8.3
1975	8.2	14.7	
1979	6.0	13.9	

therefore cannot be projected from one level of participation to another – from voting to running for office, for example.[26] Worth noting also is the fact that, as we shall see, the prominent number of Liberal candidates has not been translated into bureaucratic posts in Ottawa.

A very significant difference exists among the party affiliations of candidates who have been elected and it reflects well the federal-provincial governing party split. Most (twenty out of twenty-six) Ukrainian MPs have been Liberals and Conservatives, compared with only one-third (twenty-five out of seventy-eight) of the MPPs-MLAs. Fully thirty-one (42 per cent) of Ukrainian MLAs were CCF-NDP, fourteen were Social Crediters, and seven were Liberals. As with MPs, Alberta and Manitoba with twenty-eight MLAs each provided the majority of Ukrainian origin; Saskatchewan supplied another sixteen. (The difficulty of breaking into the Ontario legislature is clear from the failure to elect more than five MPPs since 1945, three in the 1981 election.) Ukrainian MLAs also possess less prestigious occupational backgrounds than their federal counterparts. Of the sixty-eight on whom information is available and who among themselves shared eighty-seven occupations, only nine were lawyers. Teaching appeared twenty-five times; farming and business, twenty times each.[27] For the sixty-five whose educational qualifications could be ascertained, twenty-nine had attended university and ten had been to normal school or a teachers' college. In socio-economic terms, the MLAs appear to be closer to their constituents than the MPs. Whether they are more inclined to act as ethnic spokesmen, however, is a moot point. About one-half are identified in their official biographies as of

Ukrainian descent, a proportion similar to the MPs. But the number is sharply down from 1973, a sure sign of assimilation and an indication that Ukrainian MLAs increasingly do not wish to be seen as representatives of their ethnic group.

The increase in the number of Ukrainian MLAs in provincial cabinets has been most impressive. Out of eleven MLAs in 1945, none were in the cabinet; by 1977, seven out of the twenty-four held portfolios. However, by 1981, only four out of twenty-three were cabinet ministers, possibly only a temporary phenomenon resulting from the fewer Ukrainian MLAs elected in the late 1970's, the shift in the governing party in Manitoba, and Premier William Davis's reluctance to appoint a successor to John Yaremko, who was in the cabinet until 1974. Whatever the explanation, the fact remains that Ukrainians have yet to attain real power in provincial executive councils. By 1981, apart from Roy Romanow, Saskatchewan's Attorney General, few had held the most influential portfolios.

To gauge the integration of Ukrainians into Canadian political life and their ability to represent their own interests, it would help to know the ethnic composition of the public service at all three levels of government. Unfortunately, such studies of the civil service have either been few or are very dated. All that can be said federally is that the senior level is definitely closed to Ukrainian Canadians. There have never been and there are not now (1981) any Ukrainian names among the deputy ministers or their equivalent. The distribution below this level is not known, but it would likely be heaviest in the lower ranks. An important exception is William Teron, president of the Central (now Canada) Mortgage and Housing Corporation from 1973 to 1979, the first Ukrainian to head a Crown corporation in Canada.[28] Of the various federal boards and commissions, in 1980 Ukrainians were represented on only three - the Atomic Energy Control Board, the Farm Credit Corporation, and the National Capital Commission. The ability of Ukrainians to influence federal government policy is therefore not great.

At the provincial and municipal levels, the scanty information available indicates that Ukrainians have generally occupied the lower rather than higher bureaucratic ranks. By the 1960's, their overall representation in provincial government bureaucracies and in such cities as Toronto and Winnipeg was fairly reasonable, though relatively few held managerial posts and disproportionately more were clerks, labourers, and unskilled workers.[29] In Alberta, for example, in 1967, there was not one Ukrainian among the province's seventeen deputy ministers (94 per cent were Anglo-Celts) and only one individual among the eighteen board and commission chairmen (89 per cent were Anglo-Celts).[30] The glacial speed with which ethnic representatives are recruited into top public service posts is well-illustrated by the title of a *Globe and Mail* story (December 31, 1976). Referring to the situation in Ontario, it declared: "For Deputy Ministers, Spell Anglo-Saxons."

Ukrainian ethnic interests do not enjoy high priority with policymakers, either at federal or provincial levels. Apart from speeches and resolutions in Parliament, the Canadian government has rarely been moved to implement foreign policy measures in line with Ukrainian interests. While Prime Minister Diefenbaker spoke out against the Soviet domination of non-Russian peoples in the USSR, uttering statements is a very easy form of implementing policy. In response to urging by the Ukrainian Canadian Committee, Mitchell Sharp attempted to press the Soviets to change their immigration policy and the treatment of nationalists in Ukraine. He was unsuccessful. In 1971 Prime Minister Trudeau equated Ukrainian nationalist dissidents with FLQ terrorists. During the short-lived Clark government, the Minister of Immigration, Ron Atkey, signed a two-year agreement under which at least 200 East European refugees would be sponsored by the UCC as immigrants to Canada.

Ukrainians played an important role in the development of the federal government's policy of multiculturalism,[31] and Prime Minister Trudeau acknowledged this role by speaking to a UCC congress in Winnipeg the day after announcing the policy in the Commons. However, it has been virtually impossible for the Ukrainian community to influence the implementation of that policy, which appears primarily directed to immigrant adjustment rather than cultural development.[32]

In the provinces, cultural policies are probably more amenable to influence by the Ukrainians, and a major breakthrough was made in education with the establishment of English-Ukrainian bilingual programs in Alberta and Manitoba. Their survival, however, is not assured, partly because of competition from French immersion and bilingual programs and partly because of an absence of full-time social animators needed to mobilize support for them from the Ukrainian community. In higher education, the establishment of the Canadian Institute of Ukrainian Studies at the University of Alberta, the chair of Ukrainian studies at the University of Toronto, and other academic positions are signs of successful interest group activity.

The persistence of Ukrainian political behaviour depends on there being a Ukrainian political culture in the first place and upon the continued vitality of those processes which transmit and develop it. In the past, that culture has been shaped by a number of institutions, which gave their members a chance to interact and to transmit political and other values. These institutions – family, church, voluntary association, press, library, meeting hall, student residence – are now in decline as agents of political socialization and are being replaced, in part, by non-print media, the public schools, and government cultural programs.

If economic modernization is uprooting people from the rural areas and small towns and depositing them in the large cities, it may very well encourage cultural assimilation.[33] Yet it also creates concentrations of significant enough proportions – already one person in eight in Winnipeg and Edmonton is of Ukrainian origin – that interaction is inevitably encouraged and ethnic identity and interests sustained.[34] Not that assimilation is prevented; rather, assimilation and preservation go on simultaneously. With these large concentrations of population there is undoubtedly a spill-over of the Ukrainian ethnic culture into the more general Canadian culture. Sustaining this culture has been taken up by various Ukrainian studies programs at the universities, as well as by a proliferation of local histories, memoirs, and biographies.

Of more direct relevance to ethnic political interests and their survival is the fact that the young generation of Ukrainian Canadians has seriously taken up the cause of human rights in Soviet Ukraine. This could have a reinvigorating effect similar to that produced earlier by the influx of new immigrants. It could be an even more effective mechanism for reviving ethnic consciousness because it not only links Ukrainians in Canada with Ukraine, but does so on a universalistic, philosophical basis rather than on a particularistic and ethnocentric one. Such activities are more liable to be supported outside the community, rather than being treated with suspicion or animosity, as expressions of Ukrainian ethnic interest have often been historically. Since this cause is forward-looking in that it aims at an ameliorated future rather than looking back to a melancholy, irretrievable past, it may also serve as a more efficacious ideology than those in existence to date. Certainly these new developments mean that the story of Ukrainian political participation in Canada is not yet over.

NOTES

1. V. Kubijovyč, "Ukrainian Political Refugees and Emigrants after 1945," *Ukraine: A Concise Encyclopedia*, 2 vols. (Toronto: University of Toronto Press, 1963 and 1971), I, pp. 914b-15a, and V.J. Kaye (Kysilewsky), "Social and Political Life," *ibid.*, II, p. 1169.
2. D. Sherwood and A. Wakefield, "Voluntary Associations among Ethnic Groups in Canada," [Draft of a] Study Prepared for the Royal Commission on Bilingualism and Biculturalism, n.p., n.d.
3. N.H. Nie *et al.*, "Social Structure and Political Participation: Developmental Relationships," *American Political Science Review*, LXIII (1969), pp. 361-78, 808-32.
4. *Globe and Mail* (Toronto), 24 May 1979.
5. M.R. Lupul, "The Impact of Bilingualism and Biculturalism on the Ukrainian Ethnic Group in Canada," unpublished address to the Ukrainian Professional and Businessmen's Club, Edmonton, 29 May 1964; and W. Harasym, "Four Generations of Change," in P. Prokop, W. Harasym, and M.J. Sago, *Change and Challenge in the Ukrainian Ethnic Group* (Toronto: Association of United Ukrainian Canadians, 1967), pp. 13-19.
6. J. Meisel, *Working Papers on Canadian Politics*, 2nd enl. ed. (Montreal: McGill-Queen's University Press, 1975), pp. 127-39, 150-1, 155; and B.R. Bociurkiw, "Ethnic Identification and Attitudes of University

Students of Ukrainian Descent: The University of Alberta Case Study," in C.J. Jaenen (ed.), *Slavs in Canada* (Ottawa: Inter-University Committee on Canadian Slavs, 1971), pp. 59-65.

7. Bociurkiw, "Ethnic Identification," pp. 15-110; and C.W. Hobart *et al.*, *Persistence and Change: A Study of Ukrainians in Alberta* (Edmonton: Ukrainian Canadian Research Foundation, 1978), chapters 9 and 10.
8. J. Porter, *The Vertical Mosaic: An Analysis of Social Class and Power in Canada* (Toronto: University of Toronto Press, 1965), p. 91; Statistics Canada, *1971 Census of Canada: Population: Ethnic Groups* (Ottawa: Information Canada, 1973), Table 2; W.R. Petryshyn, "The Ukrainian Canadians in Social Transition," in M.R. Lupul (ed.), *Ukrainian Canadians, Multiculturalism, and Separatism: An Assessment* (Edmonton: University of Alberta Press, 1978), pp. 74-97; and Statistics Canada, *1971 Census of Canada: Population: Ethnic Groups*, Table 3, and "Ethnic Groups by Birthplace," Table 29.
9. Hobart, *Ukrainians in Alberta*, p. 448, and Meisel, *Working Papers on Canadian Politics*, pp. 127-39, 150-1, 155.
10. O. Woycenko, *The Ukrainians in Canada* (Winnipeg: Canada Ethnica, 1967), pp. 115-17; J.M. Lazarenko, "Ukrainians in Provincial Politics," in *The Ukrainian Pioneers in Alberta* (Edmonton: Ukrainian Pioneers' Association, 1970), pp. 73-5.
11. M.A. Schwartz, "Political Behaviour and Ethnic Origin," in J. Meisel (ed.), *Papers on the 1962 Election: Fifteen Papers on the Canadian General Election of 1962* (Toronto: University of Toronto Press, 1964), pp. 264-5, 267; F.G. Vallee, M. Schwartz, and F. Darknell, "Ethnic Assimilation and Differentiation in Canada," *Canadian Journal of Economics and Political Science*, XXIII (1957), p. 548; F.C. Engelmann and M.A. Schwartz, *Political Parties and the Canadian Social Structure* (Scarborough: Prentice-Hall of Canada, 1967), p. 233.
12. For examples of contests between Ukrainians for a party nomination, and of the unwillingness of fellow-ethnics within the same party to support one another, see Meisel (ed.), *Papers on the 1962 Election*, pp. 55-6; A. Shingadia, "Edmonton Centre - A Constituency Study" (Master's thesis, University of Alberta, 1969), pp. 63-76, 89-91, 175, 178-9.
13. W. Vossen, "Ethnological Factors in the Voting of a Saskatchewan Constituency" (Master's thesis, University of Saskatchewan, 1965), pp. 43-7, 52-6.
14. *Ibid.*, pp. 52, 60; R. Baird, "The Slavic Vote," *Slavs in Canada* (Edmonton: Inter-University Committee on Canadian Slavs, 1966), p. 159; P. Regenstreif, *The Diefenbaker Interlude: Parties and Voting in Canada: An Interpretation* (Toronto: Longmans, 1965), pp. 91-2; J.E. Havel, *Politics in Sudbury: A Survey of Mass Communications, Political Behavior and Political Parties in Sudbury*, trans. and ed. by R. Keir (Sudbury: Laurentian University Press, 1966), p. 9, Table 9, p. 69, Table 42, p. 65, Table 36.

15. Meisel (ed.), *Papers on the 1962 Election*, pp. 102, 173, 263-7; P.C. Newman, *Renegade in Power: The Diefenbaker Years* (Toronto: McClelland and Stewart, 1963), p. 260; J.A. Laponce, "Ethnicity, Religion, and Politics in Canada: A Comparative Analysis of Survey and Census Data," in M. Doggan and S. Rokkan (eds.), *Quantitative Ecological Analysis in the Social Sciences* (Cambridge, Mass.: M.I.T. Press, 1969), pp. 188, 212; J.C. Terry and R.J. Schultz, "Canadian Electoral Behavior: A Propositional Inventory," in O.M. Kruhlak, R. Schultz, and S.I. Pobihushchy (eds.), *The Canadian Political Process*, rev. ed. (Toronto: Holt, Rinehart and Winston of Canada, 1973), p. 265; Hobart, *Ukrainians in Alberta*, pp. 361-2; Bociurkiw, "Ethnic Identification," p. 57, Table 23.
16. Hobart, *Ukrainians in Alberta*, p. 364; Vossen, "Ethnological Factors," pp. 78-82; M.A. Schwartz, "Canadian Voting Behaviour," in R. Rose (ed.), *Electoral Behavior: A Comparative Handbook* (New York: Free Press, 1974), p. 580, Table 12.
17. T. Peterson, "Ethnic and Class Politics in Manitoba," in M. Robin (ed.), *Canadian Provincial Politics: The Party Systems of the Ten Provinces* (Scarborough: Prentice-Hall of Canada, 1972), pp. 78-97; N. Wiseman and K.W. Taylor, "Ethnic vs. Class Voting: The Case of Winnipeg, 1945," *Canadian Journal of Political Science*, VII (1974), pp. 314-28.
18. Peterson, "Ethnic and Class Politics," pp. 97-115; D. Swainson, "Ethnic Revolt: Manitoba's Election," *Canadian Forum* (August, 1969), pp. 98-9.
19. S.M. Lipset, *Agrarian Socialism: The Cooperative Commonwealth Federation in Saskatchewan: A Study in Political Sociology* (Berkeley: University of California Press, 1959), p. 170; Baird, "The Slavic Vote," p. 159; S. Silverstein, "Occupational Class and Voting Behavior: Electoral Support of a Left-Wing Protest Movement in a Period of Prosperity," in S.M. Lipset, *Agrarian Socialism*, rev. ed. (Garden City, N.Y.: Doubleday, 1968), pp. 436-7, 452-4.
20. J.A. Irving, *The Social Credit Movement in Alberta* (Toronto: University of Toronto Press, 1959), pp. 202, 250-3, 282; Bociurkiw, "Ethnic Identification," p. 57, Table 23; and Hobart, *Ukrainians in Alberta*, pp. 356-61.
21. Electoral and biographical information has been culled from G. Normandin (ed.), *Canadian Parliamentary Guide, 1945-1980*, supplemented by Woycenko, *Ukrainians in Canada*; *Globe and Mail* (Toronto); *Calgary Herald*; and *Edmonton Journal*.
22. Altogether there were fourteen PCs, six Liberals, three CCF/NDP, and three Social Crediters. Ten represented Alberta, seven Ontario, six Manitoba, and three Saskatchewan. Five were born in Poland or Ukraine and were brought to Canada as children: two before 1917, two in the interwar period, and one after 1945. The birthplaces of two are not known. Of those born in Canada, Alberta produced seven and Ontario,

Saskatchewan, and Manitoba four each. The eight born in major cities came from only four centres: Edmonton, Saskatoon, Toronto, and Windsor.

23. Michael Starr served in the Diefenbaker government; Norman Cafik under Pierre Elliott Trudeau; and Roman Hnatyshyn and Steve Paproski were in Joe Clark's cabinet.
24. Report of the Royal Commission on Bilingualism and Biculturalism, Book IV: *The Cultural Contribution of the Other Ethnic Groups* (Ottawa: Queen's Printer, 1970), p. 78; Woycenko, *Ukrainians in Canada*, pp. 118-22; F.A. Kunz, *The Modern Senate of Canada, 1925-1963: A Re-appraisal* (Toronto: University of Toronto Press, 1965), p. 52.
25. In another context, see the discussion of the prominence of "deprived ethnic minorities" in R.D. Putnam, *The Comparative Study of Political Elites* (Englewood Cliffs, N.J.: Prentice-Hall, 1976), pp. 191-3.
26. In passing, one might note that the party affiliations of candidates not only vary from province to province but from the federal to the provincial arenas. Why this happens in the case of some parties but not others is not clear. For example, federal and provincial candidates for the Liberals tended to be predominantly from Manitoba and Saskatchewan, for Social Credit from Saskatchewan and Alberta, and for the Communists from Ontario. On the other hand, federal PC candidates came predominantly from Ontario, provincial ones from Saskatchewan and Alberta. Federal CCF-NDP candidates were more likely to come from Saskatchewan and Alberta, with their provincial counterparts from Ontario and Manitoba. Since Ontario is predominantly a Conservative province and Saskatchewan reputedly had been an NDP bastion (until the 1982 provincial election), one should not expect this difference. It may be, therefore, that some organizational features of these parties make it less likely that Ukrainians will be PC candidates in Ontario, for example, or NDP in Saskatchewan provincially.
27. The following were listed once: doctor, dentist, pharmacist, manager, railroad foreman, policeman, prospector, journalist, choreographer, salesman, and public servant. There were two who reported having been mechanics. Incidentally, the vast majority of Ukrainian MLAs have been Canadian-born; the first person of the third immigration was elected only in 1981.
28. A. Gregorovich, *Chronology of Ukrainian Canadian History* (Toronto: Ukrainian Canadian Committee, 1974), pp. 50, 60; *Calgary Herald*, 9 June 1979.
29. Report of the Royal Commission on Bilingualism and Biculturalism Book IV, Tables A-36 and A-37, p. 277, and A-39, p. 278; M.S. Donnelly, "Ethnic Participation in Municipal Government: Winnipeg, St. Boniface, and the Metropolitan Corporation of Greater Winnipeg: Report for the Royal Commission on Bilingualism and Biculturalism," September, 1965, ch. 3.
30. F.G. Hulmes, "The Senior Executive and the Fifteenth Alberta

Legislature: A Study in the Social and Political Background of Membership'' (Doctoral dissertation, University of Alberta, 1970), pp. 2, 277, 285.

31. B.R. Bociurkiw, ''The Federal Policy of Multiculturalism and the Ukrainian-Canadian Community,'' in Lupul (ed.), *Ukrainian Canadians, Multiculturalism, and Separatism*, pp. 98-128.
32. See M.R. Lupul, ''The Political Implementation of Multiculturalism,'' *Journal of Canadian Studies*, 17 (Spring, 1982), pp. 93-102; and Lupul, ''The Tragedy of Canada's White Ethnics: A Constitutional Postmortem,'' *Journal of Ukrainian Studies*, 12 (Spring, 1982), pp. 3-15.
33. Some doubts about Ukrainians' ability to forestall cultural assimilation as their pattern of residence in Winnipeg changes have been expressed by L. Driedger and G. Church, ''Residential Segregation and Institutional Completeness: A Comparison of Ethnic Minorities,'' *Canadian Review of Sociology and Anthropology*, XI (1974), pp. 30-52.
34. Hobart and his colleagues (pp. 539-41) actually found that Ukrainians in smaller towns had greater assimilationist attitudes than their compatriots in Edmonton. The *forces* of assimilation may be greater in the cities, but if the *attitudes* toward it are less favourable, then the *process* will likely be inhibited in its rate of progress.

SEVEN

Religious Life

Paul Yuzyk

The dominant role of the church in the life of the Ukrainian people in their native land prior to World War I was transmitted to the Ukrainian settlements in Canada. The new churches, Greek Catholic and Greek Orthodox, both branches of the Eastern or Byzantine rite, were strange at first to Canadians of Anglo-Celtic, French, and other West European origins. Because of the early religious vacuum in the new settlements, the Roman Catholic Church and some of the Protestant denominations also took an active part in the life of the newcomers. An intense religious rivalry ensued and the religious scene became very confused during the pioneer period. By the end of the 1920's, however, the two traditional churches, the Greek Catholic and Greek Orthodox, could claim the adherence of approximately 85 per cent of the Ukrainian faithful in Canada. This predominance subsequently declined because of the inroads of other, Canadian churches. To understand these faiths, however, it is necessary to delve briefly into their historical antecedents.

HISTORICAL BACKGROUND

Christianity came to Ukraine from Constantinople, when Grand Prince Volodymyr (Vladimir) the Great adopted the Byzantine form of Christianity in 988 as the official church of the Kievan Rus' state.[1] The first church was organized by the patriarch of Constantinople, who established the metropolitan see in the capital of Kiev. The rite, practices, theological beliefs, institutions, and architecture of the majestic Byzantine church and the advanced culture of the Greeks were assumed by the new church, except for the use of Old Church Slavonic as the language. Kiev became a second Constantinople in splendour, power, and cultural leadership, dominating the life of the eastern Slavs for the next two centuries.

When Ukraine was thus converted the whole Christian church was still united, for the rift between the patriarchs of Constantinople, Antioch,

Jerusalem, and Alexandria with Rome did not occur until 1054. Kievan Rus', despite its subordination to the ecclesiastical jurisdiction of Constantinople, showed little hostility toward the Latin West after the schism, if the numerous royal marriages between the Ruryk dynasty and members of Western dynasties are any criteria. Essentially Byzantine, the church of Kievan Rus' also assumed the title of "Orthodox." In 1240 the fall of Kiev brought the Ukrainian lands under Tatar domination for a century and a half, virtually cutting off relations with western Europe.

Poland's conquest of Galicia and her dynastic union with Lithuania in 1386 and the organic Union of Lublin in 1569 gave her ascendancy over the Ukrainian lands, including the Kiev region and the territory of the Cossacks at the bend of the Dnieper River. Poland, a strong Catholic state, pursued a policy of forcibly Catholicizing and Polonizing the Ukrainians. Efforts slackened when Protestantism made great advances in Poland during the latter half of the sixteenth century and the first half of the seventeenth. When the Counter Reformation restored the supremacy of the Catholic Church in Poland, the Jesuits turned their efforts to the Ukrainians. Some Ukrainian Orthodox bishops were thoroughly dissatisfied with the patriarch of Constantinople, who after the fall of Constantinople in 1453 had been forced to recognize the Turkish sultan. The Jesuits and the Polish king advocated union with Rome, promising improved conditions. With the support of four of the Orthodox bishops, the Act of Union[2] was officially proclaimed at a Church Council in Brest (-Litovsk) in 1596, despite the opposition of two bishops and a large section of Ukrainian clergy, gentry, and laymen, especially the Cossacks.

Thus the Uniate church (Ruthenian Greek Catholic*) came into existence, having the official support of the Polish government and the papacy. The supremacy of the pope was recognized in matters of dogma but the Byzantine rite, using Old Church Slavonic in liturgy and ceremonies, was left unchanged. Priests could continue to marry before ordination. The church was promised a seat in the Polish Senate, and Greek Catholic bishops, like their Roman Catholic counterparts, were exempt from taxation. Uniates and Latin-rite citizens were to enjoy equal rights in holding state offices. The terms were made attractive to the Orthodox, for the new church was to serve as a bridge to the eastern Orthodox churches and to Christian unity under the leadership of the pope.

Although left without a hierarchy for almost two decades, the Ukrainian Orthodox Church was not destroyed. The Zaporozhian Cossacks under Hetman Petro Sahaidachny restored the hierarchy in 1621, but following Hetman Bohdan Khmelnytsky's fateful Treaty of Pereiaslav in 1654, the Ukrainian Orthodox Church was forced in 1686 to recognize the jurisdiction of the patriarch of Moscow. Subsequently, Russian interference in the selection of bishops and clergy made the Ukrainian Or-

* The Uniate church has been known as the Ruthenian church, later under Hapsburg rule (1772-1918) as the Ruthenian Greek Catholic Church, and after 1918 as the Ukrainian Catholic Church.

thodox Church a medium of Russian domination and Russification, which lasted until the Ukrainian state was restored at the end of World War I.

The fate of the Uniate church in Galicia after the Treaty of Brest was more fortunate than that of the Ukrainian Orthodox Church. Although the Ukrainian bishops were not given seats in the Polish Senate and the prelates and clergy were denied equality with the Latin bishops, hatred of the Polish aristocracy and fear of assimilation by the Poles made the Ukrainian masses cling to their clergy and church. Moreover, when Galicia became a province of Austria in 1772 as a result of the partitions of Poland, the Hapsburgs buttressed the Uniate church as a counterforce to the Polish aristocracy, designating it officially as Ruthenian Greek Catholic. Thus, although the Uniate church was systematically destroyed in those Ukrainian regions which had been absorbed by the Russian Empire after the collapse of Poland, in Galicia, with state support, it emerged in the nineteenth century as a Ukrainian national church, the defender of the culture and rights of the Ukrainian people. The Ukrainian settlers who began to emigrate to North America in the late 1880's were preponderantly from Galicia and hence adherents of the Greek Catholic (Uniate) Church.

The brief and turbulent existence of the Ukrainian state from 1917 to 1921 left the fate of the Ukrainian churches uncertain. In Kiev the Ukrainian Autocephalous Orthodox Church[3] broke away from the Russian Orthodox Church and established itself in 1921 under hostile circumstances as an independent national church without formal ties to any patriarch. The atheistic Soviet regime subsequently destroyed the hierarchy and the clergy during the first five-year plan. The only prelate to survive was Bishop Ivan Theodorovich, who had been sent from Ukraine to the United States to head the Ukrainian Orthodox Church in North America. Today in Ukraine there exists only a Ukrainian exarchate or branch of the Russian Orthodox Church, headed by a bishop who is subordinate to the patriarch of Moscow and subject to state control.

With the fall of the Ukrainian state in 1920, Galicia (the Western Ukrainian National Republic in union with the Ukrainian state) was annexed by the new Polish state. The Greek Catholic Church, under the leadership of Metropolitan Count Andrii Sheptytsky, played a leading role in the defence of Ukrainian culture, which the Poles again attempted to undermine. However, the Soviet occupation of Western Ukraine during World War II was disastrous for the Greek Catholic Church, which was forced to unite[4] with the Russian Orthodox Church in 1946. Out of 2,700 clergy, only 216 (8 per cent) were present at the "Council of Lviv" to declare themselves for the imposed union. Hundreds of clergy and bishops, including Metropolitan Iosyf Slipyj, were imprisoned, and many died in captivity. Of the few who escaped some came to Canada. Today the Ukrainian Catholic Church exists only as an underground institution in Ukraine.

Protestantism did not take firm root among the Ukrainians until 1775, when the German Mennonites settled in the Zaporozhian region. By the second half of the nineteenth century, a pietistic and evangelical sect had emerged among the Ukrainian population. Called Stundists because of their observance of a specific number of hours (*stunden*) of devotions weekly, they eventually came to be known as Stundo-Baptists after coming under the influence of Baptist missionaries. By 1914, despite the persecution of the tsarist government and the Russian Orthodox Church, the Baptists and Evangelists claimed about two million converts in Russia. Under Soviet oppression, the Evangelical movement appears to have increased in numbers mainly because congregations can worship secretly without liturgical celebrations. Some Evangelical leaders have come to the Western world since the last war.

CHARACTER OF THE PIONEER UKRAINIAN SETTLERS

To understand religious developments among Ukrainian peasant-settlers in Canada, it is necessary to appreciate the old-country situation at their departure.[5] Whatever the peasants knew about the nature of society, the art of politics, and the benefits of religion was derived mainly from the parish priest, who enjoyed many privileges in the Austro-Hungarian Empire in exchange for loyalty to the Hapsburg emperor rather than the Romanov tsar. Because the Ukrainians in Galicia lacked their own nobility, the Greek Catholic clergy were provided with education, seminaries, and opportunities to enter university and became a hereditary caste which dominated the preponderantly rural society. Economically, the clergy were independent, being provided by the state with a residence, a tract of arable land and forest, a small salary, fees for teaching catechism in the village school, and donations from parishioners for baptisms, marriages, and funerals. The children of the married clergy (in the majority) shared in the benefits and gradually increased the ranks of the intelligentsia. The Ukrainian clerical elite thus possessed power and privileges similar to, if not quite as great as, those of the Polish nobility.

The peasant was brought up to fear God, to revere the benevolent emperor, to respect the authority of bishop and priests, and to obey his superiors. The natural state of society, governed by unfathomable universal laws which preserved peace, order, well-being, happiness, and the people's identity, required that the peasant be humble, hard-working, sincere, honest, resigned to his fate, and grateful for any blessings.

Accordingly, only a smali fraction of the intelligentsia felt impelled to accompany the peasantry on its trek to the New World. The intelligentsia that did come tended to be of peasant rather than clerical background. Many were influenced by the ideas of Mykhailo Drahomanov, whose radical populism affirmed the urgent necessity of enlightening the Ukrainian people in order to raise their social and national consciousness. In

Canada the radical populists denounced clericalism and the authoritarianism of the Catholic Church and advocated democratic lay control of parish properties and affairs in accordance with the traditions of the sixteenth-century Ukrainian Orthodox Church brotherhoods. Opposing the conservative policies associated with the Greek Catholic Church, as well as efforts by local Roman Catholic bishops to subordinate the Ukrainian immigrants to their own authority, the radical intelligentsia espoused the cause of an independent Ukrainian church and of Ukrainian nationalism.

EARLY CHURCH LIFE

In the process of settling the Prairies and organizing communities in the wilderness, the Ukrainians found the religious circumstances in Canada most perplexing, and many despaired.[6] The churches familiar to them sent no permanent priests to the new country for many years. The impoverished settlers at first built no church buildings of their own; such a responsibility had been in the hands of the state in the old country. They often gathered in private homes and chanted mass with prayers as best they could. For the christening of children and for burial services, marriages, and confession, some felt compelled to go to the Roman Catholic and Protestant clergy in the vicinity. Most disliked the practice, yet appeals for priests to authorities in the old country went practically unheeded. To fill the spiritual vacuum, the Canadian Roman Catholic Church and some Protestant denominations undertook home missionary work. The Russian Orthodox Church, too, sent itinerant priests. The resulting contest for souls greatly confused the peasant-farmers and the growing number of city workers. The bickering and bitter rivalry before World War I was in many ways reminiscent of the struggle for souls during the Reformation.

In response to the many appeals to the editor of *Svoboda*, a Ukrainian weekly published in Shamokin, Pennsylvania, several Greek Catholic priests from the United States toured the Ukrainian settlements. Reverend Nestor Dmytriw, a secular priest, was the first to visit settlements in Manitoba; in 1897 he conducted mass at Trembowla on Drifting River (near Dauphin, where a Cross of Freedom was erected and the first wooden church was built), at Stuartburn (where a church was also commenced), and at Winnipeg, Edmonton, Fort Saskatchewan, Rabbit Hill, and Edna-Star.

Reports of Dmytriw's visit brought an immediate reaction from Bishop Nicholas, the Russian Orthodox "Bishop of the Aleutians and Alaska" based in San Francisco, then under the jurisdiction of the Holy Synod at St. Petersburg, Russia. Late in June, 1897, two priests arrived in the Edna-Star community east of Edmonton, where the construction of a church was promptly approved. Alarmed, Dmytriw was back in September, accompanied by Bishop Emile J. Legal of the Roman Catholic diocese of St. Albert, who assumed offical jurisdiction and promised land for a church and financial assistance. A bitter struggle ensued between the Russian Orthodox and Greek Catholic factions, with the latter opposed to vesting the title in the Latin bishop. A second Uniate priest from the United States, Reverend Paul Tymkiewicz, visiting the community in April, 1898, supported the laity against the bishop. When the church was erected in the summer of 1899, Reverend Ivan Zaklynsky, another Greek Catholic priest from the United States, conducted the first service and again opposed Latin jurisdiction. Next year, a Russian Orthodox priest held a service in the same church, thus further complicating the situation. A court case ensued, which after bitter struggles in the Supreme Court of the Northwest Territories and the Supreme Court of Canada was appealed in 1907 to the Judicial Committee of the Privy Council in London, England, where it was decided that the church was legally the property of the Orthodox trustees. Thus strengthened, all trustees now found themselves in frequent opposition to priests and church leaders advocating hierarchical control of church property.

Winnipeg was a case in point. Archbishop Adélard Langevin[7] of St. Boniface at first opposed a separate Ukrainian parish and urged the Ukrainians to join the Polish Roman Catholic Holy Ghost Church. Nevertheless, in 1899 Reverend Damaskyn Polyvka from the United States established the Ukrainian (Greek Catholic) parish of St. Nicholas (now Sts. Vladimir and Olga). Thereupon the Ukrainian parishioners erected their own church building. When Reverend Zaklynsky came from the United States to assume clerical duties, Archbishop Langevin's demand that the church be incorporated under the Roman Catholic charter was rejected by the parishioners and the priest was ordered by the archbishop to leave. Demands for an independent Greek Catholic Church with married clergy spread throughout the Ukrainian settlements and did not subside for years.

With the Roman Catholic bishops in the United States (and Canada) strongly opposed to married secular Greek Catholic priests in North America, the Apostolic See bowed to their demands on April 12, 1894. However, only 3 per cent of the Ukrainian priests in Galicia were then celibate, and the Greek Catholic Church was thus faced with a tremendous hardship. When an American Roman Catholic bishop refused to recognize Reverend Alexander Toth (Alexii Tovt), a married secular priest from Carpatho-Ukraine, Toth and a large number of married Greek Catholic priests joined the Russian Orthodox Church in the United States. On May 1, 1897, the Sacred Congregation for the Propagation of the Faith, the Roman congregation in charge of missionary activity, placed Greek Catholic priests under the jurisdiction of Roman Catholic bishops in North America. Greek Catholic priests at conventions in Shamokin (May, 1901) and Harrisburg (March, 1902) opposed the "Latin domination" and demanded an independent, separate hierarchy responsible directly to the pope. The many defections to the Russian Orthodox Church brought a changed attitude and in 1907 the Greek Catholic Church in the United States, over the objections of the Roman Catholic hierarchy, received a bishop in the person of Father Soter Ortynsky, a Basilian monk from Galicia. Although a separate diocese was formed, Bishop Ortynsky became a suffragan (auxiliary) of each Roman Catholic bishop within whose boundaries the Greek Catholic parishes were located.

The French Roman Catholic hierarchy in western Canada was less hostile toward the Greek Catholic priests than the Irish bishops in the United States. When it became clear that Greek Catholic priests and faithful refused Roman Catholic supervision, Archbishop Langevin sent Father Albert Lacombe to Rome, Vienna, and Lviv. Regular (monastic) Greek Catholic priests were requested, but the Order of St. Basil the Great had few to spare. In 1901 Metropolitan Sheptytsky, head of the Greek Catholic Church in Galicia, sent his secretary, Reverend Vasyl Zholdak, to report on the situation in the Ukrainian settlements in North America. He recommended that three Basilians, twelve secular priests, and several nuns be sent out.

The First Permanent Priests and Bishop

As a result of the above efforts, Canada soon received the first permanent Latin-rite priest for the Ukrainians; the first permanent Greek Catholic priests, monks, and nuns; and the first bishop, under whom churches could be incorporated as Greek Catholic institutions. Archbishop Langevin's appeal in 1899 brought Belgian Redemptorist, Father Achille Delaere,[8] who learned Ukrainian and soon established several parishes. In 1906, with Rome's approval, he changed to the Byzantine rite and made his headquarters at Yorkton, Saskatchewan. Several other Belgian Redemptorists followed his example. Archbishop Langevin also prevailed upon five French-Canadian priests, Fathers Adonias Sabourin and Josaphat Jean among them, to accept the Byzantine rite and serve the Ukrainians. Father Delaere's influence helped in the appointment of the first Canadian Greek Catholic bishop in 1912 and in the founding of the Redemptorist order of the Eastern rite in Galicia in 1913 and later in Canada.

In response to Reverend Zholdak's recommendation, in 1902 Metropolitan Sheptytsky dispatched the first permanent Ukrainian clergymen to Canada. The group from Galicia comprised three priests of the Basilian order of monks (Fathers Platonid Filias, Sozont Dydyk, and Anton Strotsky), a brother, and four nuns of the Sisters Servants of Mary Immaculate, all of whom made their centre in Mundare, Alberta, near Edna-Star. They were followed by others, including a few celibate secular clergy, but there were never enough Ukrainian priests to meet the growing needs because married secular priests were not granted jurisdiction in Canada. Consequently, some parishes had to be aided by Roman Catholic clergy. The Basilians incorporated their church property with the Roman Catholic bishop under the title "The Congregation of the Greek Ruthenian Catholics United to Rome."

The attendance of Metropolitan Sheptytsky at the Eucharistic Congress in Montreal in 1910 was followed by a two-month tour of the Ukrainian communities as far as Vancouver. His promise to send more priests and to secure a bishop began a new chapter in the history of the Ukrainian Greek Catholic Church. In 1911 Archbishop Langevin prepared the ground for the first bishop by helping to establish in Winnipeg the first newspaper for Ukrainian Catholics - *Kanadyiskyi rusyn*, which in 1919 became *Kanadyiskyi ukrainets* - and by providing the Ukrainian Catholics with a two-storey parish school (St. Nicholas), which taught religion and Ukrainian in addition to the regular curriculum.

The first bishop for the Greek Catholics in Canada, Nicetas (Nykyta) Budka, the titular bishop of Patara, former prefect of the Greek Catholic Seminary in Lviv, and former chairman of the Ecclesiastical Judiciary and of Emigration Affairs, arrived in Winnipeg on December 19, 1912. Unlike Bishop Ortynsky, who earlier had come under the jurisdiction of the Roman Catholic hierarchy in the United States, Bishop Budka, with the sanction of the Canadian Roman Catholic hierarchy, was given full jurisdiction over the Greek Catholic Church, responsible directly to the pope. The new bishop immediately incorporated all the parishes under provincial charters and under an episcopal charter passed by the federal Parliament in 1913. The following year, Bishop Budka convoked a synod (*sobor*) of the priests at Yorkton, which approved the *Regulations of the Ruthenian Greek Catholic Church in Canada*,[9] consisting of careful instructions for the guidance of the clergy. These steps brought stability to the church and gave it the basis for the consolidation and expansion that followed.

Russian Orthodoxy and the Independent Greek Church

The ambiguously named Russian Orthodox Greek Catholic Church first exploited the growing tide of religious independence among the Ukrainians. There were many reasons for the pioneer settlers to gravitate toward the Russian church. By Orthodox rules, North America came solely under the Russian church because it was first on the continent; other Orthodox churches were therefore excluded. The Russian church also did not require the incorporation of parishes, which appealed to the settlers' newly acquired sense of freedom, and it used Old Church Slavonic, including the similar form of mass practised by the two Ukrainian churches. Of no small importance was the fact that the Holy Synod in St. Petersburg subsidized the church in North America to the extent of $77,950 annually and constant contributions came from the Missionary Society of Russia. The early settlers, having few means of their own, welcomed funds for church buildings and itinerant priests whose fees were minimal. Reverend Toth's conversion encouraged many Greek Catholic priests and adherents to influence other Greek Catholics to reject the "forced Union of Brest." On the other hand, it was not difficult for Russian priests to convince illiterate peasants that *rusyn* (Ruthenian) was identical with *russkii* (Russian) and Russified Ukrainian priests were used to agitate the settlers. The Russian Orthodox Church in North America, moreover, had able administrators such as Archbishop Platon (1907-14), who had experience with Uniates in Ukraine under Russia.

The greatest gains for the Russian Orthodox Church in Canada were made under the leadership of Archimandrite Arsenii Chekhovtsev in the years 1905-11 through a Winnipeg newspaper, *Kanadiiskaia nyva*, and a students' residence (*bursa*) in Edmonton. When he lost hope of becoming the Canadian bishop, he returned to Russia. The church, however, continued to expand, reaching its peak in 1916, when it claimed 110 parishes, 64 clergymen, and 117,000 faithful in North America.[10] After the Bolshevik Revolution, subsidies ended, the unpaid priests defected, and the church rapidly disintegrated.

A form of Russian Orthodoxy which also successfully exploited the religious vacuum among Ukrainians, albeit very briefly, was the All-Russian Patriarchal Orthodox Church, popularly known as the "Seraphimite" church. The founder, Stefan Ustvolsky, a monk who had formerly been associated with the Greek Orthodox monastic community on Mount Athos, called himself "Seraphim Bishop and Metropolitan of the Orthodox Russian Church for the whole of America." He was an imposter who displayed a forged document of an act of consecration by three eastern Orthodox archbishops. After rejection by a group of dissatisfied Greek Catholic priests in the United States, who were trying to establish an independent Ukrainian church, Ustvolsky came to Winnipeg where the immigration agent, Cyril Genik, and a number of his radical associates also were trying to establish a Ukrainian church that would be independent of the Roman Catholic and Russian Orthodox churches. With Genik's assistance, he quickly ordained about fifty priests and numerous deacons, some only semi-literate, who went into the rural Slavic communities, preaching both Orthodoxy independent of any patriarch and trustee ownership of property. In two years the movement claimed nearly 60,000 adherents.[11]

Provoked by their bishop's indiscriminate ordination or "sprinkling" of priests, his drinking sprees, and the ludicrous actions of his eccentric, simple-minded assistant, Makarii Marchenko, a group of priests, led by Reverend Ivan Bodrug, persuaded Ustvolsky to go to Russia in the fall of 1903 to seek sanction and support for his church from the Holy Synod. During his absence the dissatisfied clergy established the Independent Greek Church in 1904. When he returned empty-handed and learned of this diversion, he immediately excommunicated the leaders, who now refused to recognize his authority. When the Holy Synod excommunicated Ustvolsky and all the priests ordained by him, he left Canada for Russia in 1908.

The Independent Greek Church was founded by such old-country radicals as Genik, Bodrug, and Ivan Negrich, teachers and former students at Manitoba College, the latter also editor of *Kanadiiskyi farmer*, the first Ukrainian newspaper in Canada, founded in 1903. They made a secret arrangement with the Presbyterian Church for financial support and the adoption of certain Protestant teachings.[12] In 1905 a constitution was drawn up for the new church with the assistance of professors and Presbyterian ministers at Manitoba College. The Independent Greek Church was to be democratically governed. The *sobor* – the clergy and lay delegates from each parish – was to meet annually to determine policy and elect the consistory, headed by a superintendent – termed *epyskop* (bishop) in Ukrainian – responsible for ordaining clergy. Church property was to be administered by lay trustees. The shorter services were to be Orthodox in form, including vestments, but such "pagan" rituals as chanting, the use of incense and candles, the blessing of water and relics, and oral confession were to be gradually discarded. The faith was comprised of the seven sacraments and the Apostolic and Nicene Creeds. Mass confession was acceptable, but individual confession would be granted only upon request. The church, being independent, would have no ties with pope, patriarch, or the Russian Holy Synod.

Under "Bishop" Bodrug the church made rapid headway. A weekly publication, *Ranok*, was established in 1905 in Winnipeg. Special theology classes were taught at Manitoba College and *bursy* were founded in Winnipeg, Sifton, Teulon, and Vegreville. In 1907 the Independent Greek Church claimed thirty clergymen and 40,000 members,[13] causing grave concern in Greek Catholic and Roman Catholic circles. By 1912, however, with membership declining, the Presbyterian Church, claiming that little progress had been made in the direction of Presbyterianism, withdrew its subsidy, cancelled the theology classes at Manitoba College, and incorporated the remaining twenty-one clergy into its ranks. When Bodrug refused to follow and the congregations became aware of the Presbyterian action, most returned to Greek Catholicism or Russian Orthodoxy. The Independent Greek Church was much too complex an experiment for Protestants[14] and Ukrainians. Furthermore, it had to contend with the Greek Catholic Church and its new bishop and with the intelligentsia associated with *Ukrainskyi holos*, a new weekly founded in 1910 that advocated Ukrainian nationalism and a national Ukrainian church.

THE PERIOD OF INTERDENOMINATIONAL RIVALRY

The Impact of World War I

Canada's entry into the First World War put the Ukrainian settlers in an embarrassing and precarious position. Most were still subjects of the Austro-Hungarian Empire, now an enemy of Canada. Their position

First Ukrainian home, Emerson, Manitoba, 1896. (Manitoba Archives)

Ukrainian home, built c. 1910, Gardenton, Manitoba. (Manitoba Archives photo 1961)

Market, Sheho, Saskatchewan, 1909. (Manitoba Archives Collection W.J. Sisler-17)

Country wedding, 1917, Samburg, Saskatchewan. (Public Archives Canada PA-88459)

Family from the village of Ruskyi-Banyliv, Bukovyna, in Wasel, Alberta, c. 1922. (Multicultural History Society of Ontario)

Roadside chapel, Pruth, Alberta, c. 1930. (Public Archives Canada PA-113847)

Ruthenian Farmers Elevator Company, Arran, Saskatchewan, 1921. (Bobersky Collection, Oseredok, Winnipeg)

Below: Rural Christmas carollers with St. Nicholas (centre), Saskatchewan, 1929. (Bobersky Collection, Oseredok, Winnipeg)

Above: *Volodymyr Hryvnak's General Store, Wakaw, Saskatchewan, c. 1909. (S.W. Frolick, Toronto)*

Advertisement for board and room, Yorkton, Saskatchewan, 1920. (Bobersky Collection, Oseredok, Winnipeg)

Ukrainians making hay, Foley, Manitoba, 1905. (Manitoba Archives Collection W.J. Sisler-195)

Below: Ukrainian workers laying sewer pipe, Port Arthur, Ontario, 1922. (Bobersky Collection, Oseredok, Winnipeg)

String orchestra, Ridna Shkola, Fort William, Ontario, c. 1924. (S.W. Frolick, Toronto)

Ukrainian Sitch softball team, inter-city champions, Oshawa, Ontario, 1935.
(Multicultural History Society of Ontario)

Ukrainian section, Social Democratic Party, Hamilton, Ontario, 1916.
(Multicultural History Society of Ontario)

"The blessing of the flag," Ukrainian Hetman Organization, Kitchener, Ontario, 1934. (Multicultural History Society of Ontario)

Ukrainian pioneer settlers domesticating moose, Shepticky (now Lac Castagnier), Quebec, c. 1930. (Multicultural History Society of Ontario)

Ukrainian immigrants on Cunard liner, Aurania, *1934.*
(Multicultural History Society of Ontario)

Four Alberta oat kings: Paul Pavlowski (1940), John Eliuk (1948), Sidney Pavlowski (1948), William Skladan (1934-40). Fred Magera, District Agriculturalist (standing).
(Public Archives Canada PA-88539)

Ukrainian Canadian military personnel outside centre of the Ukrainian Canadian Servicemen's Association, London, England, November, 1945. (S.W. Frolick, Toronto)

Rural dramatics, Plum Ridge School, Pleasant Home, Manitoba, 1912.
(Public Archives Canada PA-88567)

Urban dramatics, P. Mohyla Ukrainian Institute, Saskatoon, Saskatchewan, 1919.
(Public Archives Canada PA-88604)

Celebration of sixtieth anniversary of Ukrainian life in Canada, Massey Hall, Toronto, 1952. (Multicultural History Society of Ontario)

Kalyna Co-op/Carpathia Credit Union Society, Winnipeg. (Oseredok, Winnipeg)

Prime Minister Louis St. Laurent addresses fourth Ukrainian Canadian Committee Congress, Winnipeg, July, 1953. (Public Archives Canada PA-124489)

Pioneers at sixtieth anniversary of Ukrainian settlement in Canada, Winnipeg, 1951. (Public Archives Canada PA-124490)

Unveiling of Shevchenko statue, Manitoba Legislative Grounds, 1961. (Oseredok, Winnipeg)

Dance group at festival, Dauphin, Manitoba, 1970. (R.B. Klymasz, Winnipeg)

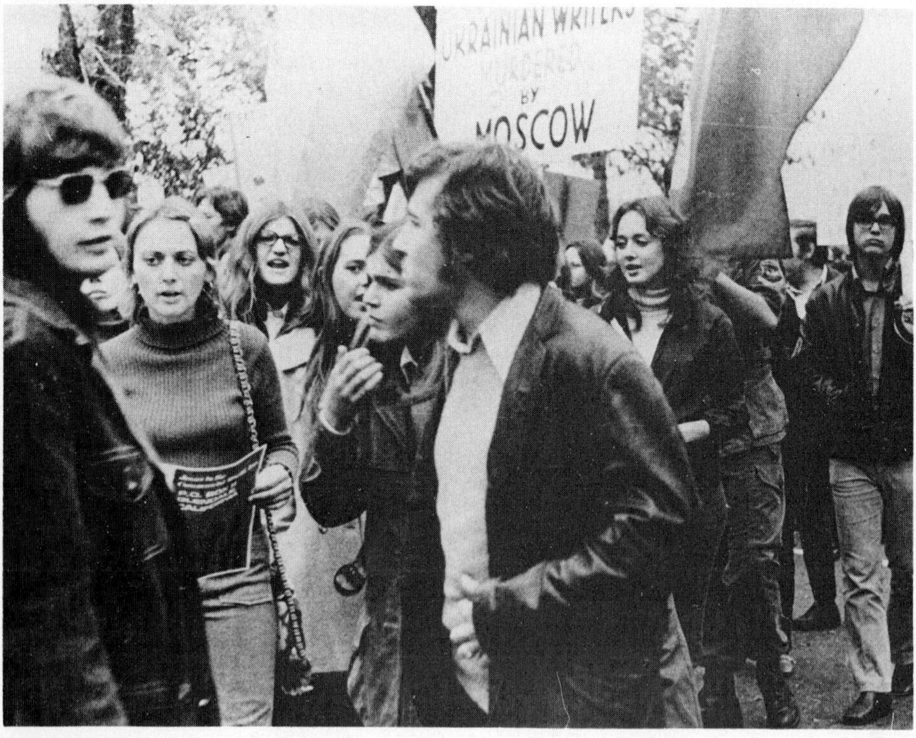

Ukrainian anti-Soviet demonstration, Ottawa, 1971.
(Multicultural History Society of Ontario)

was greatly aggravated at the outset by Bishop Budka's pastoral letter of July 27. Loyal to the Catholic Hapsburgs, convinced that Austria would grant Ukrainians a large measure of regional autonomy after the war, and concerned that the invading Russian armies would destroy Ukrainian institutions in Galicia, Budka urged Ukrainians who were Austrian citizens to come to the defence of the fatherland by joining the Austrian army.[15] Upon learning of Canada's subsequent declaration of war, he issued another pastoral letter on August 6, renouncing his previous statement and urging support for the Canadian war effort.

Nonetheless, throughout the war the intelligentsia, mainly public school teachers in bilingual (English-Ukrainian) schools and some university students backed by *Holos*, were highly critical of Bishop Budka's leadership. They condemned his pro-Austrian pastoral letter and lashed out against the "Latinization" of the Greek Catholic Church, demanding that the Belgian, French, and other celibate priests be removed. They criticized the episcopal charter that granted the bishop unrestricted powers subject only to Rome. With no explicit provision for a Ukrainian bishop, they feared that should the pope appoint a non-Ukrainian, all property would be lost. The struggle intensified in 1916 when the teachers established an interdenominational *bursa* in Saskatoon and named it after Petro Mohyla, the seventeenth-century Ukrainian Orthodox Church leader. The bishop's request that the residence come under the charter of the Ruthenian Greek Catholic Church was rejected.

Led by law students Wasyl Swystun and Michael Stechishin and by Wasyl Kudryk, editor of *Holos*, a large anti-Catholic movement set out to revive the practices of the Ukrainian Orthodox brotherhoods of the seventeenth century. The principal demands included the election of bishops and priests, with emphasis on the married clergy, and the right of laymen to manage church finances and all secular activities. The new church, which emerged before the end of the war, was to be an independent, democratic, national Ukrainian church.

The rapidly growing tide of Ukrainian nationalism greatly helped the cause of the intelligentsia, who closely followed events in their homeland. The collapse of Russian tsardom in April, 1917, the establishment of the Ukrainian Central Rada (Council) followed by the Ukrainian National Republic, and the emergence of a sovereign Ukrainian state on January 22, 1918, had an electrifying effect. The nationalistic spirit aroused was carried over into church affairs and support for an independent, national Ukrainian church, subject to no foreign interference and in charge of its own affairs, swiftly increased among Ukrainians in Canada.

The Founding of the Ukrainian Greek Orthodox Church

The formation of a "Ukrainian National Church" was strongly urged on the pages of *Holos* and *Farmer*. A conference "to discuss church and national affairs" was called by Wasyl Swystun, principal of the Mohyla

Ukrainian Institute, and endorsed by a "National Committee" of thirty leaders from the three Prairie Provinces. Attended by 154 delegates, the conference, held in Saskatoon on July 18-19, 1918, established a Ukrainian Greek Orthodox Brotherhood to organize a church in communion with the other eastern Orthodox churches.[16] The church would have the dogmas and rites of Eastern Orthodoxy; priests would be expected to marry; church property would be owned by the congregations; bishops would be elected by a general council (*sobor*) of the clergy and the delegates of the brotherhoods and congregations; and church congregations would have the right to accept and discharge priests.

Of greatest urgency to the new church was recognition by an eastern Orthodox church and the securing of priests. The first *sobor* in Saskatoon on December 28, 1918, approved and confirmed the establishment of the church and elected a committee to prepare the charter and statutes. Several Ukrainian priests of the declining Russian Orthodox Church served parishes in the Prairie Provinces, but arrangements for recognition by Metropolitan Platon of the Ukrainian Autocephalous Orthodox Church, who had come from Ukraine to New York on a visit, were not carried out. The second *sobor* in Winnipeg on November 27, 1919, was held in the presence of Metropolitan Germanos Shegedi of the Syrian Orthodox Church in the United States, who took the new church under his spiritual wing until a Ukrainian bishop could be elected. Seminary classes for clergy were conducted in Saskatoon for one year and in March, 1920, the following priests (all married) graduated: Reverends Semen W. Sawchuk, Dmytro F. Stratychuk, and Peter Sametz. All were ordained by Metropolitan Germanos, and Reverend Sawchuk, the church's administrator, conducted the first mass in the Ukrainian language in Saskatoon on June 18, 1920.

Finding a Ukrainian bishop, however, proved to be a much more difficult problem. Reverend Sawchuk travelled to Europe, but because of the hostility of the Bolshevik government was unable to make contacts in Ukraine. The matter was finally settled at the fourth *sobor* in Yorkton, July 16-17, 1924, when Archbishop Ivan Theodorovich, a bishop of the Ukrainian Autocephalous Orthodox Church in Ukraine and newly created head of the Ukrainian Orthodox Church in the United States, accepted the Canadian post, which he held until his resignation in 1946. The general council also formally decided to replace the Old Church Slavonic with the Ukrainian language in the liturgy. With Archbishop Theodorovich's seat in the United States, the affairs of the Ukrainian Greek Orthodox Church were conducted by the consistory, headed by Reverend Sawchuk. The church at the time had fourteen priests and over 100 parishes, a monthly organ, *Pravoslavnyi vistnyk*, which in 1928 became a bimonthly entitled *Visnyk*, and the support of the influential *Holos* and *Farmer*. In 1932 a seminary for the training of clergy was established in Winnipeg and the church's organizational work and membership surged ahead. In 1935 there were 180 parishes in five provinces:

Alberta, fifty-three; Saskatchewan, seventy-six; Manitoba, forty-three; Ontario, seven; and Quebec, one.

Adherents came initially from the defunct Independent Greek Church and the disintegrating Russian Orthodox Church and from dissatisfied Greek Catholics, especially those who espoused the causes of independence, married clergy, and trustee ownership of church property. A large number came from the Orthodox Bukovynians, their national consciousness aroused by events in Ukraine. While Greek Catholics, too, came to question the use of the term Ruthenian for their church, it was the Orthodox who were associated most with the growth of Ukrainian consciousness and nationalism. Their basic church orientation encouraged both a national and religious identity, propagated by the Mohyla Institute and the Michael (Mykhailo) Hrushevsky Institute in Edmonton. In 1927 leading members of the Orthodox laity established the Ukrainian Self-Reliance League, with auxiliaries for women and youth. Although concerned mainly with cultural and political matters, the League was also a strong supporter of the Ukrainian Greek Orthodox Church.

In the 1930's the church went through a stormy period. Wasyl Swystun, one of its founders and a prominent leader of the Mohyla Institute and the Ukrainian Self-Reliance League, charged Archbishop Theodorovich and the Orthodox consistory in Canada with deviating from the union with the Ukrainian Autocephalous Orthodox Church in Ukraine under Metropolitan Vasyl Lypkivsky. Swystun was supported by the cathedral parish of St. Mary in Winnipeg and a separate "brotherhood," which published a newspaper, *Ridna tserkva*. He was sustained by the Supreme Court of Canada in 1940, but the synods in Saskatoon in 1935 and 1940 condemned his actions and he and his followers were ostracized. The turbulence had no noticeable effect on church expansion. In 1941 the Orthodox Church counted 88,874 members in 203 congregations, comprising 28 per cent of the Ukrainian population.

The Catholic Counter-offensive

Bishop Budka and his clergy, mostly non-Ukrainian at the time, were naturally most disturbed that *Holos* and the Mohyla Institute should become the implacable foes of the Ruthenian Greek Catholic Church. Former Greek Catholics, who now espoused the democratic control of church finances, independently operated educational and cultural activities, and the selection of priests by independent parishes, undermined the authority of the church and ran counter to all established notions of social order. Such people were considered seditious, heretical, and schismatic: they could only destroy the sacred foundations of the traditional church. Accordingly, the distraught bishop and his clergy refused to send priests to dissident parishes, threatened excommunication, and denied church burials to unrepentent persons.

Such measures appeared actually to strengthen the anti-Catholic movement. The formation of the Ukrainian Greek Orthodox Church thus became a watershed in the history of Ukrainian Canadians, causing a deep ferment in most communities, bitter controversies over church rituals and calendar changes, and a religious tension that occasionally exploded into violence. Buildings were moved and at times even burned, families were divided, and inflammatory articles regularly filled the newspaper pages.

To counteract the Ukrainian Orthodox movement and the rapidly expanding pro-Soviet Ukrainian Labour-Farmer Temple Association, the leaders of the Greek Catholic Church had to adopt an ideology and establish a secular organization of their own. Initially they tried to ally themselves with the Ukrainian monarchists (*hetmantsi*), the supporters of Hetman Pavlo Skoropadsky, a descendant of the eighteenth-century Ukrainian Cossack hetmans, who with German support had ousted the democratic and moderately socialist Ukrainian Central Rada and governed Ukraine from April to November, 1918. The monarchists' commitment to the principles of hierarchy and authority and their positive evaluation of the church were especially appealing to the Catholic clergy. The link between monarchist circles in Europe and the Greek Catholic Church in North America was provided by Osyp Nazaruk, a disenchanted Galician radical who came to Canada in 1922 as an emissary of the Western Ukrainian National Republic. Convinced that monarchism and Catholicism provided the antidote to the "anarchism" inherent in the Ukrainian character, he moved to the United States, assumed control of Sich (Sitch), a Ukrainian-American society originally founded on democratic principles, and transformed it into a semi-military vehicle for the dissemination of monarchist propaganda. After Nazaruk left Canada, Volodymyr (Vladimir) Bossy, a recent arrival who had participated in the armed struggle for Ukrainian independence, became the leading figure in the monarchist movement. In 1924 he began organizing branches of the Canadian Sich organization and twenty-one companies were established by 1927. The Greek Catholic Church gave the monarchist group full support in its paper, *Kanadyiskyi ukrainets*, and in 1924 Bishop Budka declared the monarchist idea to be the most suitable "because it inculcates respect for the Church and Her Authority." In 1926 Bossy was made editor of *Ukrainets* after a successful conference of the Sich in Yorkton in conjunction with the congress of the Greek Catholic Church. The bishop was pleased to state that such combined efforts were beneficial. The parishes had tripled to 256, the clergy had grown from seventeen to forty-six, and at Yorkton a boys' college had been established with the aid of the Roman Catholic Church.[17]

Polemics in the *Ukrainets* against the Orthodox leaders, however, resulted in a lawsuit[18] for libel and in 1925 the newspaper was ordered to pay a fine of $7,000. When it defaulted, it was sold and eventually ceased publication in 1927. Ill and depressed, Bishop Budka left for Rome and then Lviv; he never returned to Canada.

His successor, Bishop Basil Vladimir Ladyka, nominated by the Vatican and ordained as the titular bishop of Abidi in 1929, was a Basilian priest who had arrived in Canada in 1909 and had completed theology in the Roman Catholic Grand Séminaire in Montreal. With the aid of the Basilian order and several laymen, he immediately established a newspaper, *Ukrainski visti*, in Edmonton. The paper was at first edited by prominent Sich members. In 1932 Reverend Stepan Semchuk, a secular priest, and Fred Mamchur, a teacher, founded the Ukrainian Catholic Brotherhood in Saskatoon, a lay organization whose objective was to defend the church and counteract the work of the Orthodox Ukrainian Self-Reliance League.

Bishop Ladyka, with support from the Basilians and Redemptorists in Europe, devoted his energy to strengthening and expanding the church. He obtained many new priests (mostly secular) from Western Ukraine, including Reverend Basil (Wasyl) Kushnir, who became his vicar-general and later president of the Ukrainian Canadian Committee. Important support and assistance were given by new training institutions, residential schools, and the Ukrainian Catholic Brotherhood. Intensive work stemmed the inroads of Orthodoxy and infused a new dynamism into all ranks of the church. As a result, in 1931, out of a Ukrainian population of 225,113, at least 58 per cent continued to belong to the Greek Catholic Church, as opposed to 24.6 per cent in the new Ukrainian Greek Orthodox Church. The diocese consisted of 350 parishes and listed 100 priests, of whom fifty-eight were secular, revealing a new trend.[19] Despite the criticism of Orthodox and lay leaders, it was not until 1951 that the name of the church was officially changed to "Ukrainian Catholic Church" by Canadian statute.

After the establishment of the Ukrainian Catholic Brotherhood, the role and membership of the Ukrainian Sich Association within the Greek Catholic Church declined rapidly. In 1934 the group reorganized as the United Hetman Organization and continued to wield considerable influence within the church, as evidenced by the enthusiastic welcome given to Hetman Skoropadsky's son, "Prince" Danylo, who toured Canada in 1937-38, and by the fact that for many years Wasyl Dyky, a leading Hetmanite, was editor of the church organ, *Ukrainski visti*.

The Effects of World War II

During the 1930's the structure and position of Ukrainian-Canadian society changed greatly. The population rose from 225,000 in 1931 to 306,000 by 1941, 65 per cent of whom were Canadian-born. To the earlier tide of Ukrainian nationalism was added a growing feeling of Canadian patriotism, natural with the second generation but present also among old and new immigrants. More conscious of the loss of freedom in Ukraine (the result, in part, of the admonitions and work of the Ukrainian churches), Ukrainians in Canada came to see the churches in the old country as a bulwark of liberal democracy against the twin forces of totalitarian fascism and bolshevism.

Accordingly, when Canada entered World War II, the Ukrainian-Canadian organizations and churches immediately reaffirmed their loyalty to the Canadian government and pledged their wholehearted support for the war effort. The crushing of the democratic Carpatho-Ukrainian state by Hitler's ally, Hungary, in March, 1939, helped to unite the Ukrainians against Hitler. Furthermore, the Nazi-Soviet Pact of August, 1939, between the two arch-enemies of Ukrainian independence served to strengthen the faith of Ukrainian Canadians in the cause of the Allies.

The Canadian government, pleased with such spontaneous loyalty, convinced the leaders of the various Ukrainian organizations that a strong co-ordinating body was necessary to realize common endeavours. With the formation of the Ukrainian Canadian Committee in October, 1940, all legal Ukrainian-Canadian associations, including the churches, were united in a common cause.

The Ukrainian churches did not participate directly in the formation of the Ukrainian Canadian Committee but were involved through the representatives of their lay organizations. The president of the Committee for thirty years, however, was Reverend Kushnir, representing the Ukrainian Catholic Brotherhood, and the vice-president, for almost as long, was Reverend Sawchuk, representing the Ukrainian Self-Reliance League. Ukrainian Protestant sects were also encouraged to join and they sent their representatives.

In supporting the Committee, the churches ceased open hostility for the duration of the war, thereby greatly contributing to the success of military recruiting efforts, government campaigns to sell war bonds, the work of the Red Cross, and the rehabilitation of war veterans. To minister to the spiritual needs of the approximately 35,000 Ukrainian men and women in the Canadian armed forces, the Greek Catholic Church assigned three chaplains: Reverends M. Pelech (H/Major), M. Horoshko, and T. Dobko. The three Greek Orthodox Church chaplains were Reverends S.W. Sawchuk, S.P. Symchych, and T. Kowalyshyn. All served in Great Britain and/or Europe.

After the war, the Ukrainian Canadian Relief Fund, a gigantic undertaking made possible only through the combined efforts of all the organizations and churches within the Ukrainian Canadian Committee, brought aid to the Ukrainian victims of war in Europe. It raised over $400,000 and thousands of food and clothing parcels for the unfortunate and destitute refugees in the displaced persons' camps in Europe. Arrangements with the Department of Immigration brought nearly 40,000 Ukrainian immigrants to Canada.

Although this third wave of Ukrainian immigrants caused considerable ferment in Ukrainian-Canadian society, they did join the established Ukrainian churches. A large number of refugee clergy also strengthened the hierarchies of the same churches, providing bishops and priests from the churches destroyed by the Soviet government and pastors for some of the Ukrainian Protestant denominations.

POST-WAR DEVELOPMENTS

The Ukrainian Catholic Church since 1945

The liquidation of the Ukrainian Catholic Church by the Soviet regime in Western Ukraine in 1946 and the presence in western Europe of several hundred refugee clergy prompted the papacy to study the future of the Ukrainian church in North America. In 1947 Eugene Cardinal Tisserant, secretary of the Sacred Congregation for Eastern Churches, visited several centres in Canada and on March 3, 1948, the pope announced the establishment of three exarchates for the Ukrainian Catholics in Canada. On June 21 Bishop Ladyka became titular archbishop of the central exarchate and spiritual head of the church with his see in Winnipeg, where he remained until his death in 1956. Bishop Maxim Hermaniuk, a Redemptorist who had studied in Belgium and had been Ladyka's auxiliary since 1951, succeeded him. The eastern exarchate in Toronto was headed by Bishop Isidore Borecky, a secular priest who had come to Canada in 1937, and the western exarchate in Edmonton was placed under Bishop Neil Savaryn, a Basilian trained in Canada and the auxiliary in Winnipeg since 1943. In 1951 the Saskatchewan exarchate in Saskatoon, headed by Bishop Andrew Roborecky, a secular priest trained in Canada, was carved out of the central exarchate. After Archbishop Ladyka's death, Pope Pius XII established the Ukrainian Catholic metropolitan see in Winnipeg, raising the four existing exarchates to eparchies (dioceses) headed by Metropolitan Hermaniuk. In 1974 the exarchate of New Westminster for British Columbia, headed by Bishop Jerome Chimy, a Basilian, was created within the western eparchy. Simultaneously, Bishop Savaryn became head of the eparchy of Edmonton, while Bishop Demetrius Greschuk, a former secular priest, became his auxiliary.

It is beyond the scope of this essay to survey the work of the eparchies, the monastic orders, and the various lay organizations associated with the churches. The secular priests (some married) dominate the work of the parishes, but they are not organized as a body. Systematic work and activities in the religious, educational, and cultural fields are done by the monastic orders, the backbone of the church. The Basilians,[20] who came to Canada as pioneers in 1902, are the largest order. In 1948 they were constituted as a separate province, headed mainly by Canadian-born men. Their original and chief centre is Mundare, Alberta, where they operate a large library, archives, and museum. Winnipeg is the seat of the provincial; St. Basil's College is operated in Toronto, and a seminary exists in Ottawa.

In 1945 the Ukrainian Redemptorists became an off-shoot of the order in Brussels; their centre is Yorkton where the vice-provincials have been Fathers Joseph Bala, Maxim Hermaniuk (later metropolitan), and Vladimir Malanchuk, who became bishop of the Ukrainian Catholic Church in France. In 1961 the Ukrainian Redemptorist congregation became a separate province; Winnipeg is the seat of the provincial, but the chief centre is Yorkton, with a printing press. The Redemptorists operate St. Vladimir's College for boys in Roblin, Manitoba, and a novitiate in Yorkton. The Studite Brothers, established in Canada in 1951, have a monastery in Woodstock, Ontario, and until recently the Brothers of the Christian Schools operated St. Joseph's College in Yorkton.

The membership of various congregations of nuns has been steadily increasing and their work has been expanding in such educational and social services as kindergartens, schools, orphanages, homes for senior citizens, hospitals, and stores for liturgical vestments. The oldest and largest order, founded in 1902, is the Sisters Servants of Mary Immaculate, with the provincial seat in Toronto. They manage the Immaculate Heart of Mary School in Winnipeg, the Sacred Heart Academy in Yorkton, the Mount Mary Immaculate Academy in Ancaster, Ontario (where the novitiate from Mundare was transferred in 1946), two hospitals, and several orphanages and homes for the aged. The Sisters of St. Joseph serve the Saskatchewan diocese, while the Missionary Sisters of Christian Charity are active in the Toronto eparchy.

The hierarchy of the Ukrainian Catholic Church, serving over 600 parishes and missions with numerous institutions and publications, is supported by several lay organizations with branches throughout Canada. Besides the Ukrainian Catholic Brotherhood, Ukrainian Catholic Women's League of Canada, and Ukrainian Catholic Youth, university students and graduates are organized in the Obnova (Renewal) societies. There are several branches of the Knights of Columbus with Ukrainian sections. The Ukrainian Mutual Benefit Association of St. Nicholas, founded in 1905, provides funeral expenses and life insurance for members. There are many altar societies, children's societies, sisterhoods, and brotherhoods. Each diocese has a council to co-ordinate the work of the societies in the eparchy. The national activities of all these organizations, nearly 500 units with over 25,000 members, are co-ordinated by the Ukrainian Catholic Council in Winnipeg. This vast network of organizations is the mainstay of the church.

Since the early 1960's, a vigorous movement for the establishment of a Ukrainian patriarchate has been gaining momentum. The movement has its current origins in 1963 when Metropolitan Iosyf Slipyj, Archbishop-Major and head of the Ukrainian Catholic Church, was released by the Soviet government from a concentration camp after eighteen years of imprisonment. In 1965 at the Ecumenical Vatican Council in Rome, Pope Paul VI elevated Metropolitan Slipyj to the rank of cardinal. Almost concurrently the Vatican Council issued a decree highly favourable to the traditional Eastern Christian institution of the patriarchate. Consequently, in 1969 a synod in Rome of twenty-eight Ukrainian Catholic bishops from various parts of the free world recognized the cardinal as the primate of their church and petitioned Pope Paul VI to erect a Ukrainian Catholic patriarchate. Although this initiative did not have the unanimous support of the laity, clergy, or bishops, lay organizations have strongly supported it, especially during the three visits of the cardinal to Canada in 1968, 1973, and 1976, the latter after the cardinal had assumed the title of "patriarch" without papal authorization. To its advocates, the creation of a Ukrainian Catholic patriarchate is necessary because the Ukrainian Catholic Church is numerically the largest Eastern church; because Ukrainian Catholics, who are dispersed around the world, need a unifying figure; and because they believe it would be a great moral boost to the underground church in Ukraine. They fear that pressure from Moscow, with which the Vatican has begun a diplomatic dialogue, has prevented the realization of their ambitions.

The Ukrainian Greek Orthodox Church since 1945

The leaders of the Ukrainian Greek Orthodox Church were unhappy with their acting bishop, Archbishop Ivan Theodorovich, who also headed the Ukrainian Orthodox Church in the United States and sought to rectify his own consecration, which other Orthodox churches considered uncanonical. When the archbishop tendered his resignation in 1946, Reverend Sawchuk travelled to Europe to meet with bishops of the Ukrainian Autocephalous Orthodox Church, who had fled from Soviet-occupied Ukraine. Arrangements were made for a new bishop. At the extraordinary *sobor* held in Winnipeg on November 12-13, 1947, Archbishop Mstyslaw Skrypnyk, a former politician, was elected head of the Ukrainian Greek Orthodox Church. However, he was soon in difficulty with the consistory.[21] Accordingly, at the tenth *sobor* in Winnipeg in October, 1950, Archbishop Skrypnyk resigned, later to become metropolitan of the Ukrainian Orthodox Church in the United States.

A second extraordinary *sobor* was convoked in Winnipeg on August 8-9, 1951, the most significant in the history of the church. It was decided to make the Ukrainian Greek Orthodox Church fully autocephalous by electing three bishops, thus ensuring a self-perpetuating hierarchy free of foreign entanglements. (According to canonical succession, any two bishops may consecrate a third.) The European church offered two candidates but one died in Canada on his way to the assembly, shattering for a while longer the hope of establishing a full hierarchy. The assembly unanimously elected Archbishop Michael Choroshy and offered the bishop's rank to arch-priest Wasyl Kudryk, who declined. To the great pleasure of the delegates, Metropolitan Ilarion (Ivan) Ohienko,[22] associated with the alienated St. Mary the Protectress Cathedral parish, offered his candidature, and upon accepting the terms offered in a contract approved by the delegates, was elected unanimously. By becoming a metropolitanate the hierarchy of the church was consummated and autocephaly was assured. On November 4, St. Mary's parish followed their spiritual leader and reunited with the Ukrainian Greek Orthodox Church, which now blossomed out in many directions. The new primate was a distinguished personality. A former minister of education and of confessions in the government of the Ukrainian National Republic (1918-20), a former archbishop of Kholm and Pidliashia of the Autocephalous Orthodox Church in Poland, a recognized scholar in philology, history, and theology, the author of numerous books, a publisher of many periodicals, and an energetic promoter of Ukrainian culture, Metropolitan Ohienko guided the growing work and expansion of the church until his death in 1972.

At first, the Ukrainian Greek Orthodox Church was divided into three eparchies, similar to the Ukrainian Catholic Church. The central eparchy, comprising Manitoba and Saskatchewan, was headed by Metropolitan Ohienko, who assumed the title of "Metropolitan of Winnipeg and all Canada." A new cathedral, Holy Trinity, was erected on Main Street in Winnipeg. The eastern eparchy was headed by Archbishop Michael Choroshy, with the see in Toronto. After his death in 1976, he was succeeded by Bishop Nicholas Debryn. The western eparchy, consisting of Alberta and British Columbia with the see in Edmonton, did not receive a bishop until 1959, when Reverend Andrew Metiuk, a popular priest of the parish of St. Mary the Protectress in Winnipeg, was elevated to the rank of archbishop, with the see in Edmonton. He was the first bishop to be consecrated in Canada. In 1963 Saskatchewan became the fourth eparchy, with the see in Saskatoon under Bishop Borys Yakowlewych, previously the auxiliary to Metropolitan Ohienko. When the church *sobor* in Winnipeg elected Archbishop Metiuk metropolitan in 1975, Bishop Yakowlewych was raised to the rank of archbishop of Edmonton and the western diocese. In 1978 Bishop Wasyly Fedak received jurisdiction over the diocese of Saskatoon and central Canada.

A notable achievement of the Ukrainian Orthodox Church in Canada was the establishment of St. Andrew's College in Winnipeg in 1946. Beginning as a senior high school and theological seminary, the institution affiliated with the University of Manitoba in 1960 and erected a fine large building on the campus, with a library, classrooms, and full residential facilities. The departments of philosophy and theology prepare students for the priesthood; instruction is in Ukrainian. A Bachelor of Arts degree can be obtained in conjunction with the Faculty of Arts. During the formative years Reverend Sawchuk was the rector of St. Andrew's, the only Ukrainian Orthodox college in North America. In 1979 the College's Centre for Ukrainian Canadian Studies became an integral part of the university.

The work of the church, with about 100 clergy serving over 300 parishes, is supported by the network of the Ukrainian Self-Reliance

League, the Ukrainian Women's Association of Canada, and the Canadian Ukrainian Youth Association. The organizations operate the Mohyla Ukrainian Institute in Saskatoon, St. John's (formerly Hrushevky) Institute in Edmonton, and St. Vladimir's Institute in Toronto, all basically students' residences with cultural, educational, and recreational facilities. The newspaper organ remains *Ukrainskyi holos*, owned by Trident Publishers, who issue magazines, pamphlets, and books for the organizations and the church, as well as books, texts, and materials in the broad fields of Ukrainian history, general literature, church affairs, politics, and culture.

Metropolitan Skrypnyk's departure underlined a basic problem within the Ukrainian Orthodox movement in North America, and the long and sometimes thorny process toward unity appeared to achieve success on the eve of the second World Congress of Free Ukrainians in Toronto in 1973.[23] On October 31 and November 1 the church *sobor*, the bishops, and representatives of three metropolitanates - the Ukrainian Greek Orthodox Church in Canada, the Ukrainian Orthodox Church in the United States, and the Ukrainian Autocephalous Orthodox Church in Europe - agreed unanimously that the metropolitanates constitute "One Ukrainian Orthodox Church in the Free World," which would consult at annual church synods (*sobory*) or more often if necessary. Another resolution declared that "mutual relations with the Patriarchate of Constantinople, as the traditional centre of universal Orthodoxy, remain on the basis of the Full Autocephaly of the Ukrainian Orthodox Church of the free world." The church *sobor* also gave general approval to co-operation with other churches and to the establishment of a Council of Ukrainian Churches. The spirit of co-operation was subsequently clouded by serious reservations within the Ukrainian Greek Orthodox Church in Canada.[24]

Smaller numbers of Ukrainians belong to other Orthodox churches. In Canada there are several parishes of the Ukrainian Orthodox Church of America, catering mainly to Bukovynians. Formerly under Metropolitan Bohdan Shpylka, who recognized the jurisdiction of the patriarch of Constantinople, in 1967 the church was headed by Bishop Andrew Kushchak. In Canada the "Sobor of Ivan Suchawsky" on Main Street and Flora Avenue in Winnipeg constitutes that church's cathedral. A few hundred Ukrainians continue to belong to the Russian Orthodox Greek Catholic Church of North America, so prominent in the life of Ukrainian settlers in the pioneer period. The Canadian parishes are under the jurisdiction of a metropolitan in New York. The most important question for the leaders and members of the Russian Orthodox Church is whether to recognize the jurisdiction of the Russian patriarchate controlled by the Soviet regime. The resistance to the move has been strong. A few parishes with Ukrainian members in Canada recognize the Moscow patriarchate through Archbishop Panteleimon Rudyk and Bishop Makarii Swystun in the United States.

Protestant Churches

Since Ukrainians have traditionally adhered to ritualistic liturgy and because of their nationalistic attitude, Protestantism has been generally an alien religion, and the failure of the Independent Greek Church could have been predicted. Protestantism, however, has had some success among individuals who had previously belonged to Protestant denominations in Ukraine and in recent years has been making steady progress among the Canadian-born.

Most of the twenty-one clergy of the Independent Greek Church and their small congregations later joined the United Church of Canada. Others hoped to form an Independent Ukrainian Evangelical Church. Among its most prominent clergymen have been Ivan Bodrug, Paul Crath (Pavlo Krat), Luka Standret, and Vasyl Borowsky. The advocates of a Ukrainian Evangelical Church work closely with the Ukrainian Evangelical Alliance of North America, established in 1922 in Rochester, New York, by Ukrainian-Canadian and Ukrainian-American evangelical Protestants.

The early Ukrainian Baptists in Canada were associated with the Russian Stundists until after World War I. In 1921 Reverend Peter Kindrat began to preach in Ukrainian and separate Ukrainian congregations gradually formed, especially in the 1930's when Reverend Ivan Kmeta-Ichniansky assumed the leadership in Saskatoon and established a Bible school to train pastors and preachers. After World War II, with the arrival of preachers and adherents from Ukraine, the Ukrainian Evangelical Baptist Union of Canada was headquartered in Winnipeg. The Evangelical Union is a member of the All-Ukrainian Evangelical Baptist World Alliance, which co-operates with the central Ukrainian bodies in both countries.

There are numerous Ukrainians in such other large Protestant denominations as the United Church and the Anglican, Presbyterian, and Lutheran churches. Few have separate congregations and some have only a few communities. The Canadian Pentecostal Church, the Seventh Day Adventists, the Jehovah's Witnesses, and the Lutheran church sponsor Ukrainian radio programs and publish magazines, books, and pamphlets in Ukrainian and English. These groups are not an integral part of the Ukrainian-Canadian community and do not co-operate with other Ukrainian organizations or the Ukrainian Canadian Committee.

Co-operation among the Churches

The differences between the Ukrainian Catholic Church and the Ukrainian Orthodox Church are not marked. In Canada both churches maintain the same rite, traditions, customs, and the Ukrainian language in the liturgy (although until a few years ago, the Catholic Church used Old Church Slavonic). The Orthodox Church still adheres to the old Julian calendar, while the Catholic Church has allowed most of its parishes to change to the Gregorian calendar, the one officially in use in Canada.

With the Orthodox Church in support of a married priesthood, the vast majority of priests are married and therefore cannot become bishops unless widowed; within the Ukrainian Catholic Church celibacy prevails in Canada, though occasionally married clergy have been admitted from Europe after receiving special papal permission. The Orthodox Church, proudly Ukrainian and markedly nationalistic, claims that the Catholic Church has departed from Ukrainianism by using English in sermons and at times in the liturgy in many parishes in order to appeal to mixed marriages. Because of the similarities, however, the ecumenical movement has raised the question of possible union under a common Ukrainian patriarchate. The Orthodox leaders have not been enthusiastic, fearing a patriarchate under the pope. They favour an independent Orthodox patriarchate and have recently indicated their willingness to co-operate to a limited extent in a Council of Ukrainian Churches.

There have been instances where the two churches have co-operated, particularly when Ukrainian national interests have predominated. In 1961, on the occasion of the seventieth anniversary of Ukrainian settlement in Canada, a huge bronze statue of Taras Shevchenko was unveiled on the grounds of the Manitoba legislature in Winnipeg to honour the greatest Ukrainian poet on the centenary of his death. The unveiling ceremony, attended by approximately 50,000 people, saw the Catholic and Orthodox metropolitans conduct a joint prayer service. The churches have also co-operated at the annual religious ceremony of the Cross of Freedom, erected in 1897 on the occasion of the building of the first Ukrainian church in Canada at Drifting River, near Dauphin, Manitoba; this ceremony is held regularly during Canada's National Ukrainian Festival, an annual event since 1966, attended by tens of thousands from across the country.

The greatest manifestation of religious co-operation and solidarity was demonstrated at the second World Congress of Free Ukrainians, November 1-4, 1973, in Toronto. Before approximately 15,000 people, the first conciliar prayer service was solemnly chanted around one altar in Maple Leaf Gardens by seven Catholic bishops, eight Orthodox bishops, three leading Protestant preachers, and a large number of clergymen of various denominations. An appeal on behalf of the hierarchies of the Ukrainian Catholic Church, the Ukrainian Orthodox churches, the All-Ukrainian Evangelical Baptist Alliance, the Ukrainian Evangelical Alliance of North America, and the Ukrainian Evangelical Reformed Church in Exile was read by Metropolitan Maxim Hermaniuk. Declaring solidarity with the Ukrainian World Congress and its objectives and offering prayers and blessings for its success, the statement concluded: "With one voice we urge all leaders of our national, cultural, and political life to unite all their spiritual forces and means to achieve the goal common to all our Ukrainians: the freedom of the Christian Church and the Free, Sovereign, and Independent Ukrainian State."[25] A similar manifestation of solidarity was enacted at the third World Congress in

New York on November 23, 1978. Discussions have been initiated for an ecumenical celebration in 1988 to commemorate Ukraine's adoption of Christianity one thousand years ago. Because of the reservations of some church leaders only a small degree of co-operation has been achieved so far, but a new era in church relations is developing.

Trends Indicated in the Censuses

During the many years of Ukrainian life in Canada the two traditional Ukrainian churches have firmly established themselves with hierarchies, beautiful church buildings, priests, and church and lay organizations to carry out Christian work and to maintain the Ukrainian identity. Table 13 provides some idea of the religious trends in the Ukrainian-Canadian community in recent years. The table indicates clearly that the largest Ukrainian churches have been losing support steadily, mostly to the Protestant denominations. Although the Roman Catholic element has increased, a large proportion are really Ukrainian Catholics who were not classified properly by census-takers unaware of the differences. Even so, the two traditional Ukrainian churches have lost much ground, declining from 82.6 per cent in 1931 to 52.2 per cent in 1971.

On the other hand, the general Canadian Protestant churches have consistently gained ground. The United Church, with the most rapid growth, has several Ukrainian parishes, as do the Baptists and the Presbyterians; the Anglicans and Lutherans have none. Among the others are 6,000 Pentecostals (some organized in Ukrainian congregations), Jehovah's Witnesses, Seventh Day Adventists, Methodists, Mennonites, and 30,000 who profess no religion. Bearing in mind that over

TABLE 13

Religious Denominations of Ukrainian Canadians, 1931-71 (per cent)

Denominations	*1931*	*1941*	*1951*	*1961*	*1971*
Ukrainian Catholic	58.0	50.0	41.7	33.3	32.1
Greek Orthodox	24.6	29.1	28.1	25.2	20.1
Roman Catholic	11.5	12.3	14.3	16.8	15.3
United Church	1.6	3.0	7.1	12.6	13.9
Anglican	0.3	1.0	2.6	4.0	4.6
Presbyterian	0.8	1.0	1.2	1.2	1.3
Lutheran	0.5	0.6	0.9	1.4	1.8
Baptist	0.6	0.8	0.9	1.3	1.4
Others	2.1	2.2	3.2	4.2	9.4
Ukrainian Population	225,113	305,929	395,043	473,337	580,660

Source: Dominion Bureau of Statistics and Statistics Canada, *Census of Canada,* various dates.

80 per cent of the Ukrainians who came to Canada were Catholics and about 15 per cent Orthodox, there has been a truly remarkable change by 1971, with nearly one-third of the Ukrainian population in the Protestant category.

The change is undoubtedly the result of the growing affluence of Canadian society. To the late 1930's, Ukrainians in the bloc settlements conducted their religious life in closely knit communities, preponderantly agricultural, and in equally tightly knit communities in the urban centres. The Great Depression and the rapid mechanization of farming caused an ever-growing migration to the cities, and in twenty years the Ukrainian Canadians have transformed themselves from a predominantly rural society to an urban one. In the cities, most settled in mixed districts and many did not join Ukrainian communities or Ukrainian churches. Brought up in the schools to think of themselves as Canadians, many felt it burdensome to be regarded as Ukrainians and foreigners. Non-Ukrainian churches and organizations were the natural beneficiaries in the expectation that better treatment and better jobs would follow. Social success could also be achieved through intermarriage with other English-speaking or French-speaking peoples. The traditional Ukrainian churches made a weak effort to reach out to the "assimilated," who were, accordingly, lost to Ukrainian-Canadian society. Unless there is a concerted effort by the leaders of the Ukrainian churches and the Ukrainian Canadian Committee "to bring back the lost sheep," it can be expected that the trend to Roman Catholicism and, even more, to Protestantism will continue.

THE PROBLEM OF GENERATIONS

The failure of the traditional Ukrainian churches to attract their proportion of the growing Ukrainian population can be attributed to the lack of understanding by church leaders of the changing social pattern of Ukrainian-Canadian society.[26] The first generation was brought up almost entirely in rural or small-town communities, which established churches and institutions for their own religious and cultural survival. A large proportion of the second generation rebelled against what they considered old-country religious, national, and political prejudices. The activities and attitudes of Ukrainian leaders, they thought, were harmful, hindering the progress of youth in schools and later in employment. Many among the second generation denied their origin, changed their names, and renounced the Ukrainian churches and institutions, joining the "English" churches and communities, where many intermarried and moved into the urban middle class. Brought up under a democratic system which fosters critical thinking, members of this generation found that the work of the churches and their leaders fell short of general Canadian standards. The long ritualistic services chanted in Old Church Slavonic or even Ukrainian were not well understood. Sermons of priests tended to be authoritarian, with little emphasis on the philosophical, charitable, and practical bases of religion. The intolerance practised by many priests and leaders dismayed those who took their democratic tenets seriously. Still others found it difficult to harmonize the nationalistic character of the Orthodox and Catholic churches with Canadianism. As a result, the churches suffered, gradually losing ground after 1951, even after strengthening their hierarchies.

The third generation,[27] even more thoroughly educated in the Canadian system, did not, however, have the inhibitions of its parents, because it had not experienced the intense religious and ideological rivalry of the past. Influenced by the French-Canadian renaissance of the sixties, the work of the Royal Commission on Bilingualism and Biculturalism, the emergence of multiculturalism as government policy, and the participation of prime ministers, premiers, and cabinet ministers in Ukrainian affairs, and stimulated by the devotion of the new youth organizations of the recent wave of Ukrainian immigrants to Ukrainianism, this generation has generally come to identify itself as Canadians of Ukrainian descent or cultural background, or simply as Ukrainian Canadians, similar to French Canadians. Having lost fluency in Ukrainian, they still respect it as a Canadian language and are often concerned that their children study it in the public schools. They take pride in Ukrainian culture as part of the Canadian cultural mosaic. Although not actively religious, this group regards the Ukrainian Catholic and Orthodox churches as part of their precious cultural heritage. It is a generation with an open mind, interested in the Ukrainian churches becoming more Canadian, with Canadian-born clergy and bishops to serve Canadian needs.

During the life of Ukrainians in Canada, despite urbanization and the growth of a Canadian-born population (over 82 per cent in 1971), the traditional Ukrainian churches have stood as bastions for the development of Ukrainian culture and those symbols of the Ukrainian culture which are at the heart of Ukrainian identity. The church and lay organizations have been dominated in the main by immigrant and older elements, which have generally resisted change. Alarmed by the withdrawal of the Canadian-born from the church, they have bemoaned the phenomenon but seldom entrusted that same Canadian element with leadership positions. A serious generation gap has emerged, filled with the anguished soul-searching of those sensitive to the many dilemmas created by the steady process of acculturation.

The response of the Ukrainian churches to the grievances, desires, and demands of the second and third generations has varied. The Orthodox Church has emphasized its essentially Ukrainian character, electing bishops not fluent in English from Ukrainian hierarchies outside Canada, who, in turn, have found it difficult to comprehend the problems of the Canadian-born generations. Only a fraction of the clergy is Canadian-born and educated, but this is gradually being rectified at St.

Andrew's College; few concessions, however, are made to the use of English in liturgy and sermons and to mixed marriages. On the other hand, the Ukrainian Catholic Church has been trying to adapt itself to the needs and demands of the second and third generations. Some of the bishops are Canadian-born as are an increasing proportion of the priests, monks, and nuns. In many parishes where there are significant numbers of mixed marriages, parts of the liturgy and sermons are in English; few are entirely so. The innovations, however, have not had the desired effect, judging by the large number of defections to the Roman Catholic Church. Such concessions to Roman Catholicism in the thirties and forties as adopting the new calendar, Latinizing some of the rituals and architectural structures, and the greater use of English have apparently not impressed a large segment of the Canadian-born generations, who have joined the Latin church, possibly considering the Ukrainian one anachronistic. Both churches are faced with the serious problem of recruiting clergy.

The generation gap is a very serious problem for the traditional Ukrainian churches. In order to survive in the affluent Canadian society, ways and means will have to be found by the church and lay leaders to win the confidence of the rising generation and stem the decline in attendance. The solution will probably entail government support for an educational system of continuing Ukrainian studies and programs in the Canadian context from the pre-school level upward, in some cases in the Ukrainian communities themselves. The churches, in any case, can no longer afford to wait for the youth to come to them; the bishops, clergy, and lay leaders must reach out to attract and involve them in meaningful religious and cultural experiences and to relate these to the ethnic identity and to the multicultural ideals and policies pursued by the federal, provincial, and municipal governments.

NOTES

1. For the ecclesiastical history of Ukraine, see D. Doroshenko, *Pravoslavna tserkva v mynulomu i suchasnomu zhytti ukrainskoho narodu* (The Orthodox Church in the Past and Present Life of the Ukrainian People) (Berlin: R.B., 1940); and Doroshenko, *Korotkyi narys istorii khrystiianskoi tserkvy* (Short Sketch of the History of the Christian Church) (Winnipeg: Vyd. spilka Ekleziia, 1949); M. Hrushevsky, *Z istorii religiinoi dumky na Ukraini* (From the History of Religious Thought in Ukraine) (Lviv: Naukove tov. im. Shevchenka, 1925). V. Lypynsky, *Religiia i tserkva v istorii Ukrainy* (Religion and the Church in the History of Ukraine) (Philadelphia: Vyd. Ameryka, 1925); I. Nahaievsky, *Katolytska tserkva v mynulomu i suchasnomu Ukrainy* (The Catholic Church in the Past and Present of Ukraine) (Philadelphia: Vyd. Ameryka, 1950); I. Ohienko, *Ukrainska tserkva* (The Ukrainian Church), 2 vols. (Prague: Iurii Tyshchenko, 1942); and Ohienko, *Vizantiia i Ukraina* (Byzantium

and Ukraine) (Winnipeg: Ukrainske naukove pravoslavne bohoslovske tovarystvo, 1954); S. Tomashivsky, *Istoriia tserkvy na Ukraini* (History of the Church in Ukraine) (Philadelphia: Vyd. Ameryka, 1932); E. Winter, *Vizantiia ta Rym v borotbi za Ukrainu* (Byzantium and Rome in the Struggle for Ukraine) (Prague: Iurii Tyshchenko, 1944); I. Wlasowsky, *Narys istorii Ukrainskoi pravoslavnoi tserkvy* (Outline of the History of the Ukrainian Orthodox Church) (New York: Ukrainska pravoslavna tserkva v ZDA, 1955-56); and Wlasowsky, *Outline History of the Ukrainian Orthodox Church* (New York: Ukrainian Orthodox Church of USA, 1956).

2. Several intensive and frequently polemical studies have appeared on the question of the union with Rome: V. Antonovych, *Shcho prynesla Ukraini uniia* (What the Union Brought Ukraine) (Winnipeg: Ukrainska hreko-pravoslavna tserkva v Kanadi, 1952); W. Kudryk, *Istorychni materiialy* (Historical Materials) (Winnipeg: Vyd. spilka Ekleziia, 1949); and Kudryk, *Malovidome z istorii hreko-katolytskoi tserkvy* (Little Known Facts from the History of the Greek Catholic Church), 4 vols. (Winnipeg: Trident Press, 1952-56); J.B. Koncevičius, *Russia's Attitude Toward Union with Rome* (Washington: n.p., 1927); E. Likovski, *Beresteiska uniia* (The Union of Brest) (Zhovkva: Ukrainski bohoslovtsi im. Markiiana Shashkevycha, 1916); I. Ohienko, *Podil iedynoi Khrystovoi tserkvy* (The Division of the One Church of Christ) (Winnipeg: Ukrainska hreko-pravoslavna tserkva v Kanadi, 1952); J. Pelesz, *Geschichte der Union der ruthenischen Kirche mit Rom* (History of the Union of the Ruthenian Church with Rome), 2 vols. (Würzburg: Leo Woer, 1878-80).

3. For the Ukrainian autocephalous movement, see *Diiania Vseukrainskoho pravoslavnoho tserkovnoho soboru v m. Kyievi, 14-30 zhovtnia, n.s. 1921 r.* (Proceedings of the All-Ukrainian Orthodox Sobor in the City of Kiev, October 14-30, N.S. 1921), 2nd ed. (Frankfurt-am-Main: Ukrainska avtokefalna pravoslavna tserkva, 1946); A. Lototsky, *Avtokefaliia* (Autocephaly), 2 vols. (Warsaw: Ukrainskyi naukovyi instytut, 1935); Lototsky, *Ukrainski dzherela tserkovnoho prava* (Ukrainian Sources on Church Law) (Warsaw: Ukrainskyi naukovyi instytut, 1931); V. Lypkivsky, *Ukrainska pravoslavna tserkva. Korotka istoriia* (The Ukrainian Orthodox Church: A Brief History) (Winnipeg: Konsystoriia Ukrainskoi hreko-pravoslavnoi tserkvy v Kanadi, 1934); S. Ranevsky, *Ukrainskaia avtokefalnaia tserkov* (The Ukrainian Autocephalous Church) (Jordanville, N.Y.: Nakl. avtora, 1948); W. Swystun, *Kryza v Ukrainskii pravoslavnii (avtokefalnii) tserkvi* (The Crisis in the Ukrainian Orthodox [Autocephalous] Church) (Winnipeg: Nakl. avtora, 1947); I. Theodorovich, *Blahodatnist ierarkhii U.A.P.Ts.* (The Grace of the Hierarchy of the U.A.O.C.), 2nd ed. (Regensburg: Ukrainska avtokefalna pravoslavna tserkva, 1947).

4. *Diiannia soboru hreko-katolytskoi tserkvy v Lvovi, 8-10 bereznia, 1946* (Proceedings of the Sobor of the Greek Catholic Church in Lviv, March 8-10, 1946) (Lviv: Vyd. prezydii soboru, 1946); *First Victims of Com-*

munism: White Book on the Religious Persecution in Ukraine (Rome: Analecta OSBM, 1953); W. Dushnyck, *Martyrdom in Ukraine* (New York: America Press, n.d.).

5. Sociological studies on the world views and attitudes of Ukrainians toward the church in the old country prior to their emigration have still to be researched. This section is based on numerous interviews and discussions with Ukrainian settlers and church and lay leaders in Canada over many years.
6. Early church life is discussed, though not always accurately, by P. Bozyk, *Tserkov ukraintsiv v Kanadi* (The Ukrainian Church in Canada) (Winnipeg: Kanadyiskyi ukrainets, 1927). For the religious life of the Ukrainians in Canada, see P. Yuzyk, "The History of the Ukrainian Greek Catholic (Uniate) Church in Canada" (Master's thesis, University of Saskatchewan, 1948); Yuzyk, "The Expansion of the Russian Orthodox Church in North America to 1918," unpublished paper, 1950; Yuzyk, *The Ukrainian Greek Orthodox Church of Canada 1918-1951* (Ottawa: University of Ottawa Press, 1981).
7. For Archbishop Langevin's work among the Ukrainians, see J. Jean, "S.E. Mgr. Adélard Langevin, Archevêque de St. Boniface et les Ukrainiens," in *Rapports, 1944-45: La Société Canadienne d'Histoire de L'Église Catholique* (Ottawa, 1945).
8. For the Catholic reaction to the proselytization of Ukrainians in the early period, see A. Delaere, *Memorandum on the Attempts of Schism and Heresy among the Ruthenians (commonly called "Galicians") in the Canadian Northwest* (Winnipeg: West Canada Publishing Company, 1909).
9. The regulations, published by Bishop Budka in Winnipeg in 1915 and entitled *Pravyla Rusko-katolytskoi tserkvy v Kanadi*, were restricted to the clergy because of contentious clauses. Bitter opposition to some of the regulations was instrumental in the formation of the Ukrainian Greek Orthodox Church in 1918.
10. U.S. Department of Commerce, Bureau of Census, *Religious Bodies*, 1916, p. 250. (The census also covered Canada.)
11. Bozyk, *Tserkov ukraintsiv*, p. 30; also J.A. Carmichael "Report of the Board of Home Missions," in *The Acts and Proceedings of the Thirty-Second General Assembly of the Presbyterian Church in Canada* (1908), p. 30.
12. Based on Ivan Bodrug, "Spomyny" (Memoirs), unpublished manuscript, 1949.
13. *The Acts and Proceedings of the Thirty-Third General Assembly of the Presbyterian Church of Canada* (1909), p. 7.
14. This was the opinion of the Presbyterian clergymen who worked among the Ukrainians: A.J. Hunter, *A Friendly Adventure* (Toronto: Board of Home Missions, United Church of Canada, 1929), p. 35.
15. The letter made sense in the context of Old World politics. When the war broke out, all Ukrainian parties in Galicia considered Austria to be the lesser of two evils compared to Russia. In the former, the Ukrainian

language and institutions were tolerated, if not necessarily respected; in the latter, a policy of Russification was being implemented and it was feared that invading Russian armies would destroy Ukrainian institutions in Galicia and Bukovyna. Conservative and clerical circles thus tended to believe that the Central Powers would create an autonomous or independent Ukrainian state to serve as a buffer against Russian expansionism. Hence the call to arms by the bishop.

16. For details, see Yuzyk, *Ukrainian Greek Orthodox Church*; O.S. Trosky, *The Ukrainian Greek Orthodox Church in Canada* (Winnipeg: n.p., 1968).
17. *Ukrainskyi holos*, 1 July 1925.
18. The full proceedings were reported in *ibid.*, 1 July 1925.
19. *Propamiatna knyha z nahody zolotoho iuvileiu poselennia ukrainskoho narodu v Kanadi 1891-1941* (Commemorative Book on the Occasion of the Golden Jubilee of the Settlement of the Ukrainians in Canada 1891-1941) (Yorkton: Nakl. epyskopskoho ordynariiatu, 1941), outlined the work of the Ukrainian Catholic Church and its parishes.
20. N. Savaryn, *Rolia ottsiv Vasylian v Kanadi* (The Role of the Basilian Fathers in Canada) (Mundare, Alberta: Vyd. oo. Vasyliian, 1938).
21. For the attitude of the consistory, see *Visnyk*, 15 October, 1 November 1949; 1 July, 1 November 1950.
22. See "Liudyna pratsi" (Man of Toil), in *Slovo istyny* (Word of Truth), November-December, 1950, a special issue dedicated to the metropolitan.
23. *Visnyk Svitovoho kongresu vilnykh ukraintsiv* (Herald of the World Congress of Free Ukrainians), June, 1974, pp. 14-17.
24. *Visnyk*, 1 March 1974.
25. *Visnyk Svitovoho kongresu vilnykh ukraintsiv*, June, 1974, p. 15.
26. The generation gap is a very important phenomenon in all immigrant societies and therefore requires serious study. The changing attitudes of the immigrant and his children and grandchildren in each of the generations as they adapt themselves to the affluent, increasingly industrialized, and urbanized society have had a continuing impact, with serious repercussions, seldom properly understood, on Ukrainian institutions and life in Canada. Illia Kiriak's historical novel, *Sons of the Soil* (Toronto: Ryerson Press, 1959), tried to portray the problem of generations in Ukrainian-Canadian life. Judging from a few papers presented at meetings of the Canadian Association of Slavists and the Canadian Ethnic Studies Association, some studies appear to be under way, but more attention needs to be focused on this important problem.
27. Only recently has some attention been directed to studies of Ukrainian youth. See, for example, P. Migus, "Ukrainian Canadian Youth: A History of Organizational Life in Canada, 1907-1953" (Master's thesis, University of Ottawa, 1975). Since it deals with the topic to 1953, further studies are imperative if a better understanding of the problems facing youth and the leaders of Ukrainian-Canadian organizations is to emerge.

EIGHT

Community Organizations

Ol'ha Woycenko

THE PIONEER YEARS

The types of organizations that emerged among Ukrainian Canadians during the pioneer period reflected the major types of community organizations in Galicia and Bukovyna on the eve of emigration. The most familiar corporate body for most immigrants was undoubtedly the village church. During centuries of foreign domination the Greek Catholic Church in Galicia had remained the only Ukrainian institution, the locus around which all celebrations and community social life revolved and from which the first organizations emerged. As the clergy remained the only well-educated group in the villages, they usually provided the initiative for organizational activity and jealously guarded their primacy within the newly established bodies. At first only church brotherhoods, sisterhoods, and temperance societies were organized. However, by the turn of the century, priests were often involved in the organization of parish choirs, reading halls, and even drama circles.

In the more progressive villages of Galicia and Bukovyna, the diversification and secularization of community organizations were stimulated by two movements with political, cultural, and economic implications. The first, populism (*narodovtsvo*), emerged in middle-class lay and clerical circles during the 1860's. It was inspired by the poetry of Shevchenko and the ideas expressed by other eastern Ukrainian writers. The most concrete result of the populist movement was the formation of the Prosvita (Enlightenment) Society in Lviv in 1868. Its aim was to eradicate illiteracy, raise the educational and cultural level of the peasants, and develop a national consciousness in the process. On the eve of World War I, branches of the society with their *chytalni* (reading clubs/associations) and *narodni domy* (national homes/community centres) could be found in most Galician and Bukovynian villages, where they had become increasingly popular with the peasantry.

The second movement was radicalism. The radicals were young populists who had become disillusioned with the social conservatism and lack of vision displayed by their elders. They adopted Mykhailo Drahomanov's program based on socialism, independence for Ukraine, and anti-clericalism – the latter rooted in the conviction that the clergy were not doing enough for the peasantry, either educationally or economically. In the end, the radical movement added new life to its parent, the populist movement, and gave birth to a socialist movement. All three challenged the conservatism and traditional hegemony of the clergy. As only a handful of clergymen settled in Canada during the pioneer period, the task of organizing the community fell to peasants who subscribed to these orientations and who were often unwilling to subordinate themselves to the clergy – an attitude with important implications for the development of community organizations.

Not surprisingly, the first Ukrainian organization in Canada was the St. Nicholas Brotherhood established in Edna-Star, Alberta, in 1897 by Greek Catholic immigrants.[1] The following year, Reverend Paul Tymkiewicz, a young, progressive Greek Catholic priest visiting the colony, initiated the first reading club (*chytalnia*) in Canada. In subsequent years a number of brotherhoods, sisterhoods, and reading clubs were established with the assistance of Greek Catholic priests. Ukrainians who belonged to Orthodox parishes also established brotherhoods, while in Saskatchewan several of the rural reading clubs and halls were established by ministers of the Independent Greek Church.

However, because of a shortage of priests, most reading clubs and organizations established during the pioneer period were organized on lay initiative. Immigrants who had been introduced to populist, radical, or socialist ideas in the old country also established their own reading halls with names such as Postup (Progress), Volia (Freedom), Borotba (Struggle), and Rivnist (Equality). During the early years, however, groups of every shade of ideological opinion frequently met in the same reading hall. The Shevchenko Reading Association, established in Winnipeg in 1899, was a case in point. Immigrants of almost every political and religious persuasion, with the exception of devout Catholics, belonged to the association. Only after 1905 did the various lay organizations begin to identify themselves with specific political orientations or interest groups.

Socialist sympathizers were the first to organize their own distinct organizations. In 1906 the Taras Shevchenko Educational Association was established in Winnipeg. Within a few months it gave birth to the Ukrainian Free Thought Federation, and in 1907 a Ukrainian branch of the Socialist Party of Canada (SPC) was established. Other Ukrainian branches of the party were established in Hosmer (near Fernie, B.C.) and Nanaimo by members of local workingmen's reading clubs. By 1909, there were ten Ukrainian branches of the SPC, which led to the formation of the Federation of Ukrainian Social Democrats in Canada. The following year, as a result of widespread dissatisfaction with the SPC, the federation became one of the groups which established the Social Democratic Party of Canada. Besides trying to raise the Ukrainian immigrant labourers' class consciousness, the socialists were involved in the social and cultural life of the Ukrainian community. They collected funds for political and educational causes, sponsored lectures on controversial social issues, and participated in a number of drama circles, especially in Winnipeg. In 1914 the federation changed its name to the Ukrainian Social Democratic Party in Canada, and the leadership was assumed by younger, more radical immigrants, among whom the most prominent were Matthew Popowich, John Navis (Ivan Naviziwsky), and Danylo Lobay. These men led the party until it was banned in September, 1918.

Organizations with a populist line emerged shortly after the first socialist organizations. The populists believed that it was above all necessary to eradicate illiteracy, raise the educational and cultural level of the immigrants, and cultivate national feeling rather than class consciousness and solidarity. Although they never constituted a compact, well-defined group like the socialists, the populists were identified with a number of prominent community activists, such as Taras D. Ferley, Jaroslaw W. Arsenych, and Wasyl Kudryk, who sympathized with the populist and radical movements in their homeland. Their influence was noticeable among the first Ukrainian bilingual public school teachers in Manitoba, the graduates of the Ruthenian Training School, where Ferley had been an instructor for a few years. In 1907 Manitoba's Ukrainian bilingual teachers established the Ukrainian Teachers' Association, the first Ukrainian-Canadian organization with distinctly Canadian roots. Similar teachers' associations were also established in Saskatchewan and Alberta. The associations championed the cause of bilingual public school education, urged Ukrainians to organize school districts, encouraged teachers to participate in community development (especially adult education), supported compulsory school attendance legislation, and tried to establish Ukrainian student residences or hostels (*bursy*).[2] Other organizations identified with the populists included Zaporozhska Sich (Zaporzhian Sitch), a young men's club in Winnipeg, and the National Home Association in Winnipeg, an organization that did not permit clergymen to be elected to its executive.

Of the teachers' activities, the most significant for providing a strong organizational base for the community's educational, cultural, and social development were the *bursy*. Once the bilingual era ended in 1916, they were established to stem the perceived threat to Ukrainian culture and language in Canada. They also met the practical need of extending education beyond the simple pioneer provisions of the one-room, rural school. Higher education was only available in the larger urban centres, where it was important to secure adequate but reasonable accommodation while simultaneously ensuring that the children did not forget their parents, their ancestral homeland, or their faith. The *bursy*, therefore, housed mainly rural Ukrainian students who attended city elementary or secondary schools, colleges, or universities. The residences cushioned the students' sudden contact with urban life and exposed them to Ukrainian language, literature, culture, and history through formal classes and daily living. The beginnings were invariably difficult and institutional welfare varied with the economic state of Ukrainian farmers, always the mainstay of the *bursa* movement.

The *bursy*, especially during the formative period, played a significant role in the group's educational process, for they stemmed from pioneer organizations and were conceived as non-denominational, non-partisan community institutions open to all students of Ukrainian background. Contrary to the aspirations of the founders, the *bursy* became a serious point of contention with the Greek Catholic hierarchy, leading the founders to break with Catholicism and create the Ukrainian Greek Orthodox Church of Canada. This, in turn, divided some of the emerging secular community organizations along Catholic and Orthodox lines.

The first organization to announce plans (in 1910) to establish a *bursa* was the Ukrainian Teachers' Association in Winnipeg. The name chosen was the Adam Kotsko Bursa, in honour of a student activist killed by rival Polish students at a meeting at Lviv University in July, 1910. It took time to raise the necessary funds and the *bursa* finally opened in September, 1915, under strained conditions, as the original supporters split on denominational issues. Almost half withdrew from the organizational meeting in July, 1915,[3] to establish the Greek Catholic Metropolitan Andrii Sheptytsky Bursa. The difficult beginnings did not forecast a bright future for either institution. The Kotsko Bursa closed its doors in the summer of 1917, and the Catholic residence in suburban St. Boniface followed in 1924.

The beginnings of the third student residence, the Petro Mohyla Ukrainian Institute in Saskatoon, date from 1915 when a group of students organized a Ukrainian Student's Club led by A. Kryzanowsky and A.T. Kibzey. At a convention in Saskatoon in August, called to generate interest and support, four hundred participants enthusiastically approved the establishment of a *bursa* and, most significant for the future, resolved that it be non-denominational and non-partisan. Elected to the first executive were Wasyl Swystun, A.T. Kibzey, Joseph Megas, and Michael Stechishin.[4]

The institute opened its doors for the 1917-18 school year as a secular institution, with Swystun as the unsalaried rector and teacher. Of the thirty-five students, only three attended university, ten were in high school, and the rest in elementary school. Twenty-three were Greek Catholic, six Protestant, four Orthodox, and two Roman Catholic. Only three were girls. On Sunday the students attended the churches of their choice in the morning, had the afternoon free, and studied in their rooms in the evenings. A Greek Catholic priest visited the residence often, and it was to him that the Catholic students turned for their traditional Easter confessions. With the support widespread, the institute's board pondered the purchase of a suitable building and, at the request of interested people, opened branches at Canora, Saskatchewan, and Vegreville, Alberta. The organization of Edmonton's Hrushevsky Institute (today's St. John's) followed.

The calm surface was deceiving, however. Some Catholics and Protestants began to criticize Mohyla's non-denominational character. Some Presbyterian ministers insinuated that students from farms experienced discrimination. In some Greek Catholic circles, opposition to the institute's stand on the religious question was most marked. "We want to know definitely," asked Bishop Budka's organ, *Kanadyiskyi rusyn* (25 October 1916), "whether the bursy [Kotsko and Mohyla] are in accord with the views of Greek Catholic Ukrainians or against them . . . ?" On November 1 Orest Zerebko, editor of *Holos*, replied: "Ukrainianism we place first and religious upbringing second, because all Ukrainians are members of one nationality, but not all are members of the Greek Catholic or Orthodox churches. . . . There is a need for a secular bursa, and if one did not exist it would be necessary to create one today." To Bishop Budka, the interdenominational atmosphere invited religious indifference; accordingly, when the deep, ideological split could not be bridged he opened the *bursa* in St. Boniface in the fall of 1917, followed by another in Edmonton in the spring of 1918.

A second convention in December, 1917, reaffirmed the Mohyla Institute's national and non-sectarian principles and condemned Bishop Budka, some of his clergy, and the Presbyterian *Ranok* as "enemies of national progress." When Budka denounced the Mohyla leaders as Presbyterian agents, Stechishin and others advised Catholic parishioners to take an independent stand on church incorporation.[5] The bishop retaliated by refusing the confessional and burial in sacred ground.[6] The sordid affair reached an unexpected climax in Saskatoon on July 18-19, 1918, when, at a confidential meeting attended by 154 Ukrainians from the Prairie Provinces, a majority voted to break with the Greek Catholic Church and form the Ukrainian Greek Orthodox Brotherhood to organize the Ukrainian Greek Orthodox Church of Canada. Even though Swystun dissociated the Mohyla Institute from the meeting, its leaders were among the most prominent participants.

In spite of the very serious dispute between the Catholic clergy and the advocates of secular education, there were pressing problems which called for joint action. The first was the abolition of the bilingual school system in Manitoba. Trying desperately to save it, a group was formed in January, 1916, under the name of the Ukrainian Central Committee (later renamed the Committee in Defence of Bilingual Schools). The committee met with the Premier of Manitoba, T.C. Norris, and his cabinet; it also collected signatures, presented petitions of protest, and called mass meetings and rallies across the province. Although their efforts failed, for a brief period devout Catholics and champions of secular education spoke with one voice.

The second problem was concerned with Ukraine. If the recently proclaimed Ukrainian National Republic (UNR) was to survive, it would require the consent of the Allies, representation at Versailles, and funds. Consequently, late in 1918 the Ukrainian Canadian Citizens' League (UCCL) was created in Winnipeg to further these objectives. Headed by Jaroslaw Arsenych, it met with only limited success, and even that was marred by discussions related to the religious controversy. Amid insinuations that both delegates selected by the league to attend the Versailles conference as advisers to the UNR mission sympathized with the newly created Ukrainian Greek Orthodox Church, the Catholic loyalists withdrew and established the Ukrainian National Council, which pursued the same objectives as the league. To co-ordinate at least the collection of funds for the relief of Ukrainian war victims, in 1920 a Central Committee consisting of representatives from both the league and the council was formed to make the work of the Ukrainian Red Cross Society more effective. The Central Committee, while it did not become a permanent organization, set a pattern for future unifying forces and may therefore be considered the forerunner of today's Ukrainian Canadian Committee.

Organized Ukrainian-Canadian life was, of course, completely changed by the establishment of the Ukrainian Greek Orthodox Church of Canada. This was the watershed of differentiation within the community, which divided it confessionally into Catholic and Orthodox just as other events were dividing it secularly into nationalist and Communist. The confessional division, with roots deep in Galician anti-clericalism, was consummated by the establishment of *bursy* in Winnipeg and Saskatoon, specifically designed (ironically) to provide an education without regard to faith or secular affiliation. The year 1918 was significant in still another sense. The tendency toward the simultaneous but separate development of church and secular life was replaced by the absorption, domination, or creation by the churches of secular organizations and institutions. Today there are few Ukrainian organizations in Canada which are truly non-denominational. The arrival of immigrants after World War I greatly increased organizational differentiation as the newcomers gradually established organizations that reflected post-war political trends in the old country. Thus, to the diversity of opinion concerning the role of the church brought by the first settlers were added further differences rooted in political ideologies.

THE EMERGENCE OF NATIONAL ORGANIZATIONS

In the period between 1919 and 1939 the Ukrainian population in Canada increased considerably. Almost 70,000 immigrants arrived between the wars. Many of the activists among interwar immigrants had been personally involved in the struggle for liberation, either as members of the armed forces or as members of clandestine nationalist organizations. As a result of their experiences, they concluded that Ukrainians lacked the discipline, will, and commitment to achieve statehood and independence. Populism, radicalism, and, above all, socialism were incapable of correcting this deficiency. Nor did the mundane concerns and religious quarrels of the pioneers appeal to them. Thus, the organizations established by the interwar immigrants were founded either under the banner of monarchism (*hetmanstvo*) or, more commonly, nationalism.

Thanks to the efforts of the early settlers, the newcomers found in Canada a definite Ukrainian pattern of community life. But while the older settlers had expected the newcomers to bring new vitality to established structures, the newcomers arrived with plans to establish their own organizations. The recruiting of supporters, the soliciting of funds, and the founding of newspapers followed. Such fragmentation, in addition to the feuds among older settlers, disoriented some Ukrainians, as rivalry and friction within the community steadily mounted.

Pioneer Organizations in the Interwar Period

Despite the failure to establish a permanent umbrella structure and growing strife between the old and new settlers, Ukrainian-Canadian organizational life at the local level gradually expanded to national levels in the 1920's and 1930's, as churches and political groupings sought Dominion-wide status. Most of the hitherto local *prosvity* (enlightenment societies) and *narodni domy* became part of the organizations with central headquarters and national leadership.

The Ukrainian social democrats, as we have seen, were the first to establish a federation, albeit a loose one. When the Ukrainian Social Democratic Party was banned in 1918, their movement re-emerged under a new name, the Ukrainian Labour-Farmer Temple Association (ULFTA), and became the first truly national Ukrainian organization in Canada. A new weekly, *Ukrainski robitnychi visti*, was established in 1919. At its first national convention in Winnipeg, January 16-18, 1920, the ULFTA boasted twenty branches across the country. Its development was typical of the national organizations which followed. It expanded rapidly to accommodate both sexes and various age groups, evolving a family-type structure with female and youth sections as affiliates. In 1922 it founded the Workers' Benevolent Association of Canada, which still does business under the federal Life and Fraternal Benefit Insurance Act.[7]

Committed to the Communist cause since 1918, the founders of the ULFTA were involved in the formation of the Communist Party of Canada and worked closely with it. They hoped to improve working-class conditions and to check discrimination and exploitation of immigrant workers. In its cultural-educational activities the ULFTA resembled the Prosvita societies. An impressive Ukrainian Labour Temple building was erected in Winnipeg, with space for its national headquarters and printing presses, a concert stage and auditorium for theatrical, choral, and dance groups, orchestra and lecturers, and classrooms for children and adults. Its appealing, dynamic socio-cultural programs and frequent protests against social injustices attracted a large following across the country in the twenties and thirties. Even its open and aggressive pro-Soviet stance, which set the ULFTA apart from all other Ukrainian organizations, was an asset during the 1920's when Soviet Ukraine experienced a literary and cultural revival and appeared to have attained republican status. Membership in the ULFTA allowed Ukrainian immigrants to take pride in being Ukrainian even if, as today's Russified Ukraine shows, they were living under an illusion.

In its publications the ULFTA concentrated on labour and agrarian problems, which other organizations tended to ignore.

> While the majority of Ukrainian Canadians were busily engaged in establishing their churches and safeguarding their ethnicity, little attention was paid to the economic problems of the working class and poor farmers – at least they were not very vocal in this respect. In contrast, the Communist sector spoke out for better working conditions, higher wages for the labourers, and better deals for the farmer. Their slogans appealed to the masses. Furthermore, their listeners were led to believe that the Russian Revolution and the emergence of the Communist regime was for the good of the working classes of the world.[8]

During the thirties the ULFTA experienced a major rift. Events in the USSR, especially in Soviet Ukraine, where famine and the liquidation of intellectuals disillusioned many, prompted a group of dissenters under Danylo Lobay, a long-time editor of *Ukrainski robitnychi visti*, to leave the movement. The dissenters formed the Ukrainian Workers' League (URO) with headquarters in Winnipeg, published their own paper, and tried to reveal the truth about developments in Ukraine. Yet the ULFTA managed to weather the storm, sustained by the deplorable economic conditions in Canada. In 1939 it boasted 10,000 members, of whom almost 10 per cent belonged to the Communist Party. The URO had barely 500 members at the time. Although the ULFTA was banned shortly after the outbreak of World War II as a result of the Hitler-Stalin pact, it flourished after the Soviet Union joined the Allies in 1941. When the Association of United Ukrainian Canadians (AUUC), the ULFTA's successor, was incorporated in 1946, it boasted 13,000 members, and even though this represented less than 5 per cent of Ukrainian Canadians, its leaders could influence public opinion on Ukrainian issues. It declined only in the fifties and sixties.[9]

The second Canada-wide organization to emerge was the Ukrainian Self-Reliance League of Canada (SUS). Indigenous to Canada with roots deep in the pioneer period, SUS's leaders were the early school teachers, founders of *Ukrainskyi holos*, initiators of *prosvity* and *narodni domy*, and founders of *bursy* in Winnipeg, Saskatoon, and Edmonton. Although the group did not start as an umbrella organization, *Ukrainskyi holos*, edited by Myroslaw Stechishin (1921-47), held it together ideologically. The national conventions in Saskatoon, Edmonton, and Winnipeg between 1916 and 1926 also were strong unifying forces, which led to the formation of a national structure in December, 1927. The expanding movement made a national co-ordinating body imperative. Under its wing SUS embraced the Ukrainian Self-Reliance Association (TUS) for adult males; the Ukrainian Women's Association of Canada (SUK), the national women's organization; the Union of Ukrainian Community Centres (SUND), uniting local *prosvity* and *narodni domy*; the Canadian Ukrainian Youth Association (SUMK), the youth section; and three *bursy*, the Mohyla in Saskatoon, the Hrushevsky (later St. John's) in Edmonton, and St. Vladimir's in Toronto.

Among the founders of SUS were Wasyl Swystun, the first national president, Jaroslaw W. Arsenych, Peter H. Woycenko, Reverend Semen W. Sawchuk, Wasyl Batycky, Joseph Bohonos, and the three Stechishin brothers: Myroslaw, Michael, and Julian. The organization's ideology may be summed up as follows:

> Canada is the adopted homeland; Ukrainians have settled here permanently, their children have been born and raised here, thus Canada is their native land; as full-fledged citizens with privileges and responsibilities, Ukrainians should participate in all spheres and all phases of the life of this country on an equal footing with their co-citizens; politically, there could be only one loyalty – loyalty to Canada; ethnically, Ukrainians should strive to perpetuate and cultivate their specific cultural attributes . . . ; within the framework of their Canadian citizenship, the Ukrainian Canadians should aid their kinsmen in Ukraine in their aspirations and struggle for freedom . . . ; they should help the cause morally and financially, but they must not affiliate formally with any of the political factions in the homeland or in exile.[10]

Although planned as a secular organization, it was evident from the beginning that SUS would become the lay body of the Ukrainian Greek Orthodox Church because its founders were also leading Orthodox members committed to support a fully independent Ukrainian church. The alignment with the Orthodox Church alienated some original members, who preferred freedom of religious belief and church affiliation.

In the 1920's and early 1930's SUS was dynamic, the avant-garde among Ukrainian organizations. Local missionary zeal coupled with a profound concern about the policies of Russia, Poland, Romania, and Czechoslovakia toward Ukraine brought mass protest meetings and appeals to the League of Nations and heads of state to condemn atrocities such as the forced collectivization of peasants and famine in Soviet Ukraine, the "monster trials" of Ukrainian intellectuals at Kharkiv, and the "pacification" of Ukrainian areas in Poland. By the late 1930's, however, SUS's original vitality was sapped by confessional differences and religious practices that alienated Swystun and his supporters. The war, too, disrupted the normal activities of all organized groups and post-war prosperity diverted the attention of many.

The third Canada-wide organization, the Ukrainian Catholic Brotherhood (BUK), as its name implies, had its roots in the local brotherhoods and sisterhoods of the pioneer period. A generation later, in 1932, with the steady growth of Greek Catholic parishes, a central lay organization was created. As with other Ukrainian national organizations, women's and youth associations emerged as affiliates: the Ukrainian Catholic Women's League of Canada (LUKZh) and the Ukrainian Catholic Youth (UKIu). A *bursa*, the Metropolitan Sheptytsky Institute, established in Saskatoon in 1934 was also an affiliate. The brotherhood's ideology was summed up by one of its founders, Reverend Stepan Semchuk, in the following motto: "Catholic Religion, Ukrainian Culture and Canadian Citizenship." Its attitude toward Ukraine was similar to that of SUS: to aid its aspirations within a Canadian context. Among its founders and early leaders were Fred Mamchur, George Skwarok, (Senator) William Wall (Wolochatiuk), John Kozoriz, V.H. Koman, and M. Hrynevich.

Apart from the short-lived St. Raphael's Ukrainian Immigrants' Welfare Association in Winnipeg, ongoing mutual aid organizations flourished in the interwar period, including the Ukrainian Mutual Benefit Association of St. Nicholas and the Workers' Benevolent Association of Canada. A third, founded in 1921, was the Ukrainian Fraternal Society of Canada. Two American organizations with Canadian headquarters in Toronto and branches across Canada were the Ukrainian National Association and the Ukrainian Workingman's Association.

Despite the emergence of these national organizations, a number of local organizations continued to operate independently. Notable among these were the *narodni domy* in Winnipeg and Toronto, the *prosvity* in Winnipeg and Kenora, and the Markiian Shashkevych Literary Society and the Canadian Ukrainian Institute Prosvita, both in Winnipeg. The main reason for remaining independent was that membership consisted of various faiths and political hues. Moreover, a small community could not afford to splinter if its social, cultural, and educational aims were to be realized.

Organizations of the Newcomers

The first of the organizations founded by the interwar immigrants was the semi-military Sich, established in 1924 on the initiative of Volodymyr (Vladimir) Bossy, who became editor of the Ukrainian Catholic *Kanadyiskyi ukrainets* until its demise in 1927. Monarchist in orientation and upholding the claims of the Skoropadsky family to the throne of an independent Ukraine, its leaders were I. Isaiw, A. Zaharychuk, N. Danylchenko, D.M. Elcheshen, and M. Hetman. Renamed the Canadian Sich Organization in 1928, within four years it was headed by an energetic journalist, M. Hetman of Toronto, who edited a new publication, *Ukrainskyi robitnyk*. In 1934 it changed its name to the United Hetman Organization (SHD) and added a women's section. In 1937-38 Danylo Skoropadsky, son of the former Hetman Pavlo Skoropadsky, head of German-occupied Ukraine in 1918, visited a number of Ukrainian-Canadian communities, but there is no evidence that his warm personality greatly strengthened the monarchist movement.

An anti-Soviet, democratic socialist faction followed the monarchists to Canada. After the fall of the Ukrainian National Republic in 1921, members of the Ukrainian Party of Socialist Revolutionaries (UPSR) and other democrats settled in Prague. Mykyta Shapoval was their most prominent leader. Failing to achieve a union of revolutionary democratic Ukrainian émigrés in Europe, Shapoval turned his attention to North America, sending N. Ia. Hryhoriiv and M.I. Mandryka to tour Ukrainian-Canadian settlements in 1928-29. Mandryka remained in Winnipeg when some members of the independent Ukrainian National Home Association supported him. This organization was in need of new impetus. With the founding of the Ukrainian Greek Orthodox Church and the emergence of SUS, some formerly active members became deeply involved in both. The strongly non-denominational National Home, which constitutionally would allow only laymen to its executive positions, no longer appealed to the Orthodox neophytes. When they withdrew, Mandryka began an extensive program of cultural-educational activities of the sort which had appealed to the first settlers. The "revitalized" association, however, failed to attract a large following, and even Shapoval's visit in 1930 did not help. Shortly thereafter, it returned to its original status as an independent, local body.

The monarchist and socialist groups were marginal phenomena in the Ukrainian-Canadian community. Of far greater importance were the nationalist organizations, formed primarily on the initiative of newcomers who had served in the volunteer legion of Ukrainian Sich Riflemen and in the Ukrainian Galician Army. The first was the Ukrainian War Veterans' Association (USH), organized in 1928. It made a dramatic debut by leading a campaign in defence of Ukrainian political prisoners in Galicia and Volhynia, then part of Poland. As a result of letters, memoranda, and petitions addressed to the Canadian government and the League of Nations, two Ukrainians (Atamanchuk and Verbytsky), who had been unjustly sentenced to death by the Polish courts, had their sentences commuted. USH mobilized many other organizations, including SUS, during the campaign. It was the first successful international political action undertaken by Ukrainian Canadians. In the years that followed, USH continued to make appeals on behalf of overseas Ukrainian political prisoners and collected enough money to erect a hostel for Ukrainian war invalids in Lviv. On the eve of World War II USH had almost 700 members in twenty branches scattered across the Prairie Provinces and Ontario.[11]

As more veterans arrived, some of them members of the revolutionary underground Organization of Ukrainian Nationalists (OUN), the USH realized that it would have to broaden its organizational base to expand its influence. The war veterans had "denounced the prevailing religious controversy and intolerance" and appealed for "unity to combat the Russian-inspired Communist movement among the Ukrainian Canadians and to work for the common goal of winning liberty and statehood for Ukraine."[12] To them, the existing organizations were too parochial, too narrowly concerned with Canadian issues, and insufficiently mindful of the situation in Ukraine. If the goal of Ukrainian independence was to be achieved, if the plight of Ukrainians in Poland and the USSR was to receive the international attention it deserved, the Ukrainian-Canadian community would have to redefine its priorities. Antagonism between the veterans and the leaders of the older organizations was thus practically inevitable.

The result was the creation of the Ukrainian National Federation (UNO) in 1932. Although USH continued to exist, most members also joined local UNO branches. From the outset, UNO was an amalgam of first- and second-immigration Ukrainian Canadians. Its first national president, Alexander Gregorovich, had come to Canada prior to the outbreak of World War I. Another prominent member who had arrived as an infant during the pioneer years was the future Member of Parliament, Anthony Hlynka.[13] Among UNO's other leaders were W. Kossar, T. Pavlychenko, and W. Hultay, all interwar immigrants. Like the other national organizations, UNO had a women's sector, the Ukrainian Women's Organization of Canada (OUK), and a youth organization, the Young Ukrainian Nationalists (MUN). Needless to say, UNO also built its own halls (*domivky*), and the rates of factionalism and differentiation steadily escalated.

Women's Organizations

As already noted, sisterhoods were the first lay church-oriented women's groups in Canada. They were followed by women's auxiliaries, usually attached to local *prosvity* or *narodni domy*. There was a dire need for national organizations that would reach out to women in urban centres and in isolated areas across the country. Pioneer women were burdened with many basic problems: establishing homes, bearing and rearing children, working in the fields, and tending to countless domestic tasks. They were confined to a limited, prosaic existence, though in urban centres many became involved in the activities of *narodni domy*, especially in drama and choral groups. National organizations could best give the leadership in providing specific advice on women's concerns, such as updating household management, fostering good hygienic practices, and assisting with the rearing of children in a changing environment.

Upgrading the educational levels of Ukrainian women was also essential. The illiterate needed encouragement to learn at least the basics of reading, writing, and arithmetic, while the literate needed the opportunity to acquire new knowledge. It was also important that Ukrainian women should become involved in women's councils, outside their own cultural milieu, that worked for the good of Canadian society as a whole. To achieve this end, national organizations were more important than ever. Three already noted were the Ukrainian Women's Association of Canada (SUK, 1926), the Ukrainian Women's Organization of Canada (OUK, 1930), and the Ukrainian Catholic Women's League of Canada (LUKZh, 1944). Though Orthodox, nationalist, and Catholic, respectively, they pursued common activities: the establishment of museums with workshops to preserve cultural artifacts brought from Ukraine and craft skills, and to retain and develop Ukrainian language and culture in Canada.

Planned initially as a non-denominational, non-partisan women's organization, SUK became an affiliate of SUS in 1927 and thus drew closer to the Ukrainian Greek Orthodox Church, where most local branches across the country are now located. In sharp contrast, OUK was truly a secular organization. Consisting primarily of interwar immigrants, its members worked initially with the Ukrainian War Veterans' Association until they became an integral part of UNO in 1934. Not surprisingly, the latter gave events in Ukraine much attention, offering financial assistance to various institutions struggling to survive the pressures of Polish rule.

The women's sections of the nation-wide ULFTA preceded these three organizations and differed from them in three main ways: the initiative to organize came from men, the members of the parent body; the sections never had a distinct name but were known as "women's sections" of the ULFTA; and the periodicals and publications were edited by men. Once the ULFTA's fortunes began to decline, the women's groups fared no better.

Youth Organizations

Normally, children learn the many features of their cultural heritage in the family. This, however, can never be entirely true where the family is uprooted and exposed to a totally new and at times hostile environment. In such instances, families need the support of the larger community's organizations. To this end, the national organizations that emerged in the twenties and thirties incorporated separate youth sections: the Canadian Ukrainian Youth Association (SUMK, 1931), the Young Ukrainian Nationalists (MUN, 1934), and the Ukrainian Catholic Youth (UKIu, 1939).

The general purpose of such organizations was to foster cultural, social, spiritual, and physical activities. Good citizenship, a well-rounded Christian personality, active church membership, and respect for and an understanding of the Ukrainian cultural heritage were strongly encouraged through interregional and interprovincial competitions, frequently at jamborees. The nationalist MUN differed from the Orthodox SUMK and

Catholic UKIu in that its members were primarily children of interwar immigrants and therefore largely urban rather than urban and rural.

The pro-Communist ULFTA's youth sections came into being in January, 1926, and a monthly publication, *Svit molodi*, followed in 1927. During the Depression, the youth sections joined the Young Communist League in demonstrations which made headlines in *Svit*. In June, 1930, a new periodical, *Boiova molod*, appeared. Its editors sought to fight capitalist exploitation and mass unemployment, to combat imperialistic war threats, to portray the Soviet Union's role in the class struggle, and to teach working-class youth to work against Ukrainian nationalism and fascism. Despite its aggressiveness, the journal ceased publication in 1932 and the pro-Communist youth movement began to decline.

THE POST-WAR YEARS

The war caused all organizations to limit activities to a minimum as increased demand for manpower and labour made it difficult to continue with many traditional programs. Yet during this difficult period there were two notable developments: first, a superstructure, the Ukrainian Canadian Committee (UCC), was established in 1940 to consolidate Ukrainian-Canadian opinion and co-ordinate the activities of non-Communist Ukrainian-Canadian organizations during the war years; second, the Ukrainian Canadian Relief Fund was created in 1944 to assist Ukrainian refugees in war-torn Europe. Between 1945 and 1958, this fund collected $500,000 for the relief of Ukrainians in Europe. In accordance with its constitution it also organized and co-ordinated welfare work among Ukrainians in Canada and was the nucleus out of which the Ukrainian Canadian Social Welfare Services emerged.

After the war, the formation of new organizations contributed further to the fragmentation of the Ukrainian-Canadian community. Most were established by the new wave of immigrants – the refugees and the displaced persons. In many respects these newcomers were quite distinct from the immigrants who had preceded them. Although, as always, the majority were from western Ukraine – Galicia, Bukovyna, Carpatho-Ukraine, Volhynia – a significant proportion were refugees from the Soviet regime in eastern Ukraine. The post-war immigrants were more skilled and better educated than their predecessors; for the first time professionals, scholars, technologists, and other skilled workers came in considerable numbers. Finally, a significant proportion of the newcomers were highly politicized and militant. While democrats, democratic socialists, and monarchists were to be found among the politically active newcomers, the overwhelming majority were intense nationalists. Oppression in Poland, the USSR, Romania, and Czechoslovakia during the interwar years had fueled a militant underground nationalist movement led by the Organization of Ukrainian Nationalists (OUN). The Soviet invasion of Polish-occupied western Ukrainian territories in 1939, followed by the German occupation of the entire Ukraine in 1941 and the Soviet reconquest and consolidation of all Ukrainian territories after 1945, hardened nationalist sentiment, drove Ukrainians into military formations created by both sides, and ultimately led to the emergence of the guerilla Ukrainian Insurgent Army (UPA), which fought both the Germans and the Soviets. Many of the nationalists had been in the OUN or in the UPA. Not surprisingly, many could not readily fit into the existing Ukrainian-Canadian organizations.

National Organizations

After the war, the established organizations resumed their work with varying degrees of success. The two national organizations which were affiliated with the major churches, the Ukrainian Catholic Brotherhood (BUK) and the Ukrainian Self-Reliance League (SUS), continued to expand, since both were reinforced by the arrival of new immigrants.[14] On the other hand, the monarchist United Hetman Organization (SHD), already faltering, continued to decline. During the 1950's internal dissension and the death of Danylo Skoropadsky, the last male heir to the title of hetman, weakened the movement. Moreover, as young Ukrainians of conservative tendencies were drawn into the ranks of nationalist organizations, new recruits for the monarchists disappeared.

The most dramatic decline, however, occurred within the pro-Communist camp.[15] The Association of United Ukrainian Canadians had grown by leaps and bounds during the war, but after 1946 it began a steady decline from a high point of 13,000 members. A number of factors were responsible: the arrival of articulate refugees from the USSR, who had personal knowledge of Soviet reality; the post-war economic boom, which seemed to destroy the rationale for membership in a movement dedicated to the destruction of capitalism; and the realization that Russification in Ukraine was, in fact, Soviet policy pursued deliberately and systematically. Today only a hard core of aging veterans remain within the organization, which no longer publishes membership statistics.

The nationalists, united before World War II in the Ukrainian National Federation (UNO), expected to benefit most from the influx of nationalistically oriented immigrants. This did not happen, however, for the nationalist camp divided into a number of organizations during the post-war years. During and after the war, the OUN had been rent by disputes and schisms in Ukraine and Europe. By the early 1950's, the following three nationalist factions were active outside Ukraine: the Organization of Ukrainian Nationalists, commonly known as *Melnykivtsi* (OUN[m]); the Foreign Branch of the Organization of Ukrainian Nationalists, commonly known as the *Banderivtsi* (OUN[b]); and the Organization of Ukrainian Nationalists Abroad, commonly known as the

Dviikari (OUN[z]).[16] OUN(b), which emerged as the largest faction, was a militant, disciplined, highly centralized, ultra right-wing group; OUN(m), second in terms of membership, was conservative but considerably more moderate and flexible in its internal organization; OUN(z), the smallest and youngest faction, was the most liberal and democratic.[17]

In Canada adherents of OUN(m) joined UNO, reinvigorated it, and integrated into Ukrainian-Canadian community life without a great deal of friction. Today UNO is composed of interwar and post-war immigrants and their offspring and continues to follow the precepts of its founders. It sponsors a number of fine choral groups, dance ensembles, and Ukrainian schools (*ridni shkoly*) across Canada. UNO maintains close relations with other organizations in the OUN(m) camp throughout the world.

The more militant, right-wing adherents of OUN(b) created their own organization, the Canadian League for Ukraine's Liberation (LVU), in 1949. LVU was founded to inform Ukrainian Canadians and others about the political and military struggle for Ukraine's liberation and to disseminate information about the threat of Russian imperialism and Communist totalitarianism. LVU at the present time is the largest community organization. A greater emphasis is placed on the inculcation of ideology than in the other non-Communist organizations. This is achieved through the press, at frequent celebrations commemorating the heroic deeds of Ukrainian nationalists, and by mobilizing members for participation in political demonstrations.

OUN(z) broke away from OUN(b) in the early fifties to create an organization called the Canadian Friends of the Liberation of Ukraine (UKT).[18] It has remained small in size and has made no effort to organize on a national scale. Individual members contribute articles to journals and periodicals published by OUN(z) sympathizers in Europe and the United States.

Two other, smaller organizations were formed by post-war immigrants: the Ukrainian National Democratic League (UNDS) and the Association of Ukrainian Victims of Russian Communist Terror (SUZhERO). Created primarily by refugees from Soviet Ukraine, both stood on democratic principles with no connection to the OUN.

Women's Organizations

In 1944 the Ukrainian Canadian Women's Committee was formed to coordinate the activity of SUK, OUK, and LUKZh. A decade later, the Women's Association of the Canadian League for Ukraine's Liberation (ZhLVU) was admitted to the committee. Although a number of local organizations which are unaffiliated with any of the national organizations also belong to the committee, the presidency is reserved for representatives of the four national organizations, among whom it is rotated. Charitable work and the retention and development of the Ukrainian cultural heritage continue to be the major concerns of women's organizations. On a number of occasions the organizations have worked in unison on major projects. In 1963, for example, they published a collection of the poetess Lesia Ukrainka's works in English translation. Four years later, they co-operated on the occasion of Ukrainian Day at "Expo 67." Although the women's organizations continue to be active, their membership is increasingly composed of middle-aged and elderly women.

Youth Organizations

Since 1953, the work of youth organizations has been co-ordinated (theoretically, if not practically) by the Ukrainian Canadian Youth Council (RUMK). In addition to the Canadian Ukrainian Youth Association (SUMK), the Ukrainian Catholic Youth (UKIu), and the Ukrainian National Youth Federation (MUNO) (formerly the Young Ukrainian Nationalists), which appeared during the interwar years, the Council also includes representatives of organizations created in the post-war period by the new immigrants.

The first branches of Ukrainian Youth Association – Plast were organized in 1948. A non-denominational organization, unaffiliated with any of the national organizations or political parties, Plast is the Ukrainian equivalent of the Boy Scout-Girl Guide movement. It was originally founded in Galicia in 1911. Unlike other Ukrainian youth organizations, it stresses camping, pioneering, and other outdoor-wilderness activities. The organization has a reputation for developing well-rounded Canadian citizens who appreciate Ukrainian culture and traditions.

The Ukrainian Youth Association of Canada (SUM) was organized at the same time as Plast, on which it was modelled. Unlike Plast, however, the organization was founded in Europe after the war and is affiliated with LVU. Consequently, members are exposed to LVU's ideology and particular brand of Ukrainian nationalism. Numerically, it is the largest of the youth organizations. SUM choirs and orchestras attract thousands of listeners in Canada and the United States.

The last major youth organization to appear in the post-war period was the Ukrainian Democratic Youth Association (ODUM) organized in 1950 by immigrants from eastern or Soviet Ukraine and affiliated with SUZhERO. To keep the organization "young," members who have reached the age of thirty-five must "enter the ranks of the Educational Council (*Vykhovna rada*) and assist in the upbringing of new ranks of members."[19]

In addition to these youth organizations, the Ukrainian Canadian University Students' Union (SUSK) has also worked with RUMK. SUSK was founded in 1953 in Winnipeg to unite a number of denominational and party-affiliated student organizations, as well as independent university student clubs. Its activities have fluctuated for lack of both continuity in its executive and able financial management. Since 1968, however, it has been a vocal and dynamic body, concerned with issues such as the democratization of the Ukrainian Canadian Committee, multiculturalism in Canada, and the fate of dissidents in Soviet Ukraine. Its presentation in 1974 on multilingual programming before the House of Commons Committee on Broadcasting, Films, and Assistance to the Arts was particularly impressive.

Special-interest Organizations

In addition to the national organizations which try to appeal to and recruit from the community as a whole, a number of more specialized organizations have emerged since World War II. Veterans', professional, and cultural groups belong in this category.

The first and largest among the veterans' organizations was the Ukrainian Canadian Veterans' Association (UCVA), established in June, 1945, by veterans of the Canadian Armed Forces who had been stationed in England. Immediately after the war, UCVA played an important role in assisting Ukrainian refugees. Local branches have also sponsored cadet programs, published materials concerning Ukrainian settlement in Canada, and collected data on the role of Ukrainians in the Canadian armed forces. At the local level, each club is a branch of the Royal Canadian Legion. To assure continuity, associate membership is now open to sons and daughters of the founders. Émigré war veterans' organizations have been concerned primarily with the collection of funds for the support of Ukrainian war invalids stranded in Europe. Since 1964 members of the émigré organizations have had the right to join UCVA.

The first two Ukrainian-Canadian professional and businessmen's clubs were organized in Toronto and Winnipeg in 1935 and 1943 respectively, and within a few years others appeared in major cities. Except for personal contacts, each operated independently until 1965, when the Ukrainian Canadian Professional and Business Federation (UCPBF) was formed in Winnipeg. The national executive has rotated between Edmonton, Toronto, and Winnipeg. To date, it has been most vigorous in Edmonton, where it assisted in establishing the first English-Ukrainian bilingual classes in the public schools and laid the basis for the Canadian Institute of Ukrainian Studies (and its foundation, now the Canadian Foundation for Ukrainian Studies) at the University of Alberta. It was also the main force behind the establishment of the chair of Ukrainian studies at the University of Toronto. Branches of Ukrainian professional organizations, which unite medical doctors, veterinarians, engineers, librarians, social workers, jurists, and journalists outside Ukraine, also exist. These are usually affiliated with national or international Ukrainian organizations rather than with the UCPBF, although many members belong to local Ukrainian professional and business clubs.

A number of cultural institutions – museums, archives, libraries, art galleries – have also appeared during the post-war years. They either branched out from existing organizations or emerged independently. Their appearance was retarded by the fact that the true ethnographic value of authentic folk apparel, embroidery, and other items brought by the first settlers was not recognized until the 1930's, when the Ukrainian Women's Association of Canada began to display artifacts in order to revive craft work. Today its museum collection is housed in a new building in Saskatoon. The Ukrainian Catholic Women's League also maintains museums in Edmonton, Saskatoon, and Toronto. One of the most unique establishments in Canada is Oseredok, the Ukrainian Cultural and Educational Centre in Winnipeg. Founded in 1944, it has a museum, library, archives, and art gallery. Tetiana Koshetz was its founder and first director and curator until her death in 1966. It houses many rare items, including the papers of the composer and conductor Alexander Koshetz; the papers of Colonel Ievhen Konovalets, the inter-war leader of the OUN; the papers of Ivan Bobersky; and documents bearing on life in displaced persons' camps.

Ukrainian editors and writers also established a number of organizations for members of their professions. The Association of Ukrainian Journalists of Canada came into being in 1966 in Toronto, largely on the initiative of Nestor Ripetskyj. It has held conferences with its American counterpart and publishes *Zhurnalist* irregularly.

In 1963 the Ukrainian Canadian Writers' Association – Slovo was organized in Winnipeg with Maryna Antonovych-Rudnycka as president. Like its New York counterpart, it is a forum for writers engaged in creative writing, literary criticism, and historical-literary research. At a conference in Toronto in 1973, the association became a national body, headed by George (Iurii) Stefanyk of Edmonton. To date, the organization has had difficulty in cultivating a rapport with Canadian-born Ukrainian writers who work mainly in English or French.

To encourage serious research on Ukrainians in Canada the Ukrainian Canadian Research Foundation was established in 1957 in Toronto by Stephen Pawluk, with support from the Ukrainian Canadian Veterans' Association in southern Ontario. To its credit some major works were produced, including V.J. Kaye's study of early Ukrainian settlements in Canada, his biographical dictionary of Ukrainian-Canadian pioneers, and the memoirs of the first Ukrainian member of the House of Commons, Michael Luchkovich. The foundation was also instrumental in microfilming a number of early Ukrainian newspapers and publications.

To sustain interest in the Ukrainian language, to develop it at the highest literary level, and to enrich the vocabulary of Ukrainian Canadians, the Ukrainian Language Association of Canada was established in 1964. Constantine Bida became the first president. Its publication, *Slovo na storozhi*, edited by one of the founders, J.B. Rudnyckyj, is the only linguistic journal in North America devoted to Ukrainian language problems.

CONCLUSION

Any survey of Ukrainian-Canadian community organizations confronts one with a maze. Is the Ukrainian-Canadian community over-organized? Does it form a self-sufficient cultural community in Canada as do, for example, the French or the Jews? Originally, group life was shaped along parallel but separate confessional and secular lines. The *prosvity* and *narodni domy*, which national organizations like SUS and BUK eventually absorbed, were meant to be secular. Yet they evolved into highly church-oriented groups, largely dependent on and in some instances dominated by their respective ecclesiastical bodies. There were several reasons for this: church leaders feared that membership would diminish if the faithful worked along interdenominational lines; some clergy and laymen believed that the churches should oversee all aspects of life; and church buildings were exempt from property taxes whereas the same was not always true for other community, cultural, and even scholarly institutions. Organizations which cut across denominational lines are, therefore, relatively rare and include primarily highly specialized post-war organizations.

The most serious impact of the denominational and political divisions has been the unnecessary duplication and overlapping in organizational services. In communities where one Ukrainian school would suffice, there have been two or more *ridni shkoly*, maintained in basements of Orthodox, Catholic, and non-denominational halls. The same has been true for adult education classes, youth clubs, choral, drama, and folk dance groups, and museum and archival collections. The Ukrainian-language press has also been fragmented along denominational lines. In fact, it is frequently splintered regionally within the same denomination. Each weekly experiences the same difficulties in staffing and financing, yet each duplicates a large portion of the published material. The various political factions – the interwar UNO and the post-war LVU – have only added to the duplication. Even on the intellectual level there have been unnecessary divisions: the Shevchenko Scientific Society (NTSH), the Ukrainian Free Academy of Sciences (UVAN), and several other research groups, all struggling to finance their research and publications.

Ukrainians display their folk cultural heritage on every possible occasion; they organize mass demonstrations protesting oppression in Ukraine; and they are vocal in matters of language and cultural retention and development. Such surface manifestations have created an image of a dynamic, cohesive group, championing not only their cultural rights but those of all other groups in Canada. In comparison to the community's size (580,000 in 1971) and high profile, however, the total active membership in all organizations is small: the most pessimistic estimate is 30,000, the most optimistic is 60,000.[20]

It is evident that both national and local groups have not kept pace with the changing times. Outdated programs do not attract the young, and self-appointed, self-perpetuating executives alienate youth. That some young people are interested in organizational structures that are broadly based, interdenominational, unbiased, and non-partisan is exemplified by the fact that they have been meeting privately and devising programs which qualify for various multicultural grants. In their view, time is running out for leaders who are old, apathetic, narrow-minded, or disputatious. All Ukrainian-Canadian organizations need to reexamine their structural framework and the varying ideologies they encompass – and this in relation to Canada, to each other, and to Ukraine. Clearly defined policies and a sense of direction are needed, but these can only come from leaders able to transcend differences and unite Ukrainians at least in areas of essential common interest.

NOTES

1. For provisional inventories of pioneer community organizations, see M.H. Marunchak, *The Ukrainian Canadians: A History* (Winnipeg: Ukrainian Free Academy of Sciences, 1970); O. Woycenko, *Litopys ukrainskoho zhyttia v Kanadi* (Annals of Ukrainian Life in Canada), 5 vols. (Winnipeg: Vyd. Tryzub, 1961-69), vols. I, II.
2. W. Burianyk, *Uchyteli-pionery* (Teachers-pioneers), (Winnipeg: Kolegiia sv. Andreia, 1966); J.H. Syrnick, "Community Builders: Early Ukrainian Teachers," *Transactions of the Historical and Scientific Society of Manitoba*, series III, no. 21 (1965).
3. D. Doroshenko and S. Kowbel (eds.), *Propamiatna knyha ukrainskoho narodnoho domu u Vynypegu* (Commemorative Book of the Ukrainian National Home in Winnipeg) (Winnipeg: Trident Press, 1949), p. 593.
4. *Iuvileina knyha 25-littia instytutu im. Petra Mohyly v Saskatuni* (Twenty-fifth Anniversary Jubilee Book of the Petro Mohyla Institute in Saskatoon) (Winnipeg: Nakladom instytutu, 1945), pp. 50-2.
5. *Ibid.*, pp. 88-90.
6. P. Yuzyk, "The History of the Ukrainian Greek Catholic (Uniate) Church in Canada" (Master's thesis, University of Saskatchewan, 1948), p. 127.
7. A. Bileski, W. Repka, and M. Sago (eds.), *Friends in Need: The W.B.A. Story, A Canadian Epic in Fraternalism* (Winnipeg: Workers' Benevolent Association of Canada, 1972).
8. Interview by the writer with Toma Kobzey, Winnipeg, July, 1967. Kobzey left the ULFTA with Danylo Lobay and other dissenters in 1935.
9. J. Kolasky, *The Shattered Illusion: The History of Ukrainian Pro-Communist Organizations in Canada* (Toronto: Peter Martin Associates, 1979), *passim*.
10. O. Woycenko, *The Ukrainians in Canada* (Winnipeg: Canada Ethnica, 1968), p. 191.
11. See the USH almanac *Ukrainska striletska hromada v Kanadi: 1928-1938*

(Ukrainian Sich Riflemen's Society [UWVA] in Canada: 1928-1938) (Saskatoon: Nakladom ukrainskoi striletskoi hromady, 1938).

12. P. Yuzyk, *The Ukrainians in Manitoba: A Social History* (Toronto: University of Toronto Press, 1953), p. 85.
13. Marunchak, *Ukrainian Canadians*, pp. 398-401.
14. *Ibid.*, p. 606.
15. Kolasky, *The Shattered Illusion*, pp. 177-99.
16. *Entsyklopediia ukrainoznavstva* (Encyclopaedia of Ukraine), 8 vols. (Paris/New York: Naukove tovarystvo im. Shevchenka, 1966), II, part 5, pp. 1723-7, 1863-7.
17. These differences in temperament and orientation are rooted in social differences. OUN(b) originated among local activists and students in Galicia who were dissatisfied with the so-called Leadership of the OUN in western Europe; it received its popular support from the peasant and lower-middle class masses. OUN(m) was composed of those elements who supported the Leadership; it drew its support from fairly well-educated, middle-class circles primarily. OUN(z), which was a splinter group from OUN(b), included intellectuals, publicists, and others who were dissatisfied with the authoritarian tendencies within OUN(b).
18. Marunchak, *Ukrainian Canadians*, p. 603.
19. P.M. Migus, "Ukrainian Canadian Youth: A History of Organizational Life in Canada, 1907-1953" (Master's thesis, University of Ottawa, 1975), p. 223.
20. Membership figures fluctuate and the sources are unreliable. The most reliable source, complete with statistical tables covering the period to January, 1964, is B.Z. Kazymyra, *Development of the Ukrainian Catholic Group in Canada* (Toronto: Basilian Press, 1965).

NINE

The Ukrainian Canadian Committee

Oleh W. Gerus

The formation of the Ukrainian Canadian Committee (UCC) in 1940 was an attempt to provide a faction-ridden community with an umbrella organization that could speak for the community while helping to preserve its identity. During the interwar period the Ukrainian-Canadian community was in a state of flux. The rapid growth of organizational life and the transformation of regional organizational structures into several national associations was punctuated by intense rivalry and factionalism, both religious and political.

The bitterness created by these divisions has generally been viewed in negative terms, but it did have two important early benefits. The competition intensified organizational life and gave it a national basis. The oral and literary polemics could only be sustained with nation-wide funds, and national organizations with appropriate newspapers became indispensable. Equally important, the competition stimulated a Ukrainian national consciousness in many, without which the formation of the UCC would have been impossible.[1]

The history of collective community action is associated almost entirely with Winnipeg. There, in 1912, a committee to aid Ukrainian schools in Galicia was formed. There, too, in 1916 the teachers organized the first major united action, the Committee in Defence of Bilingual Schools, to defend Manitoba's bilingual school system. And in 1918 the Ukrainian Canadian Citizens' League came into being to acquaint Ukrainian Canadians with Canada's institutions and the principles of good citizenship and to interest all Canadians in the cause of Ukrainian democracy and the case for an independent Ukraine.

Notwithstanding the league's success, the Catholics in 1919 established their own Ukrainian National Council, whose brief merger with the league for Red Cross fund-raising for overseas disintegrated in 1922. Equally unsuccessful was the attempt in 1933 to create a single body to co-ordinate protests against Polish persecution in Western Ukraine and Stalinist terror in Soviet Ukraine.

In 1938 the attempt at union was renewed. Events in eastern Europe provided the catalyst. In September the Polish government launched a major, almost medieval, anti-Orthodox campaign in the Ukrainian-populated region of Kholm, a move accompanied by the wholesale destruction of Orthodox churches. Orthodox and Catholic Ukrainians in Canada reacted with mass demonstrations and protests, and a short-lived Ukrainian Central Council of Canada, inspired by the Ukrainian Self-Reliance League (SUS), emerged in Winnipeg to co-ordinate action. The Czechoslovakian crisis followed the Polish affair. Nazi Germany's insistance that Czechoslovakia cede the German-populated Sudetenland resulted in the partition and reorganization of Czechoslovakia. The half-million Ukrainians living in Carpatho-Ukraine, which had been incorporated into Czechoslovakia since 1918, profited by winning regional autonomy and declaring their independence in March, 1939. Invaded by Hungary, the newly established Ukrainian government called on overseas Ukrainians for help. All Canadian-Ukrainian organizations responded and collected relief funds through mass rallies. The absence of central co-ordination led to chaos and a misappropriation of funds, and public pressure mounted for a cessation of internal hostilities and collective action through a central body. With war in Europe imminent, there was an urgent need for consensus on the position Ukrainians in Canada would take.

Informal discussions to achieve unity began in Winnipeg in September, 1938,[2] among Reverend Basil (Wasyl) Kushnir, chancellor of the Ukrainian Catholic Church in Canada, representing the Ukrainian Catholic Brotherhood (BUK); Teodor Datskiv, editor of *Kanadiiskyi farmer*, representing the monarchist United Hetman Organization (SHD); and the "big three" of SUS, Jaroslaw W. Arsenych, a lawyer, Taras Ferley, the former Manitoba MLA, and Myroslaw Stechishin, the volatile and disputatious editor of their newspaper, *Ukrainskyi holos*. The pivotal role in initiating the talks was played by Kushnir, who possessed that rare capacity among Ukrainian leaders, the ability to compromise. To achieve unity, he set out to reconcile political, religious, and personal antagonisms, to the frequent annoyance of the more doctrinaire elements within BUK itself. The participants agreed on the need for a central body, and Kushnir was asked to prepare a draft constitution for it. To help ensure its acceptance, however, he leaked his new-found role to the press. SUS, who had been feuding with UNO over membership and ideology, found Kushnir's sympathies toward UNO unacceptable and promptly ended the discussions. Once again political and religious polemics filled the pages of the Ukrainian press.

The hiatus gave UNO the opportunity to initiate talks on the unity question, and Professor Toma Pavlychenko of the University of Saskatchewan approached all Ukrainian organizations to issue a joint declaration on behalf of Carpatho-Ukraine. By the end of December, 1938, he had organized the Representative Committee of Ukrainian Canadians

(RCUC), an *ad hoc* group in Saskatoon with representatives from UNO, BUK, and the local SUS. This surprising co-operation was short-lived. After the publication of the special declaration in support of Carpatho-Ukraine, the SUS executive immediately withdrew the Saskatoon representative and *Ukrainskyi holos*, joined by *Kanadiiskyi farmer*, denounced the BUK-UNO venture.

The outbreak of war renewed the case for Ukrainian-Canadian unity, with both UNO and SUS concerned to bring about a central body, each on its own terms. Kushnir took definite steps to transform Saskatoon's RCUC into a national co-ordinating body; when SUS refused to co-operate, BUK and UNO established a joint committee of their own.[3] The anticipated co-operation of SHD did not materialize, for it now shared SUS's concern about working with UNO. On February 3, 1940, the RCUC was officially established with Reverend Kushnir as president and provision for future executive positions for SUS and SHD.

The announcement of the RCUC's creation produced a mixed reaction among Ukrainians. UNO and BUK held mass rallies and formed local branches. To give the RCUC greater credibility, UNO initiated a special honorary council of prominent Canadians with pro-Ukrainian sympathies. Professor Watson Kirkconnell of McMaster University, well-known in literary circles, and Professor George Simpson, an historian at the University of Saskatchewan, were members who exercised a strong, decisive influence on the process of Ukrainian consolidation.[4] The English-language press lauded the RCUC's strong display of loyalty and patriotism. SUS, as expected, attacked the RCUC in *Ukrainskyi holos* and initiated talks with SHD and the socialist League of Ukrainian Organizations (LUO). To new overtures from the RCUC to join, SUS reiterated its well-known position on UNO's participation, and the name-calling was revived.[5] The apparent public acceptance of the RCUC, however, concerned SUS and, after informal talks in March, 1940, it modified its stand on UNO, but insisted that LUO be included, a move that displeased UNO, which considered LUO to be SUS's puppet. Accordingly, on May 9, 1940, at a meeting in the Ukrainian National Home in Winnipeg, SUS, SHD, and LUO formed a counter-committee called the Ukrainian Central Committee of Canada (UCCC), with Jaroslaw W. Arsenych as president.

The intransigence of SUS, and particularly *Ukrainskyi holos*, inadvertently enhanced the prestige of the RCUC and caused dissatisfaction within SUS itself. Moderate voices in the Ukrainian community decried the feud between the two bodies and urged unity, which was eventually achieved in the fall of 1940, after the federal government intervened. The Department of National War Services under J.T. Thorson, Member of Parliament for Selkirk, saw the lack of unity among Ukrainians as inimical to the war effort. As the largest Slavic group in Canada, Ukrainians suddenly became a valuable reservoir of recruits and the urgent need for manpower cast the federal government into the role of arbitrator between the RCUC and the UCCC.

It may also be that the UCCC, with its deep commitment to collective unity, had some influence on the decision of the Department to interfere directly in Ukrainian affairs. When creating a special advisory group on Canadian Co-operation and Canadian Citizenship, National War Services turned to a number of experts on ethnic affairs, including Professors Simpson and Kirkconnell, Vladimir J. Kaye (Kysilewsky), a Ukrainian civil servant in the Citizenship Branch, and Tracy Philipps, a British Near Eastern specialist with an intriguing background.[6] Through direct contacts with the leaders of ethnic organizations and their press, the department undertook to generate Canadian patriotism among the Europeans, most of whom were employed in the vital war industry. In these circumstances, it appears that Wasyl Swystun privately invited Philipps and Simpson to Winnipeg to press for unity. When the news leaked out, Philipps' relations with the UCCC were greatly complicated, but sufficient subtle pressure was exerted on both groups by their respective advisers, Simpson and Kirkconnell, to effect a conference for Winnipeg on November 6-7, 1940.

At the conference the UCCC executive was initially represented by Jaroslaw Arsenych, Taras Ferley, Teodor Datskiv, Andrew Zaharychuk, Mykyta Mandryka, Paul Barycki, Myroslaw Stechishin, Julian Stechishin, Toma Kobzey, and Nicholas Bachynsky. The RCUC had a smaller representation with Basil Kushnir, Wolodymyr Kossar (president of UNO), Toma Pavlychenko, and Wasyl Swystun. Considering the recent hostility between the two groups, the very meeting itself was a major breakthrough.[7]

While everyone agreed that unity was important to help the war effort and that a single voice for all Ukrainians was needed, disagreement revolved around the structure of the proposed body and the specific functions of the various organizations in it. Particularly delicate negotiations concerned the presidency, with the UCCC advancing Arsenych and the RCUC insisting on Kushnir. The deadlock was resolved by Philipps and Simpson, who favoured SUS at the expense of UNO, which remained a sore spot with the latter. The presidency went to BUK (Reverend Kushnir), the first vice-presidency with the function of chairman of the executive went to SUS (Reverend Sawchuk), the second vice-presidency with the function of co-ordination to UNO (Swystun), the post of secretary-general to SUS (Arsenych), treasurer to SHD (Datskiv), and financial secretary to LUO (Chwaliboga). The new committee, called the Ukrainian Canadian Committee (UCC), assumed the assets and liabilities of the UCCC and RCUC.

The structure of the UCC was designed to meet the war's exigencies. There were no provisions for converting it into a permanent representative and co-ordinating institution, a later development which emerged naturally. In the initial stages, the UCC consisted of a fifteen-member executive divided into a presidium of six and an executive council of nine permanent and co-opted members. In addition, the UCC included the co-ordinating commission, chaired by Swystun; the advisory council, consisting of organizational members and co-opted individuals; and an honorary council of invited non-Ukrainians such as Kirkconnell and Simpson. Although the constitutional arrangements sought to provide organizational balance, BUK had the monopoly of the presidency and SUS, by virtue of its more dynamic and capable representatives, quickly asserted itself and remained the most influential factor in the UCC until the mid-sixties. Kushnir became the symbol of unity rather than the real leader, and from the minutes of meetings, it appears that his creative input into the UCC was negligible.

Public reaction to the formation of the UCC was positive. *Ukrainskyi holos* and UNO's *Novyi shliakh* hailed Ukrainian unity and both even saw themselves as instruments in bringing it about. The western Canadian press, particularly the *Winnipeg Free Press* (November 19) and the *Regina Leader-Post* (November 12), was also complimentary and urged definite Ukrainian participation in the war effort. The onus was now on the new committee to prove itself before both the Ukrainian public and the Canadian government.[8]

THE WAR EFFORT AND REFUGEE RESETTLEMENT

The UCC found itself co-ordinating the war effort, previously undertaken by individual organizations, by generating enthusiasm for military service among Ukrainians and encouraging the purchase of war bonds through mass meetings, concerts, and patriotic pronouncements. During the course of the war a large number of Ukrainians - between 30,000 and 40,000 or over 10 per cent of the total Ukrainian population in Canada - enlisted in the armed forces,[9] undoubtedly motivated in part by the UCC campaign as well as by personal patriotism and perhaps also by the desire to escape the Depression-ridden Prairies. At the same time, the UCC continued previously independent efforts to acquaint non-Ukrainians with the Ukrainian political problem in Europe.

The Ukrainian response to the war effort, both in Europe and at home, brought constant praise from the government and the English press, which equated Ukrainian activism with Canadianism. The 1942 conscription vote was the only brief embarrassment, both to the Ukrainian community and to the UCC. Wishing to free itself from its earlier pledge not to introduce military conscription, the Canadian government called a national plebiscite on April 28, 1942. Despite an intensive pro-conscription campaign by the Ukrainian press and the UCC, a number of Ukrainian communities, especially in Manitoba, rejected conscription in the face of overwhelming approval by the rest of English-speaking Canada. In an atmosphere of war hysteria and super-patriotism, the scattered Ukrainian opposition was severely criticized, with the *Winnipeg Free Press* particularly strident.[10] The UCC, its leadership and loyalty challenged indirectly, rationalized the Ukrainian vote as a form of popular protest against three factors: Canada's failure to discuss publicly the Ukrainian problem in Europe, alleged discrimination in the armed forces, and the government's co-operation with the "forces of the Left." However explained, the vote showed clearly that the UCC had still to achieve a decisive influence over the Ukrainian community.

Nevertheless, the war effort helped transform the popular image of Ukrainians as quaint peasants, fanatical nationalists, and potential revolutionaries into one of normal human beings deeply involved in Canadian society. To Ukrainians themselves, the war, with its financial and physical sacrifices on behalf of Canada, helped to instil greater self-confidence as full-fledged citizens at a crucial time. Allied victory presented the UCC with a new challenge of gigantic proportions. Among the refugees uprooted in devastated Europe were an estimated two million Ukrainians: most had been deported to Nazi Germany as slave labourers; some had fled to the West when Ukraine was reoccupied by Soviet armies; a minority had collaborated with the Germans. The legal position of Ukrainian refugees in the displaced persons' camps established by the United Nations was precarious. At Yalta in 1945 the Allies had agreed to the repatriation of citizens, and the anti-Communist Ukrainians were soon being forced to return to the USSR. The Western powers, influenced to some extent by Soviet propaganda, saw all Ukrainians who refused voluntary repatriation as Nazi collaborators and war criminals. The UCC, recognizing the serious plight of the refugees, helped to legitimize the displaced persons as *bona fide* political refugees, thus facilitating their immigration to Canada and other countries. Unfortunately, however, when forced repatriation was finally halted in 1947, only about 200,000 Ukrainian families were in the displaced persons' camps.

The UCC approached the refugee problem in two ways. It organized the Ukrainian Canadian Relief Fund to furnish material aid; it also lobbied to allow the refugees to enter Canada.[11] Its women's section, the Ukrainian Canadian Women's Committee, played a vital part in raising contributions for the Relief Fund – more than $200,000 by 1948. In London, the Central Ukrainian Relief Bureau served as the headquarters for all committees formed by the Ukrainian displaced persons in Germany, Belgium, France, Switzerland, and Italy. The Relief Bureau was financed by the UCC (with some aid from its American counterpart) and placed under the auspices of the Canadian Red Cross, which gave it greater authority, for the work of the Canadian Red Cross Relief Mission involved not only food and clothing but legal protection against deportation, the location and reunification of scattered families, and immigration assistance to Canada. The Bureau functioned until 1951, when most of the refugees had been resettled.

The immigration of the refugees to Canada was a far more difficult issue. Uncertain about the economic ramifications of demobilization and peace, the Canadian government was reluctant to admit them. The situation was further complicated by the Ukrainian Communists, in particular by the unpredictable Wasyl Swystun, who had left UNO to join the pro-Communist camp and in 1946 made a dramatic ideological about-face, launching a strong campaign against the displaced persons in Germany. He branded many of them Nazis and urged their deportation to face the "people's justice" in Soviet Ukraine.[12] The UCC reacted by sending several fact-finding missions to Europe, followed by memoranda to the Canadian government denying the allegations and stressing the asset the refugees would be to Canada. In 1946, when UCC delegations appeared before the Senate Standing Committee on Labour and Immigration, Ukrainian Communist counter-delegations also participated, but the Senate Committee favoured the UCC. This was largely because of the work of Anthony Hlynka, the Social Credit Member of Parliament for Vegreville and long-time UNO supporter, who in 1945 made an official visit to Europe on behalf of the Canadian government and the UCC, and subsequently waged a vigorous campaign in Parliament and at public meetings to relax Canadian immigration restrictions. He saw the refugees as "freedom-loving Christian people" whose existence was threatened by forcible repatriation to the USSR.[13]

The tone of the UCC representations to government showed a confidence not previously seen in Ukrainian petitions. For their contribution to the war effort, the Ukrainians expected the government to reciprocate. And indeed, in May, 1946, it did, providing first for family reunions, followed by broader entry. By 1953, most of the Ukrainian refugees were resettled, with over 30,000 coming to Canada.[14]

At first, the third immigration generally accepted Canada as a political refuge rather than a new home. Anticipating a third world war, many longed to return and continue the fight for a free Ukraine. Their numerous political organizations immediately rekindled the political factionalism which the UCC had so laboriously diffused during the war. To its immense credit, the UCC gradually incorporated most of the new organizations and prevented the atomization of Ukrainian-Canadian community life. But the effort required was considerable, as the older Ukrainian Canadians resented the ingratitude they detected in the newcomers and the latter contemptuously dismissed the Canadian orientation of their benefactors. It did not help that some newcomers obtained better employment than their hosts, which aroused the latter's envy.

THE STRUCTURE OF THE UCC

The UCC began its existence as an *ad hoc* structure, encompassing five organizations. To gather all non-Communist Ukrainian forces around itself, it altered its constitution and, by 1965, embraced thirty organizations.[15] More than half, however, were vestiges of the Ukrainian émigré experience, with a handful of adherents of little national or even local significance.

Within the UCC executive, power has been concentrated within the founding members – BUK, SUS, UNO, and later the Ukrainian Canadian Veterans' Association (UCVA) – joined recently by the Ukrainian Canadian Professional and Business Federation (UCPBF), all with their primary orientation toward Canada.[16] Rising in influence and a member of the "Big Six" was the émigré-based Canadian League for Ukraine's Liberation (LVU), a highly politicized component of the radical wing of the Organization of Ukrainian Nationalists. Because of its right-wing political philosophy and almost total preoccupation with Ukraine, it remains doubtful whether the LVU will be able to assert itself within the UCC.

The UCC has branches in six provinces – Quebec, Ontario, Manitoba, Saskatchewan, Alberta, and British Columbia. Provincial councils were formed in 1972-74 in all but Manitoba and Quebec, where the Winnipeg and Montreal locals have dominated. This decentralization was necessary to meet the resentment of the central UCC among strong locals, especially those in Toronto and Edmonton, both of which had surpassed Winnipeg as centres of organized Ukrainian life in Canada. The locals send delegates to the triennial congresses and pay an assessed fee annually to the UCC headquarters. Interest in the locals waned after the war once religious conflicts resurfaced sporadically at the parish level. At the same time many rural locals disappeared with the increased urbanization of Ukrainian-Canadian society. By 1974, only twenty-five locals functioned with varying degrees of effectiveness. Where Ukrainian life was not sufficiently well-organized to establish locals, UCC representatives (twenty-six in 1975) were appointed from the centre.

To counter the aloofness of UCC central, in recent years national councils have been convened to discuss specific policies, with the national executive, the local presidents of the UCC, and the presidents of member organizations in attendance. Pre-congress conventions with member organizations and occasional UCC conferences have been held since 1960. In 1966 field trips by executive members, so useful during the war, were revived. The need to make the UCC more visible grew as criticism of its alleged lack of leadership mounted.

The UCC executive consists of the presidium and the executive board. The presidium is composed of one representative from each member organization with the exception of the "Big Six," which have two representatives each. The executive board consists of fifteen members, twelve from the "Big Six." Although power seemingly lies with the senior member organizations, each representative on the presidium has a veto, making decision-making a delicate process necessitating considerable diplomatic skill on the part of the executive director and the president to secure a consensus. On the average, the presidium meets twice a month. With the executive composed of volunteers, the day-to-day activities are necessarily in the hands of the executive director. This office was created in 1948 and Volodymyr Kochan, a highly respected community leader from Europe, served until his sudden death in 1965. Simon Kalba, also a post-war émigré, succeeded him.[17]

Adequate financial support has been a constant and serious problem for the UCC. Since its inception, it has operated solely through the voluntary support of its member organizations and private donations. The fourth congress, in 1953, improved the situation by dividing the budget into two parts – administration and program – with the first funded out of a specified assessment of UCC locals and member organizations.[18] The program budget would come out of the Ukrainian National Fund, a form of individual voluntary contribution, introduced in 1949. After a slow start, the fund has grown substantially, a reflection on the improved economic status of the Ukrainian community. The administrative budget supports the day-to-day operations of the UCC headquarters, while the program budget underwrites the cultural and political work.

Strict adherence to the budgetary limits set by each congress has frequently prevented the executive from fulfilling such laudable objectives as the establishment of permanent representation in Ottawa. Even so, the financial position of the UCC, although solvent, has been restrictive. In its first twenty-five years, total income barely exceeded $1 million. Deficits, however, have also been rare.

UKRAINIAN NATIONAL CONGRESSES

According to the constitution of the UCC, the national congress of Ukrainian Canadians has the responsibility of appraising the UCC's performance, approving guidelines for the future, electing the executive and the board of auditors, and amending the constitution.

Each triennial congress has regularly reaffirmed the UCC's principles: to act as an authoritative spokesman for the Ukrainian community before the people and government of Canada and to strengthen and coordinate the work in all matters that are of common interest, thereby developing a sound basis for community life among Ukrainian Canadians. Each congress has issued numerous resolutions, most focusing on the preservation and development of the Ukrainian identity in Canada and the liberation of Ukraine.

Much like the creation of the UCC itself, the first congress was initiated by Ottawa as a result of the wartime situation. Both Simpson and Kirkconnell grew concerned about its apparent low profile in the war effort (after a very impressive start) and a corresponding growth in Ukrainian Communist activities. With the German invasion of the Soviet Union, the banned Ukrainian Labour-Farmer Temple Association (ULFTA), legitimized as the Association of United Ukrainian Canadians (AUUC), began promoting material aid for the Soviet Union, the West's new ally. The activism of the Communists generated publicity and sympathy for Soviet Ukraine, and ironically projected an image in non-Ukrainian quarters that the AUUC and not the UCC really represented the majority of Ukrainian Canadians. To regain its position of leadership, the need for greater UCC visibility became urgent.

The first congress was convened in Winnipeg late in June of 1943, with the slogan "Victory and Freedom." Over 600 enthusiastic delegates and guests attended and demonstrated to all Canadians that the UCC was the leader of the Ukrainian community. Present were federal and provincial government representatives, as well as Simpson and Kirkconnell. The speeches of the UCC executive – Kushnir, Stechishin, Arsenych, Kossar, and Sawchuk – painstakingly elucidated Ukrainian contributions to the war effort and underlined the loyalty of Ukrainians to the British crown.

Despite the government's determination to prevent discussion or resolutions that would embarrass the USSR, the subject of Ukrainian freedom and statehood did emerge. Ukrainian spokesmen denied the UCC was undermining the United Nations' efforts by urging Ukrainian separation from the USSR; they stressed that the principles of the Atlantic Charter, signed by the USSR, granted "the right of all people to choose the form of government under which they want to live," and that right should be applied to Ukraine. The Ukrainian Communists were attacked as a subversive minority group because the UCC represented the bulk of Ukrainian people. Government officials with their patronizing speeches emphasized Ottawa's determination to confirm the UCC as the official spokesman of "loyal" Ukrainians.

The first congress was viewed as a major triumph in national solidarity by all associated with it. The UCC received much newspaper coverage as the authoritative voice of the Ukrainian community, and the success determined its executive to hold similar congresses in the future and thus transform the UCC into a permanent national co-ordinating body.[19]

Between 1943 and 1980, thirteen congresses have been held. There can be little doubt that the Ukrainian Canadian Congress is today the highest moral authority for the entire organized non-Communist Ukrainian community in Canada – a kind of parliament in which Ukrainian political and cultural ideals are reaffirmed or modified.

It is noteworthy that the congresses have paid scant attention to socio-economic problems. The resolutions of their farm and labour commissions have been hollow, even irrelevant. Originally designed to demonstrate to the AUUC that the UCC was concerned with economic problems, the results have been meagre. The UCC has been primarily an ethnopolitical organization. Such bodies as the Ukrainian Canadian Social Welfare Services have had limited appeal either because of the Ukrainian community's general indifference or because alternative government agencies have been readily available.

The congresses themselves until recently exerted little tangible influence on the UCC. Three-day sessions once every three years gave delegates no real opportunity to make their presence felt. Though many public commissions to parallel the assembly were introduced, the chairmen were selected in advance by the UCC executive. With a prearranged congress agenda, the executive has always been firmly in control. Not surprisingly, the executive's monopoly of power and its tendency to stress backroom politics have been the two main forces behind the move for a democratically elected executive.

The 1974 congress brought to a head the long-standing pressure to transform the UCC executive into a more democratic institution. The presidential office became an elective three-year term, but only candidates proposed by the "Big Six" organizations were eligible. Other executive positions would continue to rotate among the "Big Six," as they had since 1971. Two candidates contested the presidency – Celestin Suchowersky from Edmonton, representing UNO, and Serge Radchuk, a Winnipeg lawyer, representing the UCPBF. The latter's victory appeared to signify a change in the socio-economic structure of Ukrainian society. Ukrainians in Canada had become highly urbanized with a substantial middle class. For the congress to reflect the change, community leadership had to be transferred from the traditional "teacher-priest" intelligentsia to professional and business interests with Canadian-oriented ideas and without the political and emotional traumas of their predecessors.

Another feature of the congresses has been the low quality of most position papers. The sessions have traditionally opened with a presidential address reviewing the relevance of world problems to Ukrainian concerns. Most addresses have been strong on rhetoric and weak in content. Position papers, too, have generally been very uneven, characterized by redundancy, emotional appeal, the lack of basic research, and occasionally a poor understanding of Canada.

Despite inadequacies, the congresses have become the most important single forum for the organized Ukrainian community in Canada. Because of size and time factors, not all delegates can be heard, but determined individuals can express themselves and question the activities of the UCC executive. The students (SUSK) have been singularly successful in publicly scrutinizing the reports of the executive director. The recent outspokenness of the delegates, openly challenging the entire rationale of the UCC, contrasts sharply with earlier congresses at which the executive devoted much time to self-glorification. The increased criticism may reflect not only the new Ukrainian activism, but the manner in which congresses have been handled by the executive directors. Volodymyr Kochan probably possessed an unsurpassed understanding of the dynamics of Ukrainian organized life, which he subtly manipulated to the UCC's benefit. Simon Kalba, who retired in 1980, was publicity conscious, frequently assuming a high profile which occasionally annoyed some organizations.

Although representation at the congresses has been based on a quota system with the "Big Six" entitled to 100 delegates each, in practice only SUS, BUK, UNO, and, after 1959, LVU have usually met their quotas and, not surprisingly, have dominated the proceedings.

THE UCC AND THE SOCIAL LIFE OF THE COMMUNITY

As noted earlier, the UCC, mainly because of SUS's strong pro-Canadian position, has considered itself a Canadian rather than a Ukrainian émigré institution. The attitude has reflected the realities of the Ukrainian situation in Canada, where most Canadian-born Ukrainians regard Canada as their homeland, even though many, including some who use English almost exclusively, continue to cherish their cultural heritage and wish to retain it in something other than a Ukrainian ghetto. The UCC, consistently opposed to both Ukrainian isolation and Anglo-American assimilation, has favoured multiculturalism. The Ukrainian community, it has argued, should function as an equal partner in a multi-ethnic Canada, with constitutional guarantees to retain and develop ethnic cultures.

The drive for cultural and linguistic concessions stemmed from the UCC's conviction that such gains would eventually become rights – not only for Ukrainians, but for all other interested groups. Formal recognition of Canada as a multicultural society would follow, and in such a diverse environment Ukrainian culture and identity would survive. In 1963 the federal government, responding to growing French nationalism in Quebec, established a Royal Commission on Bilingualism and Biculturalism to make recommendations on how to improve relations between Canada's French- and English-speaking peoples. While the Ukrainian position was not uniform, the UCC's brief, based on decisions at the 1962 congress and a special conference in Winnipeg in September, 1963, generally stressed that Canada, apart from Quebec, remain an English-speaking country, with government support for the preservation and development of all languages and cultures where desired.[20] The concept of Canada-wide bilingualism was rejected in favour of English as the official language of Canada, with French official in Quebec. As for Quebec's future role in Canada, the UCC proposed that the final decision be settled by a plebiscite of the Québécois themselves. Although the bilingual and bicultural concept ultimately prevailed, the combined ethnic agitation obliged the government to concede the multicultural principle. Prime Minister Trudeau's affirmation of the new policy at the 1971 congress was seen as a major triumph for the UCC's lobbying skills. The UCC recognized English and French as the official working languages of the Canadian government and its institutions, but called for amendments to the Official Languages Act that would recognize all languages rooted in Canada as Canadian languages and oblige the federal government to assume responsibility for their sustenance and preservation.

The eleventh congress in 1974 heard John Munro, the second minister responsible for multiculturalism, enunciate federal policies concerning the preservation and development of individual national cultures and languages in Canada. Multiculturalism, according to him, was a permanent policy of the federal government, recognizing Canada's uniqueness as a nation. However, the promotion of multiculturalism since 1971 appeared to some to be very limited and almost tokenistic, especially designed to silence "the ethnics" (or at least the Ukrainians) before a concerted, well-financed campaign to promote English-French bilingualism wherever possible.

The UCC and its congresses have always placed their priority on the Ukrainian language as the key to national survival at home and abroad. In its efforts to have the language recognized, the UCC had to demonstrate its usefulness to provincial governments – not just as a benefit to the Ukrainian community, but as an intellectual and practical asset. It was not to be merely an optional subject, but one equal to French, German, or Russian for matriculation purposes. The UCC has pursued this objective tenaciously, despite official opposition and Ukrainian apathy. Future success at all levels will depend upon the practical opportunities to use Ukrainian, generally a much more significant stimulant to learning languages than academic curiosity or cultural loyalty.

While the UCC's most publicized efforts were directed toward introducing Ukrainian in the public schools and universities, it did not neglect the *ridni shkoly*, the Ukrainian private school sector, where theoretically at least the environment was best suited for moulding a Ukrainian cultural identity. In reality, however, the schools, scattered across Canada and operated by a variety of religious and secular bodies, have always left much to be desired. Without adequate funds and with few qualified teachers the educational effectiveness of most has never been great. In 1971 the UCC's arm, the Ukrainian National Educational Council of Canada, was directed to establish certain standards and to provide a degree of co-ordination, particularly through its National Centre of Ukrainian School Boards. Nonetheless, no amount of institutionalized Ukrainianism could bring about the desired results if the parents themselves continued to abandon the responsibility for educating their children in a Ukrainian milieu. In view of the rapidly declining use of Ukrainian as a language of family communication, the UCC's emphasis on the language question requires a major review.[21]

The performing arts have been a major vehicle for demonstrating and cultivating Ukrainian culture in Canada, and the colourful dances and melodious and robust choirs are well-established as part of Canada's cultural scene. The UCC has effectively combined the abundant artistic talents with key historical and political events.

Some evidence of the UCC's cultural and educational involvement has been the slow but steady growth of Ukrainian studies at the university level. Beginning with the University of Saskatchewan in 1945, Ukrainian studies (essentially language and literature) have been introduced at these universities: Manitoba, Alberta, Montreal, Toronto, Ottawa, McMaster, British Columbia, Calgary, Carleton, McGill, Regina, Waterloo, Western Ontario, Windsor, and York. The promising Shevchenko Foundation, established by the UCC in 1964, has sponsored research in Ukrainian studies. In April, 1974, the UCC was also instrumental in convening the first Ukrainian academic conference in Winnipeg, which led to the establishment of an annual Conference on Ukrainian Studies within the framework of the Canadian Association of Slavists and indirectly assisted the development of the Canadian Institute of Ukrainian Studies at the University of Alberta.

The UCC's decision to enter the bilingual publishing field was motivated by two factors: the desire to inform all Canadians about the heritage of Ukrainians and their aspirations, and hopefully, to dispel such prejudices as may still exist, and to complement the campaign for Ukrainian-language instruction. The literary works by Kirkconnell and Andrusyshen, commissioned to raise the prestige of Ukrainian as a literary language, are of a high standard.[22] In the area of educational material, however, the UCC's school texts and audio-visual aids have generally suffered from underfinanced, hasty preparation.

Even though the UCC mirrors a nationally conscious Ukrainian-Canadian community, politically loyal to Canada and culturally drawn to Ukraine, the UCC's first priority is the preservation and development of the Ukrainian fact in Canada; its role vis-à-vis Ukrainian independence is supportive but indirect. The liberation struggle is the responsibility of Ukrainian political parties in exile, which the UCC supports morally but with which it has no official ties.

Nonetheless, this policy has not precluded the UCC and its member organizations from lobbying with the federal government to recognize Ukrainian claims to independent statehood. Ukrainian demands occasionally clash with Ottawa's view of the world. Cognizant of the realities of global power politics, Canada has tended to pursue a cautious, pragmatic foreign policy toward the Soviet Union.[23] It consequently refrained from *officially* supporting the Ukrainian cause in the belief that hard line anti-Sovietism would accomplish little. However, it has emphasized the human and cultural rights issues in relation to Ukraine, thereby sympathizing with the UCC position on independence mainly by implication.

In the opinion of the UCC, cultural contacts with Soviet Ukraine, however, are crucial, the difficulties notwithstanding. Perceptive Ukrainian leaders have understood that because of their small size and inclination toward assimilation, Ukrainian Canadians will be unable to sustain themselves without some meaningful cultural link with Ukraine. Thus the UCC's moral support for the Ukrainian liberation struggle has been coupled, despite strong opposition from its right-wing members like LVU, with the promotion of reciprocal cultural relations with Soviet Ukraine. As regards Canada's official relations with the USSR, the UCC has urged a policy of extreme caution. In fact, profound distrust of the Soviet Union has characterized all its submissions to the government. Even cultural relations should entail a free and open examination of competitive values, if they are to be meaningful. Thus, Ukrainian Canadians committed to Western values should be as free to express themselves in Ukraine as Soviet Ukrainians committed to Communist values are in Canada.

UCC briefs, reflecting humanitarian and political considerations, have also requested Canadian authorities to urge the Soviet government to relax emigration policy and allow a freer exodus of Ukrainian citizens. Especially important has been the question of family reunions, as many Ukrainian Canadians still have relatives in Soviet Ukraine. As the exodus of Soviet Jews has shown, emigration from Soviet Ukraine would increase substantially the size and dynamism of the Ukrainian community in Canada. However, to date, the results have been meagre: only a handful of retired senior citizens have been released to settle in Canada.

Another practical implication of the UCC's ideological commitment to Ukraine's political independence has been its role as monitor of events affecting Ukraine. It has naturally drawn the Soviet Ukrainian situation, particularly the policies of repression and Russification, to the attention of Canadian governments and to the Western world generally through executive and congress resolutions. Position papers have been submitted to Commonwealth conferences, the United Nations, and NATO, denouncing Soviet imperialism and protesting the harsh treatment of Ukrainian political dissidents. The UCC has approved demonstrations protesting the one-way exchange of Soviet cultural groups and of official delegations and visitors such as Premier Kosygin in the fall of 1971.

On occasion, the UCC's tactics have drawn considerable debate. To the nationalists, its memoranda have been too moderate and its posture as an apolitical organization unacceptable. Others have questioned the benefits of public demonstrations which only embarrass. Recently, however, with the release of a number of prominent Ukrainian dissidents by Soviet authorities, the UCC has sponsored a few well-publicized speaking tours, press conferences, and meetings with government figures.

Occasionally, the prestige of the UCC has been raised by Canadian government requests for observers to accompany official Canadian delegations to the UN and NATO conferences. Ottawa has consistently appointed Ukrainian parliamentarians to various commissions, through which the UCC could make representations. Partly on the UCC's initiative, UNESCO commemorated the 150th anniversary of Taras Shevchenko's birth in 1964. The UCC's greatest success in generating publicity for Ukraine's plight undoubtedly occurred in September, 1960, when Prime Minister Diefenbaker raised the matter of Ukraine's treatment at the United Nations. The speech precipitated hostile Soviet reaction and the UCC was castigated as the centre of "Ukrainian bourgeois nationalism" in Canada.

In 1967 the UCC played a major role in convening the first World Congress of Free Ukrainians. The idea of a global Ukrainian community had been advanced by many political organizations since the collapse of independent Ukraine, but because of ideological differences and personality clashes progress had been slow. As the most credible Ukrainian organization in the Western world and one which had managed to retain its non-political character, the UCC had the prestige which such other major Ukrainian organizations as the Ukrainian Congress Committee of America (UCCA) lacked.[24] The basis for a world Ukrainian organization existed from 1947 when the UCC, the UCCA, and representatives of Ukrainian communities in Latin America established the Pan-American Ukrainian Conference as an information agency. The latter was headed by the UCC president, Reverend Kushnir, but it was Kochan who actually spearheaded the move for a world congress.[25] In view of the scattered nature of Ukrainian centres in the world and the tradition of factionalism, success did not come easily.

The first world congress was held in New York on November 16-19, 1967, with over 200 political, social, economic, cultural, and religious organizations participating. Of the 1,000 delegates, one-quarter came from Canada. Canada's importance was further enhanced by the presence of the former prime minister, John G. Diefenbaker, and the election of Reverend Kushnir to the presidency of the World Congress. The second congress was hosted by the UCC in Toronto in 1973. The congress had two main purposes: (1) to co-ordinate and promote the activities of all democratically and nationalistically oriented Ukrainian communities in the non-Communist world which sought to preserve the Ukrainian national identity outside Ukraine; and (2) to inform world opinion of the violation of human rights in Soviet Ukraine. Although it has met three times, most recently in 1978, the overall impact of the World Congress of Free Ukrainians on the Ukrainian community outside Ukraine and on the world at large is still uncertain.[26]

CONCLUSION

The formation of the UCC, notwithstanding the initial "Made in Ottawa" label, transformed Ukrainian life from one mired in factionalism into one of the better organized Ukrainian communities in the Western world. As Ukrainians gradually came to influence many levels of Canadian society, they acquired greater financial power and social respectability, which, superimposed on their strong ethnic consciousness, made them a notable fact of Canadian life. The UCC, as the recognized spokesman for Ukrainian Canadians, often translated the latent potential of that community into meaningful cultural and political gains, no mean accomplishment considering the size of the country and the incompatibility of the several immigrations and generations.

Over the years, the federal government has developed considerable confidence in the UCC's credibility and has regularly consulted it (privately and officially) on Ukrainian affairs in Canada and abroad.[27] The fact that the UCC has a permanent headquarters and full-time staff has facilitated the ease and frequency of communication. That results have fallen short of expectations is due to small budgets, the absence of an Ottawa bureau, and policies of the federal government beyond the influence of the UCC, as well as the quality of leadership provided.

A long-standing criticism of the UCC has centred in the executive's monopoly of power. Many of its officers have served for long periods of time – Reverend Kushnir for thirty-six years, and others like Reverend Sawchuk, Anthony Yaremovich, John Syrnick, Wasyl Sarchuk, Wolodymyr Kossar, John G. Karasevich, Toma Kobzey, and Ivan Iwanchuk for extensive periods. This has been interpreted by some as a perpetuation of personal ambition behind a facade of community interest. Others have preferred to see the long years as a worthy example of selfless public service. The notion of a UCC clique is difficult to substantiate in view of the ideological differences which continue to exist among the various representatives on the executive. The long tenure of many, it could be said, has given the UCC establishment a sense of continuity and stability, most important against the background of earlier Ukrainian factionalism. The lacklustre appearance of the UCC is due not so much to the alleged conservatism and rigidity of its establishment, as to the nature of the UCC itself. A superstructure based on the principle of consensus of highly divergent member organizations cannot operate effectively if the issues become too controversial. The UCC has survived primarily because of a spirit of compromise and decision by consensus instead of majority rule, which would have accentuated the party differences and minimized common interests. Whether the organized Ukrainian community has reached the stage where majority rule can be introduced without destroying the UCC is still uncertain.

The lengthy and influential involvement of Reverends Kushnir and Sawchuk gave the UCC an aura of clericalism. Appearances, however, can be misleading. Apart from its public commitment to "Christian principles" (never clearly defined but at least understood to stand for anti-Communism), the UCC has always been a secular body. The clerical executive positions mirrored the traditional social structure of rural Ukraine, transferred to Canada, where the focus of community life had always been the parish church. The universal decline of organized religion in recent times, however, affected the prestige and influence of the Ukrainian churches and ensured that effective leadership would be in secular hands.

The future of the UCC is obviously bound up closely with organized Ukrainians in Canada. Their exact number is unknown, but it is estimated to be between 10 and 15 per cent of the total Ukrainian population. That proportion, however small it may appear, is probably higher than in most ethnic groups. Although the UCC represents only the structured side of Ukrainian life, it has always acted on behalf of the entire Ukrainian community. How long it can continue to do so with credibility will undoubtedly be the most pressing issue in the years to come.

Although Ukrainians have been steadily assimilating into the dominant anglophone society, they continue to cling to aspects of their cultural heritage, which suggests the possibility of Ukrainian cultural continuity without the benefit of the Ukrainian language. The UCC's response to this natural phenomenon has been a shift to a wider use of English in its communications and proceedings, thereby encouraging the Ukrainian anglophones to retain their cultural and organizational ties. Whether this partial transformation of the traditional Ukrainian bodies will assure their continuation, however, remains to be seen.

NOTES

1. The best study of the UCC's beginnings is W. Veryha, "The Ukrainian Canadian Committee: Its Origins and War Activity" (Master's thesis, University of Ottawa, 1967). See also my article, "Ethnic Politics in Canada: The Formation of the Ukrainian Canadian Committee," in O.W. Gerus *et al.* (eds.), *The Jubilee Collection of the Ukrainian Free Academy of Sciences in Canada* (Winnipeg: UVAN, 1976), pp. 467-80; B.S. Kordan, "Disunity and Unity: Ukrainian Canadians and the Second World War" (Master's thesis, Carleton University, 1981).
2. Interview by the author with Rev. W. Kushnir, 12 April 1974.
3. *Novyi shliakh*, 8 February 1940.
4. Why Simpson and Kirkconnell became involved is not clear. Simpson had personal Ukrainian friends in Saskatoon, especially within SUS, who respected him highly. This delighted him. He became interested in Ukrainian problems as an historian and eventually saw himself as an expert, although his scholarship was somewhat tendentious. Kirkconnell, who had lived in Winnipeg, was much preoccupied with creating a uniquely Canadian identity based on the finest aspects of ethnic cultures, whose literary masterpieces he translated into English. See his address presented to the Manitoba Mosaic Conference on October 13, 1970: "Many Voices, One Chorus," in *Report of Manitoba Mosaic October 13-17, 1970* (Winnipeg: Queen's Printer, 1970), pp. 21-30.
5. *Ukrainskyi holos*, 14, 21 February, 10, 14 March, 17 April 1940; *Novyi shliakh*, 24, 29 April, 2, 27 May 1940.
6. James Erasmus Tracy Philipps (1890-1959) had been educated at Oxford and Durham Universities and worked for the Foreign Office, primarily in the Near and Middle East during and after World War I. He travelled extensively, spoke thirteen African languages, and published on topics ranging from geography and anthropology to Islam and international relations. One of his many and varied appointments was the post of British Relief Commissioner in South Russia in 1921; he subsequently visited the USSR again in 1933. In 1939 he had married Liubka Kolessa, a concert pianist and the daughter of Dr. Oleksander Kolessa, a noted western Ukrainian linguist, literary historian, and parliamentarian. See

Who's Who 1940 (London: Adam and Charles Black, 1940), pp. 2514-15. Philipps' large role in the formation of the UCC and during its early years is well-documented in Kordan, "Disunity and Unity," pp. 33-4, 38, 44-70, 79-96.

7. Ukrainian Canadian Committee Archives, "Protokoly ekzekutyvy ta skladovykh orhanizatsii KUK" (Minutes of the Executive and Member Organizations of the UCC), November 6-7, 1940.
8. There is some early evidence that Ottawa may have underestimated the viability of the UCC. Writing to his superior, Justice T.C. Davis, on February 5, 1941, Philipps noted: "Three months have now elapsed since the (almost surgical) intervention by which they were got together. But no one has been giving them the nursing and attention which they need if they are to survive and function firmly. I am afraid that they will be wrecked if we show them no signs of satisfaction or guidance." Public Archives of Canada (PAC), Dept. of National War Services, RG 44, vol. 35, Committee on Co-operation in Canadian Citizenship.
9. W. Kirkconnell, *Our Ukrainian Loyalists* (Winnipeg: Ukrainian Canadian Committee, 1943), p. 27.
10. In Manitoba's Provencher constituency, the degree of opposition in the Ukrainian centres was as follows: Vita: 155-144; Arbaka: 121-43; Gardenton: 277-27; Rosa: 123-15; Tolstoi: 132-72; Sundown: 173-63. *Winnipeg Free Press*, 28 April 1942. On April 29, the editor, John Dafoe, accused the Ukrainian nationalists of being Nazis at heart and potential fifth columnists.
11. For details on relief work, see *Proceedings of the Second All-Canadian Congress of Ukrainians in Canada (1946)* (Winnipeg: Ukrainian Canadian Committee, n.d.), pp. 33-9.
12. W. Swystun, *Ukraina i skytaltsi* (Ukraine and the Refugees) (Toronto: n.p., 1946), p. 17. For Swystun's critical view of the UCC, see his *Ukrainskyi patriotyzm v Kanadi na slovakh i na dili* (Ukrainian Patriotism in Canada in Word and Action) (Winnipeg: T-vo kulturnoho zviazku z Ukrainoiu, 1957).
13. A. Hlynka, "The Problem of Ukrainian Displaced Persons," *Novyi shliakh*, 16 January 1946.
14. Immigration statistics vary because many Ukrainians from regions incorporated into the interwar Polish state, afraid of repatriation to the USSR, registered themselves as Poles.
15. Members were the Ukrainian Catholic Brotherhood, Ukrainian Self-Reliance League, Ukrainian National Federation, Ukrainian Canadian Veterans' Association, United Hetman Organization, Ukrainian Workers' League, Ukrainian Youth Association - Plast, Shevchenko Scientific Society, Ukrainian Free Academy of Sciences, Carpatho-Ukrainian War Veterans' Association, Ukrainian National Democratic League, Ukrainian Technical Society, Ukrainian National Association, Research Institute of Volyn, Canadian Friends for Liberation of Ukraine, Ukrainian Evangelical Alliance, Ukrainian Canadian Univer-

sity Students' Union, Ukrainian Canadian Youth Council, Ukrainian Association of Victims of Russian Communist Terror, Canadian League for Ukraine's Liberation, Ukrainian War Veterans' Association, Ukrainian Cultural and Educational Centre, Ukrainian Canadian Women's Committee, Ukrainian Youth Association of Canada – SUM, Ukrainian Teachers' Association of Canada, Brotherhood of Former Combatants of the Ukrainian Division of the Ukrainian National Army.

16. Two of the original UCC members – the United Hetman Organization and the League of Ukrainian Organizations – have faded into obscurity.
17. Before arriving in Canada from a displaced persons' camp, Kochan had distinguished himself as a Ukrainian parliamentarian in Poland and after World War II as general secretary of the Ukrainian Co-ordinating Committee in Europe. A combination of pragmatism and deep dedication to the Ukrainian cause characterized his tenure of office. Kochan had a great influence over Kushnir. Private papers of Volodymyr Kochan, in possession of R. Kochan, California State University, Long Beach, California.
18. Financial contributions from member organizations are divided into four categories according to size – \$1,500, \$330, \$275, \$110 – and from locals into three categories – \$1,500, \$750, and \$300.
19. Interview by the author with Rev. W. Kushnir, 12 April 1974.
20. *Zbirnyk materiialiv i dokumentiv u 25 littia diialnosty KUK, 1940-1965* (Collection of Documentary Material on the Occasion of the 25th Anniversary of the UCC) (Winnipeg: Nakladom komitetu ukraintsiv Kanady, 1965), pp. 110-32.
21. While 50 per cent of Ukrainian Canadians acknowledge Ukrainian as their native language, only 23 per cent use it with any regularity. See *Zvidomlennia KUK za 3 roky pratsi, 1972-74* (The UCC Report for 3 Years of Work, 1972-74) (Winnipeg: Nakladom komitetu ukraintsiv Kanady, 1974), p. 23; I. Tesla, "The Ukrainian Canadian in 1971," in Gerus *et al.* (eds.), *Jubilee Collection*, p. 515.
22. *The Poetical Works of Taras Shevchenko* (Toronto: University of Toronto Press, 1964); *The Ukrainian Poets: 1189-1962* (Toronto: University of Toronto Press, 1964).
23. See L.B. Pearson, *Mike: The Memoirs of the Rt. Honourable Lester B. Pearson*, 3 vols. (Toronto: University of Toronto Press, 1972), II.
24. Although Ukrainians, according to the 1971 census, constituted only 2.7 per cent of Canada's population, this percentage makes them proportionately the largest Ukrainian community in the Western world.
25. Private papers of Volodymyr Kochan.
26. Soviet reaction has been so negative and vehement as to suggest a major concern about the World Congress. See "The Congress of the Unfree," *News from Ukraine*, nos. 41-43, Kiev, 1978.
27. Interviews by the author with S.J. Kalba, October, 1974, September, 1977.

TEN

Ukrainian-language Education in Canada's Public Schools

Manoly R. Lupul

In the education of Ukrainians in Canada's public school systems, a crucial issue has always been schooling in the Ukrainian language or at least the teaching of Ukrainian as a subject of study. Other educational aspects – the value attached to schooling and its prevalence in Ukrainian school districts, the school regimen in the same districts, school consolidation, the status of the teaching profession, the cost of education and the size of school grants, the portrayal of Ukrainians and East Europeans in school curricula and textbooks, or the struggle of Ukrainians to obtain a college or university or even a secondary school education – have generally been secondary issues. Because of the peculiar predicament of Ukrainians in Canada – between the twin fires of Russification abroad and Anglicization in a New World impatient with minority aspirations rooted in Old World concerns – the battle for Ukrainian-language education has been an overriding concern.

The struggle, however, has not been conducted in a social vacuum, and it is well to keep the general educational situation in mind. With most Ukrainians on prairie farms, especially before 1919, rural school conditions were the most important, and these were always far from ideal. School legislation provided for a strong central authority – the department of education – responsible for all aspects of schooling: curriculum, inspection, textbooks, teacher education, formation of school districts, and election of school trustees who levied taxes. Pioneer teachers in elementary school classrooms usually had little advanced schooling: the completion of grade eight was the norm, followed by four months at normal school. With the frontier's insatiable demand for labour, average daily attendance was low and short-term or "half year" schools were common. The number of pupils who went on to high school was low, usually between 2 and 3 per cent of the school population. The hard-pressed pioneer did not value what he thought he did not need, and language education, apart from English, was of little consequence to most in the host society.

Into this unfamiliar situation stepped the bewildered Ukrainians. Most had had little or no experience with state school systems, especially the formation of school districts. The costs involved also frequently dampened enthusiasm as did the language barrier, with bilingual teachers who could speak Ukrainian and English always in short supply. A few families had sons who had reached the upper forms of the gymnasium in Galicia and knew several languages, including English, and a few young men who had been teachers in the old country knew, or quickly acquired, English. But on the whole, the level of literacy was low. In these circumstances, it is difficult to gauge the real interest in schooling, although most male Ukrainians undoubtedly realized the value of English as a working language. That Ukrainians did not rush to form school districts is not necessarily proof of a lack of interest in education. The formation of the more familiar reading associations (*chytalni*) with modest libraries in private homes in Edna-Star in 1898 and in Winnipeg in 1900 would suggest the opposite. The problems were much deeper, as their examination in the most important provincial jurisdiction shows.

MANITOBA

The subject of "Galician" education, first urged upon Premier Roblin's government in February, 1901, by a Presbyterian delegation concerned to establish instruction in English, was much complicated by the provincial legislation of 1890, which had destroyed the financial basis of the Roman Catholic schools and threatened the use of French in the state schools. Following agitation by French Canadians and Catholics across the country and a successful appeal against the legislation to the Judicial Committee of the Privy Council in London, the federal and provincial governments reached an agreement that resulted in new legislation. In March, 1897, the first language legislation in Manitoba's history declared that "When ten of the pupils in any school speak the French language, or any language other than English as their native language, the teaching of such pupils shall be conducted in French, or such other language, and English upon the bilingual system." The retention of bilingual education pleased Quebec; that it was not confined to French pleased Ontario. But bilingual combinations that included Ukrainian, German, or Polish and ignored French or made English a second language were not envisaged and, when they emerged, pleased neither.

The first Ukrainian school district, Galicia, was formed in 1899 with Wasyl Cichocky, in charge since 1898, as teacher. Also among the first Ukrainian teachers were Ivan Bodrug at Kusiw (Dauphin) and Ivan Negrich at Trembowla (Valley River). In 1903 John Baderski was appointed organizer and inspector of Ukrainian and Polish bilingual schools, but neither he nor Michael Rudnicki, who joined his Polish and equally Conservative colleague in 1904, was popular with the Ukrainians, and Rudnicki soon retired because of "some questionable real-estate transactions."[1] In 1907 Theodore Stefanyk, another Conservative and well-known community leader since 1894, was appointed to organize schools. In 1910 Paul Gigeychuk, an even more prominent Conservative and Ukrainian community leader in Winnipeg, succeeded Stefanyk, who became Winnipeg's first Ukrainian alderman in 1911. There is no evidence that, beyond a commendable knowledge of English, either appointee had any pedagogical training or teaching experience.

Schools were not easy to organize. Baderski, however, noticed that attendance improved under teachers who spoke Ukrainian and recommended "a special preparatory school for bilingual (Galician-English) teachers" – all the more important as the "isolated situation" of school districts made it difficult to obtain qualified teachers.[2] As a result, in February, 1905, the government opened the Ruthenian Training School in Winnipeg to complement the pedagogical and theological courses offered at Manitoba College. In the fall of 1907, the Ukrainians were transferred to Brandon to avoid difficulties between themselves and the Poles. The men and boys (there is no evidence of female registrants) who attended the school and similar institutions in Saskatchewan and Alberta became the earliest leaders of their people.

The frustrations were enormous, especially as the teachers were frequently attacked for their Ukrainian nationalism and/or pedagogical incompetence. Their Ukrainian consciousness manifested itself early. At their first convention in Winnipeg in 1907, they formed the Ukrainian Teachers' Association, deciding to discard the archaic "Ruthenian." A committee to press for bilingual textbooks consulted Ivan Franko in Lviv, whom the teachers admired as a Ukrainian writer. In 1908 not only did the first Ukrainian mass meeting organized in Winnipeg place much emphasis on child and adult education, but the community was urged to call itself only "Ukrainian."[3] The teachers' Ukrainian consciousness was also shown through the tenacity with which they pursued (and obtained) six successive Ukrainian instructors at Brandon.

The pedagogical competence of Brandon's graduates is more difficult to assess. Some knew much English; others very little. Some had attended the gymnasium in Europe and knew several languages; others had a modicum of elementary schooling in Canada and spoke English and Ukrainian tolerably well but could not attempt the collegiate's entrance examinations. All, however, were equally welcome to spend three years (if possible) mastering the elementary school curriculum and learning or perfecting their English, before attempting the grade nine examinations. Eleven weeks in a special classroom in an ordinary normal school usually followed, with graduates awarded special certificates to teach primarily in Ukrainian school districts. With the status of the certificates uncertain and each candidate completing only one part of the academic examination, the qualifications could pose problems, as events in Alberta subsequently showed.

Between 150 and 200 students passed through Principal J.T. Cressy's hands at Brandon, and the number of schools among Ukrainians rose from about forty in 1907 to 125 in 1916.[4] Some schools, converted into reading rooms in the evenings or on Sunday afternoons, encouraged parents to acquire literacy in English and/or Ukrainian. But schooling for all was brief and sporadic, and it was not unusual to find children with several years of intermittent schooling in the earliest grades. The salaries were generally low and debt-ridden graduates, obliged to pay the Department of Education the costs of maintenance and tuition,[5] were frequently compensated in kind rather than scarce cash. Not surprisingly, many who taught also farmed, sold insurance, entered politics, or embarked upon studies in law or medicine as soon as circumstances permitted.

Nor did the hostile attitudes of the host society always help. The Presbyterian delegation of 1901 was followed within a year by an even more influential one from Winnipeg, urging the government to repeal the bilingual clause to keep out Ukrainian teachers incapable of developing "thoroughgoing Canadians." The Roman Catholic Archbishop Adélard Langevin countered with an equally impressive mass meeting, where the traditional French Catholic thesis of an inseparable link between language and religion was applied to the Ukrainians.

The government's record of dealing with the problems of Ukrainian education was not brilliant. The problems lay not with the attitude of the Ukrainians toward English-language education but with the government, which tolerated a shortage of well-qualified bilingual teachers, refused to pass a compulsory education law, and allowed Ukrainian to be taught for only one hour per day. With the free-wheeling Roblin administration vulnerable, the Liberals, with the *Free Press* in the lead (between January 1 and March 17, 1913, it published sixty-five long articles critical of bilingual education), agitated for the establishment of two principles: compulsory education and English as the first and only language in all public schools.

Provincial elections in 1914 and 1915 brought the Liberals under T.C. Norris to power, and the new Minister of Education, R.S. Thornton, a Scottish physician, immediately requested the Superintendent of Schools, C.K. Newcombe, to prepare a special report on the bilingual school situation. The position, as Table 14 shows, was much better than had been supposed and, under less hysterical circumstances, changes might have been minimal. The absence of compulsory education, not the existence of bilingual schools, was the main problem, as the low enrolments above grade five indicate. In the 111 Ukrainian and Polish schools (the two were lumped together and only seventy-nine were actually visited), with 114 teachers and 6,513 out of the 16,720 bilingual pupils, the knowledge of English varied greatly, depending on the qualifications and attitude of the teacher, the presence of English-speaking pupils, and the proximity of the school to English-speaking settlements.

The potential for administrative chaos in the bilingual provisions

TABLE 14

Average Attendance and Enrolment in Manitoba Schools, 1915 (per cent)

Type of Bilingual School	*Average Attendance*	*Enrolment in Grades One and Two*	*Enrolment above Grade Five*
French	46	47	16
Ukrainian and Polish	59	68	2
German	65	54	8
(Provincial Average)	67	42	22

Source: *Special Report on Bilingual Schools in Manitoba* (Winnipeg: King's Printer, 1963), pp. 1-2. The provincial averages are calculated from the *Report of the Department of Education for 1914-15* (Manitoba), pp. 24-5.

(Clause 258) was also not in evidence. Eighty-five districts entitled to bilingual schools remained unilingual English due to "a condition of unstable equilibrium." In the same schools thirty-seven teachers were of non-Anglo-Celtic origin, but the children "were able to converse easily and readily in English." It is true that in five schools bilingual teaching "might have been demanded in three languages other than English" and "36 districts teaching on this plan might have been claimed in two such languages." "The arrival or departure of a single family" could alter the language situation and "in nearly one-fourth of the schools actually conducted upon the bilingual system . . . [were] groups of French, German, Polish or Ruthenian children receiving instruction in some other non-English tongues, but not their own." Although the situation was not perfect, Newcombe did not find it serious enough to recommend the abolition of the bilingual system.

Nevertheless, when Thornton presented Newcombe's findings to the legislature early in 1916, he knew that most Manitobans expected drastic changes. The prevailing theory of Anglo-conformity insisted upon the fastest possible assimilation of the immigrant and his offspring to British, Canadian, or Imperial norms – distinctions were seldom made – and of these the most important was the ability to speak English well. That Thornton understood this and much more is clear: "He saw in the assimilation to the British ideal the development of a Canadian nationality which was, by design, unilingual." That he could also rely on Ontario-born Robert Fletcher, Deputy Minister of Education since 1908, who had been minimizing bilingualism by consolidating school districts and encouraging the teacher to use Ukrainian only as "a medium of explanation, and to do his teaching in English,"[6] only strengthened his position once the bill to repeal clause 258 was introduced on February 18.

Spurred on by a Polish public meeting, the Ukrainians crowded the Vladimir and Olga School on December 26, 1915, to listen to Gigeychuk, Stefanyk, Jaroslaw W. Arsenych, and Taras D. Ferley, Manitoba's first

Ukrainian MLA. On January 7 a nine-man delegation, led by Ivan Petrushevich, editor of the Catholic *Kanadyiski rusyn*, and Arsenych, a graduate of the Brandon school and later the first judge of Ukrainian origin in Canada, received "a cool reception" from Premier Norris and several cabinet colleagues.[7] The Ukrainian Committee for the Defence of Bilingual Schools then quickly appealed for mass meetings at twenty-eight centres to "pass the resolutions supplied to them," sign the petitions sent out by the committee's secretary, and elect one representative to a January 28 convention in each electoral district to name a delegate to approach the government again.

On February 3 the delegation, led by Ferley, presented a petition with 6,000 signatures to four cabinet ministers, including Norris and Thornton. Norris was unmoved: "the multiplicity of nationalities within the province makes the present (bilingual) law impossible." All would benefit from the system of education enjoyed by the English-speaking Canadians.[8] Ferley, the Liberal returned as an Independent in 1915, tried to salvage what he could in the House. On February 28 he proposed to retain bilingual education in grades one and two where more than 75 per cent of the pupils spoke a language other than English; thereafter, only English would be used with the second language a subject of study. Where only 50 per cent spoke a second language, all instruction would be in English with the second language a subject of study during the last hour. No one supported the amendment. Next day, Norris and Thornton spoke and the government's bill passed second reading 36-8; opposed were Ferley, F.Y. Newton of Roblin, and the French-speaking members.

Although Ferley and Arsenych told the *Winnipeg Tribune* that the fight would continue, it was clear that the bilingual forces were in disarray and that an important factor had been the absence of Franco-Ukrainian co-operation:

> The Ukrainians [said Ferley] are not working with the French-Canadian interests. It is claimed in certain quarters that the French people - members and other public speakers - did not generously support the Ukrainians in the bilingual fight.
>
> The opinion gained currency that the French were prepared to sacrifice the Europeans if only the teaching of the French language were to be permitted in French schools. This, coupled with the fact that recent French-Canadian conventions held with a view to fighting the Manitoba government's policy at Ottawa have been held without reference to the other nationalities interested in the problem, has created a split in the ranks of bilingualists. The Ukrainians say they will henceforward fight their own battle without any attempt to collaborate or in any way co-operate with the French-Canadian party.[9]

With the report early in May that the Brandon school would be closed and an extra year's academic year in collegiates added to each student's program, the education of Manitoba's Ukrainians had already entered a new era – one which brought no immediate improvement in the school situation. Enrolment increased by 5 per cent between 1910 and 1915 and only 3 per cent in the next seven years, and in 1922, of the 90 per cent enrolled, 41 per cent were absent each day, a sharp drop from the 63 per cent in 1910 but only slightly better than the 46 per cent in 1915.[10] Bilingualism, then, was clearly not the weak link in Manitoba's school system, but so sensitive was the issue that no legal provision for any second language existed for almost forty years.

In 1952 the law was suddenly changed. English remained the language of instruction in all public schools, but trustees could authorize the study of other languages at three distinct times: during a period authorized for religious instruction, or one authorized in the program of studies for teaching a second language, or before and after school hours. Manitoba's Ukrainians did not stir. The last alternative had always existed and was never attractive. The substitution of language for religion posed a difficult, even unfair, dilemma unless language learning was deliberately combined with religious instruction; and in heterogeneous districts all second-language learning was effectively blocked. The middle option, on the other hand, could not be exercised until Ukrainian was authorized as a language of study.

The usual kinds of political pressure were applied to realize the middle option; conference resolutions, briefs to royal commissions, delegations to governments, personal political contacts, and speaking invitations to cabinet ministers. Finally, in 1961, at the commemorative centennial of Taras Shevchenko's death, Premier Duff Roblin, Sir Rodmond's grandson, announced that beginning in 1962 Ukrainian would be an elective subject in grades nine through twelve. Since French, German, Latin, even Icelandic, had been introduced earlier and in 1952 and 1959 Saskatchewan and Alberta respectively had made Ukrainian a secondary school option, further delay was hardly possible.

For the first three years, Ukrainian carried little status. In 1967, however, the University of Manitoba accepted it as a general matriculation subject and, with the Faculty of Arts among the first to respond favourably, a major concern disappeared. By 1970, Ukrainian could be taught through to the kindergarten level, but without suitable teaching materials its study usually began in grade four. In recent years the study of Ukrainian has been hampered by extensive language loss among rural Ukrainians, indifferent school boards like Winnipeg's where a special brief from the teachers' professional development section was needed to obtain Ukrainian as a second language below grade four in the fall of 1975, and the change in university matriculation requirements which deleted compulsory second-language study. However, in July, 1978, as a result of pressure by Winnipeg's Ukrainian Professional and Businessmen's Club, the government amended the school legislation to permit instruction in a language other than English or French for up to 50 per cent of the school day. As a result, in September, 1979, one Ukrainian kindergarten and five Ukrainian bilingual classes with 113 pupils opened in four Manitoba school divisions, indicating that Manitoba's Ukrainians were on the threshold of a new educational era.

SASKATCHEWAN

The education of Ukrainians in Saskatchewan dates effectively from 1901, when the 1892 law establishing English as the language of all schools, with trustees free to offer French as "a primary course," was changed. In this year, the law permitted trustees, on parental request, to employ "competent persons to give instruction in any language other than English" provided the course did not "supersede or in any way interfere with" instruction in the schools and "a special rate" were levied on participating parents to meet any additional costs.[11] Between 1903 and 1918 the teaching of languages other than French was relegated by the Department of Education to the last hour in the school day and confined to teaching reading and writing from texts authorized by the education ministry.

There is some evidence that in Saskatchewan Ukrainian was used to assist in teaching English and that occasionally even a few English- and French-speaking children were present. Some trustees also tried to secure Ukrainian-English teachers by advertising in the Ukrainian press, which urged trustees and teachers to take their responsibilities for teaching Ukrainian seriously.[12] But estimates vary as to the number of schools in which Ukrainian was actually taught or used. By 1916, in the comprehensive annual reports of the province's twenty-five school inspectors, only Inspector J.T.M. Anderson of Yorkton, a critic of bilingualism, indicated that Ukrainian was taught in three public schools. There was no authorized text "to be found" and there were "very few teachers competent to *teach* a second language."[13]

The absence of competent bilingual teachers was no accident. Efforts to train them were frustrated and eventually petered out altogether. In 1908 Joseph (Osyp) Megas, former editor of the *Kanadiiskyi farmer*, in his first and only report as "Supervisor of Ruthenian Schools," recommended that Saskatchewan prepare its own "Ruthenian Teachers" for "Galician settlements," and on October 13, 1909, a Training School for Teachers for Foreign Speaking Communities opened in Regina, with Megas responsible for recruiting.[14]

Regina's equivalent of Brandon, however, was doomed from the outset. The aspirations of Ukrainian students, always the most numerous, were continually thwarted, and it was clear that the teaching of Ukrainian was resisted within the Department of Education. The situation grew steadily worse. The Ontario-born principal, Joseph Greer, formerly at Fort Qu'Appelle, held only a second-class professional certificate, had had no previous experience with the foreign-born, had never taught teachers, was a poor disciplinarian, and was generally unsympathetic toward the aspirations of his students. Nor was his task an enviable one. Students were admitted with less than grade four in their own language and without a "fair" knowledge of English, the minimal requirements. The course required a full eight months, yet Greer seldom had more than six, as classes opened late and closed early. The aim was a variant of Manitoba's: a third-class professional certificate laboriously won through a grade eight exam, followed by grades nine and ten in the high school and a term at the provincial normal school. Agreements betweeen the government and the students and parents required that interest-free loans for board and room – $25 per month – be repaid in six semi-annual instalments. The growing student indebtedness and the unfortunate practice of issuing teaching permits after each six-month session increased the dissatisfaction, as student teachers mistook the permits for certificates and returned to Regina reluctantly.

On February 25, 1914, classes closed abruptly, followed by a petition to the department critical of the principal signed by every student. A three-man departmental commission, which included Julian Androchowicz, Megas's Ukrainian counterpart in the Vonda school district, exonerated Greer and recommended the expulsion of six of the student leaders. The students, however, refused to return, effectively closing the school and forcing Greer to resign. Special classes attached to the normal school followed for "foreign speaking students" with Inspectors Stevenson and Everts in charge. Mykyta Romaniuk, a young immigrant of ten months, assisted the two inspectors until December, 1915,[15] when he was accused of "subversive activities, interned, and . . . summarily dismissed." With Manitoba's example before it and the war intensifying feelings against "the foreigner" and bilingual education, a drop in enrolment from fifty-six in 1915-16 to twenty-nine a year later was all the government needed to close the special classes in April, 1917.

The school's difficulties were accompanied by a frontal attack on the language legislation of 1901 and the departmental regulations of 1903 – as Saskatchewan's Anglo-Celtic majority, concerned about the steady growth of the province's European population, released pent-up feelings embittered by the war, the conscription crisis, and the ever-elusive quick victory in Europe. Led by the Orange lodges, the movement favouring an "English only, English first" policy was formidable and included not only the Soldiers' Wives and Mothers' League and the Sons of England Benefit Society, but the Rural Municipalities Association, the School Trustees' Association, the Saskatchewan Grain Growers' Association, the Protestant clergy, and the Conservative Party.

The government, through Premier Walter Scott, issued an unexpected call for public participation to establish an educational system "more suited to [the] nature of Saskatchewan."[16] The impact was startling. By September, 1915, the Saskatchewan Public Education League was formed and Reverend E.H. Oliver, principal of the Saskatoon Presbyterian Theological College and the league's first vice-president, expressed alarm at the growing political power of the Ukrainians. The emphasis on one language, also carried by him to other parts of the province, became an integral part of "The Crusade for Better Schools." Developments in Manitoba fuelled the demand for basic educational changes, with bilingualism and the unassimilated foreign – the twin perils – at the top of most lists. School inspectors were provided with a set outline for the year 1916 and asked to note the "Nationality of People" and "any tendency to neglect the teaching of English in foreign speaking communities, naming the schools and the teachers; also state the qualifications of these teachers and indicate the general standing of the pupils in such schools."[17]

The detailed, objective reports did not still the fury over language and nationality. They showed there were few problems in education that more competent teachers could not cure – teachers who were not only Canadian-born and English-speaking, but better trained over a longer period of time, and especially skilled in teaching English to non-English-speaking children, an area the government's normal schools generally ignored.[18] The reports, in short, failed to provide an unqualified case against the much despised teachers of foreign origin. Accordingly, on the combined advice of the league, the trustees, and the school inspectors, the government, on June 17, 1917, appointed "an entirely disinterested expert," Dr. H.W. Foght, of the Bureau of Education, Washington, to survey educational conditions "with special reference to rural schools."[19]

On two occasions W.M. Martin, the new Premier who was his own Minister of Education, had tried to stem the rising tide of xenophobia at provincial conventions of Saskatchewan teachers. In April, 1917, he defended the Ukrainians, then under severe attack in the English press; a year later he tried to defuse the issue by insisting that it was education, not the language in which it was offered, that was most important.[20] His words fell on deaf ears.

In Foght's study, released in summary form on March 16, 1918, Ukrainians shared the stage with the Old Colony Mennonites, the Community Doukhobors, and the Germans. Languages were identified with the first generation and the injunction was clear: in public schools languages other than English were to be taught "only after regular school hours."[21] The Premier, faced with numerous form letters and a petition bearing 1,843 signatures, decided to limit all second-language learning to French for an hour per day. When W.R. Motherwell, Minister of Agriculture, resigned in protest, French as a language of instruction was reinstated but confined to grade one; the study of all other languages disappeared.

The Ukrainians in Saskatchewan had been following these developments closely. In 1915 Romaniuk and A.T. Kibzey, a graduate of the Regina training school dismissed as unqualified in Wroxton in 1914, called for the formation of strong teachers' organizations in each province and a convention to form national trustees' and teachers' organizations. Early in September, however, Saskatchewan's convention was postponed to 1916 for lack of delegate interest.

The 400 delegates, including several guests from Manitoba and Alberta, who eventually met in Saskatoon on August 4-5, 1916, surpassed all previous Ukrainian gatherings. Two interrelated themes - education and loyalty to Canada and the British Empire - predominated. Saskatoon's Mayor Young, President Murray of the University of Saskatchewan, and J.S. Woodsworth solemnly urged the Ukrainians to become the best possible citizens through Canada's educational institutions; Bishop Budka, Megas, Ferley, G. Skwarok, and W. Swystun just as fervently assured them that the Ukrainians had no other intentions. On the question of language, bilingualism was espoused by the Ukrainian speakers: while the learning of English was important, Ukrainian also had to be retained. A Ukrainian branch of the Saskatchewan Education League and a Ukrainian section of the Saskatchewan School Trustees' Association were promptly formed and participation was stressed. The government was urged to establish a chair of Ukrainian studies at the University of Saskatchewan, "mutually assist" the attendance of several "ambitious" Ukrainian students at the University's Agricultural College, "evolve some scheme" for teachers' pensions, enforce the compulsory school attendance clause, and enable trustees to tax all lands within a school district. The convention also called for an end to "malicious newspaper propaganda," urging instead co-operation with the recently established British-Ukrainian League in Winnipeg, designed to furnish accurate information about Ukrainians.[22]

At the Saskatchewan School Trustees' Association convention in Regina in February, 1917, a respectable Ukrainian contingent attended. A resolution for "a uniform system of school readers printed in the English language" was tabled by a narrow margin, 330-321. The fact also that P.M. Friesen, who had opposed the "English only" resolution, was elected president along with several other non-Anglo-Celts (none Ukrainian) greatly annoyed J.F. Bryant, chairman of the Regina Public School Board. At the next convention in Saskatoon in February, 1918, the jingoistic Bryant told the teachers "to assist in the maintenance and preservation of British institutions and British ideals, of British customs and British traditions throughout the fair province of Saskatchewan."[23]

The 700 Ukrainians from the Prairies who gathered at a second convention in Saskatoon on December 27-29, 1917, appeared remarkably calm about their educational situation, despite mounting difficulties. Since the provincial election on June 26, in which bilingual education was a major issue, the victorious Liberals had closed the Regina training school, forbidden the use of old-country Ukrainian textbooks, and removed Androchowicz and J. Kuhn of Yorkton as school supervisors.[24] Moreover, the hostile attitude of the Anglo-Celtic school trustees was clear. But equally clear was the fall of the tsarist regime and the emergence of an independent Ukrainian republic, which was encouraged "not [to] lay down her arms until the cause of the Allies has been completely won." With the loyalty of Canadian Ukrainians no longer in question, Megas, the chairman, sounded a significant new note:

> If the so-called foreigner in Canada has failed to respond to the call of duty the English-speaking elements have themselves largely to blame for it. The non-English . . . have been frequently exploited by the professional vote-getter and the unscrupulous who would see the nation in perdition so long as nothing interfered with his wealth-getting schemes. Coldness and reserve seems to characterise especially now the attitude of our English-speaking citizens. . . .

With the approach of the convention of the Saskatchewan School Trustees' Association in February, 1918, feelings ran high, and Ukrainians (one delegate from each school) were urged to attend and oppose changes bearing on language, school consolidation, and the replacement of school trustees by municipal councils. While the convention debate on the language resolutions was extensive, there is no evidence of Ukrainian participation. With the vote against the department's one-hour language regulation 440 to 200, the *Kanadyiskyi rusyn* undoubtedly summed up the sentiments of all concerned Ukrainians:

> The English chauvinists cannot sleep from "worry" that in "foreign" schools it is still possible to teach for *an hour*, not in English, but in a language spoken by a mother to her child. They "fear" that "single hour" more than a Hunnish invasion.[25]

However, when the Saskatchewan government ousted all languages other than English (and French within strict limitations) from its schools, the public reaction of Ukrainians was barely visible. The real and threatened restrictions on civil rights and the growing preoccupation with developments in Ukraine – both by-products of the war – encouraged a low profile. The internments, the loss of the franchise, the designation of Ukrainian as an enemy language, the bilingual press (one column in Ukrainian, the other in English), and rumours of land seizure and even deportation in the English press were all intimidating. Manitoba's example, too, was undoubtedly a factor. If the much better organized Ukrainians in Winnipeg and environs could do little in 1916 to save a truly bilingual system, what resistance could Saskatchewan's Ukrainians offer with no representation in Regina, a smaller and more dispersed intelligentsia, a more restricted training school, no local Ukrainian newspapers, and, possibly most important of all, comparatively modest linguistic provisions to defend?

The same caution characterized the hate-filled twenties, as for over a decade Saskatchewan remained the hot-bed of linguistic and social tension. Not until the Ku Klux Klan had made its appearance in 1927,

Anderson had become premier of a "Cooperative Government" in 1929, the legal status of French had been reduced to a language of study for one hour per day in 1931, and the Great Depression had overwhelmed everybody and everything was the great emotional binge aroused by World War I diverted from language, race, nationality (and creed) to the struggle for economic survival. By then, legislation in 1930 and 1931 had also realized goals first advanced at the third convention of Saskatchewan trustees in February, 1918: all school meetings had to be conducted in English and all candidates for trustees had to read and write English. The Ukrainian trustees succumbed in silence. The defence of Ukrainian newspapers and of leaders like the first Member of Parliament, Michael Luchkovich, a former teacher, had concentrated for years on the loyalty, accomplishments, and contributions of the Ukrainians to Canadian life, without reference to language education in the public schools. Wherever Ukrainian was taught there at all, it was after school hours. In 1931 the offensive to make it once more part of Saskatchewan's public school curriculum was still a generation away.

Not until 1952 was Ukrainian again a language of study in Saskatchewan's schools.[26] No law was passed and none would be; from the beginning the study of Ukrainian was at the pleasure of the Department of Education, providing thereby an interesting case study of the difficulties linguistic minorities must endure to reach even modest goals. It took ten years for the department to agree to re-introduce Ukrainian, and even then it was confined to a two-year experiment in grades eleven and twelve in two Yorkton high schools, Sacred Heart Academy and St. Joseph's College.

In the interim, steps were taken in 1944 to establish Ukrainian at the University of Saskatchewan's Department of Slavic Studies, which, after 1946, awarded credits toward a degree to students at Sacred Heart and St. Joseph's who wrote its Ukrainian 1 exam. The Department of Education, however, refused to grant Ukrainian 1 matriculation status. Only students bound for the Department of Slavic Studies could benefit from the exams, while also enrolled in the ordinary matriculation program. To the Department of Education, however, the extra burden was probably just, for the Ukrainian community was clearly using the Slavic Department as a lever to get Ukrainian into the schools. The same close relationship between university and high school was undoubtedly also responsible for introducing Ukrainian at the top of the grade structure when logically the development of linguistic fluency would suggest the opposite. The Department of Education could afford to be indifferent: effective bilingual education had been strongly opposed by most people in Saskatchewan for decades.

With an election approaching and the census since 1941 showing the Ukrainians to be the third largest ethnic group in the province, Brother Methodius of St. Joseph's approached the Department of Education again and was directed in 1952 to form a "Ukrainian Curriculum Committee" to present a brief to the Minister of Education, complete with texts and course outlines for grades nine through twelve. The brief's rationale, based "on cultural values and not on political expediency or on Ukrainian national aspirations,"[27] was inoffensive and Ukrainian was introduced with the minister's blessing. In 1954 it became an accredited modern language option in all provincial high schools "with certain reservations" depending on the size of school, enrolment, and the teacher's qualifications.

By 1958, to ease a teacher shortage that was reaching crisis proportions, Ukrainian 1 was available as a correspondence course, and by 1964 each high school course could be taken by correspondence. In 1966 Canora Composite High School was allowed to experiment with conversational Ukrainian in grades seven and eight and in the same year uniformity of materials for the Prairies was first proposed. As a result, by the fall of 1968, the Chilton-Didier audio-visual method and materials were adopted for the junior high classes, and early in 1970 the first steps were taken by the loosely organized interprovincial curriculum committee to extend them to the senior high school.

In May, 1974, provincial legislation enabled school boards to allow any language as a language of instruction. Although tied to local initiative, the ubiquitous Department of Education still had the last word through regulations which, in June, 1974, established three different sliding scales for instruction in languages other than English: for French schools, up to 100 per cent in kindergarten and up to 50 per cent after grade four; for Indian schools, up to 50 per cent in kindergarten and up to 20 per cent after grade two; and for all others, up to 20 per cent at any time. The Ukrainians did not stir; nor did the department think it necessary to justify the arbitrarily restrictive, discriminatory time allotments.[28] In 1979 full instruction was permitted in any second language at the kindergarten level and its use allowed up to 50 per cent of the time at other division levels in non-designated schools. With the change, the first kindergarten class in Ukrainian opened in Saskatoon's St. Goretti School, and with the public school authorities also interested in Ukrainian bilingual elementary school classes, their future development clearly rested with the Ukrainian community in Saskatoon and elsewhere in Saskatchewan.

ALBERTA

Ukrainians in Alberta also had their difficulties with provincial school authorities on the language question, and they were no more successful than in the two neighbouring Prairie Provinces. In fact, by mid-1914, even before the outbreak of war in Europe, the "war" in Alberta's Ukrainian classrooms was all but over. Neither the law nor the departmental regulations (the same as in Saskatchewan) were involved. The 1901 provision for non-English language study at parental expense and the 1903 regulations – carried over in September, 1906, and published annually in departmental reports until 1915 – were never issues. No movement to repeal the last hour of language study ever emerged; there is no evidence it was even noticed.

In administering its language policy, Alberta differed from Saskatchewan in two significant ways: Robert Fletcher,[29] not Joseph Megas, was appointed "Supervisor of Schools Among Foreigners" with power to act as official trustee; and the English School for Foreigners in Vegreville established in 1913 did not qualify graduates to teach even in Ukrainian settlements. The government's grip on policy always appeared firm, and even at the height of the crisis in 1913-14, when violence briefly erupted, victory was assured by the critical shortage of bilingual teachers. The first Ukrainian teacher, William Kuriets, did not graduate from an Alberta normal school until 1916[30] when no more than six Ukrainian teachers were available for some ninety-five schools in Ukrainian settlements.[31]

In his first report in 1907, Fletcher indicated that "the most serious obstacle" to progress in the organization of school districts was the attitude of the Ukrainians, who were "loath to engage qualified teachers, all of whom were English-speaking."[32] In March, 1909, a convention of Ukrainian Liberals in Vegreville petitioned Premier A.C. Rutherford's Liberal government, requesting an official school organizer, a Ukrainian training school, and permission to hire Ukrainian teachers trained in Manitoba and Saskatchewan.[33] With no action forthcoming, a ten-man delegation met the Premier in December and was told that if sufficient Ukrainian students applied, a training school would be established and the legislature would consider appointing school organizers. Ukrainian teachers from Saskatchewan or Manitoba were not mentioned.[34]

Two years later the situation remained unchanged. Early in January, 1912, therefore, another convention in Vegreville passed the three resolutions again and also asked the Department of Education to publish the School Act and regulations in Ukrainian, to include at least one Ukrainian teacher on the staff of the training school, and to approve the Ukrainian textbooks then in use.[35] The committee that met the Minister of Education, C.R. Mitchell, on February 22, was led by convention chairman, Andrew Shandro, president of the newly formed Association of Ukrainian School Trustees and a prominent Liberal, who within a year would become Canada's first Ukrainian MLA. From the subsequent exchange of published correspondence between Mitchell and Peter Svarich, the association secretary, it is clear that the government promised only a training school. Svarich treated the promise as an accepted fact and expressed pleasure that Mitchell would support the other resolutions in cabinet.[36]

In May of 1912 John R. Boyle became Minister of Education in Arthur L. Sifton's Liberal administration. The new minister was not only from the Sturgeon constituency, where the Ukrainian vote was significant, but was more appreciative of Ukrainian aspirations. On June 5, Shandro and Svarich reminded Boyle of the convention's resolutions and requested an early and clear official response. The minister's encouraging reply promised a training school by August 1 and a translation of the Act.[37]

In October, Boyle visited Svarich and announced a training school for Vegreville with tuition "up to matriculation standing." By November, Svarich could report a rented building to accommodate forty students, two bursaries, religious instruction by a clergyman after school hours and plans for two teachers, one to teach in English, the other in Ukrainian.[38] When the school finally opened on February 3, Principal W.A. Stickle was the only teacher. The initial enrolment of nine grew to twenty-three, all males sixteen to twenty-eight years of age, thus necessitating much individual instruction.

Alberta's English School for Foreigners was soon plagued with most of Regina's difficulties. A former public school principal in Calgary, Stickle, like Greer, had no special qualifications for his work.[39] Regulations followed, which disregarded student maturity, motivation, and nationality, the result as much of the Stickles' Methodist attitudes as of the government's failure to communicate the school's purposes adequately and of the students' own false expectations.[40] The emphasis on English was marked, in keeping with the school's main purpose: to enable students to master enough of the school curriculum to write the grade nine non-professional examination, preparatory to entering normal school or the school's own commercial course. In this context, Ukrainian studies were superfluous and, although assistants regularly succeeded one another, no Ukrainian teacher was ever hired. Resentment ran deep and when Mrs. Stickle's efforts to teach Protestant hymns on Sunday afternoons became an issue, the students were locked out by the principal on December 7, 1913. Classes resumed early in January, but students above grade eight were transferred to the local high school. In the spring of 1915 Stickle, although exonerated, was replaced as principal. The school, having failed to graduate Ukrainian teachers, closed at the end of June, 1918.[41]

Even though the English School for Foreigners had failed to live up to Ukrainian expectations (the very name was offensive), it was indicative of the government's negative attitude toward the initiatives taken since 1909. What the Ukrainians needed was the largest possible Ukrainian representation in the provincial legislature, and for that the moment was opportune. Both an election and a redistribution of seats were in the offing and the pro-Liberal voting record of the Ukrainians was well-known. Accordingly, the first political convention of Ukrainians in the five constituencies in which they were most numerous – Victoria, Pakan, Vegreville, Whitford, and Vermilion – was called for January, 1913, in Vegreville by an organizational committee which quickly showed its

Liberal colours, not only by its partisan resolution of support for the Sifton administration but also by the delegation chosen to see the Premier – Svarich, Shandro, Paul Rudyk, Roman Kremar, Michael Gowda, and Hryhorii Kraykiwsky (the last four from Edmonton). Sifton accepted the resolution for later use, but held out little hope for controversial boundary changes to ensure three or four Ukrainian representatives. When only the Liberals in the Whitford constituency nominated a Ukrainian candidate, the prominent Liberal Andrew Shandro, the remaining members of the delegation decided to nominate Peter Kulmatysky at the Conservative meeting in Vegreville on March 31. The Liberals countered with the earlier resolution of support and the *Edmonton Bulletin* obliged with an appropriate headline: "RUTHENIANS ARE WITH GOVERNMENT/Large Gathering Held at Chipman [*sic*] at Which Resolution Approving the Sifton Administration is Unanimously Passed." The Vegreville Conservatives were no more accommodating. The nominations committee chose F.A. Morrison over Kulmatysky and an hour-long free-for-all, which spilled into the streets, followed. Next day, Svarich called another meeting, which chose him to run as an Independent;[42] Kraykiwsky, Gowda, and Rudyk also ran as Independents in Vermilion, Victoria, and Whitford respectively. In Sturgeon, out of deference to Boyle, the Ukrainians fielded no candidate. On April 17, to their dismay, only Boyle and Shandro emerged victorious.

The attempt to establish the Ukrainians as a political – and bilingual – force in Alberta's school system had failed miserably and Roman Kremar, in particular, was most disturbed. A moderate social democrat, who immediately before the political meeting in Vegreville had become editor of the newly founded *Novyny* in Edmonton, he concluded that Ukrainian Liberals themselves had brought about the debacle by their overt partisanship which had undermined any hope of an independent Ukrainian political movement. For these same Liberals, as the training school showed, appeared merely to toy with Ukrainian educational aspirations. If further proof were needed, it was soon forthcoming. Within a month of the election, Boyle cancelled the permits of all "Galician teachers." Involved were thirteen individuals: three students from Alberta College, seven from Manitoba College, and three graduates with third-class professional certificates from Brandon.

Strictly speaking, Boyle was within his rights, for none of the permit holders had attended normal school in Alberta. To the Ukrainians, however, the thirteen were all well-educated men, their occasional deficiencies in English notwithstanding; they were certainly capable of teaching elementary school children. To Kremar, in particular, they were intellectuals and patriots, leading their own unfortunate people, in the best European tradition, before the deceptive enemy – the Anglicizers and assimilators – irrespective of party. To Boyle, however, the teachers, some of whom had actively supported the Independent candidates,[43] were part of a political movement, possibly even organized by the Conservatives to weaken traditional Liberal support among "the foreigners." With the positions so diametrically opposed and with some truth on all sides, accommodation was impossible – but with the Liberals all-powerful, it was the teachers who had to go.

And all did go but one. At Bukowina School, immediately north of Whitford Lake, William Czumer, Rudyk's "official agent"[44] and a Brandon graduate, was retained by the school trustees and placed in a hastily assembled private school across the road from the public one. The battle was now joined in earnest between the two uneven camps: *Novyny*-Kremar-Czumer-Rudyk and the English press-Boyle-Fletcher-Shandro. On July 11, Fletcher, as official trustee, filled the public-school position with a Mr. Armstrong to the objections of the trustees and a hostile crowd under police surveillance. Next day, at a special celebration honouring the first Ukrainian MLA, Czumer filed his pupils into the church at Shandro and was complimented by the priest. During the afternoon speechmaking, fisticuffs broke out and William Kozlowsky, one of the fired teachers who wished to speak about schools, had his clothes torn and glasses broken in a mêlée.[45]

When on July 29 the Bukowina trustees were declared innocent and escaped with only $13 in costs for retaining Czumer in the private school, Boyle appealed to the public and threatened to use the Truancy Act: "This is an English speaking province . . . and every Alberta boy and girl should receive a sound English education in the public schools of the province." The remarks naturally pleased the Liberal press, were endorsed by Shandro who declared himself "decidedly opposed to any bilingual schools such as existed in Manitoba," disturbed Svarich who wondered why the education ministers in western Canada could not "work out some scheme whereby a teacher qualified to teach in any one province would be equally qualified in any other province," and infuriated Kremar who referred briefly but forcefully to the language legislation, completely ignoring the more generous regulations which even then graced the department's annual report.[46]

On September 9, at a Liberal rally in Edmonton, Boyle unexpectedly took a very provocative, new direction. He referred to Ukrainians as "the Russian population . . . commonly known by English people as Galicians or Ruthenians" and denied they needed "any special type of school"; English could be taught to "foreign children very satisfactorily by any intelligent English teacher."[47] Kremar was livid; not only was Boyle's pedagogy suspect, but his understanding of East European politics betrayed a Moscophile influence. Boyle had the law amended in October to require "a valid certificate . . . issued under the regulations of the Department." Without it, no person could legally receive remuneration for teaching services and to teach without it was to risk fine or imprisonment.[48]

With the law amended, Fletcher decided in December to meet the Bukowina school situation head-on by warning Stephen Kucher, relieved of his duties as secretary-treasurer on July 11, to stop collecting taxes and gave "five of the leading belligerents," who had already paid their taxes, ten days to do so officially. When they failed, Fletcher began seizing horses on December 15. In her husband's absence, a woman who protested vigorously was apparently roughed up by Fletcher's companions, and on January 4 Armstrong was set upon in his teacherage by several women. Recognizing one of them, Armstrong sued for assault and Mary Kapitsky was fined $200 and, with her eighteen-month-old child, spent two months at the women's jail in Macleod. The next move was Fletcher's. Having discovered that Kucher had paid Czumer his monthly salary of $65 on July 15 (four days after his official removal), Fletcher sued Kucher and on March 30 won a decision in Edmonton. Next day, the Bukowina trustees asked Boyle to reinstate them and were given the standard reply: Alberta granted equal rights to all and special privileges to none.[49]

The Ukrainian counterattack was, of course, spearheaded by *Novyny*. In December, 1913, it formed a fourteen-man school committee, chaired by Kremar, and on March 22, 1914, at a mass meeting in Edmonton, the committee stressed that the teaching of Ukrainian and "a thorough training in the English language" required bilingual teachers. The language issue, however, ran much deeper. The school law had been translated into a Russified Ukrainian by the Moscophile *Russkii holos* in Edmonton, which together with the Winnipeg-based *Russkii narod* was representing the Ukrainian people as Little Russians to the host society at a time when the Ukrainian leadership was struggling to establish the Ukrainians as a people in their own right.[50] In this context it was difficult enough to be deprived of bilingual teachers, but to have the satisfaction of Ukrainians with Alberta's school system confirmed through letters to the editor from such non-Ukrainian spokesmen as Mary Nicolaeff of Morningside, E. Tikotzky and M. Prokot of Edmonton, and a meeting in Rabbit Hill on April 7, 1914, of "over 500 Russians, Little Russians and Poles" was most annoying.[51]

By January, 1915, the bilingual issue had spent itself and its injection by Kremar into the Whitford by-election on March 15 to replace Andrew Shandro, who had been unseated, was definitely anticlimactic. Shandro defeated Kremar 697-484 in a contest that the relieved *Bulletin* declared was not "so much" between two men as "between the ideals of bilingual and purely English schools."[52] In an inexplicable last move, particularly in view of events already under way in Saskatchewan, the government in an Order-in-Council on May 16, 1916,[53] reintroduced the 1903 language regulations which had disappeared with the deletion of all regulations from the department's annual report in 1915. However, the *Alberta Gazette* did not carry the executive's legislation and it went unnoticed. Thus the opportunity to study Ukrainian in the public schools lay untapped until revived well after the Second World War.

For the next thirty years, attacks on "the foreigner" and the struggles during the Great Depression and the war kept Ukrainians from pressing for the chance to learn Ukrainian in Alberta's schools. In December, 1948, the annual convention of St. John's Institute in Edmonton appointed a special committee to request the University of Alberta to introduce Ukrainian, and the campaign was under way.[54] Progress was very slow. Late in 1951, however, the Conservative and Social Credit conventions recognized the sixtieth anniversary of Ukrainian settlement in Canada with motions favouring a chair of Ukrainian studies at the university, and on January 25, 1952, Ukrainian re-entered the province's educational system through the back door in the form of two non-credit, two-month evening courses in the university's Department of Extension. In the first burst of enthusiasm 113 students enrolled; in 1953-54 there were 135 in three courses, one in literary history. Thereafter interest waned. By 1956, no courses were offered and in 1957-58 twenty-five students were enrolled in a single course. Clearly, as in Saskatchewan, the leverage of accredited high school courses was needed to make Ukrainian a viable option in the educational system.

Progress at the school level, however, was even slower. Despite the efforts of the Ukrainian Canadian Committee in Winnipeg and its local branch in Edmonton, by the spring of 1956 only the private teaching by clergy of non-credit courses in six separate schools after school hours had been achieved. In the rural centres the situation was no better. The Smoky Lake School Division tried to capitalize on the department's 1951 regulations which encouraged teacher participation in building curricula in elective areas such as the sciences, vocations, and foreign languages, but the project to offer Ukrainian at the junior high level was never implemented because problems associated with the centralization of rural schools took precedence over the preparation of course outlines and teaching materials. Not until August, 1958, did Anders Aalborg, Minister of Education, indicate in a pre-election speech that Ukrainian would become a language of study in grade eleven in the fall of 1959. Ukrainians were finally to receive what the deeply buried regulations permitted all along.

With the politicians committed, the next steps were to commit the university and to produce the all-important textbook. Neither proved easy. In November, 1958, the Faculty of Arts and Science agreed to offer an accredited summer school course for teachers and students in the Faculty of Education, and in the fall of 1959 the same course was offered for the first time as a general option. However, matriculation status for Ukrainian, largely within the university's sole jurisdiction, was resisted strongly. Not until 1964 did the Faculty of Arts accept Ukrainian as a third language, a status it held until 1969, although other faculties had accepted Ukrainian as a second language four years earlier. The attitude of the university reflected the general early outlook of the educational establishment, which probably represented public opinion at the time. At a meeting of the Department of Education senior high school curriculum committee on April 20-21, 1961, "all the members were enthusiastically in favor of the teaching of Russian. With respect to Ukrainian the Committee seemed not particularly interested in what its future might be."[55] Six months later, Ukrainian 30 was strongly opposed as a matriculation subject by the same committee.

The preparation of a suitable textbook was just as frustrating to the department's subcommittee on Ukrainian chaired by Isidore Goresky, Superintendent of Schools in Thorhild County. The situation was eased considerably in October, 1958, when the subcommittee located Yar Slavutych, a language instructor at the American Army School in Monterey, California, but the publication of his *Conversational Ukrainian* by Gateway Publishers of Edmonton was a most complicated, nerve-racking experience. By September, 1959, the text was ready, though the conversational approach involving language laboratories and tape recorders was never completely reconciled with the subcommittee's conviction that respectability required sufficient formal grammar and written exercises to pave the way ultimately for written examinations. The result was frequently "frustrated and confused" teachers, especially where the necessary mechanical equipment was not provided or used.

In the fall of 1964, with ministerial approval, Ukrainian entered the junior high school as an oral, exploratory subject in grade nine, necessitating a search for more teaching materials. The Didier audio-visual "picture" method, marketed by the Chilton Company of Philadelphia to teach Russian, was adapted to teach Ukrainian in 1965 in Thorhild County. Slavutych's *Ukrainian in Pictures* made Ukrainian possible in grades seven and eight by 1969, after a six-year French-language program was introduced in 1967.

All this activity largely ignored the elementary school. Ukrainian as a language of study was seldom extended to grades four through six in Alberta and in no grade was it a language of instruction. By 1964, however, French had become a language of instruction and by 1970 the teaching periods and regulations were sufficiently liberal to make French education a legitimate alternative. Accordingly, in April, 1971, the School Act was further amended to give all languages comparable status. With the school board's approval, Ukrainian could be a language of instruction in grades one and two (with an hour in English) and for 50 per cent of the school day in each subsequent grade. In January, 1974, five Ukrainian kindergartens opened in Edmonton and in September a government-subsidized three-year pilot project in Ukrainian bilingual education began in grade one.[56] In September of 1980 it became part of the program of two junior high schools in Edmonton. As the Ukrainian bilingual program grows in Edmonton, it encourages both the development of other bilingual combinations in that city and its gradual expansion to other parts of Alberta and to the rest of Canada.

BRITISH COLUMBIA, QUEBEC, AND ONTARIO

The public education of Ukrainians was never an issue in the Maritimes, the Yukon, or today's Northwest Territories; the few Ukrainians neither warranted nor requested special attention.[57] In British Columbia, regular provincial programs in French, Latin, Spanish, and German were supplemented by locally developed programs in Chinese, Italian, and Russian, mainly as languages of study. While the latter groups occasionally campaigned unsuccessfully for special linguistic consideration, the Ukrainians did not. Even in Vernon, where Ukrainians have constituted 20 per cent of the population and some interest has been shown in having Ukrainian taught in the local public schools, the major impediment has been insufficient local initiative to pressure an indifferent and distant government to introduce Ukrainian-language study. Although a Department of Slavic Studies was established at the University of British Columbia in 1964, the study of Ukrainian has not flourished because of low enrolments, and teachers specifically trained in Ukrainian-language instruction have always been few.

In Quebec, on the other hand, the Ukrainian community (20,325 in 1971 or 13 per cent of that in Ontario) has agitated consistently to have Ukrainian offered in the provincial schools. As early as 1912, Montreal's Ukrainians approached the Catholic School Commission and, under the leadership of Father T. Dwulit, obtained four separate classes in two schools, Sarsfield and St. Charles, at Point St. Charles, heavily populated by Ukrainian labourers, to offer instruction in Ukrainian and French. The classes continued into the mid-1920's when the Latinizing influence of the Roman Catholic School Commission caused large numbers of Ukrainian Catholics to become Orthodox and to enrol their children in the unilingual English Protestant schools. Thereafter, the only Ukrainian taught was in the *ridni shkoly* (Ukrainian schools) until 1965, when Premier Jean Lesage, in a meeting with the Ukrainian Canadian Committee in Winnipeg, promised to aid the Ukrainians in exchange for Ukrainian support of French-Canadian aspirations. The government followed with modest grants to the private or Saturday schools of all ethnocultural groups and also introduced Ukrainian as a language of study at the elementary and high school levels where sufficient demand and qualified teachers existed. Classes were established at Rosemount High School in grades eight through eleven in the late sixties, but were discontinued after three years for lack of enrolment. Parents who were not totally indifferent preferred the Saturday schools sponsored by parishes and organizations, whose enrolments, too, were on the decline. Bill 22, introduced by the Bourassa government in 1975, disturbed

Quebec's non-Anglo-Celtic minorities by forcing their children into French-language schools, but the distressed Ukrainians, outnumbered by the Italians, Greeks, and Portuguese, relied on others to confront the authorities.

Following the victory of the Parti Québécois in November of 1976, legislation spearheaded by Camille Laurin, Minister of State for Cultural Development, restricted admission to English-language schools to special categories, which excluded the children of immigrants not already in the English system or where at least one parent had not attended an English school. Immigrants who had traditionally gravitated toward the language of the English-speaking minority would now be absorbed by the French-language schools, though government spokesmen also indicated a willingness to support heritage languages as subjects of study where interest and numbers warranted. The Ukrainians have been singled out periodically as a particularly important linguistic entity in Quebec, and in the wake of the PQ government's 1978 white paper on cultural development, Quebec has joined the Prairies in permitting instruction in languages such as Ukrainian.

Generally suspicious of the PQ's intentions, most Ukrainians tend to approach Québécois aspirations with mixed feelings. They can readily sympathize with the concern to preserve the language and culture of the French "nation" in a predominantly English-speaking North America, and they can understand spokesmen in both groups who compare the French-Canadian situation to the Russification of Ukraine under tsarist and Communist rule. Such spokesmen, however, are few, and in any case they tend to oversimplify. Most Ukrainians feel that the French language, culture, and "nation" have an assured future in Canada, and they are baffled by reasoning which insists that French must be protected by law when, unlike the massive presence of Russian in most urbanized centres in Soviet Ukraine, most Ukrainians in Quebec hear nothing but French in the streets and in the communities where they live. They feel, moreover, that Quebec nationalists have not really tried to understand their desire not to be absorbed by either the French- or the English-speaking milieu. They have been drawn toward the latter for two reasons: most French-Canadian school principals have not welcomed children from immigrant homes; and faced with French Catholic schools that were more French than Catholic and English Protestant schools that were more English than Protestant, Ukrainian Catholics have generally preferred English Catholic schools and the Orthodox have sent their children to English Protestant schools for linguistic (both believe that English is more essential in North America) and religious reasons.

The situation in Ontario, though fraught with difficulties, is less dramatic than in Quebec and much influenced by the fact that Ontario's Ukrainians have lacked the political influence of their prairie counterparts. Representatives to the provincial parliament have been very few and the influence at the municipal and school-trustee levels in Toronto has been negligible. Sociologically, too, Ontario's Ukrainians have differed much from those in western Canada. Ontario received the bulk of the third immigration and still receives a trickle of Soviet Ukrainian émigrés. Speaking Ukrainian fluently and congregating in tightly knit community enclaves, they have been able to conduct most of their social life in Ukrainian. Although the incorporation of Ukrainian into Ontario's public schools is the goal of Canadian-born leaders, others with influence from the last immigration have not always been entirely supportive, concentrating instead on the development of an extensive and vigorous *ridna shkola* system in the province. Accreditation by the state of the latter's courses in advanced Ukrainian language, literature, history, geography, art, and music (*ukrainoznavstvo*) has been deemed the most desirable alternative to motivate students, but the lack both of a uniform program that could meet ministerial approval and of Canadian certified teachers has to date frustrated this goal.

The Catholic separate school system has responded to parental pressure by allowing Ukrainian to be taught as a subject during regular school time for one-half hour each day from kindergarten through grade eight in three schools: St. Josaphat's (1961) in Toronto, Holy Spirit (1966) in Hamilton, and St. Demetrius (1975) in Weston. The school boards meet all the costs, including teachers' salaries, and to maximize the Ukrainian atmosphere the schools may accept only Ukrainian students, who are bussed from all parts of the city.

At the secondary level, of the two private Catholic high schools established in 1962 to teach Ukrainian – St. Basil's in Weston and Mount Mary Immaculate Academy (girls' school) in Ancaster – financial difficulties forced the former to join the Catholic separate school system and falling enrolments gradually destroyed its unique character. In 1977-78 only seventeen out of 650 students were of Ukrainian origin. The academy also closed in 1978 because of declining enrolments.

Several attempts have been made to have the Department of Education accredit Ukrainian as a subject of study at the secondary level. In 1960 the Association of Ukrainian Pedagogues in Canada approached the Minister of Education, on whose advice 186 parents with children at Humberside Collegiate in Toronto petitioned the local board of education, which failed to reply. A similar fate met the briefs of the Canadian Parents' Committee to the Toronto board in 1967 and of Toronto's Ukrainian Canadian Committee (UCC) to William Davis, then Minister of Education, in 1969. On September 30, 1971, after the UCC approached the new education minister, Robert Welch, the Department of Education accredited locally developed courses in languages not in Ontario's schools toward a secondary school diploma on three conditions: the courses had to be taught in the senior division (grades eleven through thirteen), the teachers had to possess valid Ontario certificates, and both the board of education and the department had to approve the courses.

The stringent conditions placed the onus on parents and students and left the implementation to school principals, department heads, and language consultants. Despite considerable opposition by officials (including some of Ukrainian descent), by September, 1972, Ukrainian was offered in four Toronto high schools, in Sudbury, Ottawa, Thunder Bay, and Kenora, and subsequently in Hamilton, St. Catharines, and Windsor. By December of 1973, by ministerial decree, students in grades nine and ten could study Ukrainian. Only Sudbury, where Ukrainian in grades nine through thirteen was offered in night school, took advantage of the additional opportunity. Humberside, which responded in 1977, is the only high school which offers Ukrainian in grades ten through thirteen as day classes. In all other Toronto schools and in every other urban centre, Ukrainian has either disappeared or been relegated to the night school program.

With the passage of time, the initial enthusiasm of the Ukrainian community for the government's new language policy waned. Faced with strong opposition from local administrators, weak leadership by the UCC, and the uncertain impact on teacher employment of Ukrainian as an option at a time of falling enrolments, committed parents and teachers have found it difficult to obtain or to maintain Ukrainian as an accredited high school elective in many schools.

Opportunities at the elementary level increased on July 1, 1977, with the implementation of the government's Heritage Languages Program for all languages other than English and French. On parental initiative, school boards could offer classes after school or on non-school days to a maximum of two and a half hours per week (two and a half hours per day in the case of summer school classes), with full responsibility for hiring the staff (not necessarily certified but acceptable to the board, principal, and parents), for the curriculum, and for supervision (in a suitable facility but not necessarily a state school).

To date, the Ukrainian community's response has been impressive in the two boroughs of Metro Toronto which have accepted the program. Despite pressure from the Ukrainians and other groups, four boroughs, however, have refused to provide their 20 per cent share of the costs, thus denying Ukrainians even the modest benefits of the Heritage Languages Program.

In this difficult situation, an important positive force has been the Ukrainian subcommittee of the Ontario Modern Language Teachers' Association, which has prepared Ukrainian-language curriculum guidelines for grades ten through thirteen, published two textbooks – *Ukrainian, Conversational and Grammatical Level I* and *Level II* by a Canadian-born secondary school teacher, George Duravetz – and organized teacher seminars in Toronto and Ukraine and student tours to Ukraine. Liaison with other ethnocultural groups has also been growing, perhaps most visible in the promotion of heritage language programs in the elementary schools. The Ukrainian professional and business clubs, too, have been taking a more active interest in promoting Ukrainian education, and may, in fact, assume full leadership in the near future in a field abdicated by the UCC. Finally, the younger generation of parents and teachers in some areas have organized *ridni shkoly* outside the jurisdiction of the UCC's "Educational Council," with classes in public school facilities taught by Canadian-certified teachers employing the most recent methodology and teaching materials.

CONCLUSION

The road to the *sine qua non* for many of Canada's Ukrainians – effective Ukrainian-language education in a Ukrainian-Canadian cultural context – has been a difficult one in all provincial school systems. It has suffered from the fears or whims of politicians, the hostility or indifference of administrators, and occasionally from the unnecessary competition of the Ukrainian community's own private schools when better-equipped state alternatives were available. It has lacked adequately prepared teachers and almost every conceivable adjunct of good teaching. But most of all, probably, it has suffered from an ambiguity inherent in North American life itself: how much value can a second language have, even if spoken fluently, in a large, utilitarian, and mobile country like Canada? Moreover, what place can Ukrainian reasonably expect to have in a society where more than a quarter of the people speak French as a first or second language? And, finally, apart from the status official government recognition bestows, have Ukrainian Canadians themselves been interested in much more? The consistently low enrolments in the sixties and seventies regardless of program or place have undoubtedly been influenced by all these considerations – and in the end, perhaps, there is no better commentary on what the future may hold.

NOTES

1. M.H. Marunchak, *The Ukrainian Canadians: A History* (Winnipeg: Ukrainian Free Academy of Sciences, 1970), pp. 115, 262.
2. *Report of the Department of Education for 1904* (Manitoba), p. 46.
3. Marunchak, *Ukrainian Canadians*, pp. 119, 122.
4. *Ibid.*, pp. 121, 149.
5. As of January 1, 1911, twenty-six Brandon students owed the department $14,000, an amount which covered only one-third of the costs. *Manitoba Free Press*, 16, 18 January 1913.
6. M.A.R. Denton, "The Abolition of Bilingual Schools in Manitoba in 1916," unpublished paper in Manitoba Public Archives, February, 1973, pp. 21-30, 52-3, 59.
7. Marunchak, *Ukrainian Canadians*, p. 147.
8. *Manitoba Free Press*, 14 January, 4 February 1916. For the petition, see *ibid.*, 26 January 1916.

9. *Winnipeg Tribune*, 7, 25 March 1916.
10. B.N. Bilash, "Bilingual Public Schools in Manitoba, 1897-1916" (Master's thesis, University of Manitoba, 1960), p. 101.
11. *Ordinances of the North-West Territories*, c. 29, s. 136(2-3) (1901).
12. *Kanadyiskyi rusyn*, 23 August, 13 September 1913; 28 March, 6 June 1914; 19, 29 November, 21 December 1913; *Ukrainskyi holos*, 22 November, 6 December 1911; *Kanadiiskyi farmer*, 30 August, 20 September 1902.
13. *Annual Report of the Department of Education of the Province of Saskatchewan 1916* (Regina: King's Printer, 1917), p. 143.
14. *Ibid., 1907* (Regina: Government Printer, 1908), p. 36; *ibid., 1908* (Regina: Government Printer, 1910), p. 58. In 1909 Megas became "Supervisor of Ruthenian and Galician Schools" and from 1911 through 1913 he was "Supervisor of Schools in Foreign-Speaking Districts" (after 1914, "Communities"), a post shared from 1914 through 1917 with another Ukrainian, Julian Androchowicz of Vonda, and with H. Von Meyer (Regina) and J. Kuhn (Yorkton). The discussion of the Regina school is based largely on M.P. Toombs, "A Saskatchewan Experiment in Teacher Education 1907-1917," *Saskatchewan History*, XVII (Winter, 1964), pp. 1-11.
15. Before the appointment, the department invited sixty Ukrainian teachers to Saskatoon to hear A.H. Ball, Deputy Minister of Education, J.A. Snell, principal, Saskatoon Normal School, and Inspector J.E. Coombs. They visited the university and, at the close of the three-day session, passed a resolution urging "an improvement of the foreign training school at Regina." *Saskatoon Phoenix*, 7, 10 August 1914.
16. *Ibid.*, 4 June 1915; *Regina Leader*, 3, 23 June 1915.
17. *Annual Report of the Department of Education of the Province of Saskatchewan 1916*, p. 6.
18. *Ibid.*, pp. 85, 133-4, 136, 144, 172-3, 191.
19. H.W. Foght, *A Survey of Education in the Province of Saskatchewan Canada* (Regina: King's Printer, 1918), p. 6.
20. *Kanadiiskyi farmer*, 20 April 1917; 19 April 1918.
21. Foght, *Survey of Education*, pp. 151, 154.
22. *Saskatoon Phoenix*, 4, 5, 7 August 1916; *Kanadyiskyi rusyn*, 9, 16 August, 6, 13 September 1916.
23. *Ukrainskyi holos*, 7 March 1917; *Regina Leader*, 1 March, 12 April 1917.
24. *Ukrainskyi holos*, 2 January 1918.
25. *Kanadyiskyi rusyn*, 13, 27 (translation) February 1918; *Regina Leader*, 22 February 1918.
26. This account is based on Brother Methodius, "The History of the Ukrainian Language in Saskatchewan High Schools," *Tema* (Saskatchewan Teachers of Ukrainian, Saskatchewan Teachers' Federation), I (Fall, 1968), pp. 8-9; also on documents in the possession of Mr. Isidore Goresky, Edmonton, Alberta. (Hereafter Isidore Goresky Papers.)
27. C.H. Popowich, *To Serve Is to Love: The Canadian Story of the Sisters*

Servants of Mary Immaculate (Toronto: University of Toronto Press, 1971), p. 258.

28. M.R. Lupul, "Bilingual Education and the Ukrainians in Western Canada: Possibilities and Problems," in *Yearbook*, Canadian Society for the Study of Education, III (1976), pp. 94-6.
29. Fletcher's origins remain obscure; there is no evidence of family ties with his namesake in Manitoba.
30. W.A. Czumer, *Recollections about the Life of the First Ukrainian Settlers in Canada* (Edmonton: Canadian Institute of Ukrainian Studies, 1981), p. 103.
31. For the number of teachers, see C.H. Young, *The Ukrainian Canadians: A Study in Assimilation* (Toronto: Thomas Nelson & Sons, 1931), p. 194; for the list of schools, see J.G. MacGregor, *Vilni Zemli (Free Lands): The Ukrainian Settlement of Alberta* (Toronto: McClelland and Stewart, 1969), pp. 271-4.
32. *Second Annual Report of the Department of Education of the Province of Alberta 1907* (Edmonton: Government Printer, 1908), p. 58.
33. *Vegreville Observer*, 3 March 1909.
34. *Edmonton Journal*, 28 December 1909; *Edmonton Bulletin*, 29 December 1909; *Kanadiiskyi farmer*, 5 January 1910.
35. *Vegreville Observer*, 21 February 1912; *Ukrainskyi holos*, 17 May 1911.
36. *Kanadyiskyi rusyn*, 13 January, 23 March 1912; *Kanadiiskyi farmer*, 1 March 1912.
37. *Kanadyiskyi rusyn*, 6 July 1912. The published correspondence aroused public criticism of Svarich's motives, religious views, and political activities: *ibid*., 17, 24 August, 7, 14, 28 September, 5 October, 23 November 1912.
38. *Vegreville Observer*, 23 October 1912; *Kanadiiskyi farmer*, 25 October, 1 November 1912.
39. *Eighth Annual Report of the Department of Education of the Province of Alberta 1913*. (Edmonton: Government Printer, 1914), pp. 49-50; *Vegreville Observer*, 18 December 1912.
40. For the regulations, see *Novyny*, 27 December 1913.
41. *Vegreville Observer*, 8 May, 12 June 1918.
42. Czumer, *Recollections*, pp. 100-2.
43. See Svarich's letter, *Vegreville Observer*, 3 September 1913; also *ibid*., 10 September 1913.
44. *Ibid*., 25 June 1913.
45. Czumer, *Recollections*, pp. 113-14; *Edmonton Bulletin*, 14 July 1913; *Vegreville Observer*, 16 July 1913; *Novyny*, 22 July 1913.
46. *Novyny*, 11, 15, 22, 25 July, 5 August, 22 November 1913; *Edmonton Bulletin*, 20 August 1913; *Edmonton Journal*, 23 August 1913; *Vegreville Observer*, 27 August, 3 September 1913.
47. Quoted in *Edmonton Bulletin*, 13 September 1913. For his references in the legislature to Ukrainian as a Russian dialect, see *ibid*., 26 September, 16 October 1913.

48. *Statutes of Alberta*, 4 Geo. V, c. 16, s. 149 (2-3) (1913, second session).
49. *Novyny*, 22 August, 9, 23 December 1913; 28 March 1914; *Edmonton Bulletin*, 10, 15, 21 January, 1 April 1914; Czumer, *Recollections*, pp. 115-17; MacGregor, *Vilni Zemli*, pp. 228-9.
50. *Novyny*, 9, 25 December 1913; 24, 26, 28 March, 2, 4, 9, 11, 16, 18 April, 26 May 1914.
51. *Edmonton Capital*, 2, 4, 9 April 1914; *Edmonton Bulletin*, 20 January, 13 April 1914.
52. *Edmonton Bulletin*, 16, 19 March 1915; *Vegreville Observer*, 3 March 1915; *Edmonton Journal*, 16 March 1915.
53. Provincial Archives of Alberta, O.C. 582-16, 16 May 1916.
54. Based on I. Goresky, "Introduction of Ukrainian in Alberta High Schools," *Manitoba Modern Language Bulletin*, II (Winter, 1968-69), pp. 24-35: P. Savaryn, "Ukrainska mova v provintsiinyh shkolah Alberty" (The Ukrainian Language in the Provincial Schools of Alberta), in Y. Slavutych, *Zakhidnokanadskyi zbirnyk* (Collected Papers on Ukrainian Settlers in Western Canada) (Edmonton: Shevchenko Scientific Society in Canada, 1973), pp. 71-128; and documents in the Isidore Goresky Papers.
55. "Minutes of the Thirty-Third Meeting of the Senior High School Curriculum Committee, April 21-22, 1961," Isidore Goresky Papers.
56. M. Lupul and P. Savaryn, "The Politics of English-Ukrainian Bilingualism in Alberta," *Ukrainian Canadian Review* (Edmonton: Ukrainian Canadian Professional and Business Federation, 1975), pp. 18-22.
57. The writer is indebted to the following who assisted in the preparation of this section: Ms. Frances Swyripa; Mr. Roman Herchak (British Columbia); Mr. Bohdan Panchuk, Dr. Ivan Myhul (Quebec); Mr. George Duravetz, Mr. Michael Wawryshyn (Ontario).

ELEVEN

The Ukrainians and Private Education

Frances Swyripa

The education of Ukrainians was not confined to the public schools. Private groups supplemented their work and during the pioneer period often preceded them. Among the most significant private efforts were those by the Presbyterian, Methodist, and Roman Catholic home missionaries, followed in time by a loose network of *ridni shkoly* (Ukrainian schools) and *bursy* (student residences), with a Catholic or Orthodox parish base and/or a political-cultural orientation. While non-Ukrainian initiatives were largely confined to the early decades of the century when the newly arrived immigrants were ill-prepared to establish their own institutional structures, the *ridni shkoly* and *bursy* have evolved with the Ukrainian community and endured in varying forms to the present.

The Presbyterian and Methodist churches saw the thousands of East Europeans as an evangelical opportunity comparable to that offered by China, Japan, or India, and great efforts were made to found medical missions and school homes. Anxious to thwart their efforts (and those of the Russian Orthodox clergy), the Roman Catholics countered with home missionaries of their own, who either assisted Greek Catholics to establish private schools or initiated others until the Greek Catholics acquired a bishop of their own late in 1912. With the abolition of bilingual schools during World War I, Ukrainians concerned with the survival of their language and traditions intensified their efforts in the private sector, especially through the *bursa* movement.

THE PRESBYTERIAN AND METHODIST HOME MISSIONS

Religious and patriotic motives, coupled with concern for material and social well-being prompted by the social gospel, determined the response of Canadian Protestant churches to the Ukrainian presence in Canada.[1] The Methodists and the Presbyterians were the most enterprising, establishing rural missions in Ukrainian settlements across the Prairies. Educational, medical, and evangelical work was interwoven to "Christianize" and "Canadianize" the Ukrainian immigrants. To both churches, the school home, where Ukrainian youth were removed from their families not only for educational advantages, but to expose them also to Anglo-Canadian Protestant values and institutions on a daily basis, was the ideal means for moulding young "foreigners" into responsible Christian citizens.

Three considerations were paramount in all Protestant home missionary work. The first maintained that authoritarian churches and ritualistic religions were evil. God had brought the Ukrainians to Canada expressly to introduce them to evangelical Christianity and to the Scriptures to make them more complete human beings – to bring them "under the quickening, renewing, uplifting influences of a pure Christianity."[2] The second principle in its pure form emphasized personal salvation and universal brotherhood.[3] The religious motive, however, was frequently marred as evangelical Christianity became equated with the "superior" British-Canadian ideals and way of life, and the two were seen to be mutually interdependent. With the influx of a strange and very prolific people threatening the ethnic, economic, political, and social structure of Canada, a third principle emerged – the assimilation of Ukrainians in the national interest. Under the motto "Canada for Christ" socio-economic commitment came to parallel religious concern, as the fear of losing their identity and hegemony became very real among the Anglo-Canadian Protestant clergy.[4]

The Presbyterian Missions

By 1921, the Presbyterian Church had established sixteen mission centres, mainly in Manitoba, with residential school homes and medical facilities funded and staffed by the Women's Home Missionary Society. In this work, Manitoba College in Winnipeg played a large role as a training ground in Canadian ideals and the tenets of evangelism for future Ukrainian leaders. In 1900 Ivan Bodrug and Ivan Negrich were the first Ukrainian teachers to graduate from it. They had enrolled in 1898 and interrupted their education in 1899 to take up homesteads, but were persuaded by Reverend James Robertson, superintendent of home missionary work, to serve their people by organizing schools under Presbyterian auspices.[5] By 1903, the Presbyterians had centres of instruction at Sifton, Riding Mountain, Valley River, and Ethelbert in Manitoba and at Insinger in Saskatchewan.[6]

In 1904 Michael Sherbinin, a Russian Protestant, left his mission work among the Doukhobors to instruct Ukrainian boys and young men interested in the ministry or teaching. His first class had sixteen students, for whom the Home Mission Committee established a fund from which they could borrow $16 a month, repayable upon obtaining employment. Sherbinin divided his students into junior and senior sections and prepared them for matriculation. An hour each day was devoted to Ukrainian language and literature. To the Presbyterian Church, the future of the

Independent Greek movement and of evangelism among Ukrainians depended upon the character and success of Sherbinin's first class.[7]

The purpose of the Presbyterian school homes was the same as that of Manitoba College: "To send back each year into the life of the colony . . . boys trained in our public and high schools with a careful and systematic religious education . . . making for Christian citizenship. . . ."[8] The concept of the school home, born at Lake Geneva (Wakaw), Saskatchewan, where Reverend George Arthur first boarded four pupils and provided rooms for nine others, achieved its most elaborate expression in the pioneer institutions at Vegreville and Teulon.

The school home at Vegreville was opened by the Women's Missionary Society in August, 1910, at the suggestion of Reverend Arthur, who had boarded several Ukrainian children from the area.[9] By 1912, two boys' homes had been established there and by 1914 four buildings accommodated thirty-four boys and fourteen girls. Only students below sixteen were admitted, with those older slated for the proposed English School for Foreigners. Children from broken homes, orphans, and others with no rural public school nearby attended, as did those sent voluntarily by their parents. Often the Missionary Society's community workers who travelled the countryside persuaded parents to enrol their children. Separated from their families, the children, few of whom spoke English, which was "strictly enforced," became so homesick that "some boys actually ran away . . . with some neighbor who happened to be in Vegreville." The residential staff lightened its work substantially by giving the students various chores – from making beds to milking cows. Discipline, corporal punishment included, was strict. Despite expectations, the society's reports show that parents did not always contribute to their children's upkeep. The students studied English, religion, and the psalms, sang hymns four nights a week, attended morning services and Sunday school, and memorized the Scriptures. In the early years Reverend Maxim Zalizniak taught Ukrainian language, history, and folk songs.[10] The need for farm help during the war and the flu epidemic in 1918 hit enrolments hard. So did the Vegreville school board's refusal to accept children from outside its district until the Presbyterians equipped a temporary classroom with a teacher for intermediate pupils.[11] Despite such difficulties, the school only closed in June, 1938, once greatly improved public rural schools had increased.

The Presbyterian mission at Teulon was established in 1902 by Reverend Alexander J. Hunter, a medical missionary. A hospital followed in 1904, a boys' home in 1912, and a girls' home in 1918. Here, too, the objective was to train leaders to challenge the grip of Ukrainian "nationalists," whom Hunter blamed for the decline and failure of Protestant work. The key was access to "technological knowledge" through the public and normal schools, with the school homes furnishing the "inner life and mental and spiritual attitudes of English-speaking people."[12] Once the war was over, the Teulon boys offered night classes to teach

Ukrainian men English, reading, writing, arithmetic, and Canadian history. They also formed their own club, Zoria (Star), where they held Ukrainian classes, debates, and concerts. Under the United Church, the Teulon school homes existed as boarding schools into the 1940's.

The Methodist Missions

Unlike the Presbyterians, the Methodists focused primarily on the Ukrainian bloc north and east of Edmonton, sending Reverend Charles H. Lawford, a medical missionary, to Pakan (Fort Victoria) in 1907, where the Home Mission Board established the George McDougall Hospital six years later. The Women's Missionary Society founded school homes at Wahstao (1904), Kolokreeka (1908), and Radway (1921) and hospitals at Vegreville and Lamont. By 1914, the seven missions and twenty-four workers had approximately fifty converts. Without rural public schools, the Wahstao School Home operated as a private school for two years. Thereafter, it concentrated on orphans, children from broken homes, and those far from a public school. Kolokreeka, just north of Smoky Lake, became primarily a dormitory for girls attending high school in Smoky Lake during the 1920's. It closed in 1932 and Wahstao followed in 1937, both victims of the Great Depression. In the same year the Radway School Home became solely a residence for girls completing high school; it was sold in 1946. Each found its usefulness challenged by the steady growth of rural school districts and was eventually eliminated by improved transportation and school centralization. A fourth institution, the Ruthenian Girls' Home (1909) in Edmonton, also suffered during the Depression and closed in 1937.

Each rural school home was usually staffed by four Missionary Society workers. The head or matron, usually also the secretary-treasurer, was responsible for meals, supplies, repairs, the allocation of duties, and the reception of guests. The teacher attended to the school, supervised evening study, the library, and the playground, and assisted in Sunday school work. The community worker visited homes and organized women's groups, clubs, church services, the Sunday school, and Christian education classes. A fourth member was in charge of clothing, personal hygiene, and health, including illness. The children helped with cooking, mending, milking, gardening, and the laundry, and parents unable to pay the monthly fee of eight dollars provided supplementary food.

The Methodist institutions were resisted by Ukrainians. Even without priestly admonitions, evangelism was foreign to Ukrainian culture, and the ostracism which faced potential converts kept most at a distance. At Pakan, Lawford's deep dislike of Greek Orthodoxy and Catholicism, especially the latter's "worship of the Virgin Mary," and his personal aversion toward Ukrainians alienated many.[13] Attendance at the Kolokreeka Sunday school plummeted from fifteen to one after a Greek Orthodox priest visited the area. Nor did the inadequacy of the

Methodist staff help. Unlike the Presbyterians, Methodist home missionaries were unfamiliar with Ukrainian culture and rarely spoke the language. Many came from eastern Canada – young, single, ignorant of pioneer life, and anxious to leave because of the very difficult rural conditions.[14] Protestant missionary work had peaked in the early 1920's, though the institutions inherited by the United Church in 1925 existed one to two decades longer.

ROMAN CATHOLIC INITIATIVES AND SUPPORT

Before the arrival in 1902 of the Basilian Fathers and the Sisters Servants of Mary Immaculate from Galicia, Roman Catholic missionaries had offered classes in English to Ukrainians in the cities.[15] One such class taught by the Sisters of the Faithful Companions of Jesus was attended by about forty girls employed as domestics in Edmonton in 1901. Concerned to counter Protestant inroads, the Roman Catholic Church became involved also in the education of young, rural Ukrainians. Ukrainian boys were placed with the Redemptorist Fathers for public education and religious training, but the results were limited. The Ukrainians resisted the French and Belgian missionaries and the small number of boys reached could not counter the influence of Manitoba College. The Latin-rite church persevered nonetheless, hoping to create a system of private schools which would help to preserve Catholicism among the Ukrainians. In 1909, for example, the Roman Catholic Church Council in Quebec provided the initiative for St. Josaphat's Missionary School for boys, established in Sifton in 1912. French priests, obtained by Archbishop Langevin, adopted the Eastern rite and learned Ukrainian while a Ukrainian was also engaged to teach. The Ukrainian public, which distrusted the Roman Catholic clergy, failed to respond, and in 1916 the Sisters Servants turned St. Josaphat's into a school for girls.[16]

Much more successful were the Roman Catholic efforts to support such Greek Catholic initiatives as the St. Nicholas School in Winnipeg. Dating from 1905, when two Sisters Servants taught a Ukrainian day school organized by Father M. Hura in his parish, the school moved to the basement of St. Nicholas Church once enrolments increased. It offered the regular public school program in three languages – Ukrainian, Polish, and English – and classes in Ukrainian history, religion, handicrafts, and language. The sisters handled 106 students in 1906 and even greater numbers thereafter – until the health inspector intervened. Overcrowded in a leaky, rat-infested basement, the school obtained $25,000 through Archbishop Langevin from Catholic mission sources in Toronto to build the private Ukrainian Catholic School of St. Nicholas, today's Immaculate Heart of Mary School.

The sisters also opened two day schools in Alberta in 1905. One began in makeshift quarters in the Basilian chapel at Beaver Lake (Monaster), a short distance from today's Mundare. It quickly enrolled sixty pupils, thirty of whom lived with the sisters. A school building with classes to grade eight, erected in 1913, was replaced in 1926 by St. Joseph's School and Orphanage in Mundare. When the latter became a novitiate in 1938, its pupils went to the regular school in the village, where the sisters also taught for a time. The second school, in a house near St. Josaphat's Church in Edmonton, was replaced by a combined school and residence for the sisters in 1910 with $15,000 which Bishop Legal had obtained from a Catholic organization in Toronto. It became a regular state school taught by three sisters and two secular teachers in 1918, and four of its classrooms are today part of Sacred Heart Separate School.

In Saskatchewan the Sisters Servants opened a convent, orphanage, and private school for girls in Yorkton in 1915, with money solicited by Bishop Budka from the Sulpician Fathers in Montreal. Teaching in the Sacred Heart Institute began in January, 1917, with instruction to grade eight and courses in Ukrainian language and religion for twenty-five pupils, seventeen in residence. In 1932 high school grades were added and in 1945 the Institute, renamed Sacred Heart Academy, became a private school for girls.

St. Joseph's College for boys, also in Yorkton, was built in 1919 with $100,000 from the Catholic Extension Society in Toronto, which retained ownership. Without a male teaching order, Bishop Budka engaged the Brothers of the Christian Schools, assisted by the Redemptorists, to educate young Ukrainian males and foster the Greek Catholic priesthood. The initial Ukrainian response was poor. It was the establishment of St. Joseph's, with its non-Ukrainian teachers and non-Ukrainian ownership, that brought the Mohyla Institute in Saskatoon closer to the Ukrainian Greek Orthodox Church.[17] By 1930, St. Joseph's taught only the regular high school program, in addition to religion and Ukrainian, but the latter was not officially recognized until 1947, when the first university examinations were written. In 1963 St. Joseph's became a junior college, an affiliate of the University of Saskatchewan and thus eligible for government grants. In 1972 it acquired new status as Parkland Community College.

Roman Catholic support for such orders as the Sisters Servants, who staffed schools and hospitals, was most significant during the pioneer period. In subsequent years the sisters founded their establishments with Greek Catholic funds. Winnipeg, Mundare, Edmonton, and Yorkton remained the pioneer centres, but with the increase of Ukrainians in Ontario and Quebec after World War II, their influence also grew in eastern Canada. In 1952, for example, they established Mount Mary Immaculate Academy, a private high school for girls, at Ancaster, near Toronto. But it was the early private schools, which combined provincial curricula with Ukrainian classes wherever possible and became recognized institutions, that were the most important, as was the teaching which the sisters themselves frequently did in state schools, especially before the war.[18]

THE *RIDNA SHKOLA* MOVEMENT

While Protestant, Roman Catholic, and later Greek Catholic missionaries were engaged in establishing more formal educational institutions among Ukrainians on the Prairies, the Ukrainians themselves had been active across Canada at the grassroots level. Wherever there were sufficient pupils, a willing teacher, and parental interest, they established *ridni shkoly* or part-time Ukrainian schools to teach their children the Ukrainian language and, if possible, the literature, history, geography, and cultural traditions of the homeland.[19] Prior to World War I, Ukrainian labourers as far away as Sydney and Dominion in Nova Scotia operated two such schools, while in Montreal the Drahomanov Society sponsored one for Ukrainians in the Protestant system.[20] The *ridni shkoly*, however, only came into their own after Ukrainian was banned in the public schools of the Prairie Provinces. The first to respond were the churches and the pioneer organizations – the *prosvity* (adult education/enlightenment societies), the *chytalni* (reading clubs/associations), and the *narodni domy* (national homes/community centres). Where no building existed, concerned individuals opened their homes or obtained permission to use the local public school after hours or on Saturdays.

Through the Sisters Servants of Mary Immaculate, the Greek Catholic Church was best equipped to establish *ridni shkoly*. From such centres as Ituna, Dauphin, Winnipeg, Regina, Komarno, and Mundare, summer vacation schools were organized by travelling sisters and priests in remote rural areas. Between 1930 and 1940 in the Mundare area alone, the sisters instructed 514 children in eighty-two locations. By 1937, they were conducting vacation schools in twenty-four colonies in Manitoba, thirty-six in Saskatchewan, twenty-five in Alberta, and several out of Toronto and Ottawa for a total of 3,916 pupils.[21] In larger centres the sisters held classes two or three times weekly, usually in the parish hall from 4:30 to 6:00 p.m. and on Saturday mornings.

Ridni shkoly promoted by the *prosvity* usually experienced much more checkered careers. That sponsored by the Fort William Prosvita Society, one of the first in Canada, was typical. With ten students in 1910-11 and 179 five years later, the school had its own building by 1918, funded by parents and the proceeds from bazaars and school concerts. In 1919 a teacher arrived from Europe, but in the 1920's enrolments dropped and by 1930 the school had only eighty pupils in six grades. Rapid teacher turnover prevented the most effective instruction. During the Depression the *diak* (deacon) and priest were often replaced by qualified teachers trained in Europe or Canada, but financial pressures made payment difficult. The new immigration after 1945 brought a fresh supply of teachers, but in the 1950's total enrolments averaged between twenty and thirty pupils, meeting three times a week for two hours during the regular school term. By 1956, the combined enrolment of the six Ukrainian schools in Fort William and Port Arthur was less than that in two schools in the early years.[22]

The Ukrainian Greek Orthodox Church, too, became deeply involved in the *ridna shkola* movement, convinced that such schools were indispensible in forming a Ukrainian outlook and an appreciation of the Orthodox faith. The fifth *sobor* (synod) in 1927 specifically instructed priests to arrange for instruction in Ukrainian. Frequently, they themselves taught. The Ukrainian Women's Association of Canada (SUK) of the Ukrainian Greek Orthodox Church also actively organized *ridni shkoly* and located teachers. In 1938 the association resolved to replace textbooks from Galicia with readers portraying life in Canada, and in 1940 Illia Kiriak was engaged by the Ukrainian Self-Reliance League (SUS) to write the series. His primer *Marusia* appeared in 1947 but no others followed. In 1945, after a committee studying Ukrainian schools recommended that the Mohyla Institute promote Ukrainian among the young by helping to organize *ridni shkoly*, an extension department was established at Mohyla to collect school data, followed in 1946 by the first steps to develop a uniform method of teaching Ukrainian. That summer, Mohyla also held its first session to train Ukrainian teachers, and the following year St. Andrew's College inaugurated a similar course. In 1950 the extension office at Mohyla was transferred to Winnipeg, and in 1957 the Ukrainian Educational Council of Canada became one of the departments of the Orthodox consistory "to provide the teachers with texts, guide books, teaching aids and advice, so that the instruction will be fairly uniform in all Ukrainian schools in Orthodox communities across Canada."[23]

The first *ridna shkola* teachers, many of whom also taught in the state schools, created an interprovincial, non-sectarian, non-partisan General Committee for Ukrainian Schools at a Ukrainian teachers' convention in Manitoba in 1923 to co-ordinate and promote Ukrainian schools through an information section with statistics on schools, teachers, and pupils. Among the committee's members were Wasyl Swystun, Osyp Nazaruk, Ivan Bobersky, Jaroslaw W. Arsenych, Myroslaw Stechishin, and Taras D. Ferley. Ukrainian opposition in each province to the proposed consolidation led the Winnipeg *ridna shkola* teachers to propose, in 1932, the Society of Ukrainian Vernacular School Teachers of Canada to create greater uniformity in direction, textbooks, and teaching methods, and to extend the teachers' knowledge of Ukrainian history, literature, and language. The following year, the society indicated that there were twenty-nine teachers and 1,419 pupils across Canada.[24] Although the society survived into the post-World War II era, it was unable to unite all the Ukrainian schools. The war's outbreak also thwarted its plans to republish in Lviv the textbooks of M. Matviichuk, revised and adapted to Canadian conditions.

Nearly all early *ridna shkola* teachers were also community and cultural leaders, teaching choral singing, handicrafts, music, and staging plays and concerts. Frequently intensely patriotic (especially the interwar immigrants in charge of Ukrainian schools and cultural activities in the larger centres on a full-time basis), they injected a pronounced nationalistic tone into their school programs, which usually consisted of language, literature, geography, and history over three to five consecutive grades, frequently supplemented by music, dance, sport, drama, the folk arts, and scouting instruction.

Today the majority of Ukrainian schools continue to operate at the elementary level, teaching language to children aged seven to twelve, with the stress on cultural classes for those thirteen to sixteen. Attendance beyond that age is generally rare. However, intensive Ukrainian courses after primary school, organized into four- or five-year programs for high school students (*ukrainoznavstvo*), are conducted in all larger urban centres. Since World War II, the best Ukrainian schools have been in the cities, where the third immigration has provided a new crop of students.

Generally speaking, the Ukrainian schools remain plagued by deficiencies in quantity and quality of teaching materials, the occasional absence of suitable classroom space, and the limited training and experience of their instructors. Some among the latter possess Canadian teaching certificates and teach Ukrainian regularly in the public schools; most, however, have taught *ridna shkola* since coming to Canada shortly after the war. Fluency in Ukrainian and familiarity with Ukrainian culture have often been the major prerequisites for a *ridna shkola* teacher. Still, compared to other ethnic groups in Canada, the Ukrainians, like the Jews and Germans, have probably had the best-qualified teachers.[25]

Since its formation, the Ukrainian Canadian Committee has tried to improve conditions in the Ukrainian schools. Its Ukrainian National Educational Council of Canada has proposed standards, notably through the National Centre of Ukrainian School Boards, but a single effective co-ordinating body has yet to emerge. A report presented to its tenth congress in October, 1971, indicated that teacher quality remained questionable, as many instructors, in the main first-generation immigrants, considered themselves primarily transmitters of national ideology and culture rather than educators, and many made little attempt to improve their qualifications. Methods used conflicted with those in the public schools. The division of schools among competitors, often jealous of each other, wasted valuable space and personnel, while the need for fresh methods, contemporary subject matter, and a well-thought-out curriculum across Canada was acute. Indifference toward their leaders; the absence of reciprocal regard and toleration among the parishes and secular organizations teaching *ridni shkoly*; the need to regulate school structure, planning, and co-ordination; the neglect of kindergarten children; and little collaboration between teachers of *ridni shkoly* and those teaching Ukrainian in the public schools were (and are) questions that demand careful attention if the Ukrainian schools are to survive and prosper.[26]

A major problem confronting Ukrainian schools is their failure to attract pupils. Approximately 8,000 of an estimated Ukrainian-Canadian youth population of 125,000 attend *ridna shkola*, with the vast majority seldom going beyond the elementary grades. Distances and school centralization prevent many rural areas from maintaining Ukrainian schools. Interest, too, has waned as the young Ukrainians are now increasingly third- and fourth-generation Canadians. The decline of Ukrainian in the home has resulted in some children being sent to *ridna shkola* with little or no knowledge of Ukrainian. Canadian-born Ukrainians unconscious of or uninterested in their heritage will inevitably affect the future of the Ukrainian schools. Some organizations, acknowledging this, have developed *ridna shkola* classes for children knowing no Ukrainian from mixed marriages or third- and fourth-generation families.

In 1975-76 a total of 114 Ukrainian schools operated in the four western provinces, Ontario, and Quebec. Illustrating the population shift since the 1920's and the rise of the urban Ukrainian Canadian, fifty were located in Ontario with 3,652 students. In the Prairie Provinces, Manitoba had twenty-five schools with 1,505 students, Alberta fifteen with 831 students, and Saskatchewan seven with 341 students. Quebec enrolled 656 in nine schools and British Columbia 248 in eight schools. A total of 568 teachers were employed, almost half (282) in Ontario.[27]

A survey of Ukrainian schools in Edmonton, conducted by the Ukrainian Canadian Committee in March, 1977, yielded data which may be considered typical for all major centres in the Prairie Provinces. With few exceptions, teachers were post-1945 immigrants, having received whatever training they had in Ukraine. All possessed several years experience. A few teachers, however, were recent graduates from the Faculty of Education at the University of Alberta. Most students were under fourteen, and classes, which concentrated on teaching language (reading, writing, grammar, conversation), averaged between ten and twenty pupils, with the numbers declining only slightly since 1973. In certain instances, special classes were conducted for children speaking only English from third- or fourth-generation homes. Interestingly, the Orthodox schools had more pupils with a Canadian background that extended over a number of generations than did the Catholic schools, which were primarily attended by the children of the largely Catholic post-war immigration.[28]

The Ukrainian organizations, religious and secular, which sponsor Ukrainian schools continue to stress their relevance in spite of expanding Ukrainian bilingualism in the state schools, particularly in the Prairie Provinces. They argue that while the state school may be able to teach Ukrainian and the rudiments of history and literature, it does not and cannot impart the idealism, patriotism, and total Ukrainian cultural immersion of the *ridna shkola*.[29] Nevertheless, the more thoughtful realize that reorganization and redefinition are needed, especially with the Ukrainian bilingual classes focusing on the same age group as the Ukrainian schools. Duplication of effort is senseless, as the public schools are better staffed and equipped to teach language and, to a lesser extent, history and literature. This is not to say that the *ridna shkola* has expended its usefulness. It can still play a very important role in transmitting Ukrainian culture and in reinforcing the use of language, and, of course, it can continue to perform its traditional vital service in those provinces or localities where extension of Ukrainian into the state schools at the elementary level is impossible.

THE BURSA MOVEMENT

Although the roots of the *bursa* movement precede World War I, it was the abolition of bilingual schools on the Prairies during the war that gave the movement new impetus, especially once the Petro Mohyla Ukrainian Institute was founded in Saskatoon in 1916.[30] Financed out of community funds, the *bursy* were a logical extension of the *ridni shkoly*, designed to cap the education of those destined to lead an embattled community mindful of both Ukraine's difficult situation in Europe and of the direct and indirect assimilative forces threatening group survival in Canada. Like the graduates of the Ruthenian Training School during the pioneer period and the refugees who infused new life into the Ukrainian-Canadian community after World War II, the graduates of the *bursy* defined and articulated Ukrainian-Canadian needs and aspirations during the interwar period.

Ukrainian Orthodox Bursy

Of the *bursy*, the most venerable undoubtedly is the Mohyla Institute in Saskatoon. Conceived as a non-partisan and non-sectarian institution to serve a poor, rural population incapable of sustaining a multitude of similar institutions, it was located centrally to accommodate all students in the large, almost contiguous, bloc of Ukrainian prairie settlement east of Edmonton and northwest of Winnipeg. When religious differences affected its clientele, the institute assisted in the birth of the Ukrainian Greek Orthodox Church, thereby helping to create an irrevocable breach in the Ukrainian community in Canada.

The years 1925 to 1929 witnessed the peak of the Mohyla Institute's influence on Ukrainian-Canadian life. The building purchased in 1918 was paid for by 1925, though an operating debt of $17,000 remained. To assist in developing a library, art gallery, and museum, contacts were established with Ukrainians overseas. Michael Stechishin's European visit in 1927 made much literary material more readily accessible. Noted Ukrainian scholars and statesmen reciprocated, and some even participated in the institute's popular summer courses. Mohyla's female graduates founded the Ukrainian Women's Association of Canada (SUK) in 1926, and a museum opened in 1929. The institute itself provided the initiative for the Ukrainian Self-Reliance League (SUS) in 1927, a formal organization of members supporting the institute's ideals. The Canadian Ukrainian Youth Association (SUMK) followed in 1931. All today are Ukrainian Orthodox Church affiliates. In 1927 the institute opened a branch in Winnipeg near the University of Manitoba, but an apathetic public and uninterested teachers led to its closing in 1933 with a $3,000 debt.

Life at the institute was strictly regulated. Students rose at 6:45 a.m., studied for an hour before breakfast; attended university, business college, or high school classes; returned (if possible) to the institute for lunch; and attended Ukrainian lectures from 5:00 to 6:00 p.m. After dinner, a bell announced evening study at 8:00. The younger students retired at 10:30, the older ones at 11:00. The former always needed permission to go downtown, the latter only in the evenings. As part of their responsibilities, the older students taught Ukrainian language, history, and literature to the younger ones. In October, 1917, a students' club, Kameniari (Stonecutters) - the title of a poem by Franko depicting stonecutters with mallets (symbolizing education) clearing a roadway through rock (symbolizing illiteracy, poverty, and religious and political dissension among Ukrainians in Canada) - was formed, which embraced resident and non-resident students, without regard to religion or politics. Its members participated in Ukrainian community life, organized inter-*bursa* debates, and established student clubs in other Saskatchewan centres to organize debates, concerts, plays, and guest lectures in Ukrainian and English. A journal, *Bursak*, to encourage student writing, and an almanac, *Kameniari*, were published. The female residents organized "Mohylianky," a public-speaking club to prepare them for meetings of the students' club.

The Mohyla Institute barely survived the 1930's, as its agrarian base was hard-hit by the Depression. With the growth of rural public schools, more students could obtain a basic education closer to home. As a result, the age range of the students narrowed, thereby eliminating a serious problem as the older students had frequently found some institute activities monotonous and juvenile. With time, as the institute's residents became primarily university students - younger, better educated, and increasingly less interested in Ukrainian matters and community responsibilities - the institute realized it had either to become a university residence near the campus or perish. The move awaited economic recovery and was not made until a new building was built in December, 1964.

In 1917 the second Ukrainian convention had induced the Alberta delegates to found two *bursy* in their own province. The Taras Shevchenko Institute opened in the fall of 1917 in Vegreville on non-sectarian foundations. Two years later, it had almost twenty students whom the

Vegreville public school board refused to admit because of overcrowding. As a result, it was forced to merge with the second *bursa*, the Michael (Mykhailo) Hrushevsky Institute in Edmonton, established in October, 1918, as an affiliate of Mohyla by young men and women, mostly students and teachers in the Adam Kotsko Society.[31]

The Hrushevsky Institute, which opened with thirty-five students in the Caledonia Hotel, was immediately faced with financial difficulties and was, in fact, only saved by the absorption of Vegreville's *bursa*, whose assets, students, and general community membership gave it wider provincial support. In September, 1919, the Edmonton Bible Institute and adjacent Beulah Mission Hall were purchased for $15,000 and Reverend Michael Glowa, a Presbyterian, was hired as rector on condition that he desist from church activities. By 1920, formal association with the Ukrainian Orthodox Church was established, and by 1930 the Hrushevsky Institute had achieved economic stability and considerable cultural influence through the Adam Kotsko Society, which welcomed city students and thereby remained independent for many years before becoming solely the institute's students' union. In 1939 the institute published Dmytro Doroshenko's *History of Ukraine*, though the Depression placed a projected Ukrainian-English dictionary out of reach. Expansion and a site closer to the university were also delayed until 1949, when Robertson College was purchased and the Hrushevsky Institute became St. John's Ukrainian Institute, in keeping with its direct ties to the Ukrainian Greek Orthodox Church, with which it was fully affiliated in 1938.

Two other Orthodox institutes opened after the pioneer era.[32] In 1934 a theological seminary sponsored by the Winnipeg branch of the Mohyla Institute moved into the consistory building, where it remained until St. Andrew's College opened in 1946. Besides a four-year course leading to a degree in divinity and certificate in theology, St. Andrew's taught grades eleven and twelve and courses in Ukrainian culture. In 1953, with rural high schools improving, the two grades were dropped, and for the next ten years the college exclusively prepared clergy for the Ukrainian Orthodox Church. With the arrival of Metropolitan Ilarion, theological instruction improved, and in 1968 a university degree became a prerequisite for admission to the Faculty of Theology. In June, 1962, St. Andrew's became an associate of the University of Manitoba, and in 1964 a new building was erected on campus to accommodate seventy-six resident students. In the mid-1970's the college became an affiliate of the university with courses leading to the B.A. degree, and in 1979 its Centre for Ukrainian Canadian Studies became an integral part of the university, supported with funds from the latter's operating budget.

The most recent Ukrainian Orthodox *bursa* (the first in eastern Canada) was organized in Toronto in 1945, when the new immigration promised to swell the number of Ukrainians in Ontario. For many years, St. Vladimir's Institute confined its activities to the operation of a

Ukrainian course. In 1962 buildings were purchased near the University of Toronto and seven years later a new building became not only a residence and meeting place for students, but a cultural and educational centre for the whole community. In time, evening courses and Ukrainian summer courses developed. In 1980 the institute's premises were greatly expanded to include a large library and archives section, a museum, an art gallery, a theatre, a large lecture and meeting hall, and several study, rehearsal, and reading rooms.

Ukrainian Catholic Bursy

The first Greek Catholic *bursa*, named after Metropolitan Sheptytsky, opened in St. Boniface in the fall of 1917 in premises rented from the Roman Catholic Church. Financed by public contributions and student fees of $20 per month, the *bursa* closed in 1924 for lack of support, the only such venture by Greek Catholics in Winnipeg.

In sharp contrast, repeated attempts to establish a Catholic *bursa* were made in Alberta. In 1918, in a decision strongly supported by Bishop Budka, the Narodnyi Dim Association of Edmonton opened the Taras Shevchenko Institute in the Grand Hotel, purchased for $49,000. Even though the Basilians actively canvassed rural youth to attend, the institute, hard-hit by the post-war depression, closed in 1922. Between 1925 and 1931, the Ukrainian Catholic Institute accommodated thirty-five to fifty students annually, until the Great Depression and a marked decline in high school residents forced it to close. Two buildings - St. Basil the Great for boys and St. Josaphat's for girls, purchased near the University of Alberta in 1946 - closed to permit university expansion in the early 1960's.

In Saskatchewan the Markiian Shashkevych Bursa, established in Saskatoon by the Ukrainian Catholic Brotherhood (BUK) in 1934, prospered despite the Depression. After two years in the Belmont Hotel, it moved to its own building and was renamed the Metropolitan Andrii Sheptytsky Institute.[33] In 1950 it acquired new quarters and became solely a university residence. Other Catholic *bursy* include St. Vladimir's College, a Redemptorist residential high school for future priests, established at Roblin, Manitoba, before the close of World War II, and the College of St. Basil the Great, which opened in Weston, Ontario, in 1962.

CONCLUSION

The Protestant and Roman Catholic involvement in Ukrainian private education, emerging from a concern for Canada and the Ukrainians' souls, was a pioneer phenomenon, largely because the first Ukrainian immigrants lacked the means to establish their own institutions. The Ukrainians, in turn, accepted the educational opportunities provided without succumbing to the blandishments of either church. On the other hand, the Ukrainian *ridni shkoly* and *bursy* emerged from the Ukrainian experience itself and became inextricably linked with Ukrainian-Canadian efforts to preserve the Ukrainian language and culture in Canada by supplementing the formal education of the young. Enjoying a successful, if sometimes turbulent past, today the level of the *ridni shkoly* ranges from the very elementary to the highly sophisticated (for the select few). A measure of curricular co-ordination has been attained within each *ridna shkola* system, but no common standards and national integration exist. The future of the Ukrainian schools depends on many factors, not the least of which is their ability to recapture and hold the allegiance of nearly 600,000 Ukrainians, many separated from their Ukrainian roots by several generations of life in Canada.

As community educational institutions, too, the way of the Ukrainian *bursy* has not always been smooth. As student attitudes changed, many knew little Ukrainian, and regular classes in Ukrainian language, literature, and history were poorly attended and frequently abandoned. As enrolments fell, non-Ukrainians were accepted. However, the *bursy* that survived, their shortcomings notwithstanding, did occupy important positions in the Ukrainian community until the early 1960's. The fact that Orthodox *bursy* tended to have greater staying power than the Catholic ones may be the result of Catholic religious orders, which worked to foster pre-university educational institutions with strong ties to the community, and of Catholic separate schools in which the Sisters Servants, in particular, had their influence. Both, it could be argued, made the need for Catholic *bursy* less pressing. But as the role and influence of the institutes generally declined, energies were directed toward devising a viable role for their future in Ukrainian-Canadian life. As a result, emphasis on the education (Ukrainian or otherwise) of their residents is increasingly coupled with general community service in such areas as handicrafts and the development and operation of museums and libraries.

NOTES

1. The discussion of the Presbyterian and Methodist home missionaries is based primarily on the following sources: *Acts and Proceedings of the General Assembly of the Presbyterian Church in Canada* (1900-25); A.J. Hunter, *A Friendly Adventure: The Story of the United Church Mission among New Canadians at Teulon, Manitoba* (Toronto: Board of Home Missions, United Church of Canada, 1929); M. Wenstob, "The Work of the Methodist Church among Settlers in Alberta up to 1914, with Special Reference to the Formation of Congregations and Work among the Ukrainian People" (Bachelor of Divinity thesis, University of Alberta, 1959); M. Laycock, *Bridges of Friendship* ([Edmonton?], n.p., 1974); G.N. Emery, "Methodist Missions among the

Ukrainians," *Alberta Historical Review*, XIX (Spring, 1971); V. Olender, "The Reaction of the Canadian Methodist Church Towards Ukrainian Immigrants: Rural Missions as Agencies of Assimilation" (Master's thesis, University of Toronto, 1976).

2. W.D. Reid, "The Non-Anglo-Saxons in Canada - Their Christianization and Nationalization," *Pre-Assembly Congress, Addresses Delivered at the Presbyterian Pre-Assembly Congress* (Toronto: Board of Foreign Missions, Presbyterian Church of Canada, 1913), p. 121. Methodist statements were stronger: "In the coming of these people to our land, God is giving to Canadian Protestantism the privilege of emancipating these our fellowmen, who for centuries have as a people groaned under a system of bondage worse than African slavery." C.H. Lawford quoted in Wenstob, "Work of the Methodist Church," p. 192.
3. "Our aim in not primarily to strengthen our own particular denomination at the expense of other denominations. We wish, most of all, to bring about the brotherly relations in a Christian spirit between the different races. . . . If they are satisfied with our views and would like to work with us in our organization, we shall be very glad to have them with us, but we want them still to feel that we are comrades even though working under some other religious organization. . . . The real church is in the invisible communion of kindred spirits." Hunter, *Friendly Adventure*, pp. 102-3.
4. E.D. McLauren, "Report of the Home Mission Committee, Western Diocese, 1907-08," *The Acts and Proceedings of the Thirty-Fourth General Assembly of the Presbyterian Church in Canada* (1908), pp. 5-6; also Reid, "The Non-Anglo-Saxons in Canada," p. 120.
5. D. Romanchych, "Ukrainski kolonii v okruzi Davfyn, Man." (Ukrainian Colonies in the Vicinity of Dauphin, Man.), in D. Doroshenko and S. Kowbel (eds.), *Propamiatna knyha ukrainskoho narodnoho domu u Vynypegu* (Commemorative Book of the Ukrainian National Home in Winnipeg) (Winnipeg: Trident Press, 1949), p. 516. Bodrug and Negrich, both graduates of the gymnasium, had taught secondary school in Galicia. Cyril Genik had informed them that the Canadian churches were interested in men educated in the old country who would continue their education in Canada and become leaders of their people. After some searching, they chose the Presbyterian Church and Manitoba College.
6. For an account of the work at Insinger, see M.R. Nebel, "Rev. Thomas Johnson and the Insinger Experiment," *Saskatchewan History*, XI (1958), pp. 1-16.
7. J. Sumerville, "Report of the Home Mission Committee, Western Section, 1906-07," *The Acts and Proceedings of the Thirty-Third General Assembly of the Presbyterian Church in Canada* (1907), p. 7.
8. C. Young, "Superintendent of Northern Saskatchewan," *The Acts and Proceedings of the Forty-Fourth General Assembly of the Presbyterian Church in Canada* (1918), p. 30.

9. According to Peter Svarich, the roots of the Vegreville School Home go back to 1906, when Rev. A Broadfoot opened a mission school for twenty pupils in Svarich's house. When the Presbyterians opened three buildings in 1907, Svarich's connection ended. See *Ukrainians in Alberta* (Edmonton: Ukrainian Pioneers' Association of Alberta, 1975), pp. 184-6. Although Presbyterian reports do not mention such a school before 1912, the possibility of a forerunner bears further investigation.
10. See "The Presbyterian Church of Canada Steps In: Memoirs of Stephen Urchak," unpublished manuscript, 1974, pp. 2-7.
11. W. Simons, "Northern Alberta," *The Acts and Proceedings of the Forty-Sixth General Assembly of the Presbyterian Church in Canada* (1920), p. 42.
12. Hunter, *Friendly Adventure*, p. 19. Perhaps atypical among Presbyterian missionaries because of his scholarly interest in Ukrainian history and literature, Hunter published *Kobzar of the Ukraine* in 1922, which contained annotated translations of Shevchenko and other poets.
13. Emery, "Methodist Missions," p. 11.
14. Laycock, *Bridges of Friendship*, p. 32.
15. The discussion of Roman Catholic initiatives and support is drawn from data in the following secondary sources: J. Skwarok, *The Ukrainian Settlers in Canada and Their Schools with Reference to Government, French Canadian, and Ukrainian Missionary Influences 1891-1921* (Toronto: Basilian Press, 1959); P. Yuzyk, "The History of the Ukrainian Greek Catholic (Uniate) Church in Canada" (Master's thesis, University of Saskatchewan, 1948); M.H. Marunchak, *The Ukrainian Canadians: A History* (Winnipeg: Ukrainian Free Academy of Sciences, 1970); *Propamiatna knyha z nahody zolotoho iuvileiu poselannia ukrainskoho narodu v Kanadi 1891-1941* (Commemorative Book on the Occasion of the Golden Jubilee of the Settlement of the Ukrainian People in Canada 1891-1941) (Yorkton: Nakl. epyskopskoho ordynariiatu, 1941); *Kalendar "Holosu Spasytelia"* (Calendar of the *Redeemer's Voice*) (Yorkton: Redeemer's Voice), for 1942, 1944-45, 1950; Basilian Fathers, *Mundare Yesterday and Today* (Mundare: Basilian Press, 1969); Doroshenko and Kowbel (eds.), *Propamiatna knyha ukrainskoho*; I. Goresky, "Ukrainian Catholic Institutions," unpublished manuscript, n.d.
16. Marunchak, *Ukrainian Canadians,* p. 153.
17. For a discussion of the controversy surrounding "Latinization" of the Ukrainian Catholic Church, the use of French-Canadian missionaries, and financial ties with the Roman Catholic Church that contributed to the formation of the Ukrainian Greek Orthodox Church of Canada, see P. Yuzyk, *The Ukrainian Greek Orthodox Church of Canada, 1918-1951* (Ottawa: University of Ottawa Press, 1981), pp. 112-34.
18. By 1941, the sisters taught in government day schools in the following centres:

Place	No. of Sisters	No. of Children
Montreal	4	140
Windsor	2	72
Winnipeg	5	145
Edmonton	3	125
Yorkton	4	72
Regina	1	38
Ituna	2	54

Source: *Propamiatna knyha . . . 1891-1941,* p. 33.

19. Little serious, non-partisan research has been done on the *ridna shkola* movement, and the attempt to obtain a comprehensive picture of its historical development is still in its infancy. The following sources supplied the information for the present summary: Marunchak, *Ukrainian Canadians; Propamiatna knyha . . . 1891-1941*; O.S. Trosky, *The Ukrainian Greek Orthodox Church in Canada* (Winnipeg: n.p., 1968); N. Kohuska, *Chvert stolittia na hromadskii nyvi 1926-1951* (A Quarter Century in Community Work 1926-1951) (Winnipeg: Ukrainian Women's Association of Canada, 1952); *Zolotyi iuvilei - statti i spomyny z nahody 50-litnoi diialnosty tovarstva "Prosvita" u Fort Viliam, Onterio 1906-1956* (Golden Jubilee - Articles and Memoirs on the Occasion of the 50th Jubilee of the Prosvita Society at Fort William, Ontario 1906-1956) (Winnipeg: Fort William Prosvita Society, 1956); G.N. Duravets, "The Importance of Ukrainian Language Study: A Recommendation for the Introduction of Ukrainian Language Instruction in Ontario Secondary Schools," Education Committee of the Ukrainian Canadian Committee, Toronto, 1972; Report presented to the tenth congress of the Ukrainian Canadian Committee, Winnipeg, October 8-11, 1971, by I. Bodnarchuk on the conditions of *ridni shkoly* in Canada; Royal Commission on Bilingualism and Biculturalism, Book IV, *The Cultural Contribution of the Other Ethnic Groups* (Ottawa: Queen's Printer, 1969); and the results of a questionnaire distributed among Ukrainian schools in Edmonton in March, 1977, by the Ukrainian Canadian Committee (see n. 28 below).
20. Marunchak, *Ukrainian Canadians*, p. 150.
21. *Propamiatna knyha . . . 1891-1941*, pp. 34, 74.
22. *Zolotyi iuvilei . . . 1906-1956*, pp. 38-50.
23. Trosky, *Ukrainian Greek Orthodox Church in Canada,* p. 81.
24. Marunchak, *Ukrainian Canadians,* pp. 443, 445-6.
25. Royal Commission on Bilingualism and Biculturalism, Book IV, p. 155.
26. Papers on the tenth congress of the Ukrainian Canadian Committee, Winnipeg, October 8-11, 1971, report presented by I. Bodnarchuk, pp. 2-3.
27. Letter from I. Bodnarchuk to W.R. Petryshyn, Canadian Institute of Ukrainian Studies, University of Alberta, 8 April 1977.

28. The questionnaires are on file at the Canadian Institute of Ukrainian Studies, University of Alberta.
29. See, for example, T. Horochowych, *Batky i dity* (Parents and Children) (Toronto and Winnipeg: Ukrainian Women's Association of Canada, 1965), pp. 58-59; also D. Cherevyk "Nashi ridni shkoly" (Our Ukrainian Schools), *Visnyk*, 1 December 1976.
30. The major sources consulted in preparing this section were Doroshenko and Kowbel (eds.), *Propamiatna knyha ukrainskoho; Iuvileina knyha 25-littia instytutu im. Petra Mohyly v Saskatuni* (Twenty-fifth Anniversary Jubilee Book of the Petro Mohyla Institute in Saskatoon) (Winnipeg: Nakladom instytutu, 1945); P. Yuzyk, *Ukrainian Greek Orthodox Church; Dvadtsiat piat-litnii iuvilei instytuta im. Mykhaila Hrushevskoho v Edmontoni* (The Twenty-fifth Jubilee of the Mykhailo Hrushevsky Institute in Edmonton) (Winnipeg: Ukrainskyi holos, 1943); *Ukrainians in Alberta* (1975); Trosky, *Ukrainian Greek Orthodox Church in Canada;* and the yearbooks of the Mohyla and St. John's Institutes. Also valuable were a series of unpublished manuscripts (n.d.) by Isidore Goresky at the Canadian Institute of Ukrainian Studies: "M. Hrushevsky Institute in Edmonton," "The Petro Mohyla Institute in Saskatoon," "Ukrainian Catholic Institutions," "Institutes Established by Ukrainians," "St. Andrew's College in Winnipeg," and "St. Vladimir's Institute in Toronto." Available data on the Ukrainian-Canadian *bursy* are unfortunately reprinted from one publication to another with very little new research undertaken.
31. The Adam Kotsko Society emerged out of the Ruthenian-Ukrainian Bursa, the first to be established in Canada. It was funded by the wealthy entrepreneur, Paul Rudyk, in Edmonton in 1912. Ostensibly non-partisan and non-denominational, it operated under the auspices of the Independent Greek Church, controlled by the Presbyterians. Its life span was short. In 1913, when the Presbyterians changed its Ukrainian character and influence, some of its students formed the Adam Kotsko Society.
32. The following discuss St. Andrew's College and St. Vladimir's Institute specifically: *Kalendar ridna nyva 1948* (Calendar *Native Field* 1948) (Winnipeg: Vyd. spilka Ekleziia, 1948); *Official opening: St. Andrew's College in Winnipeg, July 4, 1964* (Winnipeg: Trident Press, 1964); *Student Exchange* (Winnipeg: Trident Press, 1968).
33. For an account of the Sheptytsky Institute, see N. Popil, "Do rannoi istorii instytuta im. A. Sheptytskoho v Saskatuni" (The Early History of the A. Sheptytsky Institute in Saskatoon), in Y. Slavutych, (ed.), *Zakhidnokanadskyi zbirnyk* (Collected Papers on Ukrainian Settlers in Western Canada) (Edmonton: Shevchenko Scientific Society in Canada, 1975), pp. 191-8.

TWELVE

The Ukrainian Press in Canada

Yuri Daschko

The ethnic press is an important part of an immigrant's socio-cultural milieu, decelerating the break with the traditional culture as it gradually accelerates integration into the new culture. The Ukrainian-Canadian press has been no exception in this regard. It has aided the Ukrainian immigrants' adjustment to the Canadian milieu and thereby contributed to their integration into Canadian society. At the same time, paradoxically, it has seemed to slow down the process of assimilation. Today, with approximately 80 per cent of all Ukrainian Canadians Canadian-born, the challenge facing the community's press is to reach the immigrants' descendants as readers and subscribers. If it cannot, it will disappear.

Over the years, at least 549 Ukrainian publications have been produced in Canada, mainly in Winnipeg (205 titles), Toronto (157 titles), and Edmonton (60 titles). These publications have included newspapers, journals, magazines, and almanacs, all of which have a substantial number of subscribers as well as advertising income. They have also included weekly or monthly mimeographed bulletins of various Ukrainian organizations, associations, credit unions, and parishes, distributed in limited editions to members at no cost and with few if any paid advertisements. The places of publication are most numerous in Ontario (16), followed by Alberta (14), Manitoba (8), Saskatchewan (7), British Columbia (3), and Quebec (1).[1] In this essay the weekly newspapers, which enjoy the largest circulation and wield the greatest influence, will be the main concern.

PURPOSE

One of the principal functions of the Ukrainian-Canadian press has been to keep abreast of Ukrainian activities in Canada and abroad, a task the mass media does not fulfil. The Ukrainian-language press has thus been an important means of intragroup communication, both nationally and internationally. To combat the feelings of loneliness, insecurity, and isolation resulting from vast distances and linguistic differences, individual immigrants and immigrant associations and parishes established contact through an immigrant press. At first, it was undoubtedly the principal source of information about Canadian institutions,[2] and as interest in international and Canadian news increased, attention to news from Ukraine decreased.

Besides transmitting Ukrainian culture, the Ukrainian press has tried to make Canada more intelligible by selecting, evaluating, and interpreting events and advising readers how to react to them. By transmitting and explaining Canada's socio-cultural heritage, it has assisted Ukrainian immigrants to integrate into Canadian society, changing their community from a replica of the cultural patterns of Ukraine into something unique.[3] On the other hand, information on entertainment or sport has had a low priority in the Ukrainian press, and has usually been very different from its mass media counterpart. The Ukrainian press has rarely included cartoon strips[4] and it has often coupled entertainment with the transmittal of social heritage by publishing poems and short stories by its readers, alongside serialized novels and Ukrainian literary classics.

The Ukrainian-language press was instrumental in raising the general educational level of many of the first wave of immigrants:

> A considerable percentage of the [first] immigrants at first knew neither how to read nor to write, yet all were anxious and eager to learn the news and information in their own papers. It was common in the pioneer days to witness a group of listeners gathered around a person who read aloud from the paper which had just arrived. In time many of the illiterates learned to read for themselves, thanks to the interest that had been aroused by the papers.[5]

The newspapers tried to teach the latest farming techniques by providing marketing and agricultural news. The motto of *Ukrainskyi holos* (Ukrainian Voice), for example, was "Education for the masses." In conjunction with this general educational work the press also helped develop a Ukrainian consciousness among the first immigrants, as distinct from a purely regional consciousness (e.g., Galician, Bukovynian).

The Ukrainian papers also represented Ukrainians to others: to the Canadian authorities, to other ethnic groups, and to Canadians in general.[6] For example, in order to monitor the attitudes of the community, the Canadian federal government and some provincial governments were in the habit of reviewing the contents of certain Ukrainian publications. Today apparently only the federal government, through the Department of the Secretary of State, carries on a continuous review of the ethnic press, including the Ukrainian-Canadian press.[7]

Finally, the recognition by the Ukrainian press of contributions made by Ukrainian Canadians to their community encourages and strengthens the group's cohesion. This recognition also helps to alleviate the frustration and depression which immigrants sometimes feel in their new environment.

CHARACTERISTICS

The first Ukrainian immigrants to Canada who wanted information about their fellow Ukrainians had to rely on Ukrainian-language newspapers from Ukraine, especially from Galicia, and from the United States. *Svoboda* (Liberty), the oldest surviving Ukrainian newspaper in the New World,[8] was founded in Jersey City, New Jersey, in 1893 by Reverend Hryhorii Hrushka, its editor. In 1894 it became the voice of the Ukrainian (then called Ruthenian) National Association, a fraternal society that *Svoboda* had helped to organize. It reflected every aspect of Ukrainian pioneer life in Canada, and also included such items as letters to the editor from Ukrainian settlers in Canada asking for advice, and news about Ukraine and oppression in their homeland.[9] Another imported newspaper, *Dilo* (Deed), was one of the most widely read Ukrainian-language newspapers in Ukraine and North America. Established in 1880 in Lviv as a weekly and later transformed into a daily, it became, in 1899, the semi-official organ of the National Democratic Party in Galicia.[10]

Because of the shortage of Ukrainian journalists, editors, and writers in Canada, the first Ukrainian-Canadian publications often had to resort to reprinting articles from such non-Canadian Ukrainian papers as *Rada* (Counsel).[11] *Ameryka* (America), published in Philadelphia by the Providence Association of Ukrainian Catholics, *Svoboda*, and publications from England, West Germany, and France are still read. *Visti z Ukrainy* (News from Ukraine) and several other papers published in Soviet Ukraine are also available to Ukrainian-Canadian readers, but their strong propaganda content mars their usefulness.

The Ukrainian-Canadian press is essentially a community press, although it includes a few commercial publications, whose main interest in paid circulation and whose opinions are not radical. The two major commercial publications are *Kanadiiskyi farmer* (Canadian Farmer), published for most of its history by a non-Ukrainian businessman, and *Vilne slovo* (The Free Word), published by a private Ukrainian publishing company.[12] Ukrainian-Canadian newspapers founded by private individuals or business firms have generally ended in bankruptcy.

Experience has shown that a non-commercial publication must enjoy the support of a particular group to survive, and naturally the political and religious views of that particular group are then found on the newspaper's pages. Such publications become partisan organs for carrying on a group's work. In addition, an organization may support a journal of opinion, which is "constantly seeking new readers outside the circle it represents. It is addressed therefore, not primarily to the members of the organization or the party it represents but to the public."[13] Comment upon and interpretation of the news then becomes more important than the news itself.

There have also been publications financed by non-Ukrainians and aimed at promoting a particular idea within the community. This type of newspaper has been supported by national or international organizations which retained the language difference as long as it was needed to reach a particular audience.[14] In the Ukrainian-Canadian community, most publications of this type disappeared by the 1920's.

CANADIAN POLITICAL PARTY PUBLICATIONS

Kanadiiskyi farmer, the first unilingual Ukrainian newspaper, was established by the federal Liberal Party in the fall of 1903.[15] The paper supported the philosophy and policy of that party in nearly all subsequent elections.[16] When the Liberals withdrew their direct financial support, the newspaper survived and flourished as a commercial enterprise, in part because of the newspaper's generally favourable orientation toward Ukrainian aspirations. The policy of the paper usually reflected the middle-of-the-road views of its changing editors, who since World War II have supported the policies of the Ukrainian Canadian Committee.[17] After the Presbyterian-sponsored Independent Greek Church launched its own paper in 1905, *Kanadiiskyi farmer* also maintained a neutral position on the religious question within the Ukrainian community, having earlier supported the Independent Greek Church.[18]

A number of short-lived papers, also subsidized by the major political parties, appeared during the pioneer era. In Manitoba the federal Conservatives subsidized *Slovo* (Word) in 1904-05 in an effort to neutralize the advantage acquired by the Liberals with the inception of *Kanadiiskyi farmer*. Almost a decade later, in 1913, the provincial Conservatives subsidized *Kanada* (Canada). Like *Slovo*, it appeared in Winnipeg and survived for less than two years. After 1918, no major Canadian political party needed to establish a Ukrainian-language newspaper because existing papers were willing to transmit party views.[19]

LEFTIST PUBLICATIONS

Initially, the Ukrainian-Canadian socialist press served Ukrainians who supported the social democratic parties in Ukraine. Eventually,

> . . . the Ukrainian socialists in Canada passed from under the utopian socialist, agrarian radical and democratic nationalist influence of the Ukrainian Radical Party into the sphere of the two Ukrainian Social Democratic organizations, and finally . . . into the orbit of the Bolsheviks.[20]

The involvement of most pre-World War I immigrants in politics stemmed from their economic insecurity and low social status; some were attracted to extremist left-wing positions because of the problems they faced during the war and the Great Depression. Only a few socialist publications have survived; at present the Communist press dominates the small Ukrainian-Canadian left.

Two Winnipeg-based Ukrainian weeklies, *Chervonyi prapor* (Red Flag) (1907-08), and its successor, *Robochyi narod* (Working People) (1909-18), were the first to promote socialist ideas among Canadian Slavs. The Russian Revolution split the Ukrainian socialist group, with *Robochyi narod*, the organ of the Ukrainian Social Democratic Party, espousing the cause of Russian Communism. In subsequent years, Ukrainian Communists published at least eighteen newspapers and periodicals, including the only major Ukrainian-Canadian daily, *Narodna hazeta* (People's Gazette) (1937-40).[21]

The first newspaper founded specifically by Ukrainian-Canadian Communists, *Ukrainski robitnychi visti* (Ukrainian Labour News), appeared in Winnipeg in 1919. Unlike *Robochyi narod*, *Ukrainski robitnychi visti* favoured international Communism. It was established by people formerly involved in the Ukrainian Social Democratic Party of Canada and *Robochyi narod* until both the party and the paper were banned in September, 1918, with several founders becoming prominent activists within the Communist Party of Canada. They worked out of the Ukrainian Labour Temple in Winnipeg and during the interwar period launched the Ukrainian Labour-Farmer Temple Association (ULFTA) with *Ukrainski robitnychi visti* as its organ. On January 1, 1935, it became a daily and on September 1, 1937, it changed its name to *Narodna hazeta*. Other interwar ULFTA titles include *Holos robitnytsi* (Voice of the Working Woman), *Boiova molod* (Militant Youth), and *Farmerske zhyttia* (Farmers' Life).[22]

All the ULFTA-affiliated publications were banned in July, 1940, because they opposed Canada's declaration of war against Nazi Germany, then allied with the Soviet Union. After the Soviet Union joined the Allies, *Ukrainske zhyttia* (Ukrainian Life) was published openly in 1941 in Toronto as a Communist weekly,[23] to be followed in 1943 by *Ukrainske slovo* (Ukrainian Word) in western Canada. In 1965 the two merged as *Zhyttia i slovo* because of a decline in subscribers.

An English-language newspaper, *Ukrainian Canadian*, was established in 1947. Initially a bi-weekly serving English-speaking Ukrainian Canadians, it became a monthly magazine in 1969. Unlike other Communist publications, it has never clearly articulated its position toward the Soviet Union. Such has not been the case with *Ukrainske zhyttia*, for example, which has supported the Soviet system and policies wholeheartedly.

Such an unquestioning attitude has been the main reason for the opposition of the vast majority of Ukrainian Canadians to the pro-Communist group. The split within Communist ranks and the formation of a splinter organization in 1935 indicate that some leftists also found the subservience unpalatable. Nevertheless, ULFTA publications retained their obsequious attitude toward the Soviet Union and its spokesman in Canada, the Communist Party of Canada, and it can therefore be seen why such publications may be viewed as belonging to the "cause-type" category. As Danylo Lobay, a former editor of the pro-Communist *Ukrainski robitnychi visti*, indicated:

> . . . the communistic organization carries a Ukrainian name and utilizes the Ukrainian language, but it works for the benefit of the Communist Party and the Russian State. Under a cover of cultural-educational activities, it rears its members and sympathizers in such a spirit that they are willing to become a blind tool of the Russian State in case of war or revolution.[24]

Existing publications of the ULFTA's successor, the Association of United Ukrainian Canadians, are still strong supporters of the Soviet government and the Communist Party of Canada.

The non-Communist publications of the left all were journals of opinion and included such papers as *Robitnyche slovo* (Workers' Word) (1916-18), the successor to *Svidoma syla* (Conscious Strength) (1915-16), both published in Toronto. It was the supporter of the socialist independence parties of Ukraine until its demise in 1918. Another semimonthly, *Robitnychi visti* (Labour News), published in Toronto from 1933 to 1937, supported the Trotskyist position. *Pravda* (Truth), established in 1936, was the newspaper of the splinter group from the ULFTA led by Danylo Lobay, who was appalled by Stalin's terroristic policies toward Ukraine. Continued as *Vpered* (Forward) until 1940, it represented the Ukrainian Workers' League, which favoured co-operation with the Ukrainian nationalists.[25]

UKRAINIAN NATIONALIST PUBLICATIONS

Many of the community publications of the first immigration supported Ukrainian nationalism. Among the most prominent pioneer newspapers to support national aspirations rather than class interests were *Kanadiiskyi farmer, Ukrainskyi holos*, and *Kanadyiskyi ukrainets* (Canadian Ukrainian). Although the papers were at odds when it came to deciding the type of government best suited for an independent Ukraine – the first two supported republicanism, the third monarchism – all were committed to the ideal of Ukrainian national independence.[26] With the influx during the 1920's of veterans of the unsuccessful war of liberation, the existing press was deemed to be insufficiently zealous about Ukraine's problems and *Novyi shliakh* (New Pathway) was established in 1930 to continue the struggle for independence: "The bullets of the rifles were replaced by the words of the press."[27]

Novyi shliakh became the journal of the Ukrainian National Federation, though it was published by a separate firm. It was based in Edmonton and Saskatoon prior to World War II and in Winnipeg after the war. Since 1977, it has been published in Toronto.

> The journal at all times . . . displayed a great deal of tolerance to other organizations and since its basic philosophy was that of Ukrainian solidarity it cooperated closely with papers of similar outlook in America and Europe.[28]

But tolerance did not prevent it from engaging in polemics with those it judged not fully behind the cause of Ukrainian independence. The diversity of outlook between the nationally conscious or moderately nationalistic pre-1914 immigrants and the newly arrived nationalist activists led to misunderstandings which were reflected in the press; but with time the intensely nationalistic group mellowed to the point where the arrival of a third wave of immigrants repeated the process of confrontation between the old and new immigrants.

The main journal of opinion of the third immigration was *Homin Ukrainy* (Echo of Ukraine), established in 1948 and allied with the right-wing OUN(b) faction of the Organization of Ukrainian Nationalists. As the journal of the Canadian League for Ukraine's Liberation (LVU), the paper viewed other newspapers, including *Novyi shliakh*, as insufficiently active in the struggle for Ukrainian independence. At the outset it was particularly concerned with publicizing the activities of the Ukrainian Insurgent Army (UPA) in Ukraine. Though still more nationalist and anti-leftist than most, it is gradually devoting more space to Ukrainian-Canadian affairs.

The hetmanite-monarchist group, relatively prominent during the interwar period, dwindled into insignificance after World War II. Its first newspaper, *Probii* (Breakthrough), established in Toronto in 1924, quickly disappeared. It was followed by *Kanadiiska sich* (Canadian Fortress), which appeared in Winnipeg between 1928 and 1930; *Sich* (Fortress), published in Montreal in 1939; *Ukrainskyi robitnyk* (Ukrainian Toiler), published in Toronto (1934-56);[29] *Nasha derzhava* (Our State), also published in Toronto (1952-56); and *Batkivshchyna* (Fatherland), which has been appearing in Toronto since 1957. Although deeply committed to Ukrainian statehood and independence, the monarchist press has never been able to attract a large following because of its devotion to the Skoropadsky family.

A periodical's concern for the latest developments in Ukraine is not necessarily a sign it is an émigré or nationalist publication. Just as the mass media takes up the cause of a group suffering from injustice, including the Soviet Ukrainian dissidents, so too does the Ukrainian press. The only difference is that because of common linguistic and cultural ties on the part of the Ukrainian-Canadian press and its readership, the situation in Ukraine is a much more important issue in that press than elsewhere.

RELIGIOUS PUBLICATIONS

Protestant

The second-oldest unilingual Ukrainian paper, *Ranok* (Morning) (1905-20), was published in Winnipeg as a monthly by the Independent Greek Church. Its first editor was Reverend Ivan Bodrug, formerly with *Kanadiiskyi farmer*, and its main concerns were the problems of the Ukrainian immigrant, especially the urgent need for moral and social reform. Its early popularity evaporated once Ukrainian Canadians discovered that it and the church were connected with the Presbyterian Church, which eventually absorbed both.

The bi-weekly *Kanadyiets* (The Canadian), which appeared in Edmonton at the beginning of 1913, was subsidized by the Methodist Church. Unlike most of its contemporaries, it thought the Ukrainian national problem relatively unimportant, which probably explains why there were so few Ukrainian Methodists to read the newspaper. In 1920 *Ranok* and *Kanadyiets* were amalgamated to form *Kanadiiskyi ranok* (Canadian Morning). The union reflected the joining of Presbyterian and Methodist churches to form the United Church. The latter subsidized *Kanadiiskyi ranok* from its inception until 1960, when *Ievanhelskyi ranok* (Evangelical Morning), the publication of the independent Ukrainian Evangelical Alliance of North America, appeared to serve the minority of Ukrainians in the United Church.

There have been other Protestant publications. Between 1923 and 1928, Paul Crath (Pavlo Krat), a United Church minister, published *Vira i znannia* (Faith and Knowledge) in Toronto. In 1950 a group of Protestant Ukrainian ministers established the short-lived *Slovo* (Word) in Toronto. Published in Saskatoon after 1951, it was supposed to propagate the formation of an independent Ukrainian evangelical church. Today its spiritual heirs publish *Ievanhelskyi ranok*. In 1940 Ukrainians who remained within the Presbyterian Church began publishing *Ievanhelska pravda* (Evangelical Truth). Both *Ievanhelskyi ranok* and *Ievanhelska pravda* support the Ukrainian Evangelical Alliance of North America. A number of Baptist and Pentecostal publications have also appeared, among them *Khrystiianskyi stiah* (Christian Banner), *Ukrainska ievanhelska nyva* (Ukrainian Gospel Field), and *Ievanhelyst* (Evangelist).

Russian Orthodox

The prominence of the Russian Orthodox Church during the first phase of immigration led to the establishment of a number of publications:

> . . . the majority was published with the aid of funds from the Russian Orthodox Mission in the U.S.A. and later a similar mission and Church in Canada. This press exhorted its readers to orient themselves towards Russia, its national, imperial indivisibility and its czarist regime . . .[30]

The journals appeared either in Ukrainian or in a Ukrainian-Russian jargon or bilingually in Russian and Ukrainian, as was *Kanadiiskaia Pravoslavnaia Rus'* (Canadian Orthodox Rus'), the official paper of the Russian Orthodox mission in Canada, which appeared in Winnipeg during 1916-17. Other newspapers included the Edmonton-based *Russkii holos* (Russian Voice) (1913-16) and the Winnipeg-based *Russkii narod* (Russian People) (1914-19), which assisted the Manitoba and Alberta governments to dismantle the provincial Ukrainian bilingual schools. Most readers of the Russophile press were Ukrainian settlers who lacked a national consciousness. During the interwar period, as that consciousness grew, the Russophile press declined, accelerated by the establishment of the Ukrainian Greek Orthodox Church and the disappearance of tsarist funds after the Russian Revolution. It left a bitter heritage, however, by incorrectly branding all Ukrainians during World War I as "Austrophiles," thereby contributing to the banning of Ukrainian-language periodicals in 1918.

Ukrainian Greek Catholic

The first Catholic periodical specifically for Ukrainian Canadians was *Kanadyiskyi rusyn* (Canadian Ruthenian), which appeared in Winnipeg in 1911 partially as a consequence of Metropolitan Sheptytsky's visit to Canada. Financed by the Roman Catholic archbishop of St. Boniface between 1911 and 1915, it waged a vehement campaign against the Independent Greek Church and against those Ukrainian Greek Catholics who refused to subordinate themselves to the spiritual authority of the Roman Catholic hierarchy.[31] With the arrival in 1913 of a Ukrainian Greek Catholic bishop, Nykyta Budka, the paper sought to reassert the spiritual and secular authority of the Greek Catholic clergy among the immigrants. In 1919 it was renamed *Kanadyiskyi ukrainets* and in 1927, in the midst of heated polemics, it lost a libel suit and was sold to cover costs.[32]

A number of Ukrainian Catholic publications followed in the ensuing years. Between 1923 and 1928 and since 1933, the Redemptorist Fathers in Yorkton, Saskatchewan, have published *Holos Spasytelia* (Redeemer's Voice), a popular religious monthly. Since 1950, the same order has published *Lohos* (Logos), a scholarly quarterly devoted to theological questions. The Ukrainian Catholic Brotherhood published *Biuleten* (Bulletin) in 1933-38 and from 1938 to 1950 *Buduchnist natsii* (The Nation's Future).[33] Today there are three Ukrainian Catholic weeklies which frequently speak on behalf of the hierarchy and the brotherhood: *Ukrainski visti* (Ukrainian News), published in Edmonton since 1929; *Nasha meta* (Our Aim), published in Toronto since 1949; and *Postup* (Progress), published in Winnipeg since 1959.

It is interesting to note that while *Nasha meta* and *Ukrainski visti* have been moderately nationalistic, *Postup* has pursued an intensely nationalistic and militantly anti-Communist line. The discussion of political matters in these newspapers reflects the close historical connection which religious topics have had with the problems of cultural survival and development.

Greek Orthodox

Established in 1918, the Ukrainian Greek Orthodox Church of Canada acquired its official organ - *Pravoslavnyi vistnyk* (Orthodox Herald), later renamed *Visnyk* (Herald) - in 1924. However, the church and its secular organization, the Ukrainian Self-Reliance League, have always enjoyed the support of *Ukrainskyi holos*, which still speaks with authority for the church hierarchy. A publication deserving special mention is *Vira i kultura* (Faith and Culture), a monthly journal established by Metropolitan Ilarion in 1953, devoted to Ukrainian theological thought and culture. Unlike such Catholic weeklies as *Postup*, the Orthodox press has been impervious to militant right-wing nationalist influences.

OTHER PUBLICATIONS

Besides political and religious publications, there have existed literary journals, satirical reviews, learned journals, business and agricultural publications, and children's magazines. In 1911 *Khata* (The Home), the first illustrated journal of literature, politics, and contemporary affairs, was published in Winnipeg. Without an intelligentsia to sustain it, however, it expired after six or seven issues. Another publication during the early period was the equally short-lived agricultural magazine, *Rilnyk* (Agriculturalist), which tried to assist farmers. The first Ukrainian-language children's publication, *Dzvinok* (The Little Bell), appeared in Winnipeg in 1918.

Thus, it can be seen that the Ukrainian-language press has been prolific and varied. Only once, during World War I, was the freedom of the Ukrainian press threatened in Canada. From the war's beginning, "foreign-language" publications were forced to conform to stricter censorship standards than their French and English counterparts. Then in September, 1918, publication in Ukrainian and in other "enemy alien" languages was prohibited. With a committee of the publishers of the four Ukrainian periodicals, *Kanadiiskyi farmer, Ukrainskyi holos, Kanadyiskyi rusyn*, and *Ranok*, continually pressing to have the prohibition removed, the federal government agreed on condition that a parallel English text was provided, a condition which prevailed until April, 1919. During World War II only the pro-Soviet Ukrainian publications were temporarily banned.

PRODUCTION

Two major components of the production process are personnel and finances, and the Ukrainian press has its problems with both. With trained personnel scarce, the typical Ukrainian newspaper editor has had to write, edit, and publish for the publication to survive. Editorial boards have been as rare as managers, compositors, and linotype operators, especially before 1945. The first editors were often their own secretaries, office boys, and proofreaders. At times they had to travel to solicit subscription and advertising. *Novyi shliakh* actually closed for a short period during the Depression, while the editor scoured Alberta for funds. Without a business manager, *Shliakh*'s editor kept books, negotiated purchases, and supervised the printing of advertisements at nominal pay (without a vacation) to prevent a temporary shutdown.[34] Personal commitment had to be high. Editors rarely had professional journalistic training, though some may have had university degrees in other fields. Practical experience was the key, as with their English- and French-speaking counterparts. Initially, clergymen, community activists, teachers, students, and skilled tradesmen were editors; only later, especially after World War II, did trained journalists occupy editorial positions.

Besides publishing, the Ukrainian editor rendered various services to recently arrived immigrants, services performed by all ethnic editors:

> Indeed, in the eyes of many newcomers, the editor becomes an omnipotent father image whose duty is to help them, advise them and care for their wellbeing. . . . An ethnic editor may have to find an obstetrician in a hurry, advise on a real estate deal, recommend a reliable plumber.[35]

His private time was consumed by various organizations, especially during the early period when he was frequently a community leader. Joseph (Osyp) Megas, for example, a former editor of *Kanadiiskyi farmer*, became a full-time organizer of bilingual schools in Saskatchewan, where he established and edited the newspaper *Novyi krai* (New Country) (1910-13), in which he urged the creation of strong political associations and rural co-operatives. Myroslaw Stechishin, a founder of the Ukrainian Social Democratic Party, edited the party's weekly, *Chervonyi prapor*. Disillusioned with the socialist cause after serving as editor of *Robochyi narod*, he accepted, in 1921, the editorship of *Ukrainskyi holos* and later became the ideologist of the Ukrainian Self-Reliance League, which he helped to establish.

Even though the third Ukrainian immigration wave has improved the situation of the Ukrainian-Canadian press, the editor's prestige has gradually diminished because of low wages and the loss of leadership to the new intelligentsia. As a result, a special editors' conference at the 1953 congress of the Ukrainian Canadian Committee underlined the need for personal contact among editors to better influence Ukrainian-Canadian public opinion. That influence, however, can never be too great, for only about one-fifth of all Ukrainian Canadians read the Ukrainian press on a regular basis. The future of the press is therefore uncertain once the present generation of editors disappears. Fluency in Ukrainian is essential to editing a Ukrainian-language paper, yet the skill is limited among youth educated in English-speaking institutions. Whether the few young correspondents and editors in the youth section of the Association of Ukrainian Journalists of Canada will be sufficient remains to be seen.

Correspondents and other contributors to the Ukrainian press have usually been unpaid. Although the most committed of the paper's supporters, they have not always been the most qualified. Nor have they been plentiful. *Novyi shliakh*, for example, had great difficulties initially and not until 1955 did it acquire reporters from among the post-World War II immigrants, who lived in Montreal, Toronto, Hamilton, Saskatoon, and Vancouver and contributed for a small honorarium or voluntarily.[36] Trained technical personnel (especially linotype operators able to handle a Ukrainian-language keyboard) have also been scarce because of non-competitive wages and poor working conditions.

Ukrainian journalists were prominent in organizing the Canadian Ethnic Press Club in Winnipeg in 1942, the Canadian Ethnic Press Association of Ontario in 1945, and the Canadian Ethnic Press Federation in 1958, which unites eighty periodical publications. From the conference of Ukrainian journalists in Toronto in 1966 emerged the Association of Ukrainian Journalists of Canada,[37] established to organize meetings of Ukrainian journalists in North America, lobby the Canadian government about postal rates and advertising, and encourage young journalists to work in the Ukrainian language by offering prizes for the best articles published in *Zhurnalist* (Journalist), issued semi-annually and alternately by Ukrainian journalists in Canada and the United States.

The creation of *Canadian Scene*, a free news service organized by a group of Torontonians in 1951 and supported out of public donations, has eased the lot of the Ukrainian editors. Bi-weekly reports on news in Canada are prepared in fifteen languages, thus obviating the need to translate while increasing the amount of Canadian-based content. Federal and provincial government agencies supply news in English or French. Although very little of the content of Ukrainian papers is derived from the regular wire services,[38] the absence of such services is largely immaterial, for the papers are mainly weeklies. General Canadian and international news is usually taken from the mass media press. Information about Ukrainians in Canada, the Soviet Union, or elsewhere is obtained from the Ukrainian Press Service, the Ukrainian Bureau of Information in Europe, the Ukrainian Canadian Committee, or other Ukrainian organizations.

Very few Ukrainian newspapers operate on a profit basis with income derived solely from advertisements and subscriptions. Additional sources include subsidies from sponsoring organizations and sustaining funds, and at critical moments personal contributions from staff. Sponsoring organizations provide an all-important ready pool of subscribers and some occasionally levy dues on chapters or locals. Sustaining funds are also derived from collections at wedding receptions, christenings, funerals, and other gatherings of Ukrainian Canadians, as well as from individual donations. Some newspapers operate as commercial print-shops and do job printing for their sponsoring organization and private individuals. Some limited companies sell public shares to finance capital expenditures. In 1910 the Ukrainian Publishing Co. Ltd. (today Trident Press Ltd.) sold shares at $25 each to establish *Ukrainskyi holos.*[39]

Large national business firms and advertising agencies are reluctant to advertise in Ukrainian-language newspapers because of their limited circulation. To strengthen the financial base, two advertising agencies, New Canadian Publications and Lingua Ads Service, were established in the 1950's in Toronto to sell advertising space for members and to supply translations of advertisements. After much lobbying by the ethnic press, the federal government agreed to advertise, and today federal and provincial government advertisements constitute the largest source of revenue for some non-Communist Ukrainian-Canadian newspapers; their withdrawal would be equivalent to a death sentence. Recently the Communist press has also begun to receive government support, but on an irregular basis.

Advertising rates are based on verified circulation figures submitted to the Audit Bureau of Circulations. Accurate circulation figures, however, are rarely available for the ethnic press. Estimates are based on information from editors and from newspaper analysts. The approximate circulation of Ukrainian-Canadian newspapers in 1969 was 172,000, with *Kanadiiskyi farmer* in the lead (16,000), followed by *Ukrainskyi holos* (14,000), *Novyi shliakh* (12,000), *Vilne slovo* and *Ukrainski visti* (9,500) each), and *Homin Ukrainy* (9,000).[40] The relationship between circulation and readership is, of course, very difficult to determine because a family may have several readers or an individual may subscribe to more than one newspaper. Until Ukrainian-language publications are able to define their market more accurately, the dearth of private national advertising will continue. Nonetheless, some advertising agencies may be reassessing the importance of the ethnic press as an advertising medium.[41]

Today most Ukrainian newspapers serve mainly the needs of immigrants, even though they form a minority within the Ukrainian-Canadian community. Only 20.2 per cent of all Ukrainian Canadians read the Ukrainian-language press regularly; 9.5 per cent read it occasionally and 4.9 per cent rarely. However, when readership is related to language fluency, 84.6 per cent of those fluent in Ukrainian read a Ukrainian-language newspaper or bulletin and 62.4 per cent read them regularly. Language retention, however, is declining. Between 1931 and 1971, the percentage of Ukrainians whose first language was Ukrainian and who still understood it dropped from 93.1 to 48.8 per cent.[42] Even worse, of the Ukrainian-Canadian population under thirty years of age, only 29.6 per cent claimed Ukrainian as a "mother tongue." Accordingly, the future of the Ukrainian-Canadian press is uncertain, especially as 80 per cent of all Ukrainian-Canadian publications continue to be printed in Ukrainian.

In order to circumvent this lack of fluency in Ukrainian, it has been suggested that English be employed as the language of publication. The editors' conference at the fourth congress of the Ukrainian Canadian Committee in 1953 thought it important "to organize a journalistic association for the purpose of publishing an English edition for those who do not know the Ukrainian language."[43] More recently, the first editorial in *Ukrainian Echo* (April, 1977), *Homin Ukrainy*'s monthly English-language supplement, declared:

> We hope to become a catalyst through which . . . involvement on the part of non-Ukrainian speaking Ukrainian Canadians will be encouraged, particularly among the young. Even if we do not visibly contribute to a linguistic revival, we consider that a closer identification with one's heritage . . . may be the first step towards this goal. In fact, we hope to gain some converts to our Ukrainian language weekly.

That Ukrainian Canadians without a knowledge of Ukrainian will read Ukrainian publications in English or French is far from certain. Besides a change in language, stylistic and content changes would help to attract those who subscribe out of interest rather than habit or loyalty. With the vast majority of Canada's Ukrainians the product of North American mass culture, it has been suggested that the Ukrainian press carry items such as stock market quotations, reviews of the non-Ukrainian entertainment scene, CFL and NHL sports, and more in-depth analysis of international and Canadian news.[44]

As necessary as is the need for changes in the format of publications, the writing style of the journalists, and the contents of articles, such changes will not necessarily cure the press's ills.[45] At the heart of the problem is the general lack of interest in Ukrainian culture beyond the superficial folkloric aspects. To build interest is the real challenge facing the Ukrainian press in Canada. Editors must resume their historic roles as leaders of the Ukrainian-Canadian community by re-evaluating the goals and methods of Ukrainian-Canadian organizations. Where once they worked to develop a Ukrainian consciousness in immigrants unaware of their heritage, today they must help to provide the organized Ukrainian-Canadian community with ideas and programs which may attract Ukrainian Canadians out of touch with their heritage.

NOTES

1. A. Malycky, "An Analysis of the Periodical Publications of Canadian

Slavs," in C.J. Jaenen (ed.), *Slavs in Canada* (Ottawa: Inter-University Committee on Canadian Slavs, 1971), p. 316.

2. According to the 1917 survey, conducted by J.S. Woodsworth of the Bureau of Social Research for the governments of Manitoba, Saskatchewan, and Alberta, 96 per cent of Ukrainians questioned did not read English: C.H. Young, *The Ukrainian Canadians: A Study in Assimilation* (Toronto: Thomas Nelson & Sons, 1931), p. 166.
3. "*Novyi shliakh.*" *Iuvileina knyha, 1930-55* (*New Pathway* Jubilee Book, 1930-1955) (Winnipeg: Ukrainian National Publishing Co., 1956), p. 11; M.H. Marunchak, *The Ukrainian Canadians: A History* (Winnipeg: Ukrainian Free Academy of Sciences, 1970), p. 498.
4. There have been exceptions. Between 1927 and 1930 *Kanadiiskyi farmer* and *Kanadyiskyi ukrainets* printed an eight-page humorous supplement known as *Vuiko* (Uncle). Earlier, between 1922 and 1927, *Vuiko* had been published as an independent Ukrainian-Canadian humorous monthly. Another humorous illustrated monthly journal was *Tochylo* (Grindstone) (1930-47). Marunchak, *Ukrainian Canadians*, p. 480.
5. P. Yuzyk, *The Ukrainians in Manitoba: A Social History* (Toronto: University of Toronto Press, 1953), p. 124.
6. V. Turek, *The Polish Language Press in Canada* (Toronto: Polish Research Institute, 1962), pp. 29-30; J. Harewood, "Ethnic Press Has a Difficult Job in Canada," in H. Palmer (ed.), *Immigration and the Rise of Multiculturalism* (Toronto: Copp Clark, 1975), p. 165.
7. "The foreign language press in Canada must be officially registered and all papers are reviewed in summary by the Citizenship Branch of the Department of Citizenship and Immigration." W.D. Borrie, *The Cultural Integration of Immigrants* (Paris: UNESCO, 1959), p. 139. The ancestral-language press is no longer required to register officially, except for the usual post office registration for mailing privileges. From the summary, the Canadian government obtains the views of ethnic groups on multiculturalism, integration, immigration, Canadian internal affairs, international affairs, and intragroup matters: see *Canadian Ethnic Press Review*, Secretary of State Department. The Ethnic Press Readership Service of the provincial secretary in Ontario and the Quebec Department of Immigration also review the ethnic press in their respective provinces.
8. The first Ukrainian newspaper in the New World was *Ameryka* (America), published by Rev. Ivan Voliansky in Shenandoah, Pennsylvania, in 1886-87. It folded after a few issues. Another *Ameryka* appeared in 1907.
9. M. Borowyk, "The Ukrainians in Canada and Their Press" (Doctoral dissertation, University of Ottawa-Ukrainian Free University of Munich, 1968), pp. 116-23. The early yearbook volumes of *Svoboda* are excellent chronicles of early Ukrainian-Canadian life.
10. *Ibid.*, pp. 125-8.
11. *Rada* was published during 1906-14 in Russian-dominated Kiev. On its

staff were M. Hrushevksy, S. Petliura, and D. Doroshenko. *Ibid.*, p. 129.

12. S.J. Jaworsky, "Newspapers and Periodicals of Slavic Groups in Canada During the Period of 1959-1965" (Master's thesis, University of Ottawa, 1971), p. 19. *Kanadiiskyi farmer* was purchased in October, 1973, by Trident Press of Winnipeg. An example of a local commercial community newspaper is *Oko* (The Eye), launched in Montreal in 1979.
13. R.E. Park, *The Immigrant Press and Its Control* (New York: Harper and Brothers, 1922), p. 331.
14. C.F. Ware, "Foreign Language Press," *Encyclopaedia of the Social Sciences* (New York: Macmillan, 1950), VI, pp. 378-81.
15. The first periodical to use Ukrainian in Canada was the bilingual *Syftonski novyny* (The Sifton News), published in Sifton, Manitoba, probably in 1901. A. Malycky, "Ukrainian-Canadian Periodical Publications: A Preliminary Check List," *Canadian Ethnic Studies*, I (1969), p. 116; Malycky, "Periodical Publications of Canadian Slavs," p. 317.
16. Marunchak, *Ukrainian Canadians*, p. 261.
17. *Ibid.*, p. 632. Although *Kanadiiskyi farmer* has generally supported the retention of Ukrainian culture and language, it was a staunch supporter of the Liberal decision to liquidate the Ukrainian bilingual schools in Manitoba. It was also indirectly responsible for the creation of the Ruthenian Training School in Manitoba. According to one account, the Conservative Party, urged on by Ukrainian activists, established the training school to counter the Liberal influence of the *Kanadiiskyi farmer*. T. Tomashevsky, "Do pochatkiv *Kanadiiskoho farmera*" (About the Beginnings of the *Canadian Farmer*), *Iuvileinyi kalendar-almanakh "Kanadiiskoho farmera" na 1963 rik* (*Canadian Farmer* Jubilee Calendar-Almanac 1963) (Winnipeg: National Publishing, 1963), p. 23.
18. *Ibid.*, p. 262.
19. For a discussion of Ukrainian-language publications supported or established by Canadian political parties, see Marunchak, *Ukrainian Canadians*, pp. 262, 275-6; Yuzyk, *Ukrainians in Manitoba*, p. 116.
20. O.T. Martynowych, "The Ukrainian Socialist Movement in Canada, 1900-1918," *Journal of Ukrainian Graduate Studies*, 1 (Fall, 1976), p. 27.
21. J.M. Kirschbaum, "The Ideological Orientation of the Canadian Slavic Press," in Jaenen (ed.), *Slavs in Canada*, p. 300. It is uncertain whether the reference is to eighteen periodicals or eighteen different titles.
22. The work of the pro-Soviet Communist press is analysed from a Communist perspective in P. Krawchuk, *Piatdesiat rokiv sluzhinnia narodu* (Fifty Years of Service to the People) (Toronto: Vydavnytstvo ukrainske zhyttia, 1957). See also J. Kolasky, *The Shattered Illusion: The History of Ukrainian Pro-Communist Organizations in Canada* (Toronto: Peter Martin Associates, 1979), *passim*.
23. Krawchuk, *Piatdesiat rokiv*, pp. 180-1.

24. O. Woycenko, *The Ukrainians in Canada* (Winnipeg: Canada Ethnica, 1968), p. 203; cf. A.R. Boyd, "The Foreign-Language Press in Canada," in I. Bernolak *et al.* (eds.), *Immigrants in Canada* (Montreal: n.p., 1955), p. 49.
25. For the range of leftist publications, see Marunchak, *Ukrainian Canadians*, pp. 475-7, 491, 497-8.
26. Yuzyk, *Ukrainians in Manitoba*, p. 115.
27. S. Rosocha, "Zamovkla zbroia-promovylo slovo" (Arms Are Silent-Words Speak), *"Novyi shliakh." Iuvileina knyha*, p. 103.
28. Marunchak, *Ukrainian Canadians*, p. 633.
29. *Robitnyk* became a non-partisan paper in 1954, but did not disappear until 1956. *Ibid.*, p. 634.
30. *Ibid.*, p. 288.
31. Borowyk, "Ukrainians in Canada and Their Press," p. 140; Marunchak, *Ukrainian Canadians*, p. 271.
32. Brother Isidore, "Ukrainian Catholic Press in Canada" (Master's thesis, University of Ottawa, 1959), pp. 30-1.
33. According to Marunchak (p. 489), *Biuleten* disappeared in 1937; Borowyk (p. 170) and Isidore (p. 37) give the date as 1938.
34. "Pochatky *Novoho shliakhu*" (The Beginnings of the *New Pathway*), *"Novyi shliakh." Iuvileina knyha*, pp. 13-28; Boyd, "Foreign-Language Press," p. 50.
35. M. Robert, "Everything that's fit to print in every language fit to read," *Maclean*'s (June, 1960), p. 25.
36. There have also been regular unpaid contributors from the United States, the United Kingdom, Argentina, Switzerland, and France. "25 rokiv na sluzhbi narodovi" (25 Years in the People's Service), *"Novyi shliakh." Iuvileina knyha*, p. 176. *Homin Ukrainy* has twenty regular unpaid contributors living outside Toronto.
37. This was not the first association of Ukrainian journalists. A group known as the Ukrainian Press Association existed in 1919, but the writer was unable to find more information about it. PAC, Robert L. Borden Papers, vol. 161, pp. 86925-6.
38. In 1971 *Ukrainskyi holos* was the only Ukrainian paper to receive a news and feature service from the Canadian Press, according to M. Graham, "The Growing Power of the Ethnic Press," in J.M. Kirschbaum *et al.* (eds.), *Twenty Years of the Ethnic Press Association of Ontario* (Toronto: Ethnic Press Association of Ontario, 1971), p. 188. This is no longer the case.
39. Borowyk, "Ukrainians in Canada and Their Press," p. 148.
40. Jaworsky, "Newspapers and Periodicals," pp. 119, 121.
41. S. Kirshner, "Ethnic press glories in diversity, but it runs on financial tightrope," *Globe and Mail* (Toronto), 6 May 1978.
42. I. Tesla, "Demography of Ukrainian Canadians," in "Immigration Ukrainian Canadian," mimeographed (Toronto: Orelets Press, 1976), p. 37.

43. Marunchak, *Ukrainian Canadians*, p. 652.
44. Ia. Zaiats, "Dlia choho nam potribna molodizhna sektsia SUZhK" (Why Do We Need the Youth Section of AUJC), *Zbirka prats chleniv molodizhnoi sektsii spilky ukrainskykh zhurnalistiv Kanady* (A Collection of Works of the Youth Section of the Association of Ukrainian Journalists of Canada) (Toronto: Spilka ukrainskykh zhurnalistiv Kanady, 1973), pp. 2, 3.
45. According to one study, only 43.3 per cent of the Ukrainian Canadians surveyed felt that better quality ethnic newspapers were needed. K.G. O'Bryan *et al.*, *Non-Official Languages: A Study in Canadian Multiculturalism* (Ottawa: Queen's Printer, 1975), p. 327. Nevertheless, newspapers such as *Postup*, which have improved their layout, have increased their subscribers.

THIRTEEN

The Fine Arts

Robert B. Klymasz

A most important aspect of the Ukrainian experience in Canada is the aesthetic dimension, expressed through the medium of artistic performance and production.[1] To some, this dimension best defines the Ukrainian heritage and its distinctive contribution to Canada's cultural development. The awareness of policies in Ukraine that disrupt normal cultural development occasionally gives the maintenance of Ukrainian arts in Canada a defensive and preservative posture – closely linked with the problem of ethnic survival in Canada and, indeed, in Ukraine itself.[2]

The resulting sense of mission can make one uncomfortable when discussing Ukrainian fine arts in Canada. Is there really such a phenomenon as Ukrainian-Canadian arts? To answer the question, the artists themselves should be queried.[3] Would they, for example, be more creative, productive, or artistic if they lived in Ukraine? Does a Ukrainian cultural background assist one's artistic maturation? Does it impede it? What is the relationship of Ukrainian-Canadian arts to Canadian arts generally?

Any serious study should try to explain why the Ukrainian experience in western Canada has often spawned artistic creativity that is generally more innovative and less purist than in eastern Canada. It should also note the weakness of viewing Ukrainian-Canadian artistic production solely in terms of criteria derived from Western civilization and the Euro-American cultural elite with aesthetic canons, which ignore, reject, or minimize ties between artistic expression and folklore or folklife, so fundamental to the Ukrainian arts.[4] It would be a mistake to apologize for this special and ultimately very enriching relationship. As an aesthetic experience, a piece of Ukrainian embroidery by an anonymous folk artist from Saskatchewan can be as rewarding as a canvas of William Kurelek's from Toronto.

The importance of the close tie between the Ukrainian arts and Ukrainian folklore cannot be exaggerated. Without the latter, the essential "Ukrainian-ness" of a particular work tends to merge it with amorphous international trends. For the Ukrainian arts, the line between "high" and "low" cultural endeavours is a continuous line, not a chasm. It is, of course, possible and perhaps even likely that in the future the test of "Ukrainian-ness" may come to depend on non-folkloric criteria, but to suppose that this would mark the maturation of the Ukrainian arts and their transformation into truly "fine" arts is highly debatable.

Although tensions between east and west and folk and non-folk characterize Ukrainian culture in Canada, it is unfortunate that the preoccupation with Ukrainian history, literature, and language has generally minimized the significance of Ukrainian arts as a source of insight into almost all aspects of the Ukrainian-Canadian experience. With little academic status, the Ukrainian arts have largely operated on an informal level as hobbies or interesting pastimes, where Ukrainians are increasingly being joined by non-Ukrainians, who help to turn the Ukrainian arts into a kind of cultural commonwealth at popular festivals, which occasionally even cut across old Ukrainian partisan lines. Outside the Ukrainian community, there is a growing recognition that the Ukrainian arts can be an antidote to the pressures of uniformity and conformity in our society and a rich source for artistic creativity.

In this essay the reader will note a conscious effort to avoid presenting a "who's who" list of names and personalities, which usually avoids the problem of evaluation and concentrates on artists with a reputation *outside* the Ukrainian-Canadian community. The emphasis is on trends reflected in music, dance, theatre, cinema, architecture, and the fine and exhibiting arts.

MUSIC

The folk tradition is a rich cultural source for the development of Ukrainian music.[5] Ukraine's geographical position on the eastern fringe of European civilization has enabled the people to retain many musical features once prevalent in West European folk music but now faded or totally absent. As a result, Ukrainian folk music is a special blend, related to yet readily distinguishable from other folk music traditions.

The classic expression of Ukrainian music is through choral singing, best exemplified in the liturgy of Eastern Christianity. The predilection for group singing may reflect an overt recognition of the sung word as a means of fostering a spirit of national consciousness and national self-awareness. This affiliation of choral song with political sensitivity occasionally turns the former into a national anthem, a kind of aural icon dedicated to a reaffirmation of Ukrainian ethnic loyalty.

As for the art itself, some Ukrainian choral activities have been most sophisticated because of the talents of such masters as A. Koshetz (1875-1944) in Winnipeg, N. Horodovenko (1885-1965) in Montreal, and L. Turkiewicz (1906-61) in Toronto. Among Ukrainians, choral singing is approached as a national art rather than a recreational outlet, pastime, or glee club. The serious approach, however, is frequently frustrated by the need to rely heavily upon untrained amateur enthusiasts, the conductors included. With very few Canadian-born composers and arrangers, the repertoire of Ukrainian choirs has been largely confined to old favourites and Soviet imports, with little exploration of new or innovative pieces. To overcome such drawbacks Ukrainian choral societies with pro-Soviet sympathies have occasionally toured Ukraine with concerts or sent promising Ukrainian-Canadian conductors to the state music conservatories for advanced training. Such training has generally produced musical activists partial to Soviet materials with a strong popular mass base and has reinforced a repertoire already heavily dominated by the folksong tradition.

The need for qualified critics to review Ukrainian musical developments in Canada is also great. Choristers tend to perform in uniformed national costumes styled especially for the concert stage, even though the authentic Ukrainian folk costume was never a wholesale copy of anyone's dress. In the renowned Koshetz choirs of the first half of the twentieth century, each member was dressed in individual folk dress to produce a rich and multicoloured visual effect. Among critics, Winnipeg's Pavlo Macenko, a classical Ukrainian musicologist, is perhaps the most noteworthy. Besides innumerable reviews and articles in the Ukrainian press, he organized conferences and workshops for church cantors and choir directors. As arranger and composer, he has belonged to the "national school" of Ukrainian music with a special attachment to folk music, an approach questioned by such leading Ukrainian modernists as George Fiala of Montreal, who consider the folk legacy convenient though not necessarily an indispensable element in the production of Ukrainian music, which should recognize and meet current musical trends and tastes.

The development of Ukrainian music in Canada has been much handicapped by the absence of well-developed music schools, without which gifted musicians have been forced to work in isolation. The resulting gap has been partially bridged by commercial Ukrainian country music, which gained popularity in western Canada during the early sixties with the general arrival of the long-playing record.

Another productive format for musical creativity and performance has been the light musical. In this as in Ukrainian country music, the most obvious feature has been the clear blend of two ethnocultural traditions, two musical styles, and even two languages. The resulting macaronic phenomenon has still to be fully recognized as artistic expression by purists within the Ukrainian community. A recent milestone among light musicals was the cabaret-style production, "On the Odessa Docks," written, directed, and choreographed by Taras Shipowick and staged at the Odessa Pavilion during Toronto's 1974 multicultural "Caravan." Its outstanding feature was a free-and-easy, English-Ukrainian script. Lacking, however, was a theme equally New World in setting and content. Its appeal notwithstanding, it had a brief life because inadequate finances permitted neither a tour of communities across Canada nor filming for television or as a movie. In spite of brilliant flashes, the fate of Ukrainian music depends almost entirely on informal, voluntary, part-time, temporary involvement.[6]

Encouraging also is the time allocated by radio stations to programs of Ukrainian music. An excellent series of eleven one-hour radio programs, "Ukrainian Concert Hall," devoted to the various aspects of Ukrainian classical music, was aired by Denis Hlynka on Winnipeg's CBC-FM station in 1972-73. Copyright restrictions have prevented its dissemination to interested stations elsewhere. Other programs have aired individual musical items or entire classical operas. Of special interest have been the periodic items of CBC radio's weekly multicultural program, "Identities."

The field of Ukrainian instrumental music has also been thriving. From violin virtuoso Steven Staryk to *lira* (hurdy-gurdy) player William Howika of Winnipeg, it includes what appears at times to be an underground army of *tsymbaly* (dulcimer) players on the Prairies, *bandura* and mandolin players in the larger cities, and a variety of such popular dance bands as "Dumka" in Edmonton, "D Drifters Five" in Winnipeg, and "Rushnychok" in Montreal. Ukrainian symphonic music is most often heard on commercial long-playing recordings imported from Soviet Ukraine. Occasionally, Ukrainian communities commission works by Ukrainian-Canadian composers and have them performed by local symphonies. In March, 1974, Edmonton's Ukrainian community sponsored the Edmonton Symphony Orchestra in an evening which featured pieces composed between 1927 and 1972 by Borys Liatoshynsky and Lev Revutsky of the Soviet Ukraine, Antin Rudnytsky of the United States, George Fiala of Montreal, and Serhii Eremenko of Edmonton. The Ukrainian-American pianist, Roman Rudnytsky, was the guest artist. In October, 1974, the eleventh Ukrainian Canadian Congress featured the Winnipeg Symphony Orchestra playing works by Mykola Lysenko, Franz Liszt, and Lev Revutsky and the world première of a specially commissioned violin concerto by George Fiala performed by guest artist Steven Staryk, which exemplified well the close relationship between the folk and non-folk strata of Ukrainian music.

An important musical aspect has been the impact of touring artists from Soviet Ukraine. Some, like baritone Dmytro Hnatiuk, have a faithful following across Canada, but it is unfortunate that almost no mainstream music critics can provide informed reviews of their performances. It is equally unfortunate that the artists themselves do not develop, but cater to, the taste of their audiences with a musical menu confined to popular items. Nor are the standards of the grandstand at Canada's National Ukrainian Festival in Dauphin any better. In 1973 one saw Montreal's capable soprano, Anna Chornodolska, belting out "Luchche bulo b" to the accompaniment of Winnipeg's Ted Komar and his accordion ensemble, and a year later, the same poor taste was exemplified by Dmytro Hnatiuk's clap-happy rendition of "Handzia" in the Opera of the National Arts Centre in Ottawa.

The field of Ukrainian popular music is especially interesting for the manner in which it reflects the mainstream hit parade in the rapid turnover of favourite stars and performers who capture the Ukrainian-Canadian community and then suddenly disappear or are absorbed by the more lucrative mainstream of North American pop music. Typical was the phenomenon of "Tony the Troubadour" (surname Stechishen), whose recordings during the forties and fifties of popular Ukrainian folksongs to guitar accompaniment anticipated the folk movement a decade later. Tony was best known among Ukrainian communities in eastern Canada; western Canada's equivalent in the sixties and seventies has been the husband and wife team of "Mickey and Bunny" (Sklepowich). Others with mass appeal have been Juliette (née Sysak), Wally Koster, and Joan Karasevich. The longest exposure has been Ivan Romanoff's weekly program of ethnic folk music on CBC national radio.

DANCE

The Ukrainian dance in Canada is understood almost exclusively to mean folk dance, with about 100 Ukrainian folk dance groups from coast to coast.[7] And of all the forms of artistic expression, the Ukrainian folk dance does retain the widest following among enthusiastic participants and countless spectators. Like most Ukrainian choirs, the folk dance operates largely at the non-professional, grassroots level and has therefore enormous potential as a unique combination of art and recreation as well as an art form which links the Ukrainian community with its cultural heritage and Canadian mainstream society generally.

In its original or natural form, the Ukrainian folk dance can still be seen on rare occasions in rural areas of western Canada, where dances like *holub, mazurka,* and *kolomyika* are performed at weddings and parties. Remembered mainly by the old, most will disappear altogether unless proper field and documentation studies are undertaken. The rich source of primary material has unfortunately been overshadowed by the more stagey, choreographed dance sequences introduced by the famed Vasyl Avramenko, the leading figure in Ukrainian dance in North America for more than a quarter century. In the fifties the Avramenko era was eclipsed somewhat by touring dance groups from the Soviet Union, and their impact on contemporary Ukrainian dance can be seen in the accent on high showmanship, vitality, sharp contrast, regimentation, and massiveness. There have been some brave, isolated attempts to counter the wholesale importation of Soviet dance styles by such groups as the Dnipro Ukrainian Dance Company (Ottawa), the Vesnianka Ukrainian Folk Dancing School (Thunder Bay), Chaika (Hamilton), and the work of innovative choreographers such as Lusia Pavlychenko

(Saskatoon), Natalka Dobrolige (Edmonton), Jaroslav Klun (Hamilton), and Nadia Pavlychenko (Toronto).

The videotape, which allows the dance company to study its choreographic routines, store the tape, or circulate it for external viewing and criticism, has been important with groups like the Evshan Ukrainian Dancers (Saskatoon) in the early seventies and the Poltava Dancers (Regina), who released "Poltava - A Heritage of Dance" in 1974, a half-hour film documentary. Both underline the need for a central data bank for such materials. Needed also is a newsletter for Ukrainian folk dance ensembles across Canada. It would also help if dance instructors did not see their respective dance groups as personal possessions and extended invitations to guest choreographers.

Since 1966, Dauphin's annual festival has presented the new and old in Ukrainian dance in close juxtaposition, with groups from the United States and Canada. Groups from the large metropolitan centres (Toronto, Winnipeg, Edmonton) exhibit an urban texture that is flashy, massive, and conformist in style, content, and essence - almost a kind of "Ukrainian power" where the dance becomes a visual manifestation of ethnic identity, a dynamic, moving icon that fulfils much the same ethnic-affirmation function performed by the popular but comparatively static Ukrainian Easter egg. Dance groups from smaller Ukrainian centres tend to be more introspective in nature, more delicate and sensitive in their feel for the Ukrainian dance. Still to be established is a permanent, full-time professional dance company capable of exploiting the legacy of the past and exploring new dance avenues in ethnic and universal forms.

THEATRE

The Ukrainian theatre in Canada was most active before World War II.[8] Today Ukrainian halls and auditoriums are left with their musty stages, old sets, and canvas drop curtains covered with advertisements for local businesses that have ceased to exist. For the most part, the earlier Ukrainian theatre was folk theatre. The performers were non-professionals who developed their roles and consulted scripts (when available) only to check the drift of action and dramatic sequences. Most plays were the old, ever-popular romance tragedies - "Marusia" or "Oi ne khody Hrytsiu" - with music, singing, and dancing. Although now abandoned, the early theatre did bequeath numerous plays that were written, published, and performed in Canada. Of special interest are those by Myroslaw Irchan (pseudonym of Andrii Babiuk, 1896-1937) and Jacob Maydanyk (1891-   ), which reflected well the tensions of the Ukrainian immigrant experience at that time.

After the war occasional amateur revivals were short-lived because of inadequate funding and tended to stress musicals such as "Natalka

Poltavka" and "Zaporozhets za Dunaiem." Ukrainian theatre fared considerably better in those urban centres with numerous Ukrainian émigrés.[9] However, much of the serious work was often eclipsed by the community's call for the more popular musical format (for example, the long-running "Tsyhanka Aza" in Toronto during the fifties) and the lack of funds to support experimental presentations. Others, totally committed to the classic Ukrainian theatre, embarked on careers in Ukrainian that could not be accommodated on Canadian soil. Translations offered only a partial solution to the problem.[10]

The co-existence of two or more cultures has a tendency to blend new phenomena. Such was the early Ukrainian theatre, which commented successfully with humour and sadness on the New World experience. In recent years a parallel development in English has drawn upon the immigrant experience. Joan Forman's one-act historical drama, *Westward to Canada* (Toronto, 1972), depicts the beginnings of Ukrainian emigration to the Prairie Provinces. Some of George Ryga's dramatic works contain tendencies that "undoubtedly spring from his upbringing in the Ukrainian farming community of northern Alberta" (R.B. Parker in his introduction to Ryga's *The Ecstasy of Rita Joe and Other Plays*, Toronto, 1971). The collective creation of Saskatoon's 25th Street Theatre, "Paper Wheat" (1977), also draws heavily upon the past. While Forman's play has yet to receive critical attention, some of Ryga's work shares that sense of humanity portrayed also in the work of his late counterpart in the graphic arts, William Kurelek (also born on a farm in Alberta). Two dramatic pieces for television by Ryga on Ukrainian-Canadian themes are "Ninth Summer," a half-hour production about a young boy's infatuation with an older girl in a small rural Ukrainian community on the Prairies, and "1927," a full-hour production which one Toronto critic has likened to John Steinbeck's novel, *The Grapes of Wrath*. "Ninth Summer" was aired on the full CBC television network in 1972 and was criticized in the press by spokesmen in the Ukrainian community who thought it highly prejudicial to the Ukrainian-Canadian image.

The need for a professional Ukrainian theatre company is as great as for a Ukrainian dance company. Especially noteworthy, therefore, are the exploratory activities of Winnipeg's "Ukrainian Theatre," which in 1979 sponsored a playwriting competition open to "all creative writers who show a high standard of work or exceptional promise." All entries were to focus on Ukrainian themes and two main prizes of $2,000 each were announced: one for a play in Ukrainian and the other for one in English. Many playwrights of Ukrainian-Canadian origin focus on the Ukrainian legacy as a sociological problem, a barrier that can threaten interpersonal relationships and estrange one generation from another. These kinds of tensions are evident in the works of the young Vancouver playwright, Ted Galay, who recently won the Canadian Authors'

Association Literary Award for "After Baba's Funeral" and "Sweet and Sour Pickles." He has also written a musical play, "Vichnoia Pamiat" (Eternal Memory).

PHOTO-CINEMA

Full of promise for the Ukrainian arts in Canada is the photo-cinema, including still photography, moving film, and videotape.[11] Until recently, such materials were either documentaries or exotic, tourist-like approaches to the Ukrainian-Canadian folk heritage. The National Film Board's early black-and-white films on Ukrainian festivities in western Canada (notably Laura Boulton's two productions in 1942, "Ukrainian Winter Holidays" and "Ukrainian Dance") are good examples of the former. The coloured film, "Treasures of the Ukraine," produced privately in Toronto during the early fifties by M.E. Lucyk, F.J. Martyniuk, and E. Wachna and devoted almost entirely to modelling Ukraine's folk costumes, illustrates well the Ukrainian tendency to mythologize on film the history, folkways, and tribulations of the Ukrainian people. Typical also is the following excerpt from a news report on the Canukr film, "Marichka":

> Hot summer breezes whip the street spraying the fence-enclosed wooden houses. At the well, an old lady sets her wooden bucket on the ground so that she can spend some time gossiping with her friend. A goatherder ambles along the poppy strewn path, stopping at the church to greet the young workers who have rested their scythes against the fence. Geese and ducks roam the streets of the sleepy Ukrainian village.[12]

Much work in depicting the Ukrainian-Canadian experience on film has been done by non-Ukrainians, sponsored by the railways, the NFB, and the CBC. A good example is the NFB's ten-minute colour production, "Kurelek," "a quiet and engrossing story that many immigrant homesteaders might have told had they had the talent and the detachment of William Kurelek whose paintings made the films."[13] Recently, filmmakers of Ukrainian origin have entered the field.[14] Typical is the NFB's "I've Never Walked the Steppes" by Jerry Krepakevich. A pioneering and even more important development was the release in 1974 of Slavko Nowytski's "Reflections of the Past," a half-hour colour film to commemorate Winnipeg's centennial. Commissioned by the Ukrainian Cultural and Educational Centre in Winnipeg, it depicts the early and difficult beginnings of Ukrainian pioneer settlement, documents the Ukrainian contribution to Manitoba's rich architectural heritage, and portrays surviving pioneers. The account, an impressionistic evaluation of the Ukrainian pioneer experience from the viewpoint of the seventies, emits an intimate feeling of appreciation for the hardship and joy of early Ukrainian life. Sound and visual techniques exploit creatively black-and-white still photographs, on-site pioneer sequences, and interviews with old-timers. Poetically conceived images from nature underscore the cyclical passage of life, the seasons, and time. The film's sensitivity and subjectivism make it a milestone in the development of Ukrainian-Canadian cinema. Neither ethnocentric nor a blatant self-image by and for Ukrainians, the film is an artistic audio-visual experience – the most successful attempt thus far to portray Ukrainians in Canada.

To date, there have been no fictitious works of artistic merit connected with the Ukrainian-Canadian experience. A possible exception is the controversial "Another Smith for Paradise," aired nationally by the CBC in 1974, a parody on many of the activities and concerns sacred to Ukrainian organizations in Canada (among them the construction of monuments that commemorate the deeds of old-country heroes). Several spokesmen for the Ukrainian community objected to the film, for it departed from the conventional belief Ukrainians have of themselves as a far-sighted, earnest, and progressive element in the Canadian mosaic. It is nonetheless certain that any comprehensive festival of Ukrainian-Canadian films would have to include "Another Smith for Paradise," which, however distorted, is a salutary contrast to the highly romanticized "Marichka." The same festival would also include the Ukrainianized sound-track versions of such NFB productions as "Canadians Can Dance," "Here is Canada," "Kurelek," "Nahanni," and "Paddle to the Sea."

Other forms of film-related production remain largely undeveloped. The potential of videotape on television has yet to be fully exploited, though it is very conducive to light, variety programing. Ivan Fecan's "A Ukrainian Christmas," a half-hour special television production in Toronto in 1973, was an interesting departure from the usual Christmas show because of Nadia Pavlychenko's choreography, the youthful cabaret-style vocal solos, and the pleasant carolling group.

In the area of still photography, most striking has been the dramatic collection of black-and-white photographs of Ukrainian pioneer churches in western Canada, the interiors included, by Edmonton radiologist Orest Semchishen. In 1974 some of his work was exhibited in Ottawa by the Still Division of the NFB as part of a special showing in the National Conference Centre.[15]

GRAPHIC ARTS, SCULPTURE, ARCHITECTURE, EXHIBITING ARTS

Prior to World War II, paintings and drawings, sculpture, and architecture operated primarily as folkloric art expressions. The emergence in recent years of an urban, mobile, cultivated middle class with a keen eye for investment opportunities has encouraged Ukrainian-Canadian artistic activity, including special commercial galleries catering almost exclusively to Ukrainians. Focus on the individual artist is a radical departure from tradition, which paid little attention to the craftsman and concentrated on the final product. The eclipse of artistic anonymity and the democratization have opened up the fine arts to a wider segment of the Ukrainian community in Canada.

With pencil, brush, or chisel, Ukrainian-Canadian artists such as Ivan Belsky (Toronto) and Ruslan Logush (Montreal) draw inspiration from symbols, favourite scenes, or famous historical events in Ukraine. Others, such as William Kurelek, Steven Repa, Peter Shostak, Leo Mol (Lev Molodozhanyn), Parasia Iwanec, draw upon Ukrainian-Canadian pioneer experience – Easter or Christmas festivities, the old farmstead, the country church. Strictly representational in nature, the autobiographical works reflect the artists' affirmation of loyalty to ethnic roots, thereafter to embark freely on an independent, personally defined path of artistic endeavour. The process was acknowledged by Ivan Belsky in Lawrence O'Toole's feature article on the artist in the *Globe and Mail*: "Most everything I did was Ukrainian but now I'm slowly, very slowly, coming into painting Canadian subjects. I remember everything from the Ukraine, so it was easy to paint the things I saw in my early life." In William Kurelek's case, the need to accommodate ethnicity posed a special problem, which he resolved as follows:

> The lesson I learned from the disillusionment that followed is strange and wonderful. It is: Put *God* first, and your country and your ethnic origin *second*. Then you will at least truly produce good for your Country and people. In addition to things which Ukrainian groups have approached me to do, I have carried out Ukrainian projects on my own and will in the future, without expecting or getting help from the Ukrainian Community. For I know if it's truly worthwhile, then God will provide for it from other sources.[16]

In general, all Ukrainian-Canadian artists face the challenge of using subject matter to maintain personal convictions without sacrificing ethnicity. Some avoid the potential conflict by moving directly into modernism and abstract work with no overt sign of Ukrainian influence, as in the structural relief and sculptured canvas work of Ron Kostyniuk at the University of Calgary. However, symbolic interpretation and visualization of Ukrainian motifs (and even content) often do appear in strange and unfamiliar guises, as in Ruslan Logush's sunflower and helianthus complex of canvases. Most in the Ukrainian community, however, are not yet ready to accept non-representational or symbolic works of art as valid forms of ethnic expression, a situation which alienates some artists.

Perhaps the boldest impression made by the non-performing Ukrainian-Canadian arts is through architectural styles, ranging from the old peasant-type prairie cottages to imposing multidomed churches in the larger urban centres. The simple rustic dwelling and the old wooden country churches and bell-tower, now largely a thing of the past, are increasingly being preserved as museum pieces and historical sites. Yet it is ironic that the very Ukrainian-Canadian press that so quickly condemns the destruction of religious and historical structures in Soviet Ukraine is not as concerned to protect and preserve equally important structures closer to home.

Besides the anonymous folk architects on the Prairies, two figures at least have had an enormous impact on church architecture in Canada. The structures of the late Reverend Philip Ruh, a Catholic missionary of non-Ukrainian origin, feature a unique, occasionally even grotesque and indiscriminate architectural mélange.[17] His work, monumental and heavy, can be seen across Canada, from St. Catharines and Grimsby in southern Ontario to the Ukrainian Catholic cathedral in Edmonton. More recently, Radoslav Zuk of McGill University's School of Architecture has made his own creative contribution, whose significance is summarized as follows:

> Considering the deeply rooted conservatism of Eastern churches, the pioneering work of Radoslav Zuk assumes additional significance extending far beyond the North American continent. In spite of the apparent simplicity of these churches, their controlled monumentality expresses convincingly the richness of the Eastern liturgy. Thus, they become not only architectural landmarks, but also landmarks of spirituality on the flat Canadian prairie.[18]

Of special note also are the variety and quantity of artistry in the churches themselves, ranging from the iron-wrought crosses on the domes to the murals, iconostasis, and embroideries inside.[19]

The folk arts and crafts are another significant part of the non-performing Ukrainian arts. The well-known Ukrainian Easter egg is a striking example of how art can be transformed into representative national art - an ethnic icon recognized by all. Today the *pysanka's* humble origins are seldom acknowledged; it has become a highly sophisticated art form, with practically every art museum in Canada housing its own collection of Easter eggs. The art is so widely practised that the leading practitioners are numerous and largely unknown. With no systematic field study of the folk arts and crafts and only scattered references in the press and other publications, the men and women who continue to use traditional techniques and motifs with wood, beads, clay, needle, and loom are mainly anonymous.

Other aspects of the Ukrainian arts in Canada range from the immigrant cartoons by Winnipeg's Jacob Maydanyk during the first half of the twentieth century to the recent poster work of the young Vera Jacyk of Toronto (that for the "Titka Kvitka" children's videotape series is especially good), and even to today's mass-produced Ukrainian T-shirt.

Artistic exhibits have gained increasing attention in recent years with a network of about thirty Ukrainian museums[20] and innumerable annual festivals. The need for forceful exhibits, properly researched, designed, and prepared, is ever-pressing. Besides attractive lighting and settings, effective displays require special posters and exhibit catalogues, and those who plan, mount, and install Ukrainian-Canadian exhibits have thus an artistic obligation to fulfil, which as yet has barely been recognized.

CONCLUSION

Although the Ukrainian arts in Canada are experiencing a modest renaissance, not all are of equal social relevance and only a small portion will survive. Still, ethnic loyalties can generate valid artistic forms; the ethnic factor – whether rooted in Ukraine, the Ukrainian-Canadian experience, or in both – can inspire an artist's work. The result may not constitute a national art, but it can be vibrant and relevant – as meaningful as any other form of artistic expression. But needless to say, ethnicity alone does not immunize against mediocre and second-rate work, and the understanding critic, now scarce, must become more commonplace. Established and traditional materials must be reinterpreted and updated to meet new demands and requirements, and those presently committed to particular canons of Ukrainian-Canadian art must learn to judge innovation and divergence if the regenerative ability of the Ukrainian fine arts is to continue and the arts themselves are to function in the future as a viable source of cultural enrichment and pride.

NOTES

1. The best general account of the Ukrainian arts is O. Dmytriw (comp.), *Ukrainian Arts*, rev. ed. (New York: Ukrainian Youth's League of North America, 1955). More authoritative is the two-volume *Ukraine: A Concise Encyclopaedia* (Toronto: University of Toronto Press, 1963-1971), with brief surveys in the second volume on the following Ukrainian-Canadian aspects: I. Keywan, "Architecture, Painting and Sculpture" (pp. 1182-3); W. Wytwycky, "Music" (pp. 1183-5); and V. Revutsky, "Theatre, Dance, Cinema" (p. 1185). For other general surveys, see P. Yuzyk, *Ukrainians in Manitoba: A Social History* (Toronto: University of Toronto Press, 1953); O. Woycenko, *Ukrainians in Canada* (Winnipeg: Canada Ethnica, 1968); and M.H. Marunchak, *The Ukrainian Canadians: A History* (Winnipeg: Ukrainian Free Academy of Sciences, 1970).
2. Soviet Russian scholars who have discussed problems of ethnicity in relation to other cultural aspects include S.A. Tokarev, "O zadachakh etnograficheskogo izucheniia narodov industrialnykh stran" (On the Tasks of Ethnographic Studies Pertaining to the Peoples of Industrial Regions), *Sovetskaia etnografiia* (Soviet Ethnography), no. 5 (1967), pp. 133-42; J.V. Bromlej, "Ethnos and the Ethnosocial Organism," *Ethnologia Slavica*, III (1971), pp. 47-57; and K.V. Chistov, "Ethnicheskaia obshchnost, etnicheskoe soznanie i nekotorie problemy

dukhovnoi kultury'' (Ethnic Community, Ethnic Consciousness and Several Problems Relating to Spiritual Aspects of Culture) *Sovetskaia etnografiia*, no. 3 (1972), pp. 73-85. For more polemical views, see M. Novak, *The Rise of the Unmeltable Ethnics* (New York: Macmillan, 1972); O. Schrag, *The Decline of the WASP* (New York: Simon and Schuster, 1971); E. Gray, ''Paradoxes in Western Creativity,'' *American Anthropologist* (1972), pp. 676-88; the critique of Gray's article by R.J. Di Pietro, ''On Creativity,'' *American Anthropologist*, LXXV (1973), pp. 312-13; R. August, ''Babeling Beaver Hunts for Home Fire: The Place of Ethnic Literature in Canadian Culture,'' *Canadian Forum* (August, 1974), pp. 8-13. For a revealing personal statement, see W. Kurelek, ''The Development of Ethnic Consciousness in a Canadian Artist,'' in W.W. Isajiw (ed.), *Identities: The Impact of Ethnicity on Canadian Society* (Toronto: Peter Martin Associates, 1977), pp. 46-56.

3. For a ''who's who'' of Ukrainian artists (many political refugees) who met in Toronto, July 3-5, 1954, at ''The First Convention of Ukrainian Artists and Writers from Canada, the United States and Western Europe,'' see M. Bazhansky, A. Kurdydk, B. Oleksandriv, and N. Harkusenko (eds.), *Knyha mystsiv i diiachiv ukrainskoi kultury* (The Book of Ukrainian Artists and Cultural Workers) (Toronto: n.p., n.d.).
4. For the folkloric aspects of the Ukrainian-Canadian arts, see B. Klymasz, *A Bibliography of Ukrainian Folklore in Canada, 1902-1964* (Ottawa: National Museum of Canada, 1969); and the National Museum of Man's exhibit catalogue, *Continuity and Change: The Ukrainian Folk Heritage in Canada* (Ottawa: Canadian Centre for Folk Culture Studies, 1972), which also appeared in a separate French edition (*Tradition et evolution: le patrimoine des Ukrainiens du Canada*). Impressionistic and rather dated views of Ukrainian folk dancing and choral singing in Canada are found in W. Paluk, *Canadian Cossacks: Essays, Articles and Stories on Ukrainian-Canadian Life* (Winnipeg: Ukrainian Canadian Review Publishing Co., 1943). For some indication of the current appeal of Ukrainian art and culture in monetary terms, see R. Desmet, *Impact Study of Canada's National Ukrainian Festival Upon the Town of Dauphin and the Neighbouring Area* (Winnipeg: Manitoba Department of Tourism, 1972).
5. Very little has been published on Ukrainian music in Canada. The only discography is a brief listing of Ukrainian country music long-playing records in R.B. Klymasz, ''Ukrainian Folklore in Canada: An Immigrant Complex in Transition'' (Doctoral dissertation, Indiana University, 1970), pp. 266-90. For a brief survey of Ukrainian music in Canada by R.B. Klymasz, see the *Encyclopedia of Music in Canada*. (Toronto: University of Toronto Press, 1981), pp. 942-3.
6. For additional details about the work of Taras Shipowick and his Odessa Group in Toronto, see O. Hlibovych, ''Talant vartyi uvahy'' (A Talent Worthy of Attention), *Svoboda*, 31 December 1976.
7. The history of Ukrainian dance in Canada is poorly documented except

for a small mimeographed publication compiled by B. Klymash (Klymasz), *Ukrainian Folk Dance: A Symposium* (Toronto: Ukrainian National Youth Federation of Canada, 1961). Peripheral material is abundant, with M.H. Botsko's brief notes on the "Kanada" dance especially noteworthy. For his selection of recent field materials on Ukrainian songs of emigration, see "Z novykh zapysiv emihrantsko-zarobitchanskykh pisen" (From Recently Collected Songs of Emigrant Wage-earners), *Narodna tvorchist ta etnohrafiia* (Folk Art and Ethnography), no. 2 (1974), pp. 88-92.

8. For the only serious treatment of the Ukrainian theatre in Canada, see B. Hiritsch, "The Development of Ukrainian Theatre and Its Role in Canada" (Master's thesis, University of Montreal, 1961), especially pp. 83-107.
9. In Edmonton, for example, important drama and theatrical activity included the staging of such classical and intellectually demanding plays as Lesia Ukrainka's *Orhiia* (The Orgy). In the seventies Toronto's Ukrainian Drama Ensemble, "Zahrava," successfully staged a number of important productions. For a favourable review of the group's version of *Myna Mazailo* by M. Kulish, see *Novyi shliakh*, 1, 8 January 1977.
10. Two notable examples are the English-language adaptation of Olha Kobylianska's novel, *Zemlia* (Land), staged in Edmonton around 1974, and the University of Toronto Drama Research Centre's production of the North American première of *Patetychna sonata* (Sonata Pathétique) by the eminent Ukrainian playwright, Mykola Kulish (1892-1942), in an English-language adaptation prepared by Moira and George Luckyj.
11. Except for the now outdated and all too brief survey by B. Berest, *Istoriia ukrainskoho kina* (History of Ukrainian Cinema) (New York: Shevchenko Scientific Society, 1962), pp. 186-93, materials regarding film and the Ukrainian experience in Canada are difficult to find. A very valuable recent work is S. Zaporzan and R.B. Klymasz, *Film and the Ukrainians in Canada 1921-1980*, Research Report No. 1 (Edmonton: Canadian Institute of Ukrainian Studies, 1982).

    The film catalogues of the National Film Board are of limited value. The Ukrainian press in Canada includes articles on Ukrainian film activities, of which the write-up on "Poltava - A Heritage of Dance" in *Ukrainian Canadian* (June, 1974) is typical. In Soviet Ukraine, U.M. Kapelhordska has written two articles outlining certain aspects of the Ukrainian-Canadian scene as well. Although tendentious, they include a survey of films on Shevchenko and their impact abroad from 1928 to 1955 in "Populiarnist' kinoshevchenkiiany za kordonom" (Popularity of Cinematic Shevchenkiana Abroad), *Narodna tvorchist ta etnohrafiia*, no. 2 (1964), pp. 108-9, and a polemical attack against "bourgeois" Ukrainian films in "Vsuperech lohitsi zhyttia" (Contrary to the Logic of Life), *ibid.*, no. 6 (1973), pp. 41-7. An appreciation of "Another Smith for Paradise" is found in an article by G. Patterson, "It's a Long Way to Paradise," *Motion* (May/June, 1973), pp. 26-7.

12. *Ukrainian Weekly* (Svoboda), 13 October 1973.
13. *Film Catalogue 1973-74* (Ottawa: National Film Board, 1974).
14. S. Zaporzan, "Review of Three Films," *Canadian Ethnic Studies*, VII (1975), p. 102.
15. For a selection of Dr. Semchishen's photographs, see H. Hohn (ed.), *Byzantine Churches of Alberta: Photographs By Orest Semchishen* (Edmonton: Edmonton Art Gallery, 1976).
16. W. Kurelek, *Someone with Me* (Ithaca, N.Y.: Centre for Improvement of Undergraduate Education, Cornell University, 1973), p. 520.
17. Ukrainian architecture in Canada is discussed in Philip Ruh's autobiography: *Fylyp Ru. Misioner i budivnychyi* (Philip Ruh: Missionary and Architect) (Winnipeg: Postup, 1960); R. Zuk, "Ukrainian Church Architecture in Canada," *Slavs in Canada* (Ottawa: Inter-University Committee on Canadian Slavs, 1968), pp. 229-34; J. Lehr, *Ukrainian Vernacular Architecture in Alberta* (Edmonton: Provincial Museum of Alberta, 1976); G. Moir and I. Thorkelsson, *Early Buildings in Manitoba* (Winnipeg: Peguis, 1973).
18. "Drei ukrainisch-katholische Kirchen in Kanada" (Three Ukrainian Catholic Churches in Canada), *Christliche Kunstblaetter* (Linz, Austria), January, 1969.
19. The rich but neglected facet of Ukrainian religious art and ritual is surveyed historically in J. Fedoriv, *Obriady ukrainskoi tserkvy. Istorychnyi rozvytok i poiasnennia* (The Rituals of the Ukrainian Church: Historical Evolution and Explanations) (Rome-Toronto: Ukrainske bohoslovske naukove tovarystvo, 1970).
20. B. Klymasz, "Ukrainian Museums in Canada," *Gazette Quarterly of the Canadian Museums Association*, IX (Winter, 1976), pp. 34-8.

FOURTEEN

Ukrainian Literature in Canada

Yar Slavutych

While only eighty-five years old, Ukrainian-language literature is rich and distinct among Canadian ethnic literatures, with fifty-five Ukrainian poets, some 160 original poetry collections, over forty authors of stories and novels, and thirty-five playwrights.[1] Besides the published authors, there have been some 250 amateur and professional writers whose poetry and prose lie buried in various Ukrainian-Canadian newspapers, magazines, and annual almanacs.

Research in Ukrainian-Canadian literature was practically non-existent before World War II. Watson Kirkconnell's notes in the *University of Toronto Quarterly* and J.B. Rudnyckyj's *Ukrainica Canadiana* (1953-72) contained only bibliographical information. Not until 1968 did the *History of Ukrainian Literature in Canada* by Mykyta Mandryka present a comprehensive study of Ukrainian-Canadian writings. Among Michael Marunchak's numerous studies, his third volume on the Ukrainian press is valuable, despite the inevitable weaknesses of a pioneer work.[2] To date, only two anthologies of Ukrainian-Canadian writing have appeared: a small *Antol'ogiia ukrains'koho pys'menstva v Kanadi* in 1941 and a larger *Antol'ohiia ukrains'koi poezii v Kanadi, 1898-1973* in 1975.[3] This essay deals only with those writers who have established major trends in the development of Ukrainian literature in Canada.

POETRY

The first Ukrainian poem written in Canada was "Kanadiis'ki emigranty" by Ivan Zbura (1860-1940), who emigrated from western Ukraine in 1898. It was published in 1899 in *Svoboda*, then the only Ukrainian newspaper in North America. The poem's form is primitively folkloristic with the content taken directly from life. The first poets were men and women without higher education, for whom poetry was a diversion after heavy work in the fields or factories or on railroads.

Ukrainian folklore brought from Ukraine or created afresh flourished among the first settlers. Among the numerous folk verses were a dozen "Canadian Songs" published in *Svoboda* at the turn of the century, which vividly portrayed the early hardships, disappointments, hopes for a better life, and nostalgia for home. Perhaps the best was Symon Palamariuk's "Pisn' pro Kanadu":

Oi, Kanado, Kanadochko,
Iaka zh ty zradlyva,
Ne z odnoho hospodaria
Tut draba zrobyla.

Oi, Kanado, Kanadochko
Ta i ty, Manitobo,
Zhyie v tobi rus'kyi narid,
Iak taia khudoba.[4]

Besides Zbura and Palamariuk, the folkloristic trend in Ukrainian-Canadian poetry was exemplified by Theodore Fedyk (1873-1949), Dmytro Rarahovsky (1878-1957), and Panteleimon Bozyk (1879-1944), and found perhaps its finest expression in the folk-poetry of Daria Mohylianka's *Dumky letiat' na Ukrainu* (Thoughts Fly to Ukraine) (Edmonton, 1962) and *Pisni moho sertsia* (Songs of My Heart) (Edmonton, 1964). The first publication of primitive folk poetry, which ranged "from flabby doggerel up to genuine human power,"[5] was by Fedyk, whose 1908 collection in Winnipeg, *Pisni pro Kanadu i Avstriiu* (Songs About Canada and Austria), ran to a sixth edition in 1926. Some 50,000 copies were claimed to have been sold, though this figure may have been exaggerated. But single copies undoubtedly reached the old country.

Besides the spontaneous folk poetry created by many versifiers, a more substantial Ukrainian literature began to appear in Canada at the turn of the century. Michael Gowda (1874-1953), who arrived in 1898 and was a prominent community leader and interpreter in Edmonton, published his interesting poem "Rus'komu narodu" (To the Ruthenian People) in *Svoboda* on August 31, 1899. "Unhappy Ukrainians," he declared, "will yet be masters in Ukraine." Gowda's other poem, of which the Ukrainian original is apparently lost, was translated into English by Edward W. Thompson and published in the *Boston Evening Transcript* in 1905. In it the author is determined to be a settler, not an immigrant, in Canada:

We are not reared within thy broad domains,
Our fathers' graves and corpses lie afar,
They did not fall for freedom on thy plains,
Nor we pour our blood beneath thy star . . .
But, Canada, in Liberty we work till death,
Our children shall be free to call thee theirs,
Their own dear land. . . .[6]

Others who wrote Ukrainian-Canadian poetry with a sense of social concern and nationalism were Paul Crath (Pavlo Krat) (1882-1952), Wasyl Kudryk (1880-1963), Semen Kowbel (1887-1966), Honore Ewach (Onufrii Ivakh) (1900-64), and Toma (Tymish) Pavlychenko (1892-1958).

Crath began as an ardent revolutionary socialist. Before coming to Canada in 1907, he had been active in the socialist underground in eastern Ukraine and later agitated for a Ukrainian university in Lviv. As early as 1909, he published *Sociialistychni pis'ni* (Socialist Songs) under the pseudonym Pavlo Ternenko, quite likely the first Ukrainian book printed in Edmonton. It dwelt on social injustices in the world and on the need to liberate Ukraine from Russia; so did his narrative poems *Sichyns'kyi v nevoli* (Sichynsky in Prison) (Edmonton, 1910) and *Za semliu i voliu*! (For Land and Liberty!) (Winnipeg, probably 1914). Upon becoming a Presbyterian minister, he ceased to write poetry.

Wasyl Kudryk, who published his collection *Vesna* (Spring) (Winnipeg, 1911), was quickly overwhelmed by the editorship of *Ukrainsky holos* and his literary career, like Crath's, ended after he became a priest in the Ukrainian Orthodox Church. In his polemics with the Vatican and in other religious writings, however, he was an ardent revolutionary. Nationalistic ideas were also treated by Semen Kowbel, whose anthem for a liberated Ukraine in 1917, concluded with the following refrain:

> From the Caucasus to the Danube River and the Carpathians,
> Rise up, Ukraine, rise up![7]

Among later poets who treated the same theme were Honore Ewach, whose booklet *Boiova surma Ukrainy* (A Warlike Trumpet of Ukraine) was published in Winnipeg in 1931, and his friend, Ivan Danylchuk (1900-42), a Saskatchewan-born poet very active in the Ukrainian Self-Reliance League of Canada.

The most ardent nationalist, however, was Toma Pavlychenko, a professor at the University of Saskatchewan and a prominent member of the Ukrainian National Federation. Reflecting upon the totalitarian regimes in the Soviet Union, Germany, Italy, and Spain, he concluded in his narrative poem *Dukh natsii* (Spirit of a Nation, 1940) that the world was ruled by the law of the jungle: "Race is oppressed by a stronger race." Employing metaphors, he challenged Ukrainian Canadians to become strong and united as a pre-condition to Ukraine's liberation: "The weed roots spread like snakes; they sucked the sap of the wet stems until the wheat-ears stood empty." "This is the eternal law that does not contemplate any change!"[8]

Although equally sympathetic to Ukraine's liberation, Honore Ewach and Ivan Danylchuk were less politically inclined and became the first to write poetry that was both philosophic and aesthetic. Ewach took an arts degree at the University of Saskatchewan, and Danylchuk steeped himself in John Keats while a student at the same university. Ewach's best poem, "Sered vichnoho prostoru" (Amidst Eternal Space), in 1921, was translated by Watson Kirkconnell:

Across the spaces of eternity,
A bullet made of porcelain I flee
Into the unknown distance, void and vast.
The air keeps rubbing at the bullet's pride,
Smoothing and polishing its cold outside
Until at the last it turns to crystal.
I shall not utterly be rubbed away,
But only alter, slowly, day by day,
Into a diamond, most hard and fair.
And all this constant change throughout the years
Is ever for the better, it appears:
This is the end of life and this its care.[9]

Ewach's philosophical narrative *Toi, koho svit lovyv, ta ne vpiimav* (He Whom the World Has Chased and Not Caught) (Winnipeg, 1932), featured the eighteenth-century Hryhorii Skovoroda, Ukraine's greatest philosopher. In "Blukanniam umucheni khmary" (The Clouds Anguished by Wandering, 1922), Danylchuk was fascinated by the sunset with the clouds gathered on the horizon around "the holy fires":

O silent evening hours,
Teach me to perceive the quietude of satisfaction,
So that my heart may be as calm,
As those little clouds above the sunset.[10]

The philosophical-aesthetic trend, found rarely in the 1920's, reappeared in *Lira emigranta* (An Emigrant's Lyre) (Winnipeg, 1936) by Myroslav Ichniansky (pseudonym of Ivan Kmeta), who came to Canada in 1929 at the age of twenty-eight and after a decade left for the United States. In his beautiful metaphors and similes, the wintry wind is "the prince of Canadian snows" and his own heart the "spring-eyed flute."[11] To Kirkconnell, Ichniansky "combines the fecundity of aspiration with the artistic consciousness of the resources of language."[12] Ivan Ohienko, in his journal *Ridna mova* (Native Language) (1937) published in Warsaw, also singled out the "picturesque imagery of Ichniansky's language."

A pastor of the Evangelical church, Ichniansky introduced a religious trend into Ukrainian-Canadian poetry, which was strengthened by the meditative verses of the Ukrainian Catholic Reverend Stepan Semchuk in his *Kanadiis'ka rapsodiia* (Canadian Rhapsody) (Winnipeg-Yorkton, 1959) and *Svitlist' dumky* (Majesty of Thought) (Winnipeg, 1970). The religious trend, however, was best expressed in the melodious language of Metropolitan Ilarion (Ivan Ohienko, 1882-1972). Another religious poet is Lev Sylenko, whose *Maha vrata* (Powerful Faith) (Winnipeg, 1969) ardently extols ancient Ukrainian mythology about Christianity and attacks both Byzantium and the Vatican for spiritually dominating Europe and particularly Ukraine.

Mykyta Mandryka (1886-1979), who exemplifies several trends, came to Canada in 1928. In Kiev in 1918 he had published *Pisni pro Anemonu* (Songs about Anemony), a collection of romantic poetry, enlarged and reprinted in Winnipeg in 1941 under the title *Mii sad* (My Orchard). Several other works followed his publication in Winnipeg in 1958 of *Zolota osin' 1905-1957* (Golden Autumn, 1905-1957): *Radist'* (Joy) (1959), *Symfoniia vikiv* (A Symphony of Ages) (1961), *Sontsetsvit* (Helianthus) (1965), *Vyno zhyttia* (Life's Wine) (1970), and *Zavershennia lita* (Accomplishment of Summer) (1975) - each better than its predecessor with social, national, meditative, and romantic themes. Especially memorable are his colourful metaphors.

With the end of World War II, about forty Ukrainian poets, writers, and literary scholars arrived, and literary clubs were organized in Toronto, Winnipeg, Edmonton, and Montreal. Among the new Ukrainian weeklies and magazines which followed was *Novi dni* (New Days), a "universal monthly" established by Petro Volyniak in 1950 and published regularly in Toronto. Five volumes of *Pivnichne siiavo* (Northern Lights), a literary and art almanac (1964-71) with Canadian overtones, were published in Edmonton. Modelled on the organization of Ukrainian émigré writers in the United States, Slovo was established in Canada in 1971 and has since published nine volumes of poetry and prose by its members. *Estafeta* (Estafette), another series of works by Ukrainian writers in North America, appeared in two volumes in Toronto.

Some of the trends in Ukrainian-Canadian literature which had begun to crystallize before the war were now reinforced. In the philosophical-aesthetic tradition was the poetry of Volodymyr Skorupsky (1912-), who arrived in 1949 and published several collections of poetry. The salient traits of his poetry were meditations in the manner of German symbolist Rainer Maria Rilke, carefully selected words and expressions and a controlled lyrical tone, best exemplified in *Aistry nevidstvili* (Asters Still Blooming) (Toronto, 1972). The poetry by Teodor Matvienko (1924-), neo-classical in style and written in polished Ukrainian, was collected in *Sonety* (Sonnets) (Toronto, 1961) and the versified narrative *Mii litopys* (My Chronicle), published as yet only in fragments.

The author of this essay prefers not to discuss his own contributions.[13] Versifying on Canadian themes, with origins at the turn of the century in the primitive "Canadian Songs," reached considerable heights with the publication of *Kanadiis'ka rapsodiia* and *Poemy* (Poems) (Winnipeg, 1970) by Reverend Stepan Semchuk, whose "Forty Below Zero," "A Canadian Rhapsody," and "To the Maple Leaves of Canada" were translated into English by Watson Kirkconnell.

Mykyta Mandryka's narrative, *Kanada* (Canada) (Winnipeg, 1961), and several of his shorter poems such as "The Land of Liberty" show well the Ukrainians' attitude to their adopted country:

O Canada! Thou limitless expanse,
Country of freedom and assured success
To all on earth who suffer dark mischance
Thou openest thy doors, with hope to bless.[14]

On the occasion of Manitoba's centennial, Mandryka wrote "Barvinok" (Periwinkle) (1969), a poem in which a flower brought from Ukraine takes root in Manitoba and is duly glorified. Similarly, *Pionery sviatoi zemli* (Pioneers of the Sacred Land) (Toronto, 1969) by Larysa Murovych (1917-) dwells on the hard-working ploughmen who turned the wild Prairies into the fertile soil that has given rich harvests. Levko Romen (1893-1981), Bohdan Mazepa (1928-78), and Dan Mur (1914-78) also wrote on Canadian topics with special insight, grateful for the opportunity to begin a new, free life. The first Ukrainian poets, occasionally too critical of Canada, have been replaced by contemporary writers who generally exude excessive praise, perhaps because discrimination is now less marked.

Romantic poetry was expressed through Bohdan Mazepa's *Zoriana dal'* (Starlit Horizon) (Edmonton, 1956) and *Polumiani akordy* (Flaming Accords) (Edmonton, 1976), whose emotive lyrics led composers Bohdan Veselovsky and Serhii Eremenko to set them to music. Borys Oleksandriv (1921-79) published mainly love lyrics in three collections in Toronto - *Tuha za sontsem* (Longing for the Sun) (1967), *Kolokruh* (The Circuit) (1972), and *Kaminnyi bereh* (The Stony Shore) (1976). Some of his poetry has social and national overtones: "Poet na Solovkakh" (A Poet in Solovky Exile) and "1933," dealing with the famine in Ukraine, stand out.

Among women poets, Vira Vorsklo's poetry is collected in *Lysty bez adresy* (Unaddressed Letters) (Toronto, 1967) and the sizable *Lada*, a goddess (Toronto, 1977). Some of her love poetry is metaphorical, with "Skelia" (The Rock) an excellent example of the meditative genre with original imagery. Oleksandra Chernenko's *Liudyna* (Man) (Philadelphia, 1960) is philosophical, as are recent verses in the almanac *Slovo* and *Antolohiia ukrains'koi poezii v Kanadi* (1975).

Social and national concerns were very much strengthened by Dan Mur's *Zhal' i hniv* (Sorrow and Wrath) (1966), *Skryzhali tuhy* (Plates of Sorrow) (1973), and *Druhotsvit* (The Second Blossom) (1979). The flashes of strong emotion which characterize his energetic rhythms can be seen in "Dukh Ukrainy" (Ukraine's Spirit). With work akin to the baroque style which flourished in Ukraine for several centuries, Mur enjoys playing with words and the result is highly musical poems such as "Provesna" (Early Spring).

A recent addition to the nationalist trend is Oleksander Smotrych's poetry, which dwells much on the colonial status of Ukraine under Russian domination. Some of the Canadian works coloured with nostalgia by Oleska Hay-Holovko (1910-) also exemplify elements of the nationalist trend. However, it is his romantic poetry, collected in *Kokhaniiada* (Loviad) and published while still in Europe, which is best.

Levko Romen's more recent drama about an herb, *Zhovtosyl* (Edmonton, 1965), is liberally sprinkled with mythological verses describing the folk beliefs of the Volhynian region in Ukraine, while his *Dub-nelyn* (The Holm-Oak) (Toronto, 1969) draws on Lemko demonology and contains Canadian Indian totemic esotericism. In her *Zhar-ptakha* (Fire Bird) (Toronto, 1971) Larysa Murovych takes this trend further, embracing even elements from Egyptian myths in her poems about pre-Ukrainian folk art. Finally, Volodymyr Skorupsky's collection of "legends," *Spokonvichni luny* (Ancient Echoes) (Toronto, 1977), is dedicated entirely to such pre-Christian Ukrainian gods as Dazhboh, Perun, and Lada. As noted earlier, Lev Sylenko worships Dazhboh in his quasi-religious *Maha vrata*.

Refusing to accept his adopted country, Volodymyr Havryliuk (1904-) is an imagist whose thoughts and preoccupations, as in *Tin' i mandrivnyk* (The Shadow and the Traveller) (New York, 1969), are in Europe or Ukraine. Oleh Zujewskyj (1920-) translates German and French symbolists into Ukrainian. His own symbolistic poetry, though occasionally esoteric and obscure, is good.

Ukrainian modernists are under-represented in Canada. Only Danylo Struk (1940-) has had his booklet *Gamma sigma* (Winnipeg, 1963) published; other promising modernists are Iryna Makaryk and Marco Carynnyk. The latter has translated from Ukrainian into English, as have Orysia Prokopiw, Mary Skrypnyk, Maara Haas, Hanna Polowy, and John Weir.

Ukrainian poetry for children has been produced in Canada on a large scale. The fables by Michael Stechishin (1888-1964) are collected in a single book *Baiky* (Fables) (Winnipeg, 1959), while the children's poetry by Bohdan Fodchuk consists of twenty books on various topics. The works by Nina Mudryk-Mryts, Lesia Khraplyva, and Svitliana Kuzmenko are the most artistic.

PROSE

As early as 1897, Reverend Nestor Dmytriw (1863-1925), editor of *Svoboda*, visited the Prairie Provinces and reported on the Ukrainian settlers in a series of articles, *Kanadiis'ka Rus'* (Canadian Ruthenia), which became a booklet. Between September 2 and November 21, 1897, Dmytriw published "Tymko Havryliuk" in *Svoboda*, about a man who left western Ukraine and settled near Winnipeg. Havryliuk's village is given as Lakhmanivka, a fictitious place suggesting ragged and tattered inhabitants. Dmytriw's "Rus'ka paska a frantsuz'kyi ksionkz" (Ukrainian Easter and the French Priest), written in Calgary in 1897 and published in the same year in *Svoboda*, depicts the differences in Ukrainian and French Easter customs. It began a series, *Obrazky z Kanady* (Pictures from Canada), which included "Vyishla za menonita" (Marriage to a Mennonite) and "Assimilation," both published in *Svoboda* in 1898.

The above series preceded by almost three years "Z hlybyny propasty" (From the Depth of the Abyss), a story by Sava Chernetsky written in Winnipeg in December, 1899, or early in 1900 and published in *Svoboda* on May 10, 1900. It is a moving account of the life of one Vasyl Lasiuk, an early settler who froze to death in his farmhouse, "300 miles from the city and 50 miles from the next railroad station." His small daughter had died two weeks earlier and his wife was in the hospital at the time. The author mixes fiction and reality, leaning heavily on the 129th Psalm: "From the depth of the abyss I call on you, God, with all the strength of my soul, come and listen to my voice." Both Dmytriw and Chernetsky only visited Canada briefly. They left for the United States, where they died.

The third writer of Ukrainian-Canadian prose was Myroslaw Stechishin (1883-1947) who, during a brief stay in Caspar, California, wrote "Pilot Butte" (1903), published in the collection *Zhuravli* (Cranes) in Scranton, Pennsylvania, in 1904. In a vivid account of the workers at the Pilot Butte CPR station near Regina, Pavlo, a Ukrainian émigré student who finds himself among illiterate workers, is so weakened by hard labour that he commits suicide by lying on the rails. Later an editor of *Ukrainskyi holos*, Stechishin wrote several short stories on Canadian themes.

Another writer, Apolinarii Novak (1885-1955), came to Canada in 1901 and worked as a labourer until he became the editor of *Kanadiiskyi farmer* in 1909. One of his first stories, "Vyhnantsi" (The Exiles), subtitled "a Canadian story," was published in Lviv in *Literaturno-naukovyi vistnyk* (The Literary-Scientific Herald).[15] The plot centres around discrimination against the "poor Galicians" who were exploited and constantly mocked by the Anglo-Saxons of the time. Two of the four stories in the first book of Ukrainian-Canadian prose - *Kanadiis'ki opovidannia* (Canadian Stories) (Winnipeg, 1910) - were by Novak. In "Pershyi den' zarobitku" (The First Day of Earnings) the author presents a vivid account of two labourers who are crushed by a huge rock when laying rails. In "Taky postavyv na nohy" (On My Feet After All) a persistent son helps his father become rich and then dies tragically. Death was large in the lives of pioneers and had a prominent place in the works of such realists as Chernetsky, Stechishin, and Novak. Wasyl Kudryk in his *Pimsta robitnyka* (A Worker's Revenge) (Winnipeg, 1911) tells of a worker's impulsive revenge against a farmer who treated his seasonal labourer improperly. After setting the farmer's property afire, the repentant worker hangs himself.

The pioneer period also produced several works of pure fantasy. In "Schastia" (Happiness), published in *Kanadiis'ki opovidannia*, Kudryk (under the pseudonym Petro Kazan) expresses a labourer's desire for happiness, which the Goddess of Happiness finally bestows. Similarly, in an adaptation from an unknown source, *Lystar i smert'* (A Knight and Death) (Winnipeg, 1910), the anonymous author (probably Kudryk or Stechishin, judging by the style) presents the dialogue between a boasting knight and omnipotent Death, which takes the knight's sword and cuts off his head.

Perhaps the most interesting writer stylistically during the pioneer period was Paul Crath (Pavlo Krat). In *Vizyta chervonoi durzhyny* (Visit of the Red Detachment) (Winnipeg), 1912), he tells about the uprising in Ukraine in 1906. The whole purpose is to incite the readers to do the same in Canada. In *Koly lekshe bude ta inshi opovidannia* (When Things Get Better and Other Stories) (Winnipeg, 1912), the social inequality in Ukraine under the Russian tsarist yoke is stressed. Himself a political refugee from the tsarist regime, in "Zhertva" (The Victims) the author pictures a man and girl who try to flee but are killed by a soldier at the Zbruch River, the boundary between the Russian and Austrian empires. In *Koly ziishlo sontse* (When the Sun Rose), Crath visualizes a wonderful future for a post-revolutionary, socialist Canada around 2000 A.D., when justice and happiness will reign supreme.

Early literature for children was written by Onufrii H. Hykawy (1885-1945), whose *Zbirnyk baiok* (Collection of Fables) (Winnipeg, 1910) was used in schools. Novak was the first to write humorous stories. In his "Skonka" (Skunk), a farmer who wishes to make some illegal homebrew is opposed by his wife and is obliged to give the mash to his pigs who become intoxicated. The pigs are said to be poisoned by rotten potatoes, and their limp bodies are hauled off into the bush. To the farmer's great surprise, they return next day bringing joy to the whole family.

In 1912 an interesting literary character, Shtif Tabashniuk, appeared in stories by Stefan Fodchuk (1899-1967) and Jacob Maydanyk (Iakiv Maidanyk) (1891-   ). Written in the Pokutian dialect of Ukrainian with corrupted English words added, the stories appeared in newspapers and had almost no literary value, but they did present a typical personage created by the Ukrainian-Canadian environment: a primitive simpleton, sly and joyful, who mocks the shortcomings of others and himself to eliminate what is considered bad in society. The change of the English words "Winnipeg" to "Manipeg" and "Immigrant" to "Manigrula"[16] undoubtedly entertained the pioneers, but the stories do not compare with Novak's humorous and imaginative "Skonka."

Kudryk's humorous stories, *Pryhody Harasyma Choronkhliba* (Harasym Chornokhlib's Adventures) (Winnipeg, 1922?), written in readily understandable and almost literary Ukrainian, are very entertaining. His "Podorozh Shevchenka po Kanadi" (Shevchenko's Journey Across Canada) shows how cultural activities among the early Ukrainian settlers in Canada acted as a shield against assimilation. As late as 1948, he wrote "Iak kum Pavlo prodavav kozu" (How Godfather Pavlo Sold a Goat), a satire on Soviet society.

The first thirty years of Ukrainian prose in Canada were marked not only by short stories and one-act plays,[17] but also by some early attempts at fiction. Mykhailo Petrowsky (1897-) wrote the first novel *Mahichne misto* (The Magic City) (Winnipeg, 1927) about a Ukrainian immigrant who leaves Canada for Miami, engages in speculation and becomes rich, only to have his adventures end in total disaster. As a literary piece, the novel suffers more than his old short stories collected in *Mrii sliozamy oblyti* (Dreams Sprinkled with Tears) (Winnipeg, 1973).

Interest in more complex prose developed during the 1930's. Honore Ewach published *Holos zemli* (Voice of the Soil) (Winnipeg, 1937), in which robust men conquer the Prairies to win a fertile soil; and their sons, who obtain an education, listen to "the call of the soil" and return to provide continuity in the development of western Canada. "A precursor of the voluminous work of Illia Kyriak [Kiriak],"[18] the novel's style is simple and clear and the language is fairly polished.

Illia Kiriak (1888-1955) elevated Ukrainian prose in Canada to a position of national importance. His trilogy *Syny zemli* (Sons of the Soil) (the first volume appeared in 1939, the last in 1945, all in Edmonton) presents three generations of Vorkuns, a hard-working family, in almost Homeric proportions. Their adjustment to life in Alberta, their activities in community halls and churches, and an intermarriage transform the novel into "a sociological document of real value."[19] Despite its occasionally vague and protracted plot, Michael Luchkovich produced a readable abridged translation for Ryerson Press, entitled *Sons of the Soil* (Toronto, 1959).

A second distinguished piece of Ukrainian-Canadian prose written before 1950 was *Bezkhatnyi* (Homeless) (Edmonton, 1946) by Oleksander Luhovy (pseudonym of Oleksander Ovrutskyi-Schwabe, 1904-62). After a romantic prologue in which the severe winter of the Canadian North is beautifully portrayed "with the fullness of tragedy,"[20] the homeless and constantly hungry Ostap, the main character, emerges as an opponent of injustice and social difficulties, who organizes the farmers into a co-operative. The novel was awarded a prize by the Ukrainian National Association in 1945, which made its publication possible a year later.

Among later novels, the half-fictional *Moie selo* (My Village) (Saskatoon, 1950; second part in 1952) by Dmytro Kolisnyk (1883-1958), who came to Canada in 1911, dealt with life in western Ukraine. Two novels, derived from personal experiences, resemble documentaries: Oleksa Hay-Holovko's *Poiedynok z dyiavolum* (A Duel with the Devil) (Winnipeg, 1950) is about the author's escape from Soviet kidnappers, and Ivan Loboda's *Vony pryishly znovu* (They Came Again) (Winnipeg, 1953) presents the author's views of the Finnish-Soviet war in 1939. Biographical elements appear in the novels by Fedir Odrach (1912-64) – *V dorozi* (On the Road) (1953), *Shchebetun* (The Wood Warbler) (1957), *Voshchad'* (Voshchad, a place name) (1972) – and in some of his collected stories, all published in Toronto.[21] A recent novel about the Ukrainian intelligentsia in Canada is *Pokolinnia ziidut'sia* (Generations Will Meet) (Toronto, 1974) by Ivan Bodnarchuk (1914-   ).

Among women writers, Maria Keywan's novel *Karvendel* (Karwendel) (Toronto, 1971) vividly depicts the life of Ukrainian displaced persons who remained in West Germany and Austria after World War II. Other women authors include Stefania Paush, who wrote *Nauchka* (Instruction) (Edmonton, 1967), Ol'ha Woycenko (1909-   ), the author of the travelogue *Inshyi svit - inshi 'dni* (Another World, Other Days) (Winnipeg, 1959), and Ol'ha Mak (1913-   ), a recent newcomer from Brazil.

The foremost Ukrainian author in Canada today is undoubtedly Ulas Samchuk (1905-   ), who has lived in Toronto since about 1950. His *Mariia* (Mary), about the Soviet-caused famine in 1933, went through four editions and was translated into French. His best work is probably *Volyn'* (Volhynia), a trilogy published in the 1930's and praised by literary scholars as one of the best works of fiction in Ukrainian in the twentieth century. On a par is *Ost* (East), another trilogy which appeared after World War II. His sole novel with Canadian content is *Na tverdii zemli* (On Hard Ground) (Toronto, 1966), an interesting account of how newly arrived Ukrainian immigrants adjust to the Canadian environment.

A western Ukrainian journalist, translator, and playwright, who wrote little in Canada but reprinted valuable earlier works, is Vasyl Sofroniv-Levytsky (1899-1977). The following appeared during his years as editor of *Novyi shliakh* (1960-77): *Klanialysia vam try Ukrainy* (Salute from Three Ukraines) (Winnipeg, 1970), an account of the author's travels through Ukrainian-populated regions of Yugoslavia, Czechoslovakia, and Poland; *Iunyi skomorokh* (The Young Scaramouch) (Toronto, 1972), a collection of plays for children and young people; *Lypneva otruta* (The Poison of July) (Toronto, 1972), selected short stories; and *Pid veselym oborohom* (Under the Jolly Roof) (Toronto, 1974), a collection of light one-act plays for variety shows.

Modernistic prose in Ukrainian-Canadian literature does not exist. The only book with some non-realistic qualities is *Buttia: 16 nikomu nepotribnykh opovidan'* (Existence: 16 Stories That No One Needs) (Toronto, 1973) by Oleksander Smotrych (1922-   ). Humour and satire, common in Ukrainian-Canadian literature before World War II, have declined considerably. Notable, however, are Borys Oleksandriv's *Svyryd Lomachka v Kanadi* (Svyryd Lomachka in Canada) (Toronto, 1951), Svyryd Lomachka's (Oleksandriv's pseudonym) *Liubov do blyzhnioho* (Love to the Kin) (Toronto, 1961), and Mykola Kolankivsky's (1912-   ) *Ambasadory: Satyry i humoresky* (The Ambassadors: Satires and Humour) (Toronto, 1968) and *Tovpa: Feiletony, humoresky, satyry* (The Crowd: Feuilletons, Humorous Sketches, Satires) (Niagara Falls, 1979). Life's trivialities, assimilation, and other negative sides of Ukrainian-Canadian life are mocked in these and similar publications.

As with poetry, the first works of Ukrainian prose in Canada were written before the turn of the century. Until the 1920's, realistic short stories dealing with the hardships, discrimination, and exploitation experienced by the immigrants on a day-to-day basis predominated. Death was a prominent theme of short stories set in Canada, while the political struggle for social justice and national liberation characterized those set in Ukraine. Humorous and satirical short stories, often written to convey a moral lesson, were also popular during the pioneer years.

The first important Ukrainian novels were written in Canada during the 1930's and 1940's. They dealt with the Ukrainian immigrants' relation to the soil and their tenacity and perseverance in the face of adversity. After World War II, a number of mature Ukrainian authors emigrated to Canada, enriching Ukrainian literature with short stories, novels, and memoirs which dealt with pre-war, wartime and post-war experiences in the Ukraine, Europe, and Canada. However, no modernistic prose was produced, while humour and satire, popular before the war, declined appreciably, and drama, prevalent during the interwar years, disappeared almost completely.

In eighty-five years Ukrainian literature in Canada developed broadly as a literature with roots in Ukraine. Folkloristic at the outset, the poetry soon developed social, philosophical-aesthetic, religious, mythological, and other trends. Prose fiction tried to reflect the difficult beginnings of Ukrainian settlers. Alongside the original literature, Ukrainian translations of high quality have been done in Canada. In addition, numerous classical works, especially those by Taras Shevchenko, Ivan Franko, Lesia Ukrainka, and Vasyl Stefanyk, have been reprinted in Winnipeg and Toronto.

NOTES

1. The author is indebted to the Immigration History Research Center, University of Minnesota, and to the Ukrainian Academy of Sciences in New York for the use of their rich depositories of ethnic literatures. He is equally grateful to Mr. John Muchin, University of Manitoba Library, and the University of Illinois Library at Urbana for their help in locating several rare publications.
2. M.H. Marunchak, *Studii do istorii ukrainstiv Kanady* (Studies in the History of Ukrainians in Canada), 4 vols. (Winnipeg: Ukrainian Free Academy of Sciences, 1969-72).
3. *Antol'ogiia ukrains'koho pys'menstva v Kanadi* (Anthology of Ukrainian Writings in Canada) (Winnipeg: Ukrainian Canadian Educational Association, 1941); Y. Slavutych (comp. and ed.), *Antol'ogiia ukrains'koi poezii v Kanadi, 1898-1973* (Anthology of Ukrainian Poetry in Canada, 1898-1973) (Edmonton: Slovo, 1975).

4. Y. Slavutych, *Ukrains'ka poeziia v Kanadi* (Ukrainian Poetry in Canada) (Edmonton: Slavuta, 1976), p. 15.
5. W. Kirkconnell, "Ukrainian-Canadian Literature," *Opinion*, III, 5 (September-October, 1947), p. 3. This brief article was reprinted in a revised version under the title "Ukrainian Literature in Canada," in *Ukrainian Year Book*, 1953-54 (Winnipeg: n.p., 1954), pp. 44-6.
6. M.I. Mandryka, *History of Ukrainian Literature in Canada* (Winnipeg: Ukrainian Free Academy of Sciences, 1968), p. 42.
7. Slavutych, *Antol'ogiia*, p. 18.
8. T. Pavlychenko, *Dukh natsii* (Saskatoon: Ukrainian National Publishing Co., 1940), pp. 9, 37.
9. C.H. Andrusyshen and W. Kirkconnell, *The Ukrainian Poets: 1189-1962* (Toronto: University of Toronto Press, 1963), p. 497.
10. I. Danylchuk, *Svitaie den'* (The Daylight Begins to Glimmer) (Winnipeg: Promin, 1929), p. 54. The original is rhymed.
11. M. Ichniansky, *Lira emigranta* (An Emigrant's Lyre) (Winnipeg: Ukrainian Bookstore, 1936), pp. 32, 87.
12. W. Kirkconnell, *University of Toronto Quarterly*, VII (1937-38), p. 568.
13. For an evaluation of Yar Slavutych's poetry, see W.T. Zyla (comp.), *Tvorchist' Iara Slavutycha* (The Poetry of Yar Slavutych) (Edmonton: Jubilee Committee, 1978).
14. Andrusyshen and Kirkconnell, *Ukrainian Poets*, p. 496.
15. *Literaturno-naukovyi vistnyk*, no. 9 (August, 1908), pp. 501-15.
16. Maydanyk's play, *Manigrula*, first published in *Kanadiiskyi farmer* (1911) and reprinted in book form in 1915, appeared in 1926 in a second edition. There were later reprints.
17. Although research on Ukrainian-Canadian drama is in its infancy, some interesting data have been compiled by Iroida Wynnyckyj, who showed in 1976 that between 1907 and 1942 at least 101 Ukrainian plays were written and published in Canada and then performed by amateur theatrical groups in various Ukrainian halls from Montreal to Vancouver. About 60 per cent were full-length plays of three, four, or five acts, with the remainder one-act plays. Of the ninety-one texts that could be located and studied, fourteen were classified as tragedy or tragi-comedy, fifty-four as drama or melodrama, and thirty-three as comedy, satire, or farce. Their highly Ukrainian-centred and introverted nature can be seen from the fact that forty-three were set in Ukraine, thirty-three among Ukrainians in Canada, and only fifteen in a non-Ukrainian milieu. Thematically, those in Ukraine were concerned with the struggle for independence (1917-21) or with the underground resistance movement in Polish-occupied Galicia and Volhynia (1921-39), and addressed themselves to ideological issues as well as universal social and moral problems. Those in Canada stressed three themes: the struggle for socio-economic betterment; love, courtship, and marriage; and such social ills as alcoholism, gambling, and wife desertion.

    Although Wynnyckyj has identified twenty-six amateur Ukrainian-

Canadian dramatists, over two-thirds of all the plays were written by six men: Semen Kowbel, Dmytro Hunkevych, Olesksander Luhovy, Pylyp Ostapchuk (Pylypenko), Myroslav Irchan, and Mykhailo Petrivsky. See I.L. Wynnyckyj, "Ukrainian Canadian Drama from the Beginnings of Immigration to 1942" (Master's thesis, University of Waterloo, 1976); A. Balan, "Six Ukrainian-Canadian Dramatists," *Promin'*, XX, 6 (1979), p. 15.

18. Mandryka, *History of Ukrainian Literature in Canada*, p. 67.
19. W. Kirkconnell, *University of Toronto Quarterly*, XIII (1943-44), p. 458.
20. D.B. Chopyk, "Litopys ukrains'koho poselentsia. *Bezkhatnyi* O. Luhovoho" (A Chronicle of the Ukrainian Settlers: *Homeless* by A. Luhovy), in Y. Slavutych (ed.), *Zakhidnokanads'kyi zbirnyk* (Collected Papers on Ukrainian Settlers in Western Canada) (Edmonton: Shevchenko Scientific Society in Canada, 1975), p. 149.
21. I. Bodnaruk discussed Odrach's prose fiction in "Tvorchist' Fedora Odracha" (The Works of Fedir Odrach), *Kanadas'ka Ukraina* (Canadian Ukraine), no. 6 (1978), pp. 14-16.

FIFTEEN

A Survey of Ukrainian-Canadian Historiography

Frances Swyripa

This survey* is limited to a chronological discussion of the most significant works on Ukrainian Canadians written in Canada in English and Ukrainian.[1] Articles are kept to a minimum and newspapers, unpublished manuscripts, government papers and reports,[2] and archival records of Ukrainians and their organizations are omitted.

ENGLISH-LANGUAGE WORKS

The bulk of the literature on Ukrainians in Canada up until the 1920's was written by Anglo-Canadians on the periphery of the coalescing Ukrainian-Canadian community and was restricted to the tangible and visible.[3] The main concern was with the impact of Ukrainians on the political and socio-economic structure of Canada. Little attention was paid to developing a distinct and self-perpetuating Ukrainian-Canadian society. The interests of the Anglo-Canadian favoured Canadianization, which entailed assimilation to British-Canadian ideals and standards.

One of the earliest interpretive attempts was *The Foreigner*,[4] a novel by Ralph Connor, the literary pseudonym of Ontario-born Charles W. Gordon, then a Presbyterian minister in Winnipeg. His portrayal of the Galician as ignorant, emotional, and immoral undoubtedly influenced the public mind. Among the more significant non-fictional works was James T.M. Anderson's *The Education of the New Canadian*,[5] with its emphasis on the role of the public school and English teacher in assimilating the "New Canadian" and preparing him for the responsibilities and privileges of Canadian citizenship. Many of Anderson's illustrations of the activities and methodology of individual teachers came from Ukrainian areas.

World War I heightened Canada's awareness of the different peoples

* Only the author and abbreviated title of specific works will appear in the text. The full title, translation where applicable, and other bibliographic data are in the notes.

who had immigrated to her shores during the preceding three decades. It also increased the knowledge of nationalities hitherto viewed only imperfectly and often mistakenly. For the first time in Canadian history, the term "Ukrainian" was used in English-language literature with some degree of consistency. Later attempts to explain the historical background and character of the Ukrainians were not solely within the context of an oppressed peasantry of Austria-Hungary and Russia, but included references to a distinctly Ukrainian national heritage.[6]

In the interwar period, English-language literature pursued two main avenues. On the one hand, emphasis on assimilation into the predominant Anglo-Canadian culture persisted. With the resumption of large-scale immigration in the late 1920's, the question of immigrant desirability again centred on a group's assimilabilty. On the other hand, the obvious diversity of peoples led some writers to recognize that the various national groups had brought spiritual and cultural resources which could enrich the quality and colour of Canadian life.[7] In general, the ethnic stereotype was gradually modified, and some came to see Ukrainian consciousness more positively. Loyalty to traditional Ukrainian things and even a desire for Ukraine's independence could help to ease adjustment. The coexistence of Anglo-conformity and ethnic diversity, often in the same work, was typical of interwar literature and indicated no clearly crystallized concept of a Ukrainian-Canadian role. For example, one writer who favoured Ukrainian immigration because of the group's economic contribution still spoke of British Canadians as "quite rightly" guiding "the ship of state toward her destined haven of nationhood."[8]

Typical was *The Central European Immigrant in Canada*[9] by Robert England, for many years continental superintendent of the Colonization Department of the CNR. England's study, based on reports compiled by teachers working in the non-English-speaking districts of Saskatchewan, approximately two-thirds of which were Ukrainian, contains numerous unfavourable descriptions of the Ukrainian character and socio-economic conditions in Ukrainian communities. More laudatory was John Murray Gibbon, the general publicity agent of the CPR, who in 1928 organized a series of "New Canadian" folksong, folk dance, and handicraft festivals throughout Canada, believing that the preservation and dissemination of immigrant cultures would enrich a rather monotonous Canadian scene.[10] His folkloristic researches culminated in the publication of *Canadian Mosaic*,[11] which sketched the historical development, settlement in Canada, and individual and general contributions to Canadian life of many groups against the background of a stereotyped image of each. Ukrainians, he believed, would perform their greatest service to Canadian culture as poets, musicians, and artists.

The major work to emerge directly from Canadian missionary activity among the Ukrainians appeared during this period. *A Friendly Adventure*[12] recorded the experiences of Reverend Alexander J. Hunter, for over a quarter of a century the Presbyterian medical missionary among Ukrainians in Teulon, Manitoba. Unlike other writers, Hunter's interpretation of the Ukrainians was based on a knowledge and appreciation of their language, literature, and history. As a result, his is a perceptive description of traditional Ukrainian religious allegiances and of the Ukrainians' historical reaction to assimilation.[13]

In 1931 sociologist Charles H. Young wrote *The Ukrainian Canadians*,[14] a study of adjustment and assimilation sponsored by the Immigration Division of the Canadian National Committee for Mental Hygiene. Young discussed Ukrainian immigration, rural and urban settlement, the factors affecting material success or failure, and Ukrainian-Canadian society as a self-contained, culturally distinct unit, its foundation Ukrainian but the superstructure growing more Canadian. Although now limited in perspective, Young's book is important because subsequent researchers relied heavily on his excellent historical summary and freely borrowed his data and conclusions about the progress of Ukrainians in Canada.

By the 1930's, Ukrainian Canadians became the subject of graduate studies among non-Ukrainians. The main concern was the teaching of English as a prerequisite to assimilation.[15] More extensive in scope, although based on limited personal interviews, was Timothy C. Byrne's "The Ukrainian Community in North Central Alberta,"[16] which examined the religious and secular divisions of Ukrainian society in the area. Charles M. Bayley's 1939 study of the Ukrainian community in Montreal was preceded by the first English-language thesis by a Ukrainian Canadian, Stephen W. Mamchur, who also examined the same community.[17]

During World War II, English-language publications concentrated on the question of Ukrainian loyalty. In his numerous pamphlets, Watson Kirkconnell stressed the dedication of non-Communist Ukrainian Canadians to the Allied war effort.[18] In reaction to his attempt to discredit the Communist faction, Raymond A. Davies, a left-wing journalist, wrote the popular and pro-Communist *This is Our Land*,[19] which attempted to exonerate the outlawed Ukrainian Labour-Farmer Temple Association.

During the war Ukrainian Canadians themselves began to emerge as English-language spokesmen for their group, although not overwhelmingly on war-related issues. Journalist William Paluk published *Canadian Cossacks*,[20] a collection of simple, pro-Ukrainian essays. Nicholas Hunchak's *Canadians of Ukrainian Origin: Population*[21] presented 1941 statistics for Ukrainian Canadians as a whole and by province, without attempting to interpret the data. Another statistical publication was the *Ukrainians in Canada Business Year Book*, issued annually from 1945 to 1956 under different titles by F.A. Macrouch.

The first English-language history of the Ukrainians in Canada by a Ukrainian Canadian, Vera Lysenko's *Men in Sheepskin Coats,*[22] appeared in 1947. Its leftist bias distorted the relative significance of movements in both Ukrainian and Ukrainian-Canadian history. The résumé of Ukrainian history focused on folk traditions and the popular ethos and ignored the struggle of the Ukrainian National Republic between 1917 and 1922. However, the understanding of assimilation as "unity in diversity" and of the impact on the individual of two converging cultures revealed considerable insight into the psychological problems facing both immigrant and Canadian-born generations.[23]

As Ukrainian Canadians at the university level began to probe the history of their group, they selected facets of the organized community. Paul Yuzyk examined the Ukrainian Greek Catholic Church in Canada.[24] Harry Piniuta and Wasyl Veryha looked at the role of the Ukrainian Canadian Committee in Ukrainian-Canadian life.[25] Father John Skwarok's study of early educational activities among the Ukrainians (from the Ukrainian Catholic point of view) discussed French and Ukrainian initiatives. Within a decade, a similar thesis appeared (from the Ukrainian Orthodox point of view) on the role of the Orthodox Church in education.[26] More analytic, although encompassing a shorter time span, was Yuzyk's 1958 historical study of the Ukrainian Greek Orthodox Church in Canada. Michael Zuk outlined the pioneer activities of the Presbyterian Church, the Independent Greek Church, and the United Church, while Murray Wenstob looked at Methodist missionary work among Ukrainians in Alberta.[27] Other theses examined Ukrainian musical culture in Canada and the beginnings, aims, contributions, problems, and role of the Ukrainian Catholic press.[28] A major publication during this period was Paul Yuzyk's *The Ukrainians in Manitoba*.[29] Despite its marked anti-Communist bias, the book is a well-documented, credible study, often approaching a general history of the Ukrainians in Canada.

Although Ukrainian Canadians have been prolific writers of Ukrainian-language memoirs and biographies, few have appeared in English. An exception is Gus Romaniuk's *Taking Root in Canada*,[30] which depicts the difficult life on Manitoba's submarginal lands settled by Ukrainians. Michael Luchkovich, the first Ukrainian Member of Parliament, also published his autobiography in English.[31] More recently, *Hardships and Progress of Ukrainian Pioneers* combined Peter Humeniuk's personal reminiscences of immigrant life in rural Manitoba with a general account of social, religious, economic, educational, and municipal developments in the Stuartburn area.[32] In 1978 Harry Piniuta published *Land of Pain, Land of Promise*, the collected and translated reminiscences of several early Ukrainian pioneers.[33]

During his lifetime, Vladimir J. Kaye (Kysilewsky) contributed greatly to Canadian immigration history. From his major study, *Early Ukrainian Settlements in Canada 1895-1900*,[34] it is clear that the groundwork for a mass movement from Galicia and Bukovyna was laid before Clifford Sifton inaugurated his own immigration policy. The book outlines Joseph Oleskiw's promotion of Ukrainian immigration to Canada and details the progress of the main Ukrainian colonies at Stuartburn,

Dauphin, Strathclair and Shoal Lake, Yorkton, Rosthern, and Edna-Star.[35]

With the seventy-fifth anniversary of Ukrainian settlement in 1966 and Canada's centennial in 1967, a rash of commemorative publications appeared. Two Soviet-oriented groups published *Tribute to Our Ukrainian Pioneers in Canada's First Century*.[36] Yuzyk's *Ukrainian Canadians*[37] highlighted personal and group achievements as proof of Ukrainian integration and right to full partnership. In the fourth volume of the Canada Ethnica series, sponsored jointly by the Centennial Commission and the Canadian Ethnic Press Federation, Ol'ha Woycenko attempted a more critical approach to the internal problems which threaten the dual nature of Ukrainian-Canadian society.[38]

Among the handful of non-Ukrainians interested in Ukrainian-Canadian development was the popular historian, James G. MacGregor, who wrote *Vilni Zemli (Free Lands)* in 1969,[39] focusing on the Edna-Star colony in Alberta. Without footnotes, bibliography, or index, the book abounds with anecdotes and fictitious passages. Another work, *The Ukrainian Pioneers in Alberta*,[40] is largely a compilation of little-edited autobiographies and biographies of Ukrainian pioneers. Two companion volumes, *Ukrainians in Alberta*,[41] contain accounts of later Ukrainian immigrants and their children. Two additional books on Ukrainians in Alberta appeared in late 1977: *No Streets of Gold* by Helen Potrebenko, a Vancouver taxi driver, and *All of Baba's Children* by journalist Myrna Kostash.[42] Both drew on personal experiences and pioneer recollections to place the history of Alberta's Ukrainians within a larger social, political, and economic framework, although *All of Baba's Children* is the more sophisticated work. Both works are the first Ukrainian-Canadian studies to look at the trials of Ukrainian immigrant and pioneer women. Potrebenko and Kostash also break new ground in their consideration of the non-agricultural labouring class in general, the left-wing movement and party organizations, union involvement, and strike action. Neither book is a scholarly study but both provide badly needed fresh viewpoints.

Recently, John Kolasky, a former activist in the ranks of the pro-Communist Association of United Ukrainian Canadians, published *The Shattered Illusion*,[43] a study of the Ukrainian Communist movement's decline in the post-war era, and the first attempt to write a critical study of a major ideologically oriented Ukrainian-Canadian organization. The final major English-language contribution to Ukrainian-Canadian historiography is Michael H. Marunchak's massive compendium, *The Ukrainian Canadians*,[44] a valuable reference work on all aspects of Ukrainian-Canadian life. Writing from a Ukrainian point of view, Marunchak stressed the European orientation of the group in Canada much more than did other students of Ukrainian-Canadian history.

In the 1970's university research on Ukrainian Canadians produced several limited case studies on a wide range of subjects.[45] In the fall of

1976 the Canadian Institute of Ukrainian Studies first published the *Journal of Ukrainian Graduate Studies* as an outlet for graduate student opinion, discussion, and research. Although issues to date have favoured Ukrainian studies *per se*, they have carried articles about Ukrainian Canadians. The two-part essay by Orest Martynowych, "The Ukrainian Socialist Movement in Canada 1900-1918," examined the evolution of Ukrainian-Canadian socialism from its roots in the Ukrainian Radical Party to its identification with the Bolsheviks. Nestor Makuch's more recent article, "The Influence of the Ukrainian Revolution on Ukrainians in Canada, 1917-1922,"[46] brought the European orientation of the Canadian community sharply into focus.

Since World War II, research into Ukrainian-Canadian development has broadened to cover several disciplines. Recently, there has been an increase in the examination of specific issues as legitimate areas of research in their own right. However, the compulsion to write Ukrainian-Canadian history only from the perspective of the Ukrainian role and contribution continues. Much English-language literature still extols the organized and conscious Ukrainian community as the guardian of a distinct Ukrainian-Canadian identity, while also favouring general political and socio-economic integration into Canadian life.

UKRAINIAN-LANGUAGE WORKS

Researchers proficient in the Ukrainian language possess a great advantage in the study of Ukrainians in Canada, as much of the source material is in Ukrainian. However, Ukrainian-language publications, confined by the language barrier, have minimal impact on general Canadian historiography. Early writers intended their publications solely for the Ukrainian community; others included only English title pages, introductions, or summaries. In recent years translations of Ukrainian works have been published, but most remain confined to a restricted audience.

Historical Ukrainian-language literature embraces three basic categories: almanacs and jubilee or commemorative publications, memoirs and biographies, and popular and scholarly studies on Ukrainian-Canadian life. Commemorative publications issued periodically by Ukrainian secular and religious organizations frequently provide a detailed account of the development, aims, and activities of a particular parish, local club, or national organization.[47] Memoirs vary with the insight, prominence, and veracity of the author, but many reflect a particular ideology and, as a result, also comment on broader aspects of Ukrainian-Canadian society. The third category, popular and scholarly research on the Ukrainian Canadians, is of greatest significance.

The first major Ukrainian-language work on Ukrainians in Canada was *Tserkov ukraintsiv v Kanadi* (The Ukrainian Church in Canada) by Panteleimon Bozyk,[48] an immigrant from Bukovyna who joined the Greek Catholic clergy after serving as a priest of the Russian Orthodox

Church in Canada. Stressing the importance of religious life among the first Ukrainian Canadians, the book devoted much space to Russian Orthodox missionary endeavours, the Seraphimite and Independent Greek Church movements, the activities of Protestant sects, and conflict between the Ukrainian Catholic and Orthodox churches in Canada. Commemorative almanacs and histories by the two main Ukrainian churches constitute a large part of the Ukrainian-language literature on Ukrainians in Canada. The publication in 1972 of a history of the Ukrainian Baptist movement in Canada, written by an adherent, suggests that the body of literature on Ukrainian religious life will expand beyond the two traditional churches.[49]

Spomyny pro perezhyvannia pershykh ukrainkhykh poselentsiv v Kanadi 1892-1942 (Memoirs of the Experiences of the First Ukrainian Settlers in Canada, 1892-1942), collected and published in Edmonton in 1942 by William A. Czumer, a Ukrainian-born pioneer school teacher, inaugurated the publication of Ukrainian-Canadian autobiographies.[50] Ukrainian-Canadian memoirs range from Ivan Nimchuk's brief autobiography, *Pochatky orhanizatsiinoho zhyttia kanadiiskykh ukraintsiv* (The Beginnings of Ukrainian-Canadian Organizational Life), to Toma A. Yastremsky's *Kanadiianizatsiia* (Canadianization), which is partially autobiographical.[51] The memoir of a Toronto businessman, Ivan Humeniuk, touches on many aspects of cultural and social life among the Ukrainians in eastern Canada.[52] Among recent, noteworthy additions has been the early memoir of Peter Svarich of Vegreville.[53]

In spite of its restricted title, *Propamiatna knyha ukrainskoho narodnoho domy u Vynnypegu* (Commemorative Book of the Ukrainian National Home in Winnipeg)[54] was the first general Ukrainian-language work on the history of Ukrainians in Canada. Written to honour the thirty-eighth anniversary of the Ukrainian National Home Association in Winnipeg, it included a great mass of undigested material on the association, Ukrainian-Canadian immigration, pioneering, educational and religious organizations, memorable occasions in Ukrainian-Canadian life, leading pioneer figures, and the beginnings of Ukrainian-Canadian literature. Similar are the two books of essays on Ukrainian settlers in western Canada published more recently by the Shevchenko Scientific Society in Canada.[55]

Ol'ha Woycenko's major Ukrainian-language contribution to Ukrainian-Canadian history is the six volume *Litopys ukrainskoho zhyttia v Kanadi* (Annals of Ukrainian Life in Canada).[56] Compiled from reports, articles, editorials, and news items in *Ukrainskyi holos*, each volume provides a Ukrainian-language index of persons and subjects and an English-language index of names and titles. To date, the series has been completed to 1959.

Michael Marunchak's major work is a four-volume series, *Studii do istorii ukraintsiv Kanady* (Studies in the History of Ukrainians in Canada).[57] Discussed are the history of Point Douglas (Winnipeg) in terms of Ukrainian and Scottish influence; Manitoba's Ukrainian settlements in the Stuartburn, Dauphin, Interlake, Shoal Lake, and Winnipeg areas during the pioneer era; and early Ukrainian newspapers, periodicals, literary activity, publishing firms, and bookstores, with particular attention to the ideological nature of the Ukrainian press. These and his large-scale general history, *Istoriia ukraintsiv Kanady* (History of the Ukrainians in Canada),[58] provided the basis for his omnibus English-language translation.

Istoriia poselennia ukraintsiv u Kanadi (The History of Ukrainian Settlement in Canada) by Julian Stechishin, published posthumously in 1975,[59] examined the first Ukrainian colonies and early social, religious, national, and educational life. Active in many of the events described, Stechishin drew on his own memory, as well as the experiences of others. Ukrainian-language theses outside the disciplines of language, linguistics, and literature have researched Bishop Nicetas Budka,[60] the Ukrainian press in eastern Canada,[61] the Ukrainian theatre,[62] and the Ukrainian churches in Montreal.[63]

Many of the Ukrainian Canadians recording their group's history have had little or no training as historians or critical researchers and writers, resulting in works that are often popular, personal, local, or partisan. Nonetheless, they do record basic or unique information highly useful to serious students of Ukrainian-Canadian history. Canadian-born scholars have generally been overshadowed by those born and educated in Europe. Many came to Canada after World War II and soon developed a keen interest in Ukrainian-Canadian studies. With the republication in 1972 by the Ukrainian Free Academy of Sciences in Winnipeg of Nestor Dmytriw's *Kanadiiska Rus'. Podorozhni spomyny* (the observations of the Pennsylvania-based Greek Catholic priest while visiting the fledgling Ukrainian colonies in Canada in 1897) as the first volume in a new series, "Sources for the History of Ukrainians in Canada," the future of Ukrainian-language historical publication brightened. Should the projected goal of publishing a parallel English series be realized, access to early documents on the Ukrainian Canadians could spur English-speaking Canadians to take a greater interest in Ukrainian-Canadian history. Such a move would also permit greater integration of Ukrainian-Canadian historical research into general Canadian historical scholarship.[64]

CONCLUSION

The question of what constitutes Ukrainian-Canadian history demands careful scrutiny. Is a Canadian of Ukrainian descent who achieves fame as a hockey player, a world wheat champion, or a pianist significant to Ukrainian-Canadian history if his contacts with things Ukrainian are minimal or totally absent? Does Ukrainian origin or a Ukrainian name necessarily mean that an individual's accomplishments illustrate the success and progress of the entire group? Do such individuals make a distinctly Ukrainian-Canadian contribution to Canadian life? Can we consider the Ukrainian-Canadian community in the future, as in the past, simply the sum total of all persons of Ukrainian origin in all walks of life?

In the early years of Ukrainian life in Canada, Ukrainian blocs were physically well-defined and Ukrainian-Canadian history largely corresponded to the general economic, political, cultural, and educational developments in the homogeneous districts. The organized Ukrainian community, reflecting European movements, was only one facet of Ukrainian life. However, as increased political and socio-economic integration intensifies the assimilation of the majority of Ukrainian Canadians into the Canadian cultural pattern, the historical experience of most Ukrainian Canadians will lose its unique quality. It is possible that historical research into the economic, political, and social development of Ukrainian Canadians will remain valid for the early decades of Ukrainian life in Canada but lose significance as a continuing field of activity. Simultaneously, research into the organized community would grow in importance. This raises another question: can Ukrainian-Canadian historiography be legitimately limited to the organized community, that narrowing sector of the ethnic group consciously propagating Ukrainian cultural traditions, promoting the Ukrainian language and culture in Canada, and actively concerned about the fate of Ukraine? Present trends would suggest that Ukrainian-Canadian historiography in the future will focus on this minority as both the guardian and visible manifestation of a specifically Ukrainian-Canadian subsociety within the Canadian framework.

Early English-language works emphasized assimilation into the Anglo-Canadian standard for the good of the country. As this tone grew less strident, a few voices advocated the retention of Ukrainian cultural values. Ukrainian-Canadian authors who still dominate the field have emphasized personal and group achievements and the unique contributions of Ukrainians to Canadian life. They have compiled lists of successful politicians, businessmen, and athletes of Ukrainian origin, calculated the number of acres of land cultivated by Ukrainian agriculturalists, reflected upon the cultural and aesthetic contributions made by exponents of the Ukrainian folk arts to Canada's multicultural heritage, and enlarged upon the role of Ukrainians in buttressing the Canadian way of life by stressing the Ukrainian people's love of liberty, their economic individualism, and their profound opposition to all anti-democratic doctrines. This tendency to examine Ukrainian-Canadian historical development within a framework determined by the prevailing ideology has been overworked. It should no longer be necessary to seek to make the Ukrainian past in Canada "respectable" to mollify the host society. Authors who continue to lend credence to their interpretations by convincing their readers of the validity of their conceptions of the past without critically examining the role of specific persons, organizations, movements, or processes do Ukrainian-Canadian history a great disservice. On the other hand, if current research in Canadian universities and some of the work published recently is any indication, the future looks promising. Students and authors have begun to look at specific phenomena and processes as legitimate in themselves; they are no longer obsessed with demonstrating that Ukrainians have managed to adapt to the Canadian way of life.

NOTES

1. Works have been published in other countries and in other languages, particularly French. For example, see E. Tremblay, *Le Père Delaere et l'église ukrainienne du Canada* (Berthierville, Québec: Impr. Bernard, 1961). The first account of the newly established Ukrainian settlements in Canada, *Kanadiiska Rus'. Podorozhni spomyny* (Canadian Ruthenia: Traveller's Memoirs) by Rev. Nestor Dmytriw, was published in 1897 in the United States. The Soviet Ukrainian historian, A.M. Shlepakov, has published two monographs: *Zhovtneva revoliutsiia i pidnesennia demokratychnoho rukhu sered ukrainskoi emihratsii v SShA i Kanadi* (The October Revolution and the Rise of the Democratic Movement among the Ukrainian Emigration in the U.S.A. and Canada) (Kiev: Vyd. AN URSR, 1957); and *Ukrainska trudova emihratsiia v SShA i Kanadi. Kinets XIX - pochatok XX st.* (The Ukrainian Labour Emigration in the U.S.A. and Canada at the end of the Nineteenth and Beginning of the Twentieth Centuries) (Kiev: Vyd. AN URSR, 1960). A growing number of doctoral theses on Ukrainian-Canadian topics are also emerging from the Ukrainian Free University in Munich.
2. The first research conducted on the Ukrainians in Canada was by J.S. Woodsworth, "Ukrainian Rural Communities: Report of Investigation" (Winnipeg: Bureau of Social Research for the Governments of Manitoba, Saskatchewan, and Alberta, 1917).
3. Typical was the first English-language work on the Ukrainians and their background, *The Galicians Dwelling in Canada and their Origin* (Winnipeg: Manitoba Free Press, 1906), a superficial summary by a Russian, Michael A. Sherbinin. Formerly a Presbyterian missionary among the Doukhobors in Saskatchewan, Sherbinin became a lecturer at Manitoba College for Ukrainians entering the teaching profession.
4. R. Connor, *The Foreigner: A Tale of Saskatchewan* (Toronto: Westminster Company, 1909). The British and American editions were entitled *The Settler: The Story of a Ukrainian Youth*.
5. J.T.M. Anderson, *The Education of the New Canadian: A Treatise on Canada's Greatest Educational Problem* (London and Toronto: J.M. Dent & Sons, 1918). In 1918 Anderson became Director of Education among New Canadians in Saskatchewan. From 1929 to 1934, he served as the Conservative Premier of the province.

6. One of the best illustrations of this transition can be seen in the annual reports on work in the Ukrainian colonies presented to the General Assembly of the Presbyterian Church in Canada from 1898 to 1925. To World War I, the reports refer primarily to "Galician" and "Ruthenian" work. However, the *Acts and Proceedings of the Forty-Sixth General Assembly of the Presbyterian Church in Canada* in 1920 contain a report that outlines the history of the Ukrainian people in terms of Ukrainian historical development and comments on the contemporary political situation in Ukraine; see also F. Heap, "The Ukrainians in Canada: An Estimate of the Presence, Ideals, Religion, Tendencies, and Citizenship of Perhaps Three Hundred Thousand Ukrainians in Canada," *Canadian Magazine of Politics, Science, Art and Literature,* LIII (1919), pp. 39-44.
7. As early as 1916, Florence R. Livesay published an annotated translation of Ukrainian folksongs, *Songs of Ukraina with Ruthenian Poems* (London and Toronto: J.M. Dent & Sons, 1916). A somewhat idyllic introductory description of Ukraine was written by Paul Crath (Pavlo Krat). In 1940 Livesay translated and published Hryhorii Kvitka's novel *Marusia.*
8. P.H. Bryce, *The Value to Canada of the Continental Immigrant* (Ottawa: n.p., 1928), p. 44.
9. R. England, *The Central European Immigrant in Canada* (Toronto: Macmillan of Canada, 1929).
10. Among Gibbon's articles were "The Foreign Born," *Queen's Quarterly*, XXVII (April, 1920), pp. 331-51; "European Seeds in the Canadian Garden," *Transactions of the Royal Society of Canada*, XXII, series III, sec. ii (May, 1923), pp. 119-29; "A Secular Bible for a New Canada," *ibid.*, XXXVI, series III, sec. ii (May, 1942), pp. 93-100; and "Folk-song and Feudalism," *ibid.*, XLII, series III, sec. ii (May, 1948), pp. 73-84.
11. J.M. Gibbon, *Canadian Mosaic: The Making of a Northern Nation* (Toronto: McClelland and Stewart, 1938). The origins of the term "mosaic" are discussed on pages viii and ix.
12. A.J. Hunter, *A Friendly Adventure: The Story of the United Church Mission among New Canadians at Teulon, Manitoba* (Toronto: Board of Home Missions, United Church of Canada, 1929). In 1922 Hunter published selected translations of Shevchenko's poetry, with commentary, in *The Kobzar of the Ukraine: Selected Poems of Taras Shevchenko* (Winnipeg: n.p., 1922).
13. In 1932 Hunter presented a paper to the Historical and Scientific Society of Manitoba, entitled "The Ukrainians; Their Historical and Cultural Background," in which he concentrated on historical manifestations of the free and democratic spirit of Ukraine. This paper was later abridged and published in *Transactions of the Historical and Scientific Society of Manitoba*, series III, no. 10 (1955).
14. C.H. Young, *The Ukrainian Canadians: A Study in Assimilation* (Toronto: Thomas Nelson & Sons, 1931).

15. See C.H. Robinson, "A Study of the Written Language Errors of 1238 Pupils of Ukrainian Origin" (B.Ed. thesis, Alberta, 1934); L. Bercuson, "Education in the Bloc Settlements of Western Canada" (Master's thesis, McGill University, 1941); L.H. Woollatt, "A Study to Discover any Characteristic Differences in Sentence Structure in the Written English of Saskatchewan Elementary School Pupils Belonging to Different National Groups" (Master's thesis, University of Saskatchewan, 1944); D.M. Sullivan, "An Investigation of the English Disabilities of Ukrainian and Polish Students in Grades IX, X, XI, XII of Alberta" (Master's thesis, University of Alberta, 1946). Related to education was J.M. Deverell, "The Ukrainian Teacher as an Agent of Cultural Assimilation" (Master's thesis, University of Toronto, 1941).

    In time, Ukrainian-Canadian students also became interested in the subject. See M. Skuba, "An Analysis of English Errors and Difficulties among Grade Ten Students in the Smoky Lake School Division" (Master's thesis, University of Alberta, 1955); A. Saruk, "Academic Performance of Students of Ukrainian Descent and the Cultural Orientation of Their Parents" (Master's thesis, University of Alberta, 1966); S.V. Cipywnyk, "Educational Implications of Ukrainian-English Childhood Bilingualism in Saskatchewan" (Master's thesis, University of Saskatchewan, 1968); C.R. Harasym, "Cultural Orientation of Rural Ukrainian High School Students" (Master's thesis, University of Calgary, 1969); B. Kubrakovich, "Place of Residence, Lingual Contact and Parental Education as Factors Affecting the Learning of Ukrainian in Grades IX and X in Manitoba Schools" (Master's thesis, University of Manitoba, 1974).
16. T.C. Byrne, "The Ukrainian Community in North Central Alberta" (Master's thesis, University of Alberta. 1937).
17. C.M. Bayley, "The Social Structure of the Italian and Ukrainian Immigrant Communities in Montreal, 1935-1939" (Master's thesis, McGill University, 1939); S.W. Mamchur, "The Economic and Social Adjustment of Slavic Immigrants in Canada, with Special Reference to the Ukrainians in Montreal" (Master's thesis, McGill University, 1934).
18. See his *Canada, Europe, and Hitler* (Toronto: Oxford University Press, 1939); *Ukrainian Canadians and the War* (Toronto: Oxford University Press, 1940); *Canadians All: A Primer of Canadian National Unity* (Ottawa: Issued by the Director of Public Information under authority of the Minister of National War Services, 1941); "Our Communists and the New Canadians" (address delivered to the Canadian Club, Toronto, 1 February 1943); and *Our Ukrainian Loyalists: The Ukrainian Canadian Committee* (Winnipeg: Ukrainian Canadian Committee, 1943).
19. R.A. Davies (Rudolf Shohan), *This is Our Land: Ukrainian Canadians Against Hitler* (Toronto: Progress Books, 1943).
20. W. Paluk, *Canadian Cossacks: Essays, Articles and Stories on Ukrainian Canadian Life* (Winnipeg: Ukrainian Canadian Review Publishing Co., 1943).

21. N. Hunchak, *Canadians of Ukrainian Origin: Population* (Winnipeg: Ukrainian Canadian Committee, 1945).
22. V. Lysenko, *Men in Sheepskin Coats: A Study in Assimilation* (Toronto: Ryerson Press, 1947). Prior to researching and writing *Men in Sheepskin Coats*, Winnipeg-born Lysenko had been a professional journalist, writing for the *Windsor Star*.
23. Vera Lysenko also wrote *Yellow Boots* (Toronto: Ryerson Press, 1954), one of the handful of English-language novels with a Ukrainian-Canadian theme. The story focuses on a young Ukrainian girl who understands the beauty and wisdom in the old peasant traditions and songs and is able to move into the New World without spiritual destruction and without relinquishing that part of her Ukrainian heritage which could be adapted and preserved in Canada.
24. P. Yuzyk, "The History of the Ukrainian Greek Catholic (Uniate) Church in Canada" (Master's thesis, University of Saskatchewan, 1948).
25. H. Piniuta, "The Organizational Life of Ukrainian Canadians, with Special Reference to the Ukrainian Canadian Committee" (Master's thesis, University of Ottawa, 1952); W. Veryha, "The Ukrainian Canadian Committee: Its Origins and War Activity" (Master's thesis, University of Ottawa, 1967).
26. J. Skwarok, "The Ukrainian Settlers in Canada and Their Schools with Reference to Government, French-Canadian and Ukrainian Missionary Influence 1891-1921" (Master's thesis, University of Alberta, 1958), published in 1959 by the Basilian Press in Toronto. O.S. Trosky, "A Historical Study of the Development of the Ukrainian Greek Orthodox Church of Canada and its Role in the Field of Education 1918-1964" (Master's thesis, University of Manitoba, 1965), updated and published by the author as *The Ukrainian Greek Orthodox Church in Canada* (Winnipeg, 1968).
27. P. Yuzyk, *The Ukrainian Greek Orthodox Church of Canada 1918-1951* (Ottawa; University of Ottawa Press, 1981); M. Zuk, "The Ukrainian Protestant Missions in Canada" (S.T.M., McGill University, 1957); and M. Wenstob, "The Work of the Methodist Church among Settlers in Alberta up to 1914, with Special Reference to the Formation of Congregations and Work among the Ukrainian People" (B.D. thesis, University of Alberta, 1959).
28. P. Bassa, "Ukrainian Musical Culture in Canada" (Master's thesis, University of Montreal, 1955); Brother Isidore, "The Ukrainian Catholic Press in Canada: Its Beginnings, Aims, Contributions, Problems, and Role" (Master's thesis, University of Ottawa, 1959).
29. P. Yuzyk, *The Ukrainians in Manitoba: A Social History* (Toronto: University of Toronto Press, 1953).
30. G. Romaniuk, *Taking Root in Canada: An Autobiography* (Winnipeg: Columbia Press, 1954). The original Ukrainian manuscript was published in 1958 under the title *Moi pionerski pryhody v Kanadi* (My Pioneer Adventures in Canada).

31. M. Luchkovich, *A Ukrainian Canadian in Parliament: Memoirs of Michael Luchkovich* (Toronto: Ukrainian Canadian Research Foundation, 1965).
32. P. Humeniuk, *Hardships and Progress of Ukrainian Pioneers: Memoirs from Stuartburn Colony and Other Points* (Steinbach, Manitoba: Derksen Printers, 1976).
33. H. Piniuta (researcher and trans.), *Land of Pain, Land of Promise: First Person Accounts by Ukrainian Pioneers 1891-1914* (Saskatoon: Western Producer Prairie Books, 1978).
34. V.J. Kaye, *Early Ukrainian Settlements in Canada 1895-1900: Dr. Josef Oleskow's Role in the Settlement of the Canadian Northwest* (Toronto: University of Toronto Press, 1964).
35. Kaye's articles include "The Ukrainians in Canada," in J. Kosa (ed.), *Immigrants in Canada* (Montreal: n.p. 1955), pp. 12-16; "Political Integration of Ethnic Groups: The Ukrainians," *Revue de l'Université d'Ottawa,* XXVI (October-December, 1957), pp. 460-77; "Dr. Josef Oleskow's Visit of Canada, August-October, 1895," *Revue de l'Université d'Ottawa*, XXXII (January-March, 1962), pp. 30-44; and "Golden Jubilee of Participation of Ukrainians in Political Life of Canada," *Ukrainian Quarterly*, XIX (Summer, 1963), pp. 167-70. His *Slavic Groups in Canada* (Winnipeg: UVAN Series Slavistica #12, 1951) sketched Ukrainian and Polish integration into Canadian economic, political, and cultural life by singling out individuals successful in various fields. In 1975 Kaye's *Dictionary of Ukrainian Canadian Biography: Pioneer Settlers of Manitoba 1891-1900* (Toronto: Ukrainian Canadian Research Foundation, 1975) was published. The compiler's death prevented the completion of volumes on Alberta and Saskatchewan.
36. *Tribute to Our Ukrainian Pioneers in Canada's First Century*, Proceedings of a Special Convention of the Association of United Ukrainian Canadians and the Workers' Benevolent Association of Canada, March 23, 1966 (Winnipeg, 1966). In 1972 the Workers' Benevolent Association published its own history. See A. Bilecki, W. Repka, and M. Sago, *Friends in Need: The WBA Story: A Canadian Epic in Fraternalism* (Winnipeg: Workers' Benevolent Association, 1972).
37. P. Yuzyk, *Ukrainian Canadians: Their Place and Role in Canadian Life* (Toronto: Ukrainian Canadian Business and Professional Federation, 1967).
38. O. Woycenko, *The Ukrainians in Canada* (Winnipeg: Canada Ethnica, 1967).
39. J.G. MacGregor, *Vilni Zemli (Free Lands): The Ukrainian Settlement of Alberta* (Toronto: McClelland and Stewart, 1969).
40. *The Ukrainian Pioneers in Alberta* (Edmonton: Ukrainian Pioneers' Association of Alberta, 1970).
41. *Ukrainians in Alberta* (Edmonton: Ukrainian Pioneers' Association of Alberta, 1975, 1981).
42. H. Potrebenko, *No Streets of Gold: A Social History of Ukrainians in*

Alberta (Vancouver: New Star Books, 1977); M. Kostash, *All of Baba's Children* (Edmonton: Hurtig Publishers, 1977).

43. J. Kolasky, *The Shattered Illusion: The History of Ukrainian Pro-Communist Organizations in Canada* (Toronto: Peter Martin Associates, 1979).

44. M.H. Marunchak, *The Ukrainian Canadians: A History* (Winnipeg: Ukrainian Free Academy of Sciences, 1970). The volume, based on Marunchak's Ukrainian-language works, is poorly translated and edited. Over the past three decades, Marunchak has been the most prolific writer of Ukrainian-Canadian history, primarily in Ukrainian.

45. M. Binns, "Cultural Pluralism in Canada: An Exploratory Study of the Italians and Ukrainians in London, Ontario" (Master's thesis, University of Western Ontario, 1971); M.S. Meleg, "Italian and Ukrainian University Students' View of Occupations in Canada: A Study of the Relationship Between Ethnicity and Occupational Prestige" (Master's thesis, University of Windsor, 1968); N.L. Penny, "Marriage Patterns in an Ethnic Community in Rural Manitoba, 1896-1970" (Master's thesis, University of Manitoba, 1972); M. Stefanow, "A Study of Intermarriage of Ukrainians in Saskatchewan" (Master's thesis, University of Saskatchewan, 1962); L. Emanuel, "Attitudes Towards Identity in a Ukrainian Parish" (Master's thesis, University of Alberta, 1975); Y.G. Kelebay, "The Ukrainian Community in Montreal" (Master's thesis, Concordia University, 1975); V. Olender, "The Reaction of the Canadian Methodist Church Towards Ukrainian Immigrants: Rural Missions as Agencies of Assimilation" (Master's thesis, Institute of Christian Thought, St. Michael's College, 1976); H. Udod, "Julian W. Stechishin: His Life and Work" (Master's thesis, University of Saskatchewan, 1974); F. Swyripa, "Ukrainian-Canadian Historiography in the English Language: A Survey" (Master's thesis, University of Alberta, 1976). This thesis was published in 1978 by the Canadian Institute of Ukrainian Studies at the University of Alberta as *Ukrainian Canadians: A Survey of Their Portrayal in English-language Works*. Also I. Wynnyckyj, "Ukrainian Canadian Drama from the Beginnings of Immigration to 1942" (Master's thesis, University of Waterloo, 1976); P. Migus, "Ukrainian Canadian Youth: A History of Organizational Life in Canada, 1907-1953" (Master's thesis, University of Ottawa, 1975); J.C. Lehr, "The Process and Pattern of Ukrainian Rural Settlement in Western Canada 1891-1914" (Doctoral thesis, University of Manitoba, 1978); O.T. Martynowych, "Village Radicals and Peasant Immigrants: The Social Roots of Factionalism among Ukrainian Immigrants in Canada, 1896-1918" (Master's thesis, University of Manitoba, 1978); P. Melnycky "A Political History of the Ukrainian Community in Manitoba, 1899-1922" (Master's thesis, University of Manitoba, 1979).

46. O.T. Martynowych, "The Ukrainian Socialist Movement in Canada, 1900-1918," *Journal of Ukrainian Graduate Studies*, 1 (Fall, 1976), pp. 27-44; *ibid.*, 2 (Spring, 1977), pp. 22-31; N. Makuch, "The In-

fluence of the Ukrainian Revolution on Ukrainians in Canada, 1917-22," *ibid.*, 6 (Spring, 1979), pp. 42-61.

47. The following titles indicate the wide variety of almanac and anniversary or commemorative publications by Ukrainian groups in Canada: *Liga ukrainskykh katolytskykh zhinok Edmontonskoi eparkhii. Pochatky i dialnist* (Ukrainian Catholic Women's League in the Edmonton Eparchy: Beginnings and Activities) (Edmonton, 1967); *Iuvileina knyha 25-littia instytutu im. Petra Mohyly v Saskatuni 1916-1941* (Twenty-Fifth Jubilee Book of the Petro Mohyla Institute in Saskatoon 1916-1941) (Winnipeg: Nakladom instytutu, 1945); *Za chest, za slavu, za narod. Zbirnyk na zolotyi iuvilei ukrainskoi striletskoi hromady v Kanadi 1928-1978* (For Honour, Glory, and the Nation: Collected Essays on the Golden Jubilee of the Ukrainian War Veterans' Association in Canada 1928-1978) (Toronto: V-vo. Novyi shliakh, 1978). Among the more significant organizational publications are the recorded proceedings of the Ukrainian Canadian Committee's triennial congresses. Only the proceedings of the first and second congresses in 1943 and 1946 were published in Ukrainian and English.

48. P. Bozyk, *Tserkov ukraintsiv v Kanadi. Prychynky do istorii ukrainskoho tserkovnoho zhyttia v brytiiskii dominii Kanady, za chas vid 1890-1927* (The Ukrainian Church in Canada: Contributions to the History of Ukrainian Religious Life in the British Dominion of Canada from 1890-1927) (Winnipeg: Nakladom Kanadyiskoho ukraintsia, 1927), republished under the title *Istoriia ukrainskoi emigratsii v Kanada za chas vid 1890 do 1930 roku* (History of Ukrainian Emigration in Canada from 1890 to 1930) (Winnipeg: Narodna drukarnia, 1930).

49. P. Kindrat, *Ukrainskyi baptystskyi rukh u Kanadi. Spohady pro pionersku dukhovnu pratsiu v Kanadi* (The Ukrainian Baptist Movement in Canada: Reminiscences about Pioneer Spiritual Work in Canada) (Winnipeg and Toronto: Doroha pravdy, 1972).

50. The English-language publication by the Canadian Institute of Ukrainian Studies in 1981 was based on the translation by Louis T. Laychuk.

51. I. Nimchuk, *Pochatky orhanizatsiinoho zhyttia kanadiiskykh ukraintsiv. Spomyny albertiiskoho pionera* (The Beginnings of Organizational Life of Canadian Ukrainians: Memoirs of an Alberta Pioneer) (Edmonton: Biblioteka Katolytskoi aktsii, 1952); T.A. Yastremsky, *Kanadiianizatsiia. Politychnyi rozvytok kanadiiskykh ukraintsiv za poslidnykh 46 rokiv ikhnoho pobutu v Kanadi* (Canadianization: The Political Development of Canadian Ukrainians in the Last 46 Years of Their Life in Canada) (Winnipeg, 1946).

52. I. Humeniuk, *Moi spomyny do rozvytku orhanizovanoho zhyttia ukraintsiv v skhidnii Kanadi* (My Memoirs Dealing with the Development of Organizational Life of Ukrainians in Eastern Canada) (Toronto, 1957).

53. P. Svarich, *Spomyny 1877-1904* (Memoirs 1877-1904) (Winnipeg: Trident Press, 1976).

54. D. Doroshenko and S. Kowbel (eds.), *Propamiatna knyha ukrainskoho narodnoho domu v Vynnypegu* (Commemorative Book of the Ukrainian National Home in Winnipeg) (Winnipeg: Trident Press, 1949). Kowbel provides an English-language summary of this monumental collection on pages 17 and 18.
55. Y. Slavutych (ed.), *Zakhidnokanadskyi zbirnyk* (Collected Papers on Ukrainian Settlers in Western Canada) (Edmonton, 1973, 1975).
56. O. Woycenko, *Litopys ukrainskoho zhyttia v Kanadi* (Annals of Ukrainian Life in Canada), 5 vols. (Winnipeg: Vyd. Tryzub, 1961-69); the sixth volume was published by the Canadian Institute of Ukrainian Studies in Edmonton in 1982.
57. M.H. Marunchak, *Studii do istorii ukraintsiv Kanady* (Studies in the History of Ukrainians in Canada), 4 vols. (Winnipeg: UVAN, Series Ukrainica Occidentalia, 1964-71).
58. M.H. Marunchak, *Istoriia ukraintsiv Kanady* (History of Ukrainians in Canada) (Winnipeg: UVAN, 1968). A second volume, *Doba mizh viinamy ta doba vyvershennia* (The Era between the Wars and the Era of Consolidation), was published in 1973.
59. J. Stechishin, *Istoriia poselennia ukraintsiv u Kanadi* (The History of Ukrainian Settlement in Canada) (Edmonton: Ukrainian Self-Reliance League, 1975).
60. A. Lishchynsky, "Preosviashchennyi kyr Nykyta Budka i ukrainska emigratsiia v Kanadi 1912-1919" (Msgr. Nykyta Budka and the Ukrainian Emigrants in Canada 1912-1919) (Master's thesis, University of Ottawa, 1955).
61. M. Borowyk, "Ukrainska presa v skhidnii Kanadi" (The Ukrainian Press in Eastern Canada) (Master's thesis, University of Ottawa, 1960).
62. B. Hiritsch, "The Development of Ukrainian Theatre and its Role in Canada" (Master's thesis, University of Montreal, 1962), Ukrainian text.
63. N.A. Hrymak-Wynnycky, "Les églises ukrainiennes à Montréal" (Master's thesis, University of Montreal, 1964), Ukrainian text.
64. To date, no comprehensive bibliography of Ukrainian-Canadian titles has been compiled. The bibliographies that do exist are discussed in F. Swyripa, *Ukrainian Canadians: A Survey of Their Portrayal in English-language Works* (Edmonton: University of Alberta Press, 1978), pp. 120-2.

Index

Press—*(Cont'd.)*
Globe: 64; *Ukrainian Canadian* (Toronto): 267; *Ukrainian Echo* (Toronto): 276; *Winnipeg Free Press:* 199; *Winnipeg Tribune:* 118; LEFT-WING: *Boiova molod* (Militant Youth): 186, 267; *Chervonyi prapor* (Red Flag): 96, 266, 273; *Farmerske zhyttia* (Farmer's Life): 267; *Holos robitnytsi* (Voice of the Working Woman): 267; *Narodna hazeta* (People's Gazette): 267; *Pravda* (Truth): 268; *Robitnyche slovo* (Workers' Word): 268; *Robitnychi visti* (Labour News): 268; *Robochyi narod* (Working People): 72, 83n, 96, 97, 267, 273; *Svidoma syla* (Conscious Strength): 268; *Svit molodi* (Youth World): 186; *Ukrainske slovo* (Ukrainian Word): 267; *Ukrainske zhyttia* (Ukrainian Life): 267; *Ukrainski robitnychi visti* (Ukrainian Labour News): 83n, 179, 180, 267, 268; *Vpered* (Forward): 268; *Zhyttia i slovo* (Life and Word): 267; MONARCHIST: *Batkivshchyna* (Fatherland): 269; *Kanadiiska sich* (Canadian Fortress): 269; *Nasha derzhava* (Our State): 269; *Probii* (Breakthrough): 269; *Sich* (Fortress): 269; *Ukrainskyi robitnyk* (Ukrainian Toiler): 108, 112, 114, 116, 121, 123n, 183, 269, 279n; MOSCOPHILE: *Rabochii narod* (Working) People): 83n; *Russkii holos* (Russian Voice): 233, 271; *Russkii narod* (Russian People): 233, 271; PROTESTANT: *Ievanhelska pravda* (Evangelical Truth): 270; *Ievanhelskyi ranok* (Evangelical Morning): 270; *Ievanhelyst* (Evangelist): 270; *Kanadiiskyi ranok* (Canadian Morning): 270; *Kanadyiets* (The Canadian): 270; *Khrystiianskyi stiah* (Christian Banner): 270; *Ranok* (Morning): 93, 152, 177, 270, 272; *Slovo* (Word): 270; *Ukrainska ievanhelska nyva* (Ukrainian Gospel Field): 270; *Vira i znannia* (Faith and Knowledge): 270; RUSSIAN ORTHODOX: *Kanadiiskaia Pravoslavnaia Rus'* (Canadian Orthodox Rus'): 271; *Kanadiiskaia nyva* (Canadian Field): 151; UKRAINIAN ORTHODOX: *Bursak* (Student): 255; *Kameniari* Stonecutters): 255; *Pravoslavnyi vistnyk (visnyk)* (Orthodox Herald): 154, 272; *Ridna tserkva* (Native Church): 155; *Ukrainskyi holos* (Ukrainian Voice): 93, 95, 99, 100, 105n, 108, 111, 112, 113, 114, 115, 118, 119, 120, 121, 122, 123n, 152, 154, 155, 163, 177, 186, 196, 197, 199, 264, 268, 272, 273, 275, 279n, 298, 303, 316; *Vira i kultura* (Faith and Culture): 272; OTHER: *Dzvinok* (The Little Bell): 272; *Homin Ukrainy* (Echo of Ukraine): 269, 275, 276; *Kanada* (Canada): 93, 266; *Kanadiiskyi farmer* (Canadian Farmer): 91, 92, 93, 94, 95, 118, 152, 153, 154, 196, 197, 222, 265, 266, 268, 270, 272, 273, 275, 277n, 278n, 303; *Khata* (Home): 272; *Novi dni* (New Days): 300; *Novyi krai* (New Country): 95, 273; *Novyi shliakh* (New Pathway): 199, 268-9, 273, 274, 275, 279n; *Novyny* (The News): 99, 231, 232, 233; *Oko* (The Eye): 278n; *Pivnichne siiavo* (Northern Lights): 300; *Ridna mova* (Native